success

Advanced
Teacher's Support Book

Contents

Introduction

Welcome to *Success*. This introduction
- describes how the course meets the needs of students and teachers
- outlines the principles on which the materials were developed
- describes the course and its components.

SUCCESS FOR STUDENTS

Success is a six-level course for upper secondary students, taking learners from zero beginner to an advanced level of English competency. It is aimed at fourteen to twenty-year-old students. The age range has been fundamental in defining the most important features of the course.

Students at this age are at the peak of their cognitive development.

They learn best when they are encouraged to use discovery techniques and engage with interesting topics related to their age. In common with learners in all age groups, they need a lot of recycling to internalise and acquire the new grammar, vocabulary and functional language input, but they can also deal with big chunks of new material.

Students at this age want to learn about the world.

Success has a highly educational content. It not only teaches English but also provides students with information about the culture of English-speaking countries and the world at large. It provides interesting and engaging exercises and texts that deal with citizenship issues, literature, history, geography, art, science and technology as well as the challenges of everyday life.

Students at this age are young adults who want to be independent in their learning.

Success promotes maturity in its approach to learning through self-assessment strategies, topics and tasks which encourage the learner to think about what they read, rather than just respond to it.

Success provides everything students of English need to cross the border between their school life and the outside world.

Success is designed for learners who are at a critical point in their education. The exams they take, whether school-leaving/university entrance exams or public exams such as those of Cambridge Assessment, will determine their future.

All exams now follow Common European Framework requirements, which means that they are skills-oriented with a special emphasis on communication. *Success* has a very strong skills syllabus and task types from different exams are practised throughout the course.

Special features in the *Success* Workbook such as exam tips and self-assessment tests also help students deal with exam tasks.

The tests included in the Testing and Evaluation Programme are designed to give students a sense of progress and achievement.

SUCCESS FOR TEACHERS

Although the course has been designed for use in state-sector schools, it is also suitable for use in private language schools and the activities will work well with both small and large groups – of up to thirty students.

Lesson preparation

The format of the units in the Students' Book guarantees successful lessons. Clear headings and the logical sequencing of exercises ensure that *Success* will be very easy for you to teach from with little preparation.

The fact that the order of sections changes in every unit makes the lessons varied and interesting.

Further support is given in the Teacher's Support Book with ideas for warm-ups, extra activities and photocopiable activities while the Workbook offers additional flexibility to the pattern of the unit. Extra material (eg Culture Shock sections) provides ideal material for special one-off lessons.

The Workbook offers further exercises for homework. As the exercises strongly reflect themes and language from the Students' Book input, you do not need to spend too much time explaining homework tasks to your students.

Evaluation and assessment

Monitoring students' progress is particularly important in the light of exam preparation. Students need to be confident that they can pass the relevant exams at each stage of their learning.

Success provides you with a unique testing and evaluation system that includes different types of tests as well as help with the grading and planning of the entire school year. The Test Master CD-ROM provides all the testing materials in an electronic version, making it easy for you to customise it to your particular classroom situation.

Dealing with mixed-level classes

Placement tests in the Testing and Evaluation Programme help you to place your students in groups according to their level, and allow you to make the right choice of book from the six levels of *Success* for your class.

For very able students, more challenging exercises on vocabulary (Extend your vocabulary) are included in the Workbook from the Pre-Intermediate level onwards. These students should be encouraged to do more projects suggested in the Testing and Evaluation Programme as they give students the opportunity for freer language production.

They will allow all students to contribute to the class irrespective of their abilities. Even the weakest students can participate and enjoy a real sense of success.

PRINCIPLES BEHIND THE COURSE

Success is an ELT course written specifically for secondary school students. It draws from the most cutting-edge developments in ELT methodology and practice and is clear, accessible and novel.

The ten most important features of the course concept are the following:

- A controlled environment for teaching and learning.
- Student and teacher motivation.
- An interactive approach to learning.
- Thinking training.
- Memorisation techniques.
- An equal emphasis on skills and grammar.
- A strong focus on vocabulary input and practice.
- Expanding general knowledge.
- Building cultural awareness.
- A principled testing and evaluation system plus exam preparation.

The above features make *Success* a very well balanced course which gives you security, and a real sense of progress to students.

1. A controlled environment for teaching and learning

One of our most important aims was to publish a course where learning is very carefully monitored.

A problem sometimes encountered in course books is that of un-previewed language and grammar. It can be frustrating for both you and the students when, for example, an elementary lesson on the Present Simple also contains examples of the Past Simple or even Present Perfect. Your assurances that 'this will be covered later' can stifle the students' own sense of achievement. We have been very careful to avoid this in *Success*. We have carefully monitored the language progression and have avoided using new grammar in the skills sections. Each speaking exercise is well guided through the use of prompts and examples.

The same approach has been carefully implemented throughout all the components.

The second important aim was to create materials that provide methodologically sound lessons on the page. You do not need to adapt the material and no extra preparation or input is required. In other words, if you teach from *Success*, you will be very successful with little effort.

2. Student and teacher motivation

The *Success* course was designed to help you motivate students and also be very rewarding to teach from.

One of the key ways of achieving this is that throughout the course there is a clear direction for learning. Unit objectives are clearly stated at the beginning of each unit. Lessons and tasks have carefully-prepared stages leading up to clear communicative outcomes.

The varied unit structure, the liveliness of the presentations and exercises, and the sheer interest of the texts make the material extremely engaging. There is often an element of puzzle-solving which, added to the high quality of photos, illustrations and audio material, will add to students' motivation and desire to learn.

Most importantly, many of the presentations in *Success* are amusing and thought provoking, which we hope will make the material memorable, thus promoting acquisition and learning. You and your students will often find yourselves smiling at a funny cartoon or a humorous text. The topics covered are usually familiar but with a fresh and interesting angle, eg Intermediate Unit 6, 'Amazing animals' shows how our favourite pets perceive their owners rather than the other way round. Grammar presentations, texts and exercises often contain an unexpected twist at the end which will surprise students and engage them further on the road to learning, eg in Advanced Unit 4 students are introduced to gadgets essential in student life, only to discover in the listening task why some of them turned out to be rather unsuccessful.

We are sure that studying from *Success* will be a very enjoyable experience!

3. An interactive approach to learning

We believe that the unique feature of *Success* is the fact that students are much more actively involved in every stage of the learning process than in other courses. The involvement is particularly transparent in the following sections of the book:

Grammar: the inductive approach makes the grammar presentations in *Success* particularly interesting and memorable. Students analyse examples of language and arrive at the grammar rules themselves: this helps them understand and remember the rules better.

Skills strategies: while other courses offer language tips about skills strategies, we give students the opportunity to experience the strategy through doing exercises that illustrate them. Students can then understand the strategies boxes (*Train Your Brain*) much better, and even help create them.

Reading and listening skills: we believe that these sections are developed in a very involving way. They very often work like puzzles where students have to complete the reading with the missing paragraph or title, or guess the ending of the listening before they listen to the last part of it. The variety of exercises and their unique character motivate the students and help them remember the material.

Speaking: as in most courses these sections include a box with the functional language highlighted. However, what is unique in *Success* is the fact that all the exercises are constructed in such a way that students have to either complete the box themselves or refer to it many times, so by the end of the lesson they can use the new phrases almost effortlessly.

Vocabulary sections: These are not just a selection of exercises based around a particular lexical set. They are mini lessons which very often finish with a speaking exercise in which students have to use the vocabulary they have just learnt.

4. Thinking Training

The key to all the techniques described above is the fact that *Success* is designed in such a way that it not only teaches English for daily communication purposes and exams, but also helps students become more independent learners.

It is particularly important for the students who will use *Success*, as they are at the very important stage of transition from structured and controlled school education to more independent university studies.

Success provides what we call Thinking Training, which consists of:

- Training in drawing conclusions connected with grammar.
- Training in skills strategies.
- Training in social skills (emphasis on communication, register, intonation).
- Training in exam skills (exam strategies in the Workbook).
- Training in self-evaluation (self-assessment tests in the Workbook).
- Training in planning the goals for the year (Evaluation semester/year plans in the Testing and Evaluation Programme).

We believe that this training is fundamental for building students' confidence and thus for their future development.

5. Memorisation techniques

The *Thinking Training* would not be complete without memorisation techniques which make it possible for students to remember their own conclusions about the language as well as new vocabulary and structures. The course has been developed in the light of knowledge about how the brain works. To help students remember grammar, vocabulary and new phrases, the following principles have been taken into consideration:

1. New language is always presented in context. Learners remember the interesting context, which then helps them remember the new structure or vocabulary.
2. Exposure leads to acquisition so new language is constantly revised within the unit and within the course. For example, the new grammar introduced

in the opening spread is recycled in the Reading, Listening and Writing sections.

3. There are references to the language students have already come across in the course, which are called *Think Back!* Students are encouraged to find the information they need in the sections of the Students' Book that they have already covered. This activates the knowledge students already have.
4. The Revision sections after every second unit help consolidate the material in all its aspects (grammar, vocabulary, pronunciation and skills).
5. The material from the Students' Book is revised and consolidated in the Workbook.
6. The Teacher's Support Book provides exercises which refer to the material covered in the previous unit or section (*Warm-up* in the Teacher's Support Book). The bank of photocopiable activities helps to revise material in a communicative way.

6. An <u>equal</u> emphasis on skills and grammar

In keeping with current trends in language teaching, we provide very solid skills training but at the same time, we are aware that skills cannot be practised without a solid base in grammar. They have therefore been given equal emphasis.

Grammar presentation and practice

Success provides a structured and thorough grammar syllabus which will not create unforeseen problems or surprises. The specific contents of the syllabus are organised in a logical way, which makes grammar easier to understand.

Depending on the level and particular unit, there are up to three grammar points presented in a unit. Grammar is always presented in context. The presentation usually opens the unit, particularly at the lower levels, and the language is then consolidated and practised in all other sections, which is very important from the point of view of recycling and remembering new structures.

The grammar presentation uses a variety of text types (dialogues, short reading texts, cartoons, famous quotations). Students first analyse examples from the presentation (*Work it out* section), then check if they were right by looking at the *Check it out* sections. *Mind the trap!* boxes draw students' attention to areas of special difficulty and help to pre-empt errors. This particular way of teaching grammar encourages students to analyse and come to conclusions about grammar patterns and rules. The course deals with this important area effectively, yet without labouring the point.

Grammar analysis is followed by controlled practice exercises, which provide a focus on accuracy, before moving on to freer practice exercises.

Grammar is consolidated and practised in the Revision sections after every second unit.

There are more grammar exercises in the Workbook.

Skills strategies training

Skills training in *Success* is organised in the following way:

1. The Students' Book covers general skills strategies such as identifying speculation or text types and reading or listening effectively. These are 'life skills' students will need in different situations outside the classroom, regardless of whether they are taking any language exams or not.

2. The Workbook introduces exam skills which help students deal with specific exam task types such as multiple choice, true/false and matching.

Skills strategies training is not limited to simple rules in a box. Students first 'experience' the strategy and then complete the *Train Your Brain* box with the information they already have about the given strategy. One example of the approach is the teaching of prediction for reading in Unit 5 of *Success* Elementary. Students only read part of the text at a time and are encouraged to guess what will happen on the basis of titles, pictures and their knowledge of the world, as well as clues within the text. The sequence of exercises leading up to the *Train Your Brain* box shows how the strategy works in a very practical way. This inductive approach to teaching skills is unparalleled in *Success*.

Teaching Reading

The Reading sections present topics and language in a wide variety of text types such as notices, signs, text messages, website pages, questionnaires, reports, brochures, advertisements, letters, emails, literary extracts and semi-authentic or authentic journalistic material, all written in a lively style.

Each reading passage is accompanied by a wide range of exercises to encourage students not only to understand what they read, but also to notice the language used. They analyse the text in detail, focusing on new vocabulary while reinforcing and building on the grammar and vocabulary they have recently learnt.

Reading strategies are introduced and practised systematically and thoroughly throughout the book.

For reading strategies see the Students' Book contents page.

Reading is practised further in the Workbook.

There are also photocopiable activities for practising reading skills in the Teacher's Support Book.

Teaching Listening

Listening is probably the most extensively practised skill in *Success*. There are special Listening sections in every unit, and shorter listening tasks in all the other Students' Book sections, including the Revision and Culture Shock sections.

The skills of listening are developed in *Success* through a wealth of listening text types, including radio (reports, phone-in, interviews, quizzes), dialogue, monologue, announcements, speeches and mini-lectures, and songs. There is a wide range of task types, both for single answer, true/false, text completion, table completion etc, and more extensive and freer note taking, with opportunities for students to compare their answers or report their findings. Listening texts mainly include standard British English and regional British accents, but some contain accents of other English-speaking countries such as the USA and Australia, all properly marked in the Teacher's Support Book.

Additionally, there are special Listening sections which cover all the listening tasks students are likely to come across both in real life and in exams. They introduce strategies for listening which are then used repeatedly in the book.

For listening strategies see the Students' Book contents page. Listening is consolidated and practised in every other Revision section. Listening is practised further in the Workbook. There are also photocopiable activities for practising listening skills in the Teacher's Support Book.

Teaching Speaking

Speaking is often the area with which students experience the most frustration. They need considerable help and guidance to improve their accuracy, but not at the expense of fluency. *Success* aims to give a wide range of speaking tasks to cater for all student types and give ample, regular practice. Speaking exercises in the classroom have to be particularly easy to administer, but also be worth the effort you put in. They should have a very high pay-off with a sense of satisfaction for both you and the students.

There are speaking activities in all sections of the course. The special Speaking sections introduce functional language (*Speak Out*), either connected with situations (eg buying goods in a shop) or everyday phrases (eg expressing interest). Students learn how to use these phrases in context and practise them meaningfully in dialogues. At the higher levels, students are introduced to speaking strategies which will help them to express themselves in a more sophisticated way as well as prepare them for various exams.

In addition to this, there are speaking activities in every lesson of *Success*. These exercises have been carefully designed so that they progress from guided to more open ones.

There are extra speaking tasks in the Revision sections. In the Teacher's Support Book there are up to three photocopiable communicative activities for each unit. They provide extra speaking practice for each lesson.

Speaking is practised further in each unit of the Workbook where there are exercises which practise the language from the *Speak Out* box.

Teaching Writing

Writing is an essential part of the student's competence and requires special emphasis. *Success* addresses key text types, especially those required in exam situations. These include letters, notes, messages, emails, discursive and descriptive essays, reports and summary writing. The course provides both appropriate guidance and opportunities for freer practice. All types of writing are covered and there is a strong focus on micro skills such as punctuation, linking words and avoiding repetition in order to build and develop the overall writing skill. *Success* also focuses on the communicative value of writing by making students aware of who they are writing to.

There are writing tasks in every unit including seven to ten extended Writing sections in each book, depending on the level. Tasks move from controlled writing activities to longer writing exercises. Students analyse the specific features of a model text by doing the exercises. This leads up to a summary of the features in a *Train Your Brain* box. Students then write and check their own text using the *Train Your Brain* box to help them.

Writing is practised further in the Workbook where the Writing section contains model texts for students to follow.

7. A strong focus on vocabulary input and practice

The activation, extension and enrichment of vocabulary is an essential element of *Success*. The course pays attention to the revision and recycling of lexis in the belief that students at this level have particular difficulty in maintaining their fluency and need help in developing strategies for learning vocabulary in context. There is a strong focus on the practice of fixed and semi-fixed phrases, based on recent research showing that we acquire language more quickly and effectively by learning in chunks rather than single items.

New vocabulary is presented where relevant through grammar and reading lessons, as well as in separate Vocabulary sections. The separate Vocabulary sections include word formation exercises, word webs, and exercises on prepositions and phrasal verbs. From Pre-Intermediate onwards, *Mind the trap!* boxes here focus students' attention on any exceptions to the rule and areas of special difficulty. Vocabulary is consolidated and practised in the Revision sections.

The new vocabulary from the Students' Book is revised in the Workbook in special sections called the Vocabulary Workbook. The exercises included in this section practise all the vocabulary from the word list and help students remember the words they have just been introduced to.

From the Pre-Intermediate level, at the end of the Vocabulary Workbook section, there is a special exercise called 'Extend your vocabulary' where students practise the vocabulary they know as well as learn new meanings of familiar words or expressions.

The word lists in the Workbook are presented on a grey panel next to the exercises. Students should first do the exercises and refer to the word list. After they have completed the exercises, they should be able to remember the words. By covering the exercises (or folding the word list), they can check if they remember them all.

8. Expanding general knowledge

Success has a highly educational content. Students learn, for example, about history, geography, music, the environment, developments in science and technology, as well as about people who have played an important role in politics, art and culture. It encourages students to discuss contemporary social issues which are relevant to their age.

For a map of educational content see pages 14–15 in the Teacher's Support Book.

9. Building cultural awareness

The content of *Success* is designed to represent the culture of Britain and other English-speaking countries that are multicultural and multiracial. The course also introduces characters from the countries where students are likely to use the book so that they can relate to the issues easily.

Culture Shock sections focus on specific cultural facts and issues which provide further information and background about Britain and other English speaking countries.

10. A principled testing and evaluation system plus exam preparation

Testing in *Success* is very carefully planned and includes a strong link between the Revision sections in the Students' Book with the self-assessment tests in the Workbook as well as the tests in the Testing and Evaluation Programme. The fundamental rule is that there should be no surprises for the students, which means that they should know the format of the test well in advance.

Successful evaluation involves planning the distribution of different test types during the year. We help teachers in this by providing templates for year plans and spreadsheets for grading students. Teachers can adjust the templates to their own teaching situation by working on the documents provided in Word format on the Test Master CD-ROM.

We hope that you will enjoy working with *Success*.

Authors: *Jane Comyns Carr, Bob Hastings, Stuart McKinlay, Jenny Parsons;* Publisher: *Teresa Pelc.*

Components

Success Advanced Students' Book (160 pages)

Authors: Bob Hastings, Stuart McKinlay

Organisation

The Students' Book contains **12 thematic units, each consisting of 10 pages.** Each unit is clearly divided into sections, i.e. Grammar and Listening, Reading and Vocabulary, Vocabulary, Listening and Speaking, Writing. Each unit follows its own pattern and the sections differ in length according to what the particular topic/grammar point/vocabulary set requires.

Every two units are followed by a **2-page Revision** section called Think Forward To Exams which draws students' attention to the material they have covered. The majority of the task types in this section are exam oriented and help students prepare for the exams.

End matter contains:

- Student Activities for information-gap exercises.

- Culture Shocks – four lessons based around different aspects of British culture.

- Grammar *Check it out* section.

Class CDs

The recorded material is a very important feature of *Success*. There are usually four CDs for each level of *Success* (only the Intermediate level has three CDs, and the Advanced level offers as many as five CDs), which is more than any other course in this segment.

Class CDs include:

- Dialogues and listening activities from the Students' Book.

- All the reading texts from the Students' Book.

- Songs from the Students' Book.

Success Advanced Workbook (120 pages) with audio CD

Authors: Lindsay White, Rod Fricker and Rosemary Nixon

The *Success* workbook has unique features which were developed to help students with taking exams. It activates the language needed for exams which was introduced in the Students' Book.

As well as the grammar and vocabulary practice which is common to find in the workbook for other courses, the *Success* Workbook provides skills practice.

The unique features of the *Success* Workbook are as follows:

Exam Strategies

As the Workbook provides a lot of exam task types, students' attention is drawn to how these tasks should be approached so that they use the same techniques in the actual exam. Next to each exam tip there is a list of exercises it relates to and students are encouraged to use the strategy with these particular exercises.

Grammar

The grammar exercises are graded and go from easier, controlled tasks, to more challenging, contrastive exercises. At the back of the Workbook there is a section called Exam English in Use which offers CAE Use of English type tasks as well as error correction tasks.

Skills

The units provide further practice of Reading, Listening, Speaking and Writing. Most of the tasks which go with these sections are exam oriented. Reading texts are recorded on the Workbook CD to provide further listening and pronunciation practice. Speaking exercises help students memorise the functions introduced in the Students' Book. Writing sections include a model text which students follow in their homework assignments.

Vocabulary

The new vocabulary from the Students' Book is revised in the Workbook in special sections called the Vocabulary Workbook. The exercises included in this section practise all the vocabulary from the word list and help students remember the words they have just been introduced to.

From the Pre-Intermediate level, at the end of the Vocabulary Workbook section, there is a special exercise called 'Extend your vocabulary' where students practise the vocabulary they know, as well as learn new meanings of familiar words or expressions.

The word lists in the Workbook are presented on a grey panel next to the exercises. Students should first do the exercises and refer to the word list. After they have completed the exercises, they should be able to remember the words. By covering the exercises (or folding over the word list), they can check if they remember them all.

Self-assessment sections

After every second unit there is a self-assessment test with language and skills tasks. It is related to Think Forward To Exams sections in the Students' Book and is designed to prepare students for the tests provided in the Testing and Evaluation Programme.

As the key to the tests is provided in the Workbook, students can assess their progress and decide if they need further practice.

Organisation

- Exam strategies tips related to the exercises in the Workbook.

- 12 units with further practice of the key grammar, vocabulary, and skills lessons from the Students' Book.

- Cumulative self-assessment tests after every other unit with an answer key included in the Workbook.

- *Success* Workbook CD with listening exercises and reading texts.

Success Advanced Teacher's Support Book (224 pages)
Author: Rod Fricker

Success Teacher's Support Book is a unique publication which contains a wealth of additional materials for teachers. The Teacher's Support Book mirrors the Students' Book in its organisation and thus is very easy to navigate.

The Introduction provides information about unique features of the *Success* Students' Book as well as the other course components. It describes how the course prepares students for exams. The map of educational content in the form of an index lists all the names of people mentioned in the course as well as geographical names, cultural events, film or book titles. It is an easy reference for teachers who are looking for specific information in the book.

The teaching notes for each lesson start with information on how a given unit prepares students for exams. It is followed by a box which outlines what materials are available for the given unit. It is very often the case that teachers may expect difficult questions from students about the particular grammar, vocabulary, pronunciation, etc. Teacher's Support Book *Special difficulties* section provides answers to the anticipated problems. *Culture notes* provide a wealth of information connected with the people, history and photos in the Students' Book.

Warm-up activities refer back to the material covered before and provide a nice start to a new lesson. *Optional activities* offer suggestions for the exploitation of the Students' Book material.

The bank of photocopiable activities contains 36 activities (three per unit) and it includes skills oriented activities.

Organisation

- Introduction
- Components description
- Evaluation and Testing system in *Success*
- *Success* exams preparation
- Map of educational content – index
- Lesson notes with tapescripts
- Grammar and skills photocopiable resources
- Workbook answer key and tapescript

Success Advanced Testing and Evaluation Programme with Test Master CD-ROM

Author: Rod Fricker

The *Success* Testing and Evaluation Programme is more than just a collection of tests. It offers a coherent system of evaluation and grading which covers a wide range of test types.

The Testing and Evaluation Programme includes:
1 Presentations
2 Visual material discussions
3 Written assignments
4 Projects
5 Language tests
6 Skills tests
7 Mid-of-the-book test
8 End-of-the-book test

As well as the wide variety of tests, the Testing and Evaluation Programme includes:
1 Tips on administration of the tests
2 Evaluation year/semester plans
3 Suggestions about grading scales
4 Spreadsheets for grading students
5 **The *Success* Advanced Test Master CD-ROM which includes everything that is in the test book but in an editable format.**

SUCCESS the channel of choice
Success Elementary and Pre-Intermediate DVDs
(2 × more than 70 minutes)

Author: Jonathan Lloyd

SUCCESS the channel of choice is an entertaining, amusing and informative video drawing on a mix of TV programme formats performed by a small group of actors who aim to be a success on a shoestring! They aim to give us a slice of a normal day's TV viewing – news, drama, documentaries, quizzes and even sport or reality TV! We also watch the characters' everyday struggle with keeping the TV station going as well as with their complicated emotional lives.

There are seven episodes on each (Elementary and Pre-Intermediate) DVD. Each episode revises the grammar from the two units it follows.

SUCCESS the channel of choice
DVD Workbook (88 pages)

Author: Rod Fricker

The DVD Workbook provides grammar, vocabulary and speaking exercises for each episode. Viewing the episode and doing the exercises from the DVD Workbook gives enough material for an entertaining 45-minute lesson. The DVD Workbook contains notes on both levels of the *SUCCESS the channel of choice* DVD.

Evaluation and testing system in *Success*

Frequent testing and evaluation gives students a sense of achievement and prepares them for difficult exams in the future. It is also a source of information for teachers as to whether remedial teaching is necessary. The evaluation and testing system in *Success* comprises:

A. Revision sections in the Students' Book

After each two units in the Students' Book there is a Revision section (Think Forward To Exams) which checks vocabulary, grammar and skills for the two units.

B. Self-assessment tests in the *Success* Workbook

The self-assessment tests in the *Success* Workbook are linked to the Revision sections in the Students' Book and prepare students for the Skills tests in the Testing and Evaluation Programme.

C. Skills tests in the Testing and Evaluation Programme

They are directly linked to the self-assessment tests in the *Success* Workbook and test the skills of reading and listening on the topics related to the two units of the Students' Book they follow.

D. Variety of other types of tests in the Testing and Evaluation Programme

They are linked to speaking, writing, grammar and vocabulary exercises in the Students' Book and the *Success* Workbook.

The two main reasons for giving students regular tests are: the need to be able to assess their progress and the need to give them the confidence to continue learning. Therefore, our tests appear regularly: after every two units of *Success* and test only the material that has been presented in these two units. What is more, we test it in such a way that the students should get most of the answers correct if they have studied the material adequately. The purpose is not to trick students or show them how much there is still to learn but to demonstrate that systematic work brings benefits. If they work systematically during the semester, most students should get high marks on the tests.

COMMUNICATIVE APPROACH TO TESTING VOCABULARY, GRAMMAR AND SKILLS

The self-assessment tests in the *Success* Workbook and the tests in the Testing and Evaluation Programme help to assess students' progress in such areas as: vocabulary, grammar, writing, reading, listening and speaking. The year plans and scales of grading have been constructed in such a way that the weight of the final grade consists of the following:

65% skills + 35% grammar and vocabulary

It reflects the communicative concept of *Success* as well as current trends in testing and evaluation. The grading sheets show very clearly what areas a student is good at and help teachers come up with more detailed evaluation of the student's progress. It also helps with remedial teaching. For example, students who consistently fail to deliver good writing should be advised to do more writing and perhaps should complete all the written assignments contained in the Testing and Evaluation Programme.

TESTS AND TYPES OF ASSIGNMENTS IN THE *SUCCESS* TESTING AND EVALUATION PROGRAMME

The *Success* Testing and Evaluation Programme is not just a collection of tests. We are proposing a coherent system of evaluation and grading which covers language and skills tests as well as oral exams, written assignments and class projects. To make the most of our proposal, different tests should be carefully planned over the semester or school year. In order to help teachers with this difficult task we provide examples of evaluation semester/year plans linked to the grading system.

The Testing and Evaluation Programme includes:

1 **Presentations.** There are twelve presentations, which correspond to the Students' Book units.

2 **Visual material.** There are six sets, three for each semester.

3 **Written assignments.** There are twelve topics of written assignments, which correspond to the Students' Book units.

11

4 Projects. There are twelve class projects to be prepared in groups of 2–3 students.

5 Language tests. There are twelve A and B Language tests, which revise the grammar and vocabulary presented in each unit of the Students' Book.

6 Skills tests. There are six A and B Skills tests which test the skills of listening and reading, on the topics related to the two units they follow.

7 Mid-of-the-book test. There is an A and B test that revises vocabulary and grammar from Units 1–6 of the Students' Book.

8 End-of-the-book test. There is an A and B test that revises vocabulary and grammar from Units 1–12 of the Students' Book.

As well as the wide variety of tests, the Testing and Evaluation Programme includes:

1 Tips on administration of the tests

2 Evaluation year/semester plans

3 Suggestions about grading scales

4 Spreadsheets for grading students

5 **The *Success* Advanced Test Master CD-ROM which includes everything that is in the test book but in an editable format.**

Evaluation year/semester plans

Among the most important problems all teachers face in their teaching practice is students' motivation and systematic work. The key to solving these two problems is providing interesting teaching material as well as a successful evaluation system which would help to stimulate students towards achieving top results throughout the school year.

Success helps to address these issues by providing very interesting lessons in the Students' Book and a coherent testing and evaluation system in the Testing and Evaluation Programme.

The proposal is based on research which has been carried out over recent years and proved that teachers either use similar systems or would like to use them if they did not involve so much preparation. Teachers asked for a variety of tests which could be used in a flexible way depending on their teaching situation. As we know, there are many classroom scenarios. Some classes require a lot of remedial teaching to bring students to the same/similar level. Some classes continue from the course book which they started studying the year before. Some classes cover the Students' Book in a year and others struggle regardless of the fact that they have the same number of hours per week. We cannot provide templates for all teachers/classes but we can give examples of what a good plan should consist of as well as provide all the

ingredients needed for that plan. Teachers can mix them in the way which is best for their group of students and according to their own judgement. All the materials are provided on the Test Master CD-ROM and teachers can make all the necessary adjustments to all the tests and the semester plans.

Advantages of the plan:

1 Motivation – students appreciate that their teacher thought about their learning process and feel cared for. Most of them pay their teachers back by being equally well prepared for the tests.

2 Students' independence – students feel that they can choose to take the test or skip it as they establish the target number of points they want to achieve for themselves. It makes them feel that they are able to manage their own learning process.

3 Systematic work – students work very systematically to score as many points as possible without constantly needing to be reminded of it by teachers.

4 Clear and objective evaluation – students, teachers and parents know the rules for the assessment for the year. The rules are the same for everybody, which helps to build trust between teachers and students.

5 Comparable grading system – the system can be shared between teachers of the same school. It makes the grades easy to compare within the different classes/students of the same school.

6 Flexibility – the system of evaluation in points can be easily 'translated' into grades.

7 Systematic progress reports – both students and parents receive frequent reports about their progress.

8 Exam preparation – the points system helps students to get used to the way they will be evaluated in the exam.

Success exams preparation

COMMON EUROPEAN FRAMEWORK

Success and CEF

The *Success* grammar, vocabulary and skills syllabuses are linked to the Council of Europe's Common European Framework. The CEF is a document created by the Council of Europe as part of their policy to promote foreign language learning, cultural contacts and understanding between the people of Europe. The CEF suggests that learners use a European Language Portfolio as a record of their language learning experience and progress.

Levels within the Common European Framework

Descriptions of different language levels are phrased in the form of *can do* statements. They state what students *can do* at each level. There are six levels: A1 is the lowest, C2 is the highest.

A1. Basic User. This is the lowest level which is described within the Framework. It is also described as Breakthrough Level.
A2. Basic User. This is also described as Waystage Level.
B1. Independent User. This is also described as Threshold Level.
B2. Independent User. This is also described as Vantage Level.

C1. Proficient User. Learners at this level are also described as having Effective Operational Proficiency.
C2. Proficient User. Learners at this level are also described as having Mastery.

The Beginner and Elementary levels of *Success* cover the key objectives of level A1. Other levels of *Success* fit in across the levels – the Pre-Intermediate level of *Success* covers the objectives of levels A2 and B1 of the framework, Intermediate covers levels B1 and B2 and Upper Intermediate covers levels B2 and C1. The Advanced level covers level C1.

CAMBRIDGE EXAMS

The *Success* syllabus also takes into consideration the range of exams from the University of Cambridge exams suite. Although the level is obviously graded to your students' needs, you will find all of the task types in one or more of the Cambridge exams.

The table below shows how all of the levels of *Success* fit together with both CEF and the UCLES exams:

Success	Common European Framework Level	UCLES Main Suite Exam
Beginner	A1	–
Elementary	A1	–
Pre-Intermediate	A2/B1	KET
Intermediate	B1/B2	PET
Upper Intermediate	B2/C1	FCE
Advanced	C1	CAE

SUCCESS AND EXAMS

Success has two main aims: to help students gain a general level of competence in English and prepare for exams. *Success* includes all of the features that you would expect to see in a general English course – listening, reading, speaking and writing tasks and in addition to this there are a variety of exam-style exercises which are graded to the students' level.

Exercise types

Success includes a varied range of exercise types which will give students the practice they need in order to prepare for exams. True/false, multiple choice, gap-fill exercises are some of the many exercise types students will need to be familiar with and *Success* includes all of these.

EXAM STRATEGIES

There are tips and strategies in both the Students' Book and Workbook to equip students with the tools they need to pass an exam successfully.
The Workbook includes a section on how to deal with exam-style tasks. Additionally, the vocabulary is organised into topics to help with revision.

Map of educational content – index

People

Geographical Names

Places, Arts and Entertainment

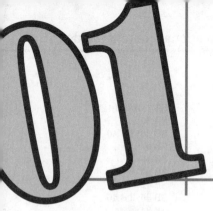

Pleased to meet you

Read, listen and talk about relationships, dating, personality types.
Practise common problems with tenses, Future Perfect and Continuous.
Focus on managing conversations.
Write narratives.

EXAM FOCUS

Topic: Family life and socialising

Speaking
Managing conversations: SB p.13, ex.6
Roleplay: SB p.13, ex.7
Giving presentations: SB p.13, ex.8

Reading
Gapped text (paragraphs): SB p.9, ex.3

Grammar and vocabulary
Verbs in brackets: SB p.11, ex.9
Wordbuilding: SB p.7, ex.6; p.7, ex.7

Writing
A story: SB p.15, ex.14

Unit 1 Materials
....
Success Workbook Unit 1
....
Photocopiable resources 1, 2, 3
....
Testing and Evaluation Programme tests

VOCABULARY AND SPEAKING

This section introduces idioms using body parts vocabulary and wordbuilding using prefixes to make opposites of adjectives.

Special difficulties: Students often tend to overuse idioms so it is important to know which are very common in everyday language, eg *keep a straight face*, and which sound a bit old-fashioned, eg *give someone the cold shoulder*.

Warm-up Review of tenses. *My grammar problem.* Tell Ss to write down the area(s) of grammar in English they find most difficult. This should be quite specific, eg future forms, Present Perfect Simple and Continuous, not vague, eg tenses. Ss then mingle and find how many other people have the same problem. Elicit the grammar problems and how many people have problems with each. It is best not to try to deal with them all at this point but just to be aware of what the Ss see as their main problems for future reference.

1 Ss open their books and look at the cartoons without looking at the idioms. Ask them to describe the situation in each, eg A *There are four people in a café. Three of them are laughing but one man looks serious. Maybe they are laughing at him and he is embarrassed or upset.* Ss then complete the captions in pairs and discuss together what the idioms mean. Elicit the answers and tell Ss that they should be careful when using idioms if they want to sound natural. In these sentences *don't turn your nose up at it, pulling his leg* and *gave her the cold shoulder* may sound less natural than the other idioms.

Answers 1 E **2** B – to be unable to act calmly and sensibly **3** F – to stay calm **4** A – to stop oneself from laughing **5** D – to play a joke on someone by making them believe something that isn't (or is) true **6** C – to reject

2 Ss find the idioms alone. Set a strict time limit for this (one minute) and then Ss work in pairs to think of the meanings. Tell Ss to write the idioms using the pronoun *one('s)/oneself* as in the example. This is unusual in spoken English, although Prince Charles uses it a lot in place of *I/my/myself*, but useful in formal or impersonal written English. Elicit ideas and correct if necessary.

Answers 1 fall head over heels in love – to suddenly feel a very strong feeling of love for someone; laugh one's head off – to laugh uncontrollably **2** have a mind of one's own – to have your own opinions; make up one's mind – to think about something and come to a decision; be out of one's mind – to be crazy **3** see eye to eye – to agree with someone; cry one's eyes out – to cry uncontrollably **4** put on a brave face – not show that you are upset **5** get something off one's chest – to share a problem or secret; keep a stiff upper lip – not show any emotion, not show that you are upset; under someone's thumb – controlled by someone, subservient to them; tear one's hair out – to show that you are angry or upset; hold one's tongue – to keep quiet, stop yourself from responding; put one's foot in it – to say the wrong thing; a pain in the neck – annoying

3 Before Ss do the quiz, ask them: *Are you easy to get on with?* Ss discuss this in pairs, giving reasons for their answers. Then they do the quiz and find out if they were correct about themselves or not.

4 Ss look at the sentences and decide which idioms would and would not be possible for each. Then they listen to check their ideas.

Tapescript CD 1 Track 2

One

Mandy: *[English West Country accent]* Ted! What are you doing? That's an electricity pylon!

Ted: *[neutral English accent]* I know! Oh, wow! It's brilliant up here!

Mandy: It's really dangerous!

Ted: I can see for miles.

Mandy: Ted! Come down. You're going to fall.

Ted: No, I'm going all the way to the top!

Mandy: No, Ted, no!

Two

Tammi: *[American (Californian) accent]* Hey, Mozart! I love that!

Billy: *[American (Californian) accent]* Yeah, it's so relaxing.

Tammi: Hmm … Hey, do you like my new top, Billy?

Billy: Yeah, it's cool. Blue's my favourite colour.

Tammi: Mine too! What are you reading?

Billy: Oh, it's an old horror story by Stephen King.

Tammi: I adore his books.

Billy: Yeah, they're so good, aren't they? … Oh, Lucy called and invited us to the cinema.

Tammi: What's the film?

Billy: A documentary about global warming.

Tammi: Well, if you like, but I don't like documentaries much.

Billy: No, neither do I. Let's just stay in and eat a pizza.

Tammi: Double cheese and pepperoni?

Billy: That's my favourite!

Three

Van: *[Ulster accent]* You seem a bit tense, Dan. What is it?

Dan: *[Ulster accent]* Nothing.

Van: Come on, you can tell me … What's up?

Dan: What's up!? I'll tell you what's up! I'm fed up with Brenda. She never listens to a word I say. I hate my job and my new boss hates me, so that's just perfect. … Shut up! These idiots think they own the road! And we've been sitting in this traffic jam for hours and because of it we're probably going to get to the concert late. And the tickets cost me a fortune that I can't afford. And … ow! I've got toothache!

Van: Is that all?

Dan: Yeah, but I feel a lot better now.

Four

Ivy: *[Scottish accent]* Sally! Sally Smith!

Sally: *[neutral English accent]* Oh! Ivy!

Ivy: Oh, I haven't seen you for ages. How are you?

Sally: Oh, I mustn't grumble. Things are going well. I'm married now.

Ivy: To Dave?

Sally: Yeah, of course … Oh and look at you! Congratulations!

Ivy: Thanks! What for?

Sally: How long have you been pregnant?

Ivy: What?

Sally: When are you expecting the baby?

Ivy: Sally, I'm not pregnant.

Sally: Oh! I'm really sorry, I thought …

Ivy: Yes, I was thinking maybe I should go on a diet!

Sally: Oh Sally! I'm so sorry …

Answers 1 out of his mind 2 see eye to eye 3 got his problems off his chest 4 put her foot in it

5 In pairs, Ss try to do as many of these as possible without a dictionary. If there are any adjectives they cannot define, they should then check. Elicit answers and definitions of the odd words out.

Answers 1 calm, unemotional 2 independent, strong-willed 3 hesitant, indecisive 4 obedient, unassertive 5 annoying, exasperating 6 cheerful, fun-loving 7 careless, insensitive 8 oversensitive, temperamental

6 Make sure Ss know that, for the first part of the activity, they should only look at the adjectives with prefixes and that the other adjectives in the exercise cannot be made negative in this way, eg *calm* does not have a negative prefix. Ss try to do the second part of Exercise 6 without checking, and then check in their dictionaries.

Answers 1 inconsiderate 2 inefficient 3 immature 4 disobedient 5 irrational 6 unaffectionate 7 insecure 8 unselfish

Mind the trap!

After looking at the Mind the trap! box, you can ask Ss to try to write the opposites of the adjectives in Exercise 5 that do not take negative prefixes. There may be more than one possible answer for each adjective, eg *calm – nervous, anxious; strong-willed – weak-willed; hesitant – decisive; stubborn – flexible; annoying – pleasant; exasperating – pleasant; cheerful – miserable; fun-loving – serious; careless – careful; cocky – modest; oversensitive – insensitive; temperamental – even-tempered.*

7 Ss work in pairs to guess the nouns. They should not look them up at this stage. Elicit the answers and spellings. Look at the form of the words, i.e. they are all uncountable except for *creation* and *social skills*. Ss then write their sentences. Nominate pairs to read out sentences in open class.

Answers 1 charisma 2 charm 3 confidence 4 courage 5 creation/creativity 6 energy 7 respect 8 self-consciousness 9 social skills 10 style

8 Give Ss an example of how much information they should include, eg *My cousin is really annoying. He's stubborn and impatient. I find it hard to talk to him. He's a real pain in the neck. We're always arguing.* Then in groups of three or four Ss discuss each type of person in turn, i.e. a relative, then a friend etc. At the end of the activity, each student could write about one or more of the people as in the example above.

ADDITIONAL PRACTICE: Photocopiable resources. Resource 1: *Body talk*. Page 166

READING AND VOCABULARY

> This section introduces a number of phrasal verbs on the topic of people and relationships.

Culture notes

H.L. Mencken (1880–1956) was an American journalist and writer and is said to be one of the most influential writers of the early 20th century. He is best known for *The American Language*, a study of how English is spoken in the USA. It was published in 1919.

Clint Eastwood (born 1930) is an American actor and film director. He got his first big acting role as Rowdy Yates in the TV cowboy series *Rawhide* in 1958. His first film as director was *Play Misty for Me* in 1971. He has won two Oscars but as director and for Best Film, not as an actor. He became mayor of Carmel in California in 1986 and served for two terms.

The earliest surviving **love spoon** dates from 1667 although they are believed to have existed before then. They were not only a token of love but also a way of showing the girl's father that the man was skilled with his hands. They are still given today as wedding, anniversary and christening gifts.

Medieval love poetry is thought to have originated in Provence. The Provencal language is closely related to French, Italian and Spanish and so the poems spread quickly throughout Europe. This form of poetry spread in the middle of the 12th century by troubadours, composers and performers of poetry who travelled and read their poems.

Warm-up Revision of vocabulary from the last lesson. *F1.*
Put Ss in groups of four or five. On the board, draw an oval shape which represents a Formula 1 race track. This is split into twenty sections. Each group chooses a name, eg Ferrari, McLaren, Lotus, Renault etc. Write the initial letters at the start of the track. For the first part of the activity, Ss have to write a body part. Dictate some of the idioms from the last lesson, eg 1 *See _____ to _____*. Ss write the body part. Test eight idioms and then groups swap answer papers with another group. Go through the answers and move the 'cars' on the board depending on how many words each group got right. Repeat the process with six adjectives which take a negative prefix, eg *considerate*. This time Ss write just the correct prefix. Again Ss swap papers and the cars are moved. Finally, test six nouns formed from adjectives. The winning car is the one furthest around the track after three activities.

1 Put Ss into groups of three. Set a time limit for Ss to discuss the two quotes and try to encourage them to use typical language for giving opinions, agreeing and disagreeing. Remind them that activities such as this are useful exam practice, not just a way to warm Ss up for the reading task. Elicit what the quotes mean first and then whether they agree with them.

2 Tell Ss not to look at the text yet, just the picture. Elicit what can be seen. Ss then look at the topics in Exercise 2. Elicit what all the words mean, eg *mating, chaperones, chivalry* etc. Set a time limit of one minute for Ss to choose topics for themselves and to compare ideas with a partner. Then set another time limit of two minutes for Ss to scan the text and find which topics are mentioned. Elicit answers and where the topics can be found in the text, i.e. 2 paragraph 1; 3 paragraph 3; 4 paragraph 4 and 5; 5 paragraph 1 mentions marriages breaking up; 6 paragraph 5 mentions chivalry although it does not state whether it is medieval; paragraph 2 talks about knights rescuing women from lonely towers and gives the date 1228; 7 the introduction and paragraph 6; 8 paragraph 2, possibly paragraph 6.

Answers 1 ✗ 2 ✓ 3 ✓ 4 ✓ 5 ✓ 6 ✓ 7 ✓ 8 ✓

3 Tell Ss to read the first paragraph in Exercise 3, about fans, and decide which of the topics in Exercise 2 it corresponds to (coded messages). This will help Ss decide where the paragraph should be inserted into the original text. Ss do the same for the other paragraphs where possible. When they are ready, again tell Ss to look at the first paragraph and how it starts: 'And then there were fans'. This indicates that before the paragraph, there was another type of coded message mentioned. Ss now work in pairs to complete the exercise. Go through the answers eliciting the clues to be found in the original text and the paragraphs from Exercise 3, i.e. 1 'Much less violent' than 'capturing wives by force'; 2 'women as objects to be adored' – 'women haven't always been passive victims'; 3 'overcome these social obstacles' – 'had to be introduced', 'have to be reintroduced'; 4 'never at night' – 'courting couples would share a bed'; 5 'imaginative ways to keep in touch' – 'Take, for example, wooden spoons'; 6 wooden spoons, gloves – 'And then there were fans'.

Answers 1 D 2 F 3 B 4 G 5 C 6 A

4 Remind Ss that there may be information in both parts of the text. To make this task quicker, put the Ss into groups of six. Each student has one of the topics only and then the Ss tell each other what they found out.

Answers **A** – advantage, **D** – disadvantage
1 A It spread genes around. **D** Not nice for the women. **2 A** Rich people could ensure they didn't have to share their money; less likely to break up than other marriages. **D** More of a business arrangement than a romantic one. **3 A** Gave the woman the right to ask a man to marry her. **D** It only happened once every four years. **4 A** Ensured couples behaved properly. **D** The couple had little or no privacy. **5 A** The couple could talk together in private, they were forced to behave properly (an advantage for the woman's reputation). **D** They were forced to behave properly (a disadvantage for

18   Students' Book ➡ pages 8–9

the couple themselves). **6 A** It allowed men and women to communicate secretly (an advantage for the couple). **D** It allowed men and women to communicate secretly (a disadvantage for the couple's parents).

5 Tell Ss to find the phrasal verbs in the texts and decide what they mean. Then they write the collocations in their notebooks. Elicit the meanings and show Ss where the phrasal verb has a literal meaning, eg *to bump into a door*, and where it has a non-literal meaning, eg *to turn down help*.

Answers 1 break up – a conversation / a fight / a relationship / with your boyfriend **2** fall for – a trick / a new classmate **3** turn down – some help / the volume **4** strike up – a conversation / a relationship **5** bump into – the door / a new classmate **6** come up with – a trick / a good idea **7** settle down – to do some work / with your boyfriend **8** do with – some help / a good idea

6 Ss look at the pictures and the descriptions and try to act out the gestures in pairs. Then they discuss what the gestures mean and compare ideas as a class. Play the recording once for Ss to write the answers and then again for them to check. Tell Ss they should get used to listening carefully to recordings twice, even when they think they have got the answers correct after the first listening.

Tapescript CD 1 Track 4

Elizabeth: *[RP accent]* Mr Biggins. How lovely to see you again!
George: *[RP accent]* Ah, hello, Miss Barnet. The pleasure is all mine. But please, call me George.
Elizabeth: Very well, but then you must call me Elizabeth.
George: Oh, yes. Of course.
Elizabeth: You know, George, I do not recall ever seeing you at a ball before.
George: No, I'm not terribly keen on dancing, you know.
Elizabeth: You must learn.
George: Hmm, Miss Ba ..., Elizabeth, erm ... do you know who that lady over there is?
Elizabeth: Yes, it's Lady Caroline Fitzpatrick.
George: You know, I rather think she might be attracted to me.
Elizabeth: Why do you think that George?
George: Well, I was looking at her – smiling, you know ... and she started waving her fan at me like this.
Elizabeth: Oh George!
George: What?
Elizabeth: You don't understand the language of fans, do you?
George: Don't I?
Elizabeth: No, if a lady closes her fan and waves it energetically in front of her face, she's telling you not to be rude!
George: Oh dear ... Elizabeth, I think I'm getting better at this fan language thing.
Elizabeth: Oh, yes?

George: Hmm. I was looking at Miss Larkin a moment ago, and she held her fan half-opened next to her left cheek. That means 'Come and talk to me', doesn't it?
Elizabeth: No, George. I'm sorry, it doesn't. It means 'No'.
George: No?
Elizabeth: Yes.
George: Oh.
Elizabeth: If a lady wishes to speak to you, she'll close her fan, hold it lightly on her shoulder and look away from it ... like this ...
George: Ah! I see. And what does it mean if someone is touching her lips with a closed fan?
Elizabeth: It means 'Kiss me!'.
George: Oh! I say!
Elizabeth: An open fan held in front of the face in the right hand ... like this ... means 'Follow me!'.
George: Right.
Elizabeth: George!
George: Yes?
Elizabeth: Follow me!
George: Oh, right ...
Elizabeth: Oh, George!
George: This is delightful, Elizabeth ... Oh! You're doing something with your fan ... let me guess what you're trying to tell me ... You're holding an open fan to the left of your head with your eyes looking down ...
Elizabeth: Yes.
George: Does it mean you're bored?
Elizabeth: No! You silly man! It means, 'I love you!'.
George: Oh, Elizabeth!

Answers 1 Don't be rude **2** No **3** I want to talk to you **4** Kiss me **5** Follow me **6** I love you

7 Ss have already looked at arranged marriages so use this as an example and try to elicit more advantages or disadvantages. One way Ss could do this is to imagine that one of them is a child brought up in a traditional family but in a western culture. All your friends are free to choose their own partners but you are not. He/She argues why he/she should be allowed to go out with anyone he/she likes. The other students are parents who are explaining why their way of life and traditional arranged marriages are a good thing. Ss roleplay and then discuss the arguments both sides used. Ss then go on to discuss the other points. Set a time limit of three minutes for each question and discuss all as a class at the end of the activity.

GRAMMAR AND LISTENING

This section reviews tenses and looks in detail at complex future forms.

Special difficulties: The first part of the lesson is a revision of Present Perfect forms. The teacher should be prepared to explain if any problems arise here as there is no grammar explanation of these forms in the unit.

Warm-up Review of phrasal verbs from the previous lesson. *Act out the phrasal verb.* Put the Ss into eight groups and give each a situation to act out. Write the eight phrasal verbs on the board: *break up, fall for, turn down, strike up, bump into, come up with, settle down, do with.* The Ss must not say their phrasal verb during their roleplay. When Ss have watched another group, they guess the phrasal verb being shown.

Possible situations:

You have just broken up with your boyfriend.

You have fallen for a new boy in your class.

Your parents want you to turn down the volume on your CD player.

You meet someone at a party and strike up a conversation.

You bump into an old friend in the street.

You come up with a great idea for Friday evening.

You can't settle down to do your homework.

You could do with some help with your Maths homework.

1 Ss discuss what they can see in the photo and read the description of the programme. Allow two minutes for Ss to discuss the questions in pairs and then elicit ideas in open class.

2 Again set a time limit of two minutes. Tell Ss not to simply give their opinion and stop talking but to look at all possible combinations and give reasons.

3 Think Back! Ss discuss their answers in groups of three or four. After the listening, discuss the uses of the different tenses.

Tapescript CD 1 Track 5

Tina: *[American accent]* So remember, in part one you're going to hear the guys talking about their girlfriends, and then you've got to guess who they're in love with. When you think you know, text 087654321 and give us your answer. Just write the names of the couples and you can win a fabulous holiday in a five-star-hotel in romantic Venice. So, let's hear what Simon has to say ...

Simon: *[London accent]* The thing about her is that she always does everything so well. She's a perfectionist. She's so creative and stylish – totally unlike me, but you know what they say – opposites attract, right?

I mean, she loves shopping and I love football, but we get on so well. We're made for each other. I'll never forget the time we met. I was at a really dull party and I was getting bored so I went out for some fresh air. Anyway, she was bored too and wanted to leave so she'd gone out to the garden to see if it was still raining, and basically it was love at first sight. We started talking and I just fell for her and she fell for me. We've been seeing each other for more than a year now, and in fact, we're thinking of getting married. We've seen a flat we like and well, it's expensive, but ...

Tina: OK, now let's listen to James ...

James: *[London accent]* We think it's important to enjoy life, but about a year ago I was feeling depressed, I was lacking in confidence and I was probably a bit of a pain in the neck and we started arguing a bit. And one day I got a letter from her. I was sure she was going to break up with me. But she was just writing to tell me she loved me. When I read the letter, I burst into tears. I cried my eyes out. You know what I love about her? She always looks on the bright side of life. She's always cheerful. She was unemployed for a while but she got a new job last month in a software company and she loves it. She's really funny too. I laugh my head off at some of the things she says! And she's always doing things to surprise me. For example, she's booked a weekend for us in a health spa! She says it'll be fun. I hope she's right.

Tina: Right, now it's our last contestant. Tommy!

Tommy: *[London accent]* I've been head over heels in love with her since we met. Chris had invited me round for Christmas dinner and she was there. She was laughing when I walked into the room, and there was like an instant connection between us. It was embarrassing because she'd been going out with Chris for ages and he's my best friend. But we sat next to each other and we just got on so well. I mean, she laughed when I told her a joke! And I'm terrible at telling jokes! The next day she wrote to me, and after I'd read the letter, I went round to her house. We've been going out together ever since then. Fortunately, Chris was really cool about it. She's been unemployed for a while so she's going to go to college to study Art. She's considerate, fun-loving, mature and she has a lovely smile.

Answers 1b (Present Simple for facts) **2a** (emotional response to a habit – annoyance or pleasure) **3b** (*think* as a state verb) **4a** (*think* as an action verb) **5a** (*when* referring to *after*) **6b** (*when* referring to *at the time*) **7a** (a single past action at an unstated time) **8b** (a continual process which started in the past and is still happening now) **9b** (a single past action which happened before a different past time, although this second past time isn't mentioned in the text) **10a** (a continual process which started at a point before a different past time and was still in progress at that second time – again not mentioned here) **11b** (a finished past situation) **12a** (an unfinished situation that started in the past and is still true now) **13a** (the two events happened simultaneously or almost simultaneously) **14b** (one activity happened and finished before the other activity started)

4 Allow Ss to look at Exercise 4 and discuss what they remember from the first listening. Play the recording again and discuss Ss' ideas and reasons.

5 Ss complete the sentences alone and then compare in pairs or small groups. For alternative answers, as in gap 9, Ss should be able to justify that choice, i.e. 1 Present Simple for facts; 2 *was trying – when* meaning *at the time*; 3 *been thinking* – a continual process before a second past time; 4 Present Perfect with a present result; 5 Present Continuous for a temporary activity happening around now; 6 Past Simple to agree with *was*; 7 Present Perfect – a situation that started in the past and is still happening now; 8 Past Continuous – use of *when* to mean *at the time*; 9 Present Continuous – a continuous form to show it is an emotional response to a habit; Ss may also use: *He was always pulling* – at the time he asked me to marry him although since then he has changed.

Answers 1 have 2 was trying 3 been thinking 4 has sold 5 is working 6 talked 7 have been 8 was having 9 is always pulling

6 Ss decide in pairs who the couples are, then listen to check. Elicit answers and recap on who was right in Exercise 2. Clues: Maggie talks about a software company and we know she is keen on computers. She also says she needs to lose a few kilos and we know she has booked up at a health spa. Natalia says they met at a friend's house. Tommy said they met at Chris' house. Yasmina and Simon both talk about plans to get married.

For tapescript see page 206.

Answers 1 James 2 Tommy 3 Simon

7 Ss work in pairs to decide who it may or may not be and why, eg *(a) probably isn't Yasmina and Simon because they're planning on getting married.*

Tapescript CD 1 Track 7

Tina: So Maggie, will you be coming to the party after the show?
Maggie: Of course, Tina. I wouldn't miss it for the world.
Tina: Great ... Now it's time for 'Make your predictions!' Where will you be a year from now? What will you be doing? What will have happened in your lives? And don't forget ... you'll all be coming back here in one year's time to see if your predictions have come true or not. Yasmina?
Yasmina: In a year's time we'll have been married for six months ... happily married, I hope. And we'll have had a wonderful honeymoon in the Caribbean. And I hope I'll be expecting a baby!
Tina: Natalia?
Natalia: Well, unfortunately Tina, a year from now we'll be living far away from each other. I'll be leaving London

at the end of the summer and if everything goes to plan, I'll have been studying Art in Edinburgh for about eight months. I don't know how I'm going to cope without him.
Tina: James?
James: By this time next year we'll have been going out together for three years. With a bit of luck I'll have graduated by then, and maybe we'll be working for the same company. That'd be cool.

Answers a Natalia b Yasmina c Tina d James e Tina

Work it out

8 Before Ss look at Exercise 8, ask them how many different tenses there are underlined in Exercise 7 (three) and see if the Ss can name them. Ss then do the matching activity alone.
Note: The Future Continuous can also be used instead of *going to* to show a more tentative question/answer, especially just before making a request.

Answers 1 e 2 c 3 a 4 b 5 d

Check it out

Refer Ss to the Check it out section on page 154 to make sure they fully understand the structure.

9 Ss work together to choose the correct form and to justify it, referring to the uses in Exercise 8, i.e. 1 – use 2; 2 – use 4; 3 – use 5; 4 – use 1; 5 – use 3.

Answers 1 will be celebrating 2 will have broadcast 3 will have been bringing 4 will you be doing 5 will be sitting

10 Remind Ss of the phrasal verbs in the last section of the book and tell them to try to use some of these in their answers. Elicit ideas in open class before Ss look at what really happens.

11 Ss try to do this alone and then check in pairs, referring back to Exercise 8 to justify their answers.

Answers 1 What **will you be doing** at this time tomorrow? 2 ✓ 3 By the end of the year, **we'll have been going out** together for nine months. 4 It won't be hard to find me. **I'll be wearing** a bright red hat. 5 ✓ 6 If we don't get a move on, the film **will have finished** before we get there.

12 Tell Ss that, although simple future forms may be possible, eg *When I get home today, I think I'll have a bath / I'm going to watch TV*, they should use the three tenses focused on in this unit. Elicit answers and correct where necessary.

ADDITIONAL PRACTICE: Photocopiable resources. Resource 2: *Past, Present and Future.* Page 167

SPEAKING AND LISTENING

This section introduces ways of managing conversations.

Special difficulties: At first, the fact that Ss are concentrating on specific phrases to include in their conversations may detract from the conversations themselves. However, they should get as much practice as possible so that they start using these phrases naturally and without thinking.

Warm-up Review of future forms. *Jeopardy.* Have some answers to questions prepared. Put the Ss into two groups and tell them that you are going to give them an answer and they must think of a question, using the Future Continuous or Future Perfect that would give that answer. One student from each group comes to the front of the class and faces away from the board. Write the answer on the board, eg *I'll be watching television.* The other Ss ask their student questions trying to elicit the answer, eg *What will you be doing after school? What will you be doing at 10p.m.?* etc.

Possible answers:

I'll have finished my homework.
I'll have got married.
I'll be walking to school.
I'll be relaxing.
I'll have gone to bed.

1 Check *to break the ice* before Ss brainstorm the two questions. Set a time limit of about three minutes for the groups to discuss their ideas and then discuss them as a class.

2 Give Ss two minutes to decide on how to start each conversation and nominate different pairs to act them out. Then play the recording and elicit from Ss how they compared with the roleplays they saw acted out.

Tapescript `CD 1 Track 8`

One
Man: *[Australian accent]* Sorry to bother you, but do you think I could have a look at your paper?
Woman: *[neutral English accent]* Oh! Eh ... yes, of course. Here you are.
Man: Thanks a lot.

Two
Girl: *[American accent]* Hi, can I get you something to drink? The orange juice is really good. It's a bit strong, but I think you can take it.
Guy: *[East European accent]* Oh! Yes, thanks, that would be lovely.
Girl: Just a second ... Here you are.

Three
Guy: *[Northern English accent]* Excuse me, do you happen to know who the teacher is?
Girl: *[Northern English accent]* What teacher?
Guy: The teacher of this course ... Programming 1.
Girl: No, sorry. I don't know anything. I'm new here.

---

3 Ss look at the bits of conversation and again try to write their own roleplay conversation before they listen to the recording. After the listening, ask Ss how the people in them felt about each other, eg the woman in 1 sounded bored of the man's conversation.

Tapescript `CD 1 Track 9`

One
Man: Sorry to bother you, but do you think I could have a look at your paper?
Woman: Oh! Eh ... yes, of course. Here you are.
Man: Thanks a lot. Have you heard what's been going on in Australia?
Woman: The forest fires, you mean?
Man: Yeah, it's terrible, isn't it? I'm from New South Wales myself.
Woman: Oh really?
Man: And the thing is ... and then he said to me, 'I'm not proud to be English!' and I said, 'No wonder!'
Woman: Oh, very good ... Well, it's been great talking to you, but I have to get off here. It's my stop. Bye.
Man: Goodbye.

Two
Girl: Hi, can I get you something to drink? The orange juice is really good. It's a bit strong, but I think you can take it.
Guy: Oh! Yes, thanks, that would be lovely.
Girl: Just a second ... Here you are.
Guy: Thanks a lot.
Girl: Cheers.
Guy: Cheers.
Girl: My name's Emily, by the way.
Guy: Roman.
Girl: Oh, are you Italian? My grandmother's ...
Guy: No, I'm not Italian. I'm Polish. My name is Roman.
Girl: Oh, sorry. Whereabouts in Poland are you from?
Guy: Well, actually, I was born in Lublin, but I moved to Rochester in Kent when I was about ... Well, I'd better be going or I'll miss my ride home.
Girl: Oh, that's a pity. I've really enjoyed talking to you. Give me your number and I'll call you later.
Guy: OK, it's 0171 ...

Three
Guy: Excuse me, do you happen to know who the teacher is?
Girl: What teacher?
Guy: The teacher of this course ... Programming 1.
Girl: No, sorry. I don't know anything. I'm new here.
Guy: Yeah, this is my first time here too. But my cousin did this course a few years ago, and he said to watch out for one of the teachers, a Mrs Simpson. She's supposed to be terrible.
Girl: Oh, I hope we don't get her then.
Guy: Yeah! If you ask me, we shouldn't have any classes on Friday afternoons anyway.
Girl: No, I agree ... Oh, look! Here's the teacher now.
Mrs Simpson: Good afternoon. My name's Mrs Simpson, and I'll be teaching you Programming 1. Come along now.
Girl: Are you coming then?
Guy: Em ... I wish I could stay, but I've just remembered I've got to do something urgent. It's really important ...
Girl: But what ...?
Guy: Bye.

Students' Book ➡ pages 12–13

SPEAK OUT

4 When Ss have completed the table, go through the answers. Then Ss practise saying the phrases in pairs.

> **Answers 1** Sorry to bother you, but do you think I could ...? **2** Hi, can I get you something to ...? **3** Excuse me, do you happen to know ...? **4** Have you heard … **5** Whereabouts in (Poland) are you from? **6** If you ask me, ... **7** Well, it's been great talking to you, but ... **8** I'd better be going or ... **9** I wish I could stay, but ...

5 Ss read through the conversations to decide where the people might be and what their relationship is, i.e. Melinda is a businesswoman of some sort, David is a student. They are at a business meeting or conference of some sort. Jane and Betty are in a café. They may have both been shopping as they are talking about shopping or they could be workers on a lunch break. Elicit ideas and then Ss complete the sentences with words from the Speak Out box.

> **Tapescript** CD 1 Track 10
>
> **The tapescript is the same as the text in the Students' Book except for the gaps (given in the Answers box) and the phrases below:**
> **(...) Melinda:** [Irish accent] That sounds interesting. Tell me more.
> **David:** [Northern English accent] Well ... and if you like, I could send you an email with more details.
> **Melinda:** Yes, why don't you do that David? Well, it's been great talking to you, but ...
> **David:** Oh! I mustn't keep you any longer. I'm sure you're busy. Thanks very much for listening to me.
> **Melinda:** No, it's been a pleasure.
>
> **(...) Betty:** [London accent] What do you think about that new shoe shop in the centre?
> **Jane:** [London accent] Well, if you ask me ... Very good. Oh, no! Is that the time? I really must be going.
> **Betty:** Relax. Have another coffee. We're having such a good time.

> **Answers 1** bother you **2** Pleased to meet you. I've heard so much about you. **3** The reason I wanted to talk to you is **4** I mustn't keep you any longer. I'm sure you're busy. **5** Do you mind **6** Where did you get them? **7** What do you think about **8** Is that the time? **9** must be going

6 Tell Ss that there is not just one thing wrong with the conversations but that they may have to change the whole thing. Look at number 1 with the whole group and elicit what is wrong, i.e. *He shouldn't start talking about himself straightaway, it is more polite to ask the other person a question first. He shouldn't boast about his own successes. Asking people how much they earn is very rude.* Ss do the same with the other conversation openers and then write their own versions. There may be more than one correct answer, eg 1 *Pleased to meet you. My*

name's Jack. Have we met somewhere before? / Sorry, but I couldn't help overhearing that you're a doctor. I'm a doctor too. My name's Jack. Where do you work?

> **Answers 1** There should be no reference to being successful or earning a lot and no question about earnings, eg *Pleased to meet you. Sorry, but I couldn't help hearing that you ...* **2** There could be a mention of the watch in a complimentary way but not mentioning the price, eg *Sorry, but I couldn't help noticing your watch. It's very nice. Where did you get it?* **3** Everything should change to a much more general greeting. *Hello, pleased to meet you. Are you new here?* **4** The second sentence should be replaced by a question asking where the person got them, eg *I love your shoes. Where did you get them?* **5** The person could start by asking, in a neutral tone, if the other person has heard about some political story. They could then judge, from the reaction, what the other person's views are and continue accordingly, eg *Have you heard about the government's new ideas on education? What do you think about them?* **6** A more polite excuse for leaving should be made, also thanking the host for the invitation, eg *Is that the time? I really must be going. Thank you so much for everything.* **7** Less slangy/informal words should be used, eg *I really must be going, gran, I've got lots to do.* **8** Replace with the phrase *But enough about me ...,* eg *That's enough about me. Tell me something about what you've been doing.*

7 Put Ss into pairs, A and B. A must start conversations 1, 3 and 5. B must start conversations 2, 4 and 6. When they have thought of some ideas for their own conversations, A starts by telling B where they are (at a party) and their relationship (strangers). A starts the conversation and B has to continue without any preparation. When the conversation is finished, the process is repeated for conversation 2 until they have acted out all six.

8 Try to ensure that a fairly equal number of people choose each statement to discuss. Set a time limit of five minutes for Ss to prepare their ideas and then nominate pairs to come to the front of the class to give their presentations. Try to stop them from writing everything that they want to say. Instead, encourage them to make very brief notes to help guide their presentation.

ADDITIONAL PRACTICE: Photocopiable resources. Resource 3: *I've always wanted to meet you ...* Page 168

WRITING

This section introduces ways to add colour and variety to a story.

Special difficulties: There is a lot of vocabulary for Ss to learn and they may try to overuse it or use it wrongly. Encourage Ss to do extra reading away from the coursebook and notice how the writers have used verbs and adverbs in their writing.

Warm-up Review of managing conversations. *(Un)lucky numbers.* Give each student in the class a number without telling them what their numbers are. Write all the numbers on the board and ask one student to choose two of them. The students who those two numbers correspond to have to come to the front of the class and act out a roleplay. When they have finished, select two more students by the same method.

Possible roleplay ideas:
* *You are at a party. Neither of you knows anyone else there.*
* *You are on a coach to England. The journey will take 24 hours. You don't know each other.*
* *You are queuing for tickets to a concert. One of you is reading a music magazine.*
* *It's the first day at a new school. You are sitting in the classroom waiting for your teacher.*

1 Ss decide which of the ideas are important and which are not and have to try to say why, eg *Poetic language isn't important if it's a science fiction story. Short sentences are good in thrillers.* etc. Discuss Ss' ideas as a whole class.

2 Look at question 2 with the whole class and elicit some titles that Ss know. Write these on the board. Ss now work alone either thinking about one of the books written on the board or a different one that they know. If they say they have never read a short story, tell them to think of a normal novel instead. Allow two minutes for Ss to think alone and make notes and then put them into groups of four to discuss their books. Nominate Ss to talk about their books to the class.

3 Ss discuss the questions in pairs. Make sure they do not start reading the story but make guesses based only on the opening sentence, title and picture. After two minutes, elicit ideas from the whole class.

Answers The title and first line suggest the story is about a girl. We know she has fallen in love with Bryan but he is unromantic. The choice she has to make is possibly between Bryan and another, more romantic boy. Or, possibly he has to choose between his computer and the girl.

4 Set a time limit of two minutes for Ss to get the gist of the story. Tell them they will read it in more detail later.

Answers The choice is for Bryan to make. He has to choose between his love for the computer and his girlfriend.

5 Put Ss into groups of four. They each work on three of the words, looking up words they do not know and then sharing their knowledge as a group. At the end of the activity, each group should have definitions for all the verbs in the multiple choice activity. Play the recording and then elicit the answers as well as any definitions you feel necessary. **Note:** The recording differs from the text only with regards to the underlined words (given in the Answer box).

Answers **1** stroll **2** whisper **3** gazed **4** glittering **5** mumbled **6** stared **7** glanced **8** glistening **9** muttered **10** glared **11** shouted **12** stormed

6 Tell Ss they have got two sentences to finish the story effectively. Set a time limit of two minutes. Nominate Ss to read out their endings and then play the recording.

Tapescript `CD 1 Track 12`

'It's time to choose! Your computer or me!' And she stormed dramatically out of the room.
The next day, Bryan sent her a present. Trembling, she opened up the box. Inside was a simple white three-pinned plug with a length of cable hanging off the end. It looked as if it had been cut off with a pair of scissors.

Answer Bryan chooses the girl.

7 Give Ss thirty seconds to find the adverbs and elicit where they are so that all the Ss know. Ss then work in pairs, looking up the adverbs in dictionaries if necessary and discussing the question.

Answers The adverbs add emotions to the narrative. By telling us how the actions were done we can tell how people were feeling, eg you can *sigh unhappily, angrily, impatiently* and they all show a different emotion to *sighing wistfully.*

8 Look at the example sentence with the Ss and elicit that *tenderly* makes us realise that the princess feels love for the frog. Elicit her emotions if she kissed the frog *quickly, sadly, furiously* etc. Ss then do the exercise in pairs. Elicit answers and what this tells us about the people's emotions.

Possible answers **giggle** nervously (eg if you are worried), happily (eg if someone tells you a joke), awkwardly (eg if you are embarrassed) **glance** impatiently (eg at your watch when waiting for someone), nervously (eg to see if anyone is following you), quickly (all glances are quick by definition; this emphasises the speed and leaves other emotions unstated) **kiss** passionately (eg when you are meeting after a long time apart), tenderly (eg on a romantic date), quickly (eg because you don't want your parents to catch you) **sigh** sadly (eg while watching a sad film), tenderly (eg watching your child in a school play), impatiently (eg waiting for someone to get ready to go out) **stumble** awkwardly (eg tripping over a loose paving stone), frantically (eg trying to stop yourself from falling), blindly (eg in an unlit street on a moonless night) **yell** furiously (eg because you've just discovered that your sister has borrowed your CDs without asking), enthusiastically (eg at a sports event), impatiently (eg to hurry someone up when you want to go out)

9 Ss may not understand all of the terms but tell them to work in pairs and try to guess. When they have looked at the text and given their ideas, tell them the correct answers and what the devices are, i.e. 1 participle clause – the sentence starts with a present or past participle: 'Shrugging his shoulders he ...', 'Touching him tenderly on the arm, she ...', 'Engrossed in his game, he ...', 'Trembling, she ...'; 2 a rhetorical question – one that does not require an answer, eg a question you ask yourself: 'Was that asking too much?', 'What was she doing here?', 'Was she wasting her life?'; 3 a simile – a comparison using *like* – 'he was more like a machine than a human being, 'he treated her like a servant'; 4 direct speech – the actual words spoken: 'Did I tell you that Josh and Frances ...', 'Whatever for?', 'They're in love.', 'Love is an obsessive delusion ...', 'Bryan, I've got something to tell you.', 'Just a minute.', 'It's time to choose!'

Answers **1** b **2** a **3** d **4** c

10 Remind Ss of how the participle clauses were formed with a present participle (*-ing* form) starting the sentence. Ss work in pairs.

Answers **1** Turning away from the screen, he stared at her. **2** Glancing at herself in the mirror, she saw her eyes glistening with tears. **3** Muttering something to himself, he turned away. **4** Glaring at him, she shouted out, 'It's time to choose!'

11 Before Ss look at the exercise, elicit a film that is well-known by most of the students. Ask them to give you one character from the film who has a problem at some stage in the film. Now ask them to think of a question that the character might have asked themselves at that time. Elicit a few examples. Ss now do the exercise in pairs.

Answers **1c** (a thriller/crime story/action story; the character is worried that he can't escape) **2b** (a romance; she's nervous) **3d** (a fantasy; he's frightened and not knowledgeable about spells or witches) **4a** (a comedy/fantasy; he's shocked, he feels as if he's dreaming)

12 When Ss have found the answers, decide what the writers are trying to say by making the comparison, i.e. 1 beautiful, red; 2 musical, a beautiful sound; 3 quickly, in a disorganised fashion; 4 quickly with nothing left behind; 5 very strong and sudden; 6 trembling, keeping together for safety, scared of the outside world; 7 fat and round. Ss may have different answers. Accept them if they can justify them, eg *The servants stood together like a flock of sheep* – sheep stay together for safety as well.

Answers **1** the petals of a rose **2** playing upon an exquisite violin **3** a flock of sheep **4** a stain of breath upon a mirror **5** a knife **6** frightened forest things **7** a beer barrel

TRAIN YOUR BRAIN

13 Tell Ss that all the answers are in the exercises they have done during the lesson. Ss work alone and check in pairs.

Answers **1** opening sentence **3** adverbs **4** direct speech **5** rhetorical questions **6** participle clauses **7** similes **8** finish/ending

14 Ss should write the story at home or under test conditions. However, if there is time, they could brainstorm ideas for the type of story it is and a very basic plot.

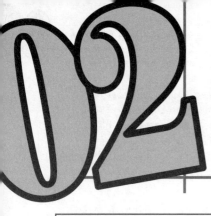

Is it art?

Read, listen and talk about art and culture.
Practise adverb and adjective collocations, cleft sentences and emphasis.
Focus on evaluating and expressing preferences.
Write a competition entry.

EXAM FOCUS

Topic: Culture

Speaking
Evaluating and expressing preferences: SB p.19, ex.7
Problem solving: SB p.20, ex.9

Listening
Notes completion: SB p.24, ex.2

Reading
Multiple matching: SB p.20, ex.4

Grammar and vocabulary
Sentence transformations: SB p.23, ex.3, ex.4

Writing
Competition entry: SB p.25, ex.11

Unit 2 Materials
....
Success Workbook Unit 2
....
Photocopiable resources 4, 5, 6
....
Testing and Evaluation Programme tests

VOCABULARY AND SPEAKING

This section reviews base and strong adjectives and the adverbs which can modify them on the topic of art.

Special difficulties: As well as knowing which adverbs can be used with which type of adjectives, it is important for Ss to know that not all combinations of adverb + adjective work, eg *very good, terribly good* and *extremely good* work but *slightly good* does not.

Culture notes

Simonedes of Ceos (c.556–468BC) was born on Kea. As a young man, he wrote poetry for the festival of Apollo, celebrated in the autumn when the crops were harvested, and then moved to Athens. He lived at the court of Hipparchus but, after the murder of Hipparchus in 514BC, he left Athens. He spent the final years of his life on Sicily. Although a prolific writer, only a few of his works survive. Among his most famous works are his odes to the heroes of Marathon and the Battle of Thermopylae.

Anthony Gormley (born 1950) is best known for his giant 'Angel of the North' sculpture which stands on a hill overlooking Gateshead near Newcastle. It is 20m tall and its wings are 54m from end to end. Gormley studied Art at Cambridge University and, after three years in Sri Lanka studying Buddhism, he did postgraduate studies in London. Buddhism is an important influence on his life and the value of 'being', not thinking or doing but simply existing. He won the Turner Prize in 1994 for a sculpture called 'Testing a World View'.

Zdzisław Beksiński (1929–2005) was a Polish painter, photographer and sculptor and is best known as a fantasy artist. He was born in Sanok in the south-east of Poland and studied Architecture in Kraków. In the 1970s and 1980s he produced some of his most famous work in his 'fantastic period' in which he painted surrealistic, post-apocalyptic images.

Manga comics actually means 'comics comics' as *manga* is the Japanese word for *comics*. Manga appeal to all ages in Japan and the industry is worth of $4 billion a year. Modern manga dates from the end of Second World War although the word dates from the late 18th century.

Warm-up Review of verbs from the story writing section.
Show it. Put Ss into groups of three. In each group one student is given the role 'speak', another 'walk' and the third 'look'. Ss find all the verbs in Exercise 5, page 15 for their role, eg *speak – mutter, whisper, yell* etc, *walk – stagger, stumble, stroll* etc, *look – gaze, glare, peep* etc, and decide how to act them out. The other two Ss have to guess what verb is being acted. When they have finished, allow some Ss to act out their verbs in front of the whole class.

1 Before Ss look at the book, ask who is interested in art and what kinds of art they know the names of in English. Ss then do the task. Elicit answers and definitions of the different kinds of art.

Answers 1 – 5, 2 – 3, 3 – 4, 4 – 2, 5 – 1

2 Set a time limit of five minutes for Ss to discuss the questions and look up any adjectives they are not sure of. Elicit ideas and definitions in open class. Ask Ss if there are any of the paintings which they do not like and elicit some negative adjectives which could describe them.

3 Ss match the adjectives alone. If necessary, drill the strong adjectives showing where the stress lies: **terri**fied, **pet**rified, a**ston**ishing, **fas**cinating, re**mark**able, a**tro**cious, pa**thet**ic, ap**pall**ing,

horrified, exhausted, furious, livid, impossible, magnificent, marvellous, superb, exquisite, miserable, heartbroken, thrilled, delighted.

Answers 1 c 2 b 3 g 4 i 5 h 6 j 7 e 8 f 9 a 10 d

4 Tell Ss they will hear the recording twice. The first time they should complete the task. Elicit the answers and then tell Ss to listen again and try to think which two paintings are being described. Elicit ideas and reasons for their choice, i.e. the first is picture 4 – key words: *buildings, river, sunset*; the second is probably picture 3 – key words: *I could paint better myself.*

Tapescript CD 1 Track 13

One

[RP accent] ... which is particularly enchanting. Now, over here on our right is an absolutely marvellous example of Impressionism, painted, of course, by Claude Monet quite late in his career. Today, as we look at this utterly exquisite painting, it's simply impossible for us to imagine the controversy it caused when Monet first presented it. Er, excuse me. The chap in the really appalling baseball cap ... Yes, yes, you! Please refrain from taking photographs or I shall be obliged to ask you to leave the tour! Where was I? Yes, the critics of the time were absolutely horrified and thought the Impressionists were primitive and vulgar. Of course, these famous buildings have been painted by countless artists but the main focus of Monet's painting isn't the buildings or the river, but the light itself. The way which Monet has captured the whole atmosphere during a winter sunset is simply remarkable.

Two

Lee: *[Ulster accent]* How are you feeling now, Karen?
Karen: *[Ulster accent]* Terribly nervous!
Lee: Don't worry, love. It's only a tooth.
Karen: I know, but I'm finding it pretty difficult to keep calm.
Lee: This waiting room can't be helping. Absolutely atrocious wallpaper ...
Karen: Really dire magazines ...
Lee: And why are the paintings in dentist's waiting rooms always really bad? They always look as though they bought them from a flea market for 50p or something. I mean look at that one. It's absolutely pathetic! I could paint better myself!
Karen: It reminds me of the birthday cards I used to get from my gran. I'm sure it's making my toothache worse!

Answers 1 marvellous, exquisite, impossible, appalling, horrified, remarkable 2 nervous, difficult, atrocious, dire, bad, pathetic

5 Ss listen to the recording and write the adverb + adjective combinations they hear. Allow them a second listening to check and complete their answers and then elicit what they heard, i.e. *absolutely marvellous, utterly exquisite, simply impossible, really appalling, absolutely horrified,*

simply remarkable, terribly nervous, pretty difficult, absolutely atrocious, really dire, really bad, absolutely pathetic.
Ss then do the matching alone.

Answers 1 b 2 c 3 a

6 The use of *pretty* as a qualifying adverb can cause problems if not said properly. To strengthen the adjective, the stress must be on the adjective, not the adverb, i.e. *It was **pretty** good* = not very good. *It was pretty **good*** = very good. With strong adjectives, *pretty* should only be used with this second meaning, i.e. strengthening the adjective, eg 3 *It was pretty **magnificent**.*

Answers 1 absolutely/utterly/simply/totally/really/ pretty astonishing/fascinating/remarkable
2 absolutely/utterly/simply/totally/really/pretty atrocious/pathetic/dire/appalling; absolutely/utterly/ simply/totally/really/pretty miserable/heartbroken
3 absolutely/utterly/simply/totally/really/pretty magnificent/marvellous/superb/exquisite; absolutely/ utterly/simply/totally/really/pretty exhausted
4 absolutely/utterly/simply/totally/really/pretty thrilled/ delighted
5 absolutely/utterly/simply/totally/really impossible
6 absolutely/utterly/simply/totally/really/pretty furious/ livid

7 Tell Ss to first use base adjectives to describe their feelings and then to change them to use strong adjectives. Elicit ideas from Ss. After each answer, ask other Ss if they agree. If they do, they should use a synonym, eg student 1 says they would feel absolutely delighted if they were top of the class and a second student agrees by saying *Yes, I would be utterly thrilled.* If not, they should use adjectives true for them, eg student 1 says they would be absolutely horrified if they had to give a speech and student 2 says *Would you? I'd be really happy.* This ensures that the second student has to listen to and understand the first and cannot just say *I agree* or *Me too.*

8 Make sure that all Ss understand what the different types of art are and then they write the sentences alone. Elicit sentences and, after each one, ask the student why they hold those views and try to involve the whole class in a discussion.

ADDITIONAL PRACTICE: Photocopiable resources. Resource 4: *Letter of complaint.* Page 169

LISTENING AND SPEAKING

This section introduces ways of evaluating and expressing preferences.

Special difficulties: As with all speaking tasks, Ss may sound unnatural at first as they consciously try to use the new phrases but this is an important step in order to allow them to learn the phrases and, later on, be able to use them more naturally.

Warm-up Review of base and strong adjectives. *What are we talking about?* Ss work in groups of four. Each group thinks of a film they have all seen. Then they join up with a second group and each person in turn gives their views of the film, the acting, special effects etc, without naming it. They must use a range of adverbs and adjectives in their descriptions. After they have finished, the other group try to guess what film they are talking about. You can repeat the process by asking them to describe an event at school, a place in town, a band etc.

1 Tell Ss to imagine they are in an exam and have just been given this task. They have got two minutes which they must fill with their ideas and also show they can work together by asking their partner for his/her opinion. After two minutes, nominate Ss to act out their discussion in front of the class.

Answers (to be given after Exercise 2) They are the editors and author of a new guidebook to London. They are in an office looking at possible photographs for the cover of the guidebook and trying to decide which is best.

2 Ss read the questions before they listen to the recording. Ss discuss their answers in pairs and then as a whole class. For question 2, elicit examples of books/products/CD covers etc that may have influenced Ss to buy something that they might not otherwise have bought.

Tapescript `CD 1 Track 14`

Minty: *[RP accent]* OK – you're probably asking yourselves why I've called you in here this morning. We want to make a final decision on the book cover and I thought it would be best to get the opinion of both the editors who've worked on the project.

Guy: *[RP accent]* Great!

Minty: And the author too, of course. So, before we start choosing the photo, I thought it might be useful to remind ourselves of what we're looking for. OK?

Zara: *[RP accent]* Good idea.

Minty: Well, we've just produced what is surely an absolutely unique guidebook to London and it's crucial that the photo on the cover really stands out in the bookshops.

Guy: Mm-hmm.

Zara: Definitely.

Minty: OK. And the cover photo really has to appeal exactly to the type of reader we've been writing for, in other words someone who's young and dynamic.

Guy: But who also wants to have a fun time ...

Zara: ... and is looking for something that's different ...

Minty: Right! Justin, are you OK with that?

Justin: *[Northern English accent]* Yeah, fine!

Minty: So we're all agreed – the photo we want on the cover of our guidebook should be fun, dynamic and unusual. OK, guys. Here's the first one.

Answers 1 They are looking for something to appeal to young, dynamic people, something that's different and fun.

3 Before Ss look at the phrases, play the recording once and ask them to decide what order the three photos are discussed in. Elicit ideas and reasons why, eg *Photo 2 is first – it's fun and dynamic. Photo 1 is second – the subjects are quite traditional*, etc. Give Ss the correct order, i.e. first photo 2, second photo 1, third photo 3. Ss now read through the phrases and make sure they understand how they could be used. Elicit some answers from them before they listen to the recording and then elicit what was said on the recording and ask the class what they think of the ideas on the recording.

Tapescript `CD 1 Track 15`

Minty: So we're all agreed – the photo we want on the cover of our guidebook should be fun, dynamic and unusual. OK, guys. Here's the first one.

Guy: That's an absolutely superb photo. I think it's exactly the kind of message we want to put across in our book.

Zara: Yes, it's such a modern, dynamic photo – it'll look totally brilliant on the cover. And of course it ties in very well with our target reader. What do you think, Justin?

Justin: It's not bad, I suppose.

Minty: Here's the second one. Can you see that OK, Guy?

Guy: Yes, fine. Well, I have to say I *do* like the contrast between old and new – absolutely perfect for the book.

Minty: Well, I like it, and the contrast is great, but I wanted something really modern on the cover and I'm not sure this one does that. The subjects look quite traditional in this one, actually. What do you think, Zara?

Zara: I think you've got a point there, Minty. It's nothing out of the ordinary, really – it just looks like any other book. It doesn't really go with the young, alternative image we want to project, does it?

Minty: What about you, Justin?

Justin: Well, who am I to judge, really?

Minty: Well, you did write this guidebook! It'd be nice if you had an opinion! Anyway, here's the last one.

Zara: It's quite striking, I suppose. But it's not a patch on the first one.

Guy: No, it's definitely not as good as the first one. To be honest, it's pretty hard to make out what's going on in it. And it's a bit gloomy, as well.

Minty: I'm glad you think that! Personally, I think it's pretty appalling for a cover photo. It'll just put people off! So, it seems as though we've all got a soft spot for the first photo. It's by far the best one, isn't it? Are you happy with that, Justin?

Justin: Well, if I'm honest, I don't think any of these photos are anything to write home about. Well, you see what I had in mind for the cover was something iconic, based on the map of the underground but with all the chapters in the book marked as different stations ...

Minty: Hmm, well there's a thought! OK, I think we all deserve some coffee now ...

Answers It's exactly the kind of message we want to put across in our book. It ties in very well with our target reader. (Photo 2) It doesn't really go with the young, alternative image we want to project. (Photo 1) It's pretty hard to make out what's going on in it. It'll just put people off! (Photo 3)

SPEAK OUT

4 Ss look at the six phrases and decide what they mean, eg a – typical, boring, not new; b – I don't know; c – bad; f – That's an interesting idea. Play the recording again and Ss complete the table alone.

Answers 1 I do like 2 It's by far the best one 3 It's nothing out of the ordinary. 4 It's pretty appalling. 5 Who am I to judge? 6 There's a thought!

Mind the trap!

Go through the Mind the trap! box with Ss and stress the last sentence as Ss can overuse idioms and sound strange. Again, extra reading or watching of films can help Ss identify how idioms are used by native speakers.

5 Play the recording as Ss read along. Ss then replace the overused phrase (tell Ss to keep the first example in the dialogue and change the other two). Nominate Ss to act out their new dialogue in open class.

Answers *nothing to write home about* is overused. Replace with: It's a bit mediocre, It's a bit second rate, It's not a patch on ..., It's definitely not as good as ..., It's nothing out of the ordinary.

6 Ss list all the words and work in groups to discuss what the words mean and any other words they know on the topic. Elicit all and give Ss a written record of any new words.

Answers Nouns: photos, snaps, shots, tripod, digital/ traditional camera Adjectives: photogenic, blurred Verbs: take photos/shots, develop photos

7 Remind Ss that this is a chance to practise using the phrases from Speak Out so, whenever they give an opinion, they should ensure that they use one of the phrases, making sure they do not overuse any particular one. Nominate Ss to summarise what their groups said at the end of the activity.

8 Remind Ss that these sorts of questions are used in the speaking exam so, again, they should carry out the task as if they were in an exam. They should try to keep talking on each topic for one minute, asking each other questions and showing interest in what their partner says. Discuss all of the questions with the whole class when they have finished.

ADDITIONAL PRACTICE: Photocopiable resources. Resource 5: *I see what you mean, but ...* Page 170

READING AND VOCABULARY

> This section introduces some useful collocations through a reading on modern art exhibitions.

Culture notes

The Bodyworks exhibition was created by Professor Gunther von Hagens who was brought up in East Germany. He invented the technique of plastination in 1977 which is how he preserves bodies. Before the Bodyworks exhibition came to London it had been seen by about eight million people worldwide. Von Hagens has a list of 3,200 people who wish to be 'plastinated' after their deaths.

Ron Mueck (born 1958) is an Australian hyperrealist sculptor. In 1996, he made a model of Pinocchio for his mother-in-law who is also an artist. She used the piece in one of her exhibitions and it was seen by Charles Saatchi who commissioned more work from Mueck. Mueck then became famous with his sculpture 'Dead Dad', a two-thirds sized model of his father.

The National Gallery was founded in 1824 and houses over 2,300 paintings. It stands at the north of Trafalgar Square in central London and the collection belongs to the British public so entry is free. Around 4–5 million people visit the gallery each year.

Brick Lane is a street in the East End of London, home to a large Bangladeshi population and is sometimes known as Banglatown. It got its name from the manufacture of bricks and tiles there in the 15th century. In the 19th century it was home to a large Jewish population and it is also famous as the site of one of Jack the Ripper's murders in 1888.

The Atlantis Gallery was built in the old Truman Brewery. The brewery closed in 1988 and is now home to bars, shops, restaurants, clubs and the gallery. The brewery was the second largest in Britain and is even mentioned in *David Copperfield*, by Charles Dickens.

Warm-up Review of evaluating and expressing preferences. *What are we talking about?* Ss work in groups of five or six. Dictate six well-known people, places or things that most, if not all, Ss will know about, eg a café in their town, a singer, a sports team, a painting in the school, a statue in their town, a song. For each thing mentioned, Ss give their opinion using a phrase from the previous lesson. When they have finished, one group decide on one of the things and each person gives their opinion without telling the class which of the things they are talking about. The other Ss have to try to guess based on what each person says, i.e. if they know that one of the students giving their opinion hates art and says *It leaves me cold*, they might guess that the object being described is the painting. Repeat so that each group gives their opinions for one of the things.

1 Ss should use dictionaries if they are not sure of the meanings of the adjectives. Allow two minutes for Ss to give and justify their opinions and then elicit ideas and justifications from the class.

2 Put Ss into pairs. They both read both opening paragraphs and discuss what they understood together. They then discuss the three questions together. Elicit ideas in open class.

3 Set a time limit of five minutes for Ss to read their text thoroughly, underlining or noting key words and phrases and trying to understand the overall meaning without looking up individual words. Ss then close their books and tell each other what was written and the answers to the questions in Exercise 2.

Answers **Text A** **1** Sculptures are made of silicon and polyester. **2** The lifelike quality is most shocking, the size of the models is also surprising. **3** The reviewer was positive – intelligent and thought-provoking. **Text B** **1** Sculptures are made of human corpses. **2** Delighted schoolchildren shocked the reviewer. **3** The reviewer was negative – no warmth, freak show, cheap sensation, left with a bad taste in the mouth.

4 Ss read the questions in Exercise 4 and try to answer them without looking back at their text. Then they read their partner's text to see if they can find the answers. Elicit the answers and reasons for them, i.e. 1A Ron Mueck, 1B says 'the creators of the exhibition'; 2A 'following a tour of several European capitals', 2B 'has attracted some eight million visitors to date across the world'; 3A Nothing explicitly stated, 3B 'one of the most keenly anticipated exhibitions'; 4A 'my expectations were decidedly low', 4B not explicitly stated; 5A not explicitly stated, 5B 'Innocuous though this sounds ...'; 6A 'packed gallery', 6B 'throngs of excitable teenagers'; 7A 'At times I had the rather disconcerting feeling', 7B 'I felt as if I was attending a Victorian freak show.'; 8A not stated, 8B 'the crowds of excited schoolchildren … who didn't seem perturbed'; 9A 'intelligent, thought-provoking', 9B 'is bound to be a resounding success' – no mention that it deserves to be.
Note: Do not give any vocabulary definitions at this point as the next activity is a vocabulary one.

Answers **1** A **2** both **3** B **4** A **5** B **6** both **7** both **8** B **9** A

5 Ss work together, either looking together at the same text or one looking at A and the other at B. Elicit all the words and drill any problematic ones.

Answers **1** to crouch **2** listlessly **3** to dwarf **4** wrinkle **5** humbling **6** throng **7** innocuous **8** faint-hearted **9** to hunch **10** perturbed

6 Ss try to work out the collocations in pairs without looking back at the text. Then they find them in the text to check their answers. Elicit answers and ask follow-up questions to make sure Ss understand them, eg *What's on display at the local museum? What do you have low expectations about and why? What questions about life would you like to pose?* etc.

Answers 1 h 2 a 3 g 4 i 5 c 6 b 7 e 8 d 9 f 10 j

7 When Ss have completed the sentences, elicit the answers and discuss sentences 1 and 10 as a whole class making sure Ss use suitable phrases for giving opinions, agreeing and disagreeing.

Answers 1 have low expectations 2 on display
3 needless to say 4 keenly anticipated 5 a resounding success 6 out of keeping with 7 a lucrative career
8 evoke sympathy 9 pose the question 10 pander to (the public's) expectations

8 Set time limits of one or two minutes per question and tell Ss they must try to keep talking for the whole time, not stop halfway through. This is training for the speaking exam where they have to fill the time, even if they think they have nothing to say. After Ss have discussed all the questions, elicit ideas in open class and allow Ss to agree and disagree politely with each other.

9 Give Ss two minutes to read through the descriptions alone and to make notes of key words which describe the different exhibits, eg ceramic bath, video – burning money. Ss then choose which they would have and tell their group, giving their reasons. If there is disagreement, Ss must try to justify their own choice and find faults with the other exhibits chosen or accept the other ideas and reject their own.

GRAMMAR

> This section introduces cleft sentences using the readings from the last lesson.

Warm-up Reminder of the readings. *What do they refer to?* Put Ss into groups of three or four. Make sure their books are closed. Tell them they are going to try to remember as much as possible about the two exhibitions in the previous lesson. Give them key words and, after each one, Ss discuss what they remember as a group. Nominate one group each time to summarise their discussion. Other groups can then add any other points that they remembered.

Points for groups to discuss:
The size of the subjects
Evoke sympathy
Excited schoolchildren
Lifelike
Cheap sensation

1 Once Ss have decided which they think is most memorable, ask them why they think that. With 1 and 3, the important verb (*to strike, to depress*) is brought to the front of the sentence so is emphasised. Similarly, in 2, the adjective, *successful*, is emphasised. 4 and 5 are not so clearly dramatic. Ss may argue that 4a is more dramatic because the word *shocking* is more important than in 4b. In 5b, a dramatic effect is created by delaying the verb, building up the suspense of what the authors have done. Even if Ss disagree with the answer, it is good to find out why.

> **Answers** Sentences b are more dramatic/memorable.

Work it out

2 When Ss have answered the questions, give them a written record of the form.

What + verb + object + verb *to be*
What upsets me is …
What worries me is …

What + verb *to be* + adjective + verb *to be*
What is interesting about English is …
What was strange about our last test was that …

What + subject + verb + verb *to be*
What I like about school is …
What I don't understand about cleft sentences is …

It + verb *to be* + noun + relative pronoun + verb *to be*
It is my mother who is …
It was on holiday that I first …

Ss copy these down in their notebooks and try to complete the sentences.

> **Answers** **1** to be (With sentences starting *It …* the relative pronoun doesn't have to be followed by the verb *to be*, eg *It was the landscapes which I found most impressive.* The examples in Mind the trap! show this as well.) **2** Sentence 4b **3** have done (Although the auxiliary *have* is always required in a Present Perfect sentence, we would also use the auxiliary *do/did* in simple tenses, eg *What the author did was to … / does is to …*)

Check it out

Refer Ss to the Check it out section on page 154 and tell them to use this if necessary to check their answers to the exercises in this section.

> **Mind the trap!**
>
> Go through the Mind the trap! box with Ss and, if the previous extension activity was used, refer them to the sentence stem used: *It was on holiday **that** I first …*

3 Look at the original sentences with the class and elicit that they are in the Past Simple. Make sure that Ss know that all the other sentences should agree with the tense. Sometimes more than one way of writing the information is possible. The answers given are the most natural sounding but Ss could write, eg 2a *What Jonathan wrote was a scathing review of Gerry's exhibition in the 'Express' last Friday.* – which is also correct.

> **Answers** **1 a** What the mayor opened was an exhibition of Gerry's paintings. **b** What the mayor did was (to) open an exhibition of Gerry's paintings. **c** It was at the Liddell Gallery that the mayor opened an exhibition of Gerry's paintings. **d** It was last week that the mayor opened an exhibition of Gerry's paintings. **e** It was the mayor that/who opened an exhibition of Gerry's paintings. **2 a** What Jonathan wrote in the *Express* last Friday was a scathing review of Gerry's exhibition. **b** It was in the *Express* last Friday that Jonathan wrote a scathing review of Gerry's exhibition. **c** What was scathing was the review of Gerry's exhibition that Jonathan wrote in the *Express* last Friday. **d** It was last Friday that Jonathan wrote a scathing review of Gerry's exhibition in the *Express*.

4 Remind Ss that, before they write anything, they should make sure that the tense they use agrees with the tense in the original sentence. The words in capitals do not have to come at the start of the sentence. Ss then write the sentences alone and check in pairs.

Answers 1 What is very impressive is the level of detail. 2 It was the spectators' reaction that/which was odd. 3 What shocked me was the price of the tickets. 4 What he did was to make lifelike sculptures for the rest of his career. 5 It is in mid-October that the exhibition ends. 6 It was in Paris that she established her reputation. 7 What surprises me is the fact that he is unknown. 8 What she's done is to create her own style of painting.

5 Ss find the sentences and discuss in pairs how they could be said in their own language and whether there are similar structures in L1 or not.

Answers 1 However close you get to them 2 Innocuous though this sounds 3 who didn't seem perturbed by these sculptures in the slightest 4 No matter what you say 5 I do feel differently about smoking   Versions from the texts are more emphatic.

6 Ss work in pairs using the answers to the last exercise as a guide. Elicit answers and tell Ss that, although these phrases are useful, the most important thing at this stage is to remember how to make cleft sentences and not to get confused by the various structures.

Answers 1 No matter what they think – I know you're very talented. 2 I know you don't believe me but I really did want to come with you. 3 However late you arrive/No matter how late you arrive – you must phone us. 4 I generally don't like silent films – although I do really like Charlie Chaplin. 5 She wasn't interested in the slightest in what we were saying to her. 6 Hard though it seems, this exercise isn't impossible.

7 Allow five minutes for Ss to write the sentences and compare them with their partner. Then elicit ideas in open class.

ADDITIONAL PRACTICE: Photocopiable resources. Resource 6: *Dramatic opinions*. Page 171

WRITING AND LISTENING

This section introduces tips for writing an article for a competition entry.

Warm-up Revision of cleft sentences. *Line up.* Have some prepared cleft sentences with each word written in large letters on a separate piece of paper. They must be large enough for the whole class to see. Nominate as many Ss as there are words in the first sentence to come to the front of the class. Each student gets a word which they look at and remember. They also show the rest of the class.

Ss at the front give back their words and now, by telling each other their words, they have to stand in the correct order to make a sentence. In the meantime, the other Ss are working out the sentence, having seen the words, and can give help, eg *Tom, you're first.* When Ss at the front think they are in the correct order, they shout out their words in turn and see if they are correct. Repeat as many times as necessary with different Ss.

Ideas:

What we did last night was create a new website. (10 Ss)

It is this group's seriousness that is most impressive. (9 Ss)

What thrilled me was my English test result. (8 Ss)

1 Some Ss may know the artist so, before Ss open their books, write his name on the board and ask Ss if they have heard of him. Try to put Ss together so that both or neither student in a pair knows him. Elicit ideas from those who do not know him first and then ask those that do know him if the others were correct.

2 When Ss read through the notes, try to elicit ideas of what could go into the gaps before playing the recording, eg 1 and 2 could be about where it is performed, how it is performed or by whom it is performed.

Tapescript `CD 1 Track 18`

Speaker: *[Scandinavian accent]* Ladies and Gentlemen. It is my pleasure to address you tonight during this closing ceremony of the first Lahti Festival of Performance Art. Before I hand out the jury's main prize of the festival, I'd like to take a moment to reflect on the wonderful two weeks of international performance art we have witnessed, here in Lahti. Performance art, in its broadest definition, is art which is performed live and in public places. But having watched so many inspirational performances during the past two weeks, I would like to offer a further definition. Performance art is something which is provocative, radical, and above all, memorable. It makes us, the public, look afresh at our daily routines as we move around our cities. I believe that our festival, our first in Lahti, has been a resounding success. We look forward to many more. Before I present the main prize, I'd like to say a few words about the winner, Cezary Bodzianowski. Mr Bodzianowski studied at the Academy of Fine Arts in Warsaw, before he moved to Belgium for four years to study at the Art Academy in Antwerp. He has been performing his absurd, one-man theatre in city streets across Europe and the United States since the early 1990s, most recently at the Tate Modern Gallery in London. But the majority of his performances take place in his hometown of Łódź in Poland.

Apart from passers-by who sometimes accidentally get involved, people rarely participate or even notice his spontaneous public performances. But I am quite sure that many citizens of Lahti have caught a glimpse of his subtle interventions over the last few days ...

Answers 1 live 2 in public places 3 memorable 4 daily routines 5 Fine Arts 6 four years 7 Europe 8 The majority of his

3 Ss read through the competition rules and underline the key words which would be important for them to focus on if they were writing an entry, i.e. *about someone, positive effect, your town/area, perhaps isn't aware, about 250 words, what makes this person a positive influence*. Ss then read the entry and decide if it answers the question or not (yes, it is about someone, what they do, why they are a positive influence and they are from the writer's home town).

Answers He brings joy to the people of the town and cheers people up with his unique brand of performance art.

4 Elicit what the different kinds of performance art in question 1 are and then set a time limit of one minute for each question. Discuss Ss' ideas as a whole class.

5 Elicit what an anecdote is (a personal account of an event that happened to the speaker/writer). Ss find the three examples in the text. Nominate Ss to answer.

Answers 1 The first two paragraphs are an anecdote although written in the second person. 2 The first sentence of the last paragraph is gently persuasive about Cezary being a worthy recipient of the award. 3 Most of the third paragraph is factual.

6 Ss look at the questions and try to find evidence in the text to back up their ideas. Try to prevent them from looking at the Train Your Brain box. Do not elicit the answers at this stage.

Answers 1 Neutral. There are some phrases which are fairly formal, eg 'Although I believe', but other places which are more informal, eg the extra information given in brackets in paragraphs 2 and 4. 2 Intriguing and enthusiastic. The writer obviously likes Cezary's work and also writes in such a way that readers find the story fascinating. 3 b It describes the person and his work and gives real life examples. 4 No. Even the anecdote is written in the 'you' form rather than as something that happened to the writer. 5 The final paragraph.

TRAIN YOUR BRAIN

7 Ss check their answers to Exercise 6. Elicit what they found out in the Train Your Brain box and examples to support those answers from the text.

8 Make sure Ss know that, although there are seven contexts and only five texts, all seven can be matched. There are no distractors. When Ss have finished, ask them which entry they would like to read more of and why.

Answers 1 b, g (a teacher) 2 e (a social worker/ volunteer) 3 d, f (a school friend) 4 a (a Youth Club leader) 5 c (the captain of a rugby team)

9 It may be a good idea to write the people from Exercise 8 on the board and elicit more ideas from Ss, adding them to the list, eg *a friend, a family member, a politician, a famous musician or sports star, a writer* etc. That will give everyone a lot of choices from which to decide on their person. Tell Ss to choose alone because it has to be someone they really believe in.

10 Allow Ss two minutes to think in pairs about the question and then discuss the advantages and disadvantages of each context as a whole class. Again this will enable the Ss to share ideas.

11 Ss should write the entry either for homework or under exam conditions in class. When they have finished, give a mark for different aspects of the writing, not just grammatical correctness, eg 5 marks for style and organisation, 5 for interest, 5 for accuracy and 10 for actual content and description. Ss therefore understand that it is not enough to be good at English but must also take care over the Train Your Brain points in the writing sections.

THINK FORWARD TO EXAMS REVISION 1
UNITS 1–2

INTRODUCTION

The review sections in the Students' Book give students a chance to revise the vocabulary and grammar of the previous two units of the book as well as giving them important exam practice in reading, listening and speaking skills. They mirror similar review sections in the workbook which can be set as homework.

There are different ways of approaching the review sections in the Students' Book and it is up to the teacher to decide which would suit their group best.

As a continuation of the normal coursebook. Activities are introduced with prediction tasks and the teacher uses a variety of individual, pair and group work. The instructions have been written for this type of activity.

Individual exam practice. Students can be given a time limit and asked to complete the tasks alone under exam conditions. The work can then be marked by the teachers and used as the basis for mid-term grades or the Ss can mark their own work using the activities as a form of self-assessment to see where they need to concentrate their studying.

Collaborative work. This involves aspects of both the previous approaches. The students work in pairs or groups but there is no lead-in to the activities or help so they are approaching the activities as a form of test but without the stress of working alone.

VOCABULARY AND GRAMMAR

1 Ss read the text quickly to get an idea of what it is about. Ss compare ideas in pairs and then, without looking at the choices offered, try to think of what words or phrases could go into the gaps. Elicit ideas. Sometimes only one word is possible, eg 1 *off*, but other gaps are more open, eg 4 could be any negative characteristic. If Ss come up with *ass* for 5, point out that this is an impolite and very informal phrase that they should not use in a classroom. Ss then look at the choices and complete the exercise alone. Elicit the answers and what the words and phrases mean.

> **Answers** 1 b 2 a 3 b 4 b 5 d 6 d 7 c 8 d 9 c 10 c 11 b 12 b

2 Ss work in pairs. Tell Ss to look at each word in turn and try to define it. The odd one out should then be obvious. If Ss do not know, tell them to guess, not to look in dictionaries. Go through the answers and elicit the meanings of the different words. As a follow-up, ask Ss to make their own odd one out activity. Ss work in pairs and then join up in groups of four to test each other.

> **Answers** 1 stutter (it's a way of speaking, the others are to do with light shining) 2 sculpture (the others are types of painting) 3 exquisite (it is positive, the others are negative) 4 creepy (it is the only negative adjective)

3 Ss read the text quickly to get an overview of what it is about. Elicit ideas (a meeting with an old school friend who is now an artist). Ss then complete the gap-fill in pairs. Tell Ss that, sometimes, the word needed is a collocation (eg 1) but sometimes they really need to understand the text to get the correct word (eg 4 where it would be easy to write *has* if you didn't read it carefully).

> **Answers** 1 into 2 since 3 What 4 lacks 5 silence 6 good 7 exhibition 8 own 9 fan 10 leaves 11 expectations 12 absolutely/really/totally/utterly/simply/pretty 13 out 14 Needless 15 out

4 Ss read quickly through the text to get the general idea of what it is about. Elicit that it is about someone who is waiting at an airport for their sister to arrive and thinking back to the past about their relationship and wondering what will happen during this meeting and visit. Tell Ss to complete the gaps alone and then check their ideas in pairs. Elicit the answers and, if there are any errors, try to elicit or explain why the correct answer is as it is. Sometimes more than one structure is possible.

> **Answers** 1 have been sitting 2 haven't spent 3 feel/am feeling 4 will stay/will be staying 5 get 6 did 7 were growing 8 will have had 9 were always fighting 10 will never forget/have never forgotten 11 discovered 12 were fighting 13 had never beaten 14 would go 15 could

5 Look at the first sentence with Ss. Elicit what Ss think the second sentence should be. Write down any ideas on the board, even if they are incorrect. Ss then work as a class to try to decide which, if any, of the ideas on the board are correct. Give Ss the correct answer and then Ss work in pairs to complete the exercise. Elicit answers and encourage peer correction if necessary.

> **Answers** 1 will have been/worked here for 2 will have forgotten 3 Will you be dressing/Are you going to be dressing 4 What I (really) like about 5 movement has done is (to) get 6 matter what the critics say 7 It was the sculpture that 8 though it may seem

LISTENING SKILLS

1 Ask Ss what they think small talk is. Elicit ideas and when and with who they use it, eg with friends at parties, on the way home etc. Ss read through the statements and decide, in pairs, whether they think each is true or false. Elicit ideas with reasons. Tell Ss they will listen to the recording twice. The first time, they should make notes about the most important things the people say. Then they answer as many of the questions as possible and finally listen again to check their answers. Elicit answers and justifications in open class: 1 'when we talk to strangers in public places, with work colleagues over a coffee, with people we don't know too well like waitresses, hairdressers and taxi drivers, (...) with your friends and family'; 2 'No mention of politics or religion and nothing too personal'; 3 'who won last night's game'; 4 'After all, it does seem rather rude just to stand there not saying anything'; 5 'but it's really common in places where you may be in the company of strangers for a length of time. For example, at bus stops, dentist's waiting rooms, the check-out queue at the supermarket, in lifts and perhaps even in public toilets'; 6 'small talk is a kind of verbal dance'; 7 'You've got to look for the clues, that is, read the body language'; 8 'Some people are natural small-talkers. Others find it hard.'

Tapescript `CD 1 Track 19`

Speaker: *[Northern English (Yorkshire) accent]* Put your hands up if you never indulge in small talk! ... Nobody? Well, I'm not surprised. We may not like it, but we all use it. Here in Britain, we use it when we talk to strangers in public places, with work colleagues over a coffee, with people we don't know too well like waitresses, hairdressers and taxi drivers, and I bet you can't say you've never used it with your friends and family when there's been an uncomfortable silence.

But what is it? What is small talk? How is it different from other kinds of conversation? Well, the key thing about it is that it's safe. And, don't forget, we need to obey the rules of British etiquette, so you shouldn't talk about anything controversial when you're playing the small talk game. No mention of politics or religion and nothing too personal either. You're not going to tell a stranger how much you earn, you shouldn't analyse your marital problems with the person in front of you in the bus stop queue, and it's not usual to discuss the details of your recent operation with the postman. No, in those situations you should really stick to nice safe topics such as local news, who won last night's game, what's been happening in a popular soap, or of course, the most popular British small talk topic available to one and all – the weather! What would we do without it? Why do we do it? Why do we bother with small talk? Well, one obvious reason is to fill up embarrassing silences and another is just to kill time. That's why we often do it when we're standing in a queue waiting for something. We also do it to be polite, to make other people feel more comfortable and to make them think that we're open and friendly. After all, it does seem rather rude just to stand there not saying anything, doesn't it?

You can find small talk almost everywhere, but it's really common in places where you may be in the company of strangers for a length of time. For example, at bus stops, dentist's waiting rooms, the check-out queue at the supermarket, in lifts and perhaps even in public toilets – although my husband tells me that this is something that most men tend not to do. It's very common in parties or in conferences like this one. In cases like these it often seems that small talk is a kind of verbal dance, a necessary ritual we have to go through to find someone we can talk to about something that really matters to us.

You can't do it any time you want to. You've got to look for the clues, that is, read the body language of the person in front of you to see if it's appropriate or not. You can't just walk up to the first stranger you see and ask them if they think it's going to rain. No, you have to establish some kind of eye-contact first, smile or make a facial expression that tells them you're ready to communicate. Then you can make an instant judgement from the way they react about whether it's a suitable moment for small talk or not. There are some obvious situations where starting up a conversation is not appropriate. For example, if someone is reading or listening to an iPod or speaking on the phone, do think twice before speaking to them. And you really shouldn't interrupt two people who're already having a conversation to ask them if they think Chelsea's first goal should have been a penalty or not. Prepare to be met with a frosty reception!

Some people are natural small-talkers. Others find it hard. It may even seem impossible. Whatever your case, you can't deny that it's a useful social skill. And the good news is that, like most skills, it's something you can learn, something you can get better at. And that's what I'm going to talk about in the rest of the talk. How can we improve our small talk skills? First of all ...

Answers 1 F 2 T 3 F 4 T 5 T 6 F 7 T 8 F

SPEAKING SKILLS

1 Ss choose their topic alone or, working in pairs, Ss choose one each. Remind Ss that they can make notes of key words and ideas they want to talk about but they should not try to script their presentation. When they are ready, Ss give their presentation to each other in pairs. Nominate Ss to present their talk to the class.

2 Tell Ss that they should discuss each choice together giving reasons why they like or do not like it. Remind Ss of phrases they can use to agree and disagree with each other and that, if they cannot think of anything to say, they can ask their partner's opinion. Again, nominate one or two pairs to carry out the conversation in open class and then discuss the Ss' opinions on the different art works as a class. **Note:** The person in painting 2 is of the Polish astronomer Copernicus. The painting hangs in Toruń Town Hall and could be a copy of a self-portrait.

Our changing world

Read, listen and talk about the environment, society, the future.
Practise passive and active forms, talking about the future.
Focus on describing changes, making predictions.
Write in the appropriate style for your reader.

EXAM FOCUS

Topic: The environment; Society

Speaking
Making predictions: SB p.34, ex.5, ex.6

Listening
Multiple choice: SB p.36, ex.3

Reading
Multiple matching: SB p.30, ex.3

Grammar and vocabulary
Sentence transformations: SB p.34, ex.6

Writing
Writing in an appropriate style: SB p.37, ex.10, ex.12

Unit 3 Materials
Success Workbook Unit 3
Photocopiable resources 7, 8, 9
Testing and Evaluation Programme tests

VOCABULARY AND LISTENING

This section introduces collocations and phrasal verbs through a listening on the topic of the news.

Warm-up Introduction to the topic of the lesson. *Our society.* Put Ss into six groups. Each group is given a topic to discuss: *house prices, air travel, road deaths, car use, gender equality, computer games.* Tell Ss to brainstorm any information on their topic that they can think of, trends over time, prices, laws, problems etc. Set a time limit of five minutes and then each group presents their ideas.

1 Ss look at the headlines in their books and, after matching them to the correct pictures, guess what the headlines mean. Tell Ss not to use dictionaries but just to guess if they do not know as they will listen to the real meanings later. Elicit ideas in open class.
Note: Picture C shows stockbrokers buying and selling shares on a stock market.

Answers 1 E 2 C 3 A 4 F 5 B 6 D

2 Play the recording once. Ss note what each text is about and compare what they understood with their partner. Ss then complete the table. Go through the answers. Tell Ss that there are subtle differences in the meanings of the words and that they should be careful how they use them. The collocations in the lesson will help but point out that: *drop, decline, shrink* and *grow* are all neutral words for increases and decreases. *To slash* is the other odd one out as someone must slash something, eg prices slashed (by shops), spending slashed (by governments). The other words can be used for increases and decreases occurring on their own.

For tapescript see page 206.

Answers **fall/decrease** collapse, slump, plummet, drop, decline, shrink, slash **rise/increase** rocket, mount, surge, shoot up, soar, grow

3 Allow Ss one minute to look through the questions and discuss, in pairs, what they can remember from the first listening. Play the recording. Allow Ss to compare answers again before eliciting answers. Explain that *first-time buyers* are people who have never had a house before and are now buying one for the first time. A *congestion charge* is money that has to be paid in order to drive into a city. London introduced a charge in 2003. Cameras read car number plates as they enter the city and drivers have to pay in advance or on the day of travel. If they do not pay, they are fined.

Answers **1** First-time home buyers **2** Up to 30 percent **3** About the future of their industry **4** Because despite their being problems for some people, others are happy with the situation. **5** Speed control devices in private cars **6** Congestion charges, price of petrol, environmental awareness **7** A government report **8** Increased competition and a drop in sales

4 Ss complete the task alone and check in pairs. Elicit answers and check *popular, popularity* and *populist* (someone who tries to appeal to as many people as possible, eg a politician who claims to represent ordinary people although he/she may only be pretending in order to win votes). Make sure Ss know why *rockets* is wrong in 2 (it implies a big increase but there have only been two more deaths), *tumbled* is wrong in 4 (it means a large decrease so cannot be used with *slightly*) and why *shrink* is wrong in 5 (because it is the candidate who is actively making the taxes fall so we need to use *slash*).

Answers 1 shooting up; soaring **2** mounts
3 plummeted; slumped **4** decreased; declined **5** slash
6 rocketed; surged **7** collapsed; tumbled

5 Look at the adjectives and nouns with Ss. Ask which of the adjectives means *bad* (*disastrous*) and *good* (*tremendous*). The others are neutral, i.e. they could be used for both positive and negative although *spectacular* is unlikely to be used negatively. Now ask which two adjectives show a small amount (*gradual, steady*). Play the recording twice to allow Ss to write the collocations and check their answers.

Tapescript CD 1 Track 21

1 Rita: ... and there's been a huge rise in the number of deaths on the road.
2 Jarvis: New figures show there's been a dramatic collapse in the housing market ...
3 Jarvis: ... in the housing market as a result of the disastrous slump in the world economy.
4 Jarvis: We'll be talking to some first-time home buyers who are delighted with the sudden reduction in prices.
5 Jarvis: Accidents involving drivers under the age of thirty have registered a significant increase of more than 20 percent over last year's figures.
6 Rita: There has been a gradual decrease in the use of cars in city centres right across the country.
7 Rita: Apparently, there's been a steady decline of almost 12 percent in the amount of city centre driving over the last five years.
8 Rita: Congestion charges, the tremendous surge in the price of petrol and a gradual increase in environmental awareness are given as the reasons for the change.
9 Jarvis: There's been a spectacular growth in the number of women in top jobs.
10 Rita: Due to increased competition in the computer games market and a sharp fall in sales since Christmas, prices have been slashed.

Answers 1 huge rise **2** dramatic collapse **3** disastrous slump **4** sudden reduction **5** significant increase **6** gradual decrease **7** steady decline **8** tremendous surge **9** spectacular growth **10** sharp fall

6 Ask Ss to cover Exercise 5 and try to complete this exercise in pairs. Then they look at Exercise 5 to check their answers.

Answers 2 There has been a significant rise in the number of visitors. **3** There has been a dramatic surge in music downloads. **4** There has been a substantial decrease in violent crime. **5** There has been a considerable decline in the quality of TV. **6** There has been a dramatic slump in crowds at football matches. **7** There is a sharp increase in the use of eco-bikes. **8** There is a gradual reduction in the amount of cheating.

7 Make sure Ss understand what sentences 2 and 8 refer to (visitors to the Ss' country/town; cheating in exams at school). Elicit sentences in open class and allow Ss to agree or disagree using the vocabulary in Exercise 5.

Mind the trap!

Go through the box with Ss and ask Ss how they could make a sentence starting with *Prices* and using the verb *raise* (or *slash*) – they could use the passive, i.e. *Prices are being/have been raised/slashed.*

8 Allow Ss to discuss the collocations and write sentences in pairs. Elicit ideas. Ss may have different answers so allow them to try to justify what they have written where there is disagreement.

Suggested answers 1 Hot-air balloons rise into the sky. **2** People raise money for charity. **3** Raise your hand. (Possibly *My hand is rising* if it is outside your control.) **4** The sun rises in the east. **5** Raise your eyebrows. **6** The temperature is rising. We need to raise the temperature quickly. **7** Don't raise your hopes. Hopes are rising for a full recovery. **8** Salaries are rising. My boss raised my salary. **9** You must rise early. **10** Don't raise your voice. Her voice rises when she gets nervous. **11** The bread is rising in the oven. **12** I want to settle down and raise a family.

9 Allow Ss to look through the phrasal verbs before they start the activity. Ss try to do the matching alone. After the activity, elicit the answers and examples that could illustrate the meaning, eg *Terrorists sometimes blow up buildings.*

Answers A 1 e **2** a **3** d **4** f **5** c **6** b
B 1 c **2** b **3** d **4** f **5** a **6** e

10 This activity may need a substantial amount of time for preparation and allowing each pair to act out their news broadcast in front of the class. It may be better for Ss to get together in groups of six to act out their radio bulletins rather than all Ss listening to all the other pairs. Ss work in pairs to decide on what stories to include. Each student can then be responsible for writing half of the stories. They should decide which of the words from Exercise 5 they are each going to use so that they do not both use the same ones and can then write the news stories at home and act out the news bulletin during the next lesson.

ADDITIONAL PRACTICE: Photocopiable resources. Resource 7: *Explaining the graphs.* Page 172

READING AND VOCABULARY

This section introduces vocabulary related to environmental issues.

Special difficulties: Care must be taken with international words which look the same in L1 and L2 but have different pronunciation. It is important to ensure that Ss do not rely on their native pronunciation of such words.

Culture notes

Carbon offsetting is a system whereby companies and individuals can purchase carbon offsets depending on how much carbon dioxide their activities produce. The money is used for emissions-reducing projects such as tree planting, renewable energy and the destruction of industrial pollutants. Some people claim that carbon offsetting is not always beneficial for the environment. It allows people to pay for their polluting without having to change their behaviour, eg someone may 'offset' their international plane travel by planting trees when it would be better for them to cut down on their flying. Some offsetting activities may actually be harmful, for example, if the trees planted are fast-growing species which are grown in places where they disrupt the native species.

Warm-up Review of vocabulary from the previous lesson.
Put them together. Have a list of adjectives and nouns written on a sheet of paper, each word numbered as follows:

Adjectives: *1 disastrous 2 dramatic 3 gradual 4 huge 5 sharp 6 significant 7 sudden 8 spectacular 9 steady 10 tremendous*

Nouns: *1 collapse 2 decline 3 decrease 4 fall 5 growth 6 increase 7 reduction 8 rise 9 slump 10 surge*

Put Ss into five groups. Each group choose two numbers from 1–10. Tell each group their four words, eg 1 *disastrous collapse*, 8 *spectacular rise* etc. They have to make two sentences which are true about their country using their four words. Elicit all and decide whether the sentences are true or false.

1 Allow Ss five minutes to discuss the five questions. After the Ss have checked them, discuss what the class think and whether they agree with the information on page 146 or not.

2 Before Ss look at the pictures, ask them to close their books and imagine the world in the year 2050. Ask them to think alone about technology, pollution, war and nature and decide whether they are optimistic or pessimistic. After one minute, Ss discuss their ideas in pairs and then as a class. Ss then open their books. This could be done in groups of three with each student looking at a different picture. Then they discuss what they think their picture represents and then read only one text. After reading, they again get back into their groups of three and tell each other what they read.

Answers **A** It's a vision of what happens if global warming gets out of control. People died of starvation and disease. **B** When it seemed as if global warming would get out of control, people changed their lifestyles and now live in a less material but happier world. **C** Global warming was brought under control through technological advances and people now live in a cleaner world.

3 If Ss read only one text in Exercise 2, they should read through the visions and decide which relate to their text. Then they find evidence in their text to justify their decisions. When they have finished, they get back together as a group and share their answers. If the number of answers matches the number of boxes, they should have completed the task correctly and can then read the other two texts to see what they say. If not, they have to read all three texts and try to work out the answers as a group. Elicit answers and the relevant extracts from the texts, i.e. 1 'The turning point came in 2027'; 2 'As temperatures soared (...) widespread flooding (...) droughts (...) people starve (...)'; 3 fuel tax, bike lanes, subsidies etc; 4 droughts, 'harvests failed and people began to starve' / droughts, famine; water shortages, scarce water resources; 5 'enormous mirrors (...) a complete failure', 'spraying (...) water (...) came to nothing'; 6 super-efficient electrical cables; 7 'flooding and paradoxically (...) droughts'; 8 'fewer than 500 million people'; 9 'The great lifestyle change' / Carbon Credits, allowances, taxes etc; 10 'saved endangered species'.

Answers 1 B 2 A 3 C 4 A, B 5 B 6 C 7 A 8 A 9 B, C 10 C

4 Ss list the words and phrases from the book. When they have finished, ask if they can add any more ideas to the lists they have made and go through the meaning of any words that Ss are not sure of.

Answers **Consequences:** ice sheets melt, less heat reflected back into space, methane released, destruction of rainforests, sea level rises, temperatures soar, flooding, droughts, deserts spread, harvests fail, people starve, refugees, disease, cyclones, storms, forest fires, famine, water shortages, global economy collapses, war
Technological solutions: spray sea water into the sky, renewable energy, CO_2-reduction technologies, alternative energies, carbon sinks, super-efficient electrical cable, wind farms, wave platforms, hydrogen fuel cells, biofuels
Environmental policies: emissions targets, ban unnecessary air travel, tax private cars, subsidise public transport, ration meat, encourage vegetarianism, make homes, shops and offices carbon neutral, carbon credits, aviation fuel taxed, bike lanes, subsidise energy saving buildings, eco-friendly houses, carbon offsetting, trees planted, international agreements

5 Ss work in pairs and try to use as many of the vocabulary items from Exercise 4 as they can. Elicit ideas in open class before playing the recording. Tell Ss to make notes of key words while they are listening and to compare later what they wrote with a partner. Elicit important words and an overall idea of what the picture shows.

Tapescript `CD 1 Track 23`

Alexis: *[Northern English accent]* Hey, George, where's the rest of this article?

George: *[Northern English accent]* Oh, sorry, Alexis, I threw it out.

Alexis: Oh! I wanted to read the last text about the future! Have you read it?

George: Yeah.

Alexis: What's it about? It's not as depressing as the other ones, is it?

George: No, it's really optimistic actually. It's about this Indian scientist who develops a process to produce the power of the sun at room temperature.

Alexis: Nuclear fusion?

George: Yeah, that's it.

Alexis: At room temperature?

George: Uh huh.

Alexis: When?

George: Oh, in 2039 or something like that.

Alexis: That's really unlikely. I suppose it might happen one day, but not so soon.

George: Yeah, well, anyway. He does that and the result is that we have virtually limitless clean energy which can be extracted for practically nothing from the hydrogen found in sea water.

Alexis: It would be brilliant, but ...

George: But this scientist, right, he suspected that if energy was free, it might actually speed up the destruction of the environment. He thought that if engines didn't pollute, more roads would be built for all those brand-new eco-friendly cars, and more trees would be chopped down and more countryside would be covered in concrete and more and more unnecessary consumer goods would be manufactured and more ...

Alexis: Right, so what did he do?

George: He created a company called 'NukeFuse'.

Alexis: 'NukeFuse'?

George: Yeah.

Alexis: What for?

George: Well, it was a non-profit-making company, so it marketed the new energy at different prices for different customers. If someone wanted power for a desalination plant to provide fresh water, it was free, but if a car manufacturer wanted the energy, it was only slightly cheaper than petrol or coal.

Alexis: Good idea.

George: And so by 2050 the world has been transformed. Hunger has been practically eradicated. Clean fresh water is available everywhere. Climate change has been halted. Oh yeah, and next year, the first elections for World President are gonna be held!

Alexis: Yeah, right! I mean, I'm optimistic, but that's just ridiculous.

George: No, not necessarily, I mean think about it. If they actually make this happen ...

Answers An optimistic view. Clean energy is obtained from hydrogen in sea water. A company sells it, charging more to some people than others depending on what they want it for.

6 Allow Ss to read through the questions and discuss anything they remember from the recording, in pairs, before playing it again.

Answers 1 A way of producing the power of the sun at room temperature. **2** It provides virtually limitless, cheap, clean energy. **3** That free energy would cause more environmental problems. **4** People who wanted energy for 'good' uses got it free whereas those who wanted it for things such as cars had to pay. **5** Clean, almost without hunger, no climate change. **6** They're optimistic although Alexis isn't convinced that things will be this good.

7 Tell Ss to attempt the task as if it were an exam problem solving task. Ss discuss each picture in turn, giving their views on how likely or unlikely it is and why, then trying to come to an agreement.

8 When Ss have finished, elicit what the sentences mean in simple language, eg 1 big floods; lots of damage; communities near sea-level.

Answers 1 widespread flooding; incalculable damage; low-lying communities **2** energy-saving/eco-friendly measures; eco-friendly/energy-saving vehicles; emissions targets **3** harness solar energy; halt climate change; eradicate hunger **4** technological fix; tipping point; devastating consequences

9 Ss look at the cartoon and discuss the joke in pairs. Then they join up in groups of four and think of other contradictions. Elicit ideas in open class.

Answers The people are protesting about car use but the man on the left has driven to the demonstration. **Other contradictions** For example politicians claiming to be against pollution but expanding airports and roads. Pop stars who fly by private jet to a special environment awareness pop festival. The audience at such a festival who leave masses of litter on the ground. People who care about animal welfare who eat cheap chickens and other meat from supermarkets.

GRAMMAR

This section reviews passive forms and extends the students' knowledge of how and when to use them.

Warm-up Review of vocabulary from the previous lesson.
Backs to the board. Nominate two Ss to come to the front of the class and face the other Ss. Write a word on the board from the last lesson. The other Ss have to attempt to define the word without saying it. The two Ss at the front are not allowed to look at the word. As soon as one of them guesses the word, change the two Ss and write a new word on the board.

Possible words to use:

Global warming

Drought

Flood

Wind farm

Subsidise

Sea levels

Carbon footprint

Work it out

1 It might be worth giving Ss an easy example sentence to start with. Write on the board: *I gave my brother a book.* Ss identify the verb (*give*) and the person who does the giving (*I*).
Now write: *I was given a book for my birthday.* Ss again identify the verb (*give*) but this time cannot say who does the giving because it is not written. Ss then do the exercise alone and compare in pairs. Leave the two sentences on the board for later.

Answers a We b Sea levels c Hurricane Theresa
d – e – f – g – h hydrogen fuel-cells

2 Elicit that sentences d–h are all examples of the passive in which it is not necessary to name the agent although, as in h, it is possible. Ss then look at Exercise 2 in pairs. There may be disagreement over exactly which sentence illustrates which point, eg sentence d could match with reason 1, 2 or 4.

Suggested answers 1 h 2 g 3 e 4 d 5 f 6 c 7 a 8 b

Optional activity: Look at the first reason for using the passive (the action is more important than the agent) and elicit ideas of when this may be likely to be true. For example, when something happens to us and we are talking we would be likely to emphasise what happened (to us or our things) rather than who did it, eg *I was told off last night. I was caught using my mobile phone in Maths.* Ss then work in groups of two or three to write their own sentence. Repeat for the other reasons given. Ss then read out one of their sentences and the rest of the class has to

guess which reason it corresponds to. As was said before, more than one reason may apply.

Check it out

Refer Ss to the Check it out section on page 155 to help them if they are still unsure about when to use the passive.

3 Look at sentence 1 with Ss. Ask: *Does the economy collapse or does someone collapse it?* (it collapses). Elicit that, as *collapse* is an intransitive verb, the sentence must be active. Ss then have to decide what tense the sentence should be in. Remind them that the texts on global warming were written from the viewpoint of 2050 so were looking back into the past.

Answers 1 collapsed 2 decimated 3 be done 4 was rationed 5 being planted 6 been brought

Mind the trap!

If you still have the two sentences from Exercise 1 on the board, ask Ss what the object of the first sentence is. The answer is that there are two objects: *a book* and *my brother*. Therefore there are two possible passive forms:
A book was given to my brother by me.
My brother was given a book by me.
Ss now look at the Mind the trap! box to see which other verbs can have two objects.

4 Ss read through the text first to get an overall understanding of it. Then they do the transformation task and discuss who they think is talking in pairs. Play the recording and elicit what the Ss heard. Ss should not have had any problems with the change from an object pronoun (*us*) to a subject pronoun (*we*) but it could be pointed out or elicited that this change has taken place.

Tapescript `CD 1 Track 24`

[RP accent] People of Earth. Listen to me. You are going to be shown something amazing. The secret of free energy will be explained to you. It is not being sold to you; it is being offered to you. No payment will be required for this. But we must be provided with your full cooperation. Many civilisations across the universe have already been taught this secret. And so far we have always been given what we need ... Your complete obedience.

Answers 1 You are going to be shown something amazing. 2 The secret of free energy will be explained to you. 3 It is not being sold to you. 4 It is being offered to you. 5 No payment will be required for this. 6 We must be provided with your full cooperation. 7 Many civilisations have already been taught this secret. 8 We have always been given what we need.

5 In this activity, both forms may be possible grammatically but one will sound better because of the reasons given in Exercise 2. Ss do the task alone and then compare ideas in pairs. Sometimes both forms are equally possible.

Answers 1 ✓ 2 A field of huge mirrors has been installed 3 The sun's rays are reflected 4 ✓ 5 ✓ / Massive quantities of electricity can be generated (either possible) 6 The station is going to be expanded 7 ✓ / enough power will be provided (either possible) 8 the energy can only be stored 9 the solar power is needed 10 air-conditioning units are used 11 ✓ 12 prices are expected to fall

6 Allow the groups to discuss the sentences first and then elicit ideas and justifications in open class.

Answers 1 is caused 2 has been proved 3 be done 4 will soon be found 5 being told; to be ignored 6 is not taken; will be wiped out; will be destroyed

Optional activity: Ss work in four groups. Dictate topics to Ss. For each topic the students must write down one famous example. For each, give an example on the board and tell Ss not to use the same idea as yours.

Topics and examples:
A painting (eg the *Mona Lisa*)
A food connected with a certain country (eg pizzas)
A type of car (eg Skoda)
A book (eg *Harry Potter*)
A character in a current film or series of films (eg James Bond)
An auxiliary verb (eg *have*)
A song popular now
A song or piece of music from the past (eg *Four Seasons*)
A film and its director (eg *Titanic*, James Cameron)
The losers in a major sports competition (eg France, 2006 World Cup Final)

Look at your first example (the *Mona Lisa*) and tell Ss that they must make a passive sentence which starts with this name, eg *The Mona Lisa was painted by Leonardo Da Vinci*. Do the same for the second sentence, eg *Real pizza is made in Italy*. One group now come to the board. Tell them to write one of their words on the board. The other groups have to try to be the first to write a passive sentence starting with that word. As soon as one group has finished, elicit the sentence and, if correct grammatically and factually, award them a point. Each group writes about three words on the board for the other groups to guess, trying to choose the most difficult. If no one can make a passive sentence which is factually correct, the group who gave the word can gain a point by making their own sentence.

ADDITIONAL PRACTICE: Photocopiable resources. Resource 8: *They match but are they right?* Page 173

SPEAKING

This section reviews and extends ways of making predictions.

Culture notes

Niels Bohr (1885–1962) was a Danish physicist who won the Nobel Prize for Physics in 1922. He was born in Copenhagen but worked on the Manhattan Project, to produce the first atomic bomb, under the name Nicholas Baker. He was against the arms race and urged the Americans to share their knowledge with the Russians.

Bertrand Russell (1872–1970) was a philosopher, historian, mathematician and logician. He was a pacifist who opposed nuclear arms and the war in Vietnam and he was jailed for pacifist activities during the First World War. In 1950 he won the Nobel Prize in Literature in recognition of his varied writings in which he promoted humanitarian ideals.

Charles F. Kettering (1876–1958) was an inventor. He held over 300 patents and worked for General Motors for many years. He invented electric starting engines for cars which replaced those that had to be started manually with a crank lever. He developed lead petrol and also helped to develop solar power.

John F. Kennedy (1917–1963) was President of the USA from 1961 until he was assassinated in November 1963. He was the youngest person to be elected president, at the age of forty-three, but not the youngest ever president as Theodore Roosevelt succeeded to the presidency at the age of forty-two, as he was vice-president when president McKinley was assassinated. Kennedy's own assassination happened in Dallas and is the subject of many conspiracy theories about who organised and carried out the killing. During his famous presidential inauguration speech in January 1961, he said 'Ask not what your country can do for you, ask what you can do for your country', asking that everyone help to make the country and the world a better place.

Warm-up Review of passive forms. *What's the activity?* Tell Ss you have written an activity on a piece of paper. To find out what that activity is, Ss must ask questions about it but the teacher can only answer *yes* or *no*. The other rule is that the questions must be in the passive. Write the verb *do* and two examples on the board: *Is it done by everyone in the world?* (no) *Will it be done by anyone in this room today?* (yes). Ss think of five more questions and then guess what the activity is (*do homework*). Repeat the process with a second activity and write the verb *make* on the board. This time, do not give any example sentences and nominate pairs to think of questions (*make the bed*).

1 Ss discuss the ideas in small groups. Elicit ideas and ask Ss if they have ever used a fortune teller or know someone who has.

Answers 1 horoscopes, tarot cards, tea leaves, palm reading, crystal balls, etc 2 **Advantages:** being able to prepare yourself **Disadvantages:** fate is out of your hands. If you know something bad is going to happen on a particular day, how can you stop it?

2 Ask Ss if anyone has (or would like to have) their own website. If so, ask them what sort of things they have got on the homepage and other pages. Ask whether they use any photos of or quotes from famous people to show who they admire or what their views on certain issues are. Ss then read the webpage and discuss the answers in pairs or small groups. Elicit ideas in open class.

Answers 1 Probably because they sum up her own views. 2 Ss' own ideas 3 Ss' own ideas 4 Men aren't brave enough. Other reasons: eg biologically impossible

SPEAK OUT

3 Ss complete the Speak Out box alone. Elicit the words and ask Ss to make a sentence using each on any topic they wish. When they have finished, discuss with the class what they think of the predictions she makes and, if they disagree with her, what they think will happen.

Answers **definitely won't happen** no way; inconceivable
almost certainly won't happen extremely doubtful; a very slight possibility
probably won't happen unlikely
will probably happen may; there's a good chance, strong likelihood
will almost certainly happen the chances are
will definitely happen certain; I'm convinced

4 Tell Ss that, if they read the opinions carefully, they will find that only one prediction is possible logically. Elicit ideas for statement 1 and then play the recording for that prediction. Stop the recording and repeat the process for number 2 and continue for all six predictions.

Tapescript CD 1 Track 25

[Scottish accent] **1** I suppose Goth fashions might become more popular and mainstream one day, but I'd hate it if they did. If everyone started dressing like me, I'd have to find a new style, wouldn't I?
2 My little brother listens to house music all the time. I think it's awful. He thinks it'll last for ever, but I think it's highly improbable it'll still be around five years from now.
3 It's not going to happen any day soon, but some time in the future there is likely to be a big change in the fashion industry and you won't have to be really tall and thin in order to be a supermodel.
4 Call me an optimist, but there's no doubt in my mind that one day we will live in a world without crime or

violence! Seriously, there's a strong likelihood that we'll all have microchips in our heads that will stop us committing crimes.

5 Everyone's banging on about global warming and stuff and saying it's sure to destroy the planet, but I'm not too worried. Scientists may well find a new form of energy that's ecological and doesn't cost much. The only thing is it's unlikely to make everyone happy.

6 This is the last one cause I've got to study for an exam tomorrow. What a pain! Still, not to worry, I'm sure there won't be any exams in the future. We'll all study at home with computers and get marks for all the work we do.

Answers **1** It's possible **2** It's extremely doubtful **3** the chances are **4** inevitable; In all probability **5** a good chance; I shouldn't think **6** I'm convinced

5 Ss discuss the ideas in pairs. This could be extended by joining pairs together in groups of four to discuss their ideas. If Ss are very interested in the topics, elicit ideas in open class.

6 Ss work in pairs to do the transformations. Then they join up in groups of four to compare their answers and then discuss the predictions. Elicit all the answers and make sure Ss have corrected any mistakes.

Answers **1** It is bound to rain tomorrow. There is no doubt that it will rain tomorrow. **2** Our national team is sure not to win the World Cup. There's not a hope of our national team winning the World Cup. **3** There's a strong likelihood that we'll have an exam next week. In all probability, we'll have an exam next week. **4** It is doubtful that house prices will fall. There's a very faint chance that house prices will fall. **5** I may well have to move abroad to find a job. The chances are that I'll have to move abroad to find a job. **6** The future is unlikely to be like it is in the movies. I shouldn't think the future will be much like it is in the movies.

7 Tell Ss to work alone at first, thinking about what to say about each topic and making notes if necessary. Allow one minute and then put Ss into groups of four to compare ideas. Elicit the most dramatic predictions from each group.

ADDITIONAL PRACTICE: Photocopiable resources. Resource 9: *Argue your point.* Page 174

LISTENING AND WRITING

This section introduces tips on writing in the appropriate style for various forms of writing task.

Culture notes

Médecins Sans Frontières means 'Doctors without borders'. It was created by a group of French doctors in 1971 as they believed that everyone had the right to medical treatment regardless of where they came from. It provides medical help in over seventy countries. The organisation won the Nobel Peace Prize in 1999.

The Ebola Virus is named after the Ebola River where the illness was first diagnosed in 1976. The strain of Ebola that broke out in Zaire is the most deadly virus known with a 90% fatality rate. It is transferred by blood or other bodily fluids. It is now thought to be carried by a species of fruit bat which has been found to carry the virus but not suffer from it.

NGOs (Non Governmental Organisations) are political organisations set up by private individuals and free from state interference. International organisations have been important since the mid-nineteenth century in the fight against slavery and for women's rights. However, the term NGO came into popular use with the formation of the UN (United Nations) in 1945 which allowed for 'a consultative role for organisations which are neither governments nor member states'.

The first **Car-free Days** were organised in 1996 in Reykjavik, Iceland and Bath, England. France organised a national Car-free Day in 1998 and the European Commission made it a Europe-wide initiative in 2000, calling it 'In town without my car!'

Croydon is a suburb of London. It is 15km south of the centre of London and became a part of Greater London in 1965. It is now a leading financial and business centre with the largest amount of office space outside of central London.

Warm-up Review of making predictions. *What am I thinking about?* Elicit topics on which you could make predictions, eg school, pollution, global warming, transport, sport etc. One student comes to the front of the class and chooses a topic from the board. Then they write a prediction about it. The student tells the class the likelihood only, eg *It's bound to happen* or *I'm sure I won't.* The other Ss have to try to guess what the student is thinking about. Give them five chances and, if they cannot guess, the student tells them what his/her prediction was. Repeat with a different student.

1 Ss discuss the quote in pairs for one minute and then as a class.

2 Give Ss thirty seconds to read through the list of things and prepare themselves for what they are about to listen to. Ss should make notes of what each person says and then match them to the things at the end of the listening. Elicit answers and key words which helped the Ss decide, eg 1 hospital, virus, contagious, infected, cure, vaccine; 2 practise, rehearse, group, community centre, stage, rehearsal room, recording studio; 3 cycling, traffic jams, bike lanes, commuting.

For tapescript see page 206.

Answers 1 food and health **2** entertainment and leisure **3** travel and transport

3 Allow Ss time to read through the questions and think about what they heard before. Play the recording again. Elicit the answers and the reasons Ss have for choosing them. Not all the answers are clear cut and there may be some disagreement. Allow Ss to justify their answers if different. 1c is possible, he did want to fly around the world but not as a tourist. However, his real reason for joining the organisation was that he felt he 'needed a change' in his life. 2 People spend more on themselves than on helping others, i.e. they are selfish. 3 There is nothing for young people to do in their town. They started the group for something to do, therefore we can assume they were bored. 4 People did not complain, they signed their petition. 5 The doctor just advised him to lose weight, not how to do it. His reasons were to lose weight and avoid traffic jams. 6 It is cheaper, quicker, cleaner, and good for your health. The bike lanes are in response to the needs of cyclists, not the other way round.

Answers 1 b **2** c **3** b **4** b **5** c **6** b

4 Again, allow Ss to look through the list before playing the recording. Ss have heard the recording twice so may be able to remember what was said. Play the recording again and then elicit answers.

Answers set up a pressure group, talked to community leaders/church groups, wrote to government representatives, made a poster, printed and handed out leaflets, organised a demonstration, started a petition

5 Look at the things that the second speaker did not do and ask whether these would have been useful (joining a political party would be a bit unnecessary but setting up a blog or website and writing to a local paper might have been very useful things to do). Ss now discuss the problems in Exercise 5 in pairs and then as a class.

Answers Speaker 1 Leaflets, websites, letters and meetings would probably be the best idea as they want to persuade not protest. **Speaker 3** Pressure groups, petitions, writing to government representatives and even joining a political party might be useful as they need to force government to change its policies.

6 Set a time limit of two minutes for Ss to discuss the questions and elicit ideas in open class.

Answers 2 It is important to consider your readers' expectations and conform to accepted stylistic and linguistic conventions. Your friends would think it strange if you wrote a very formal email whereas a future employer or a government representative may not take your letter seriously unless it is written correctly and politely. Poems and stories have to interest the reader or they may not finish reading, and a school essay has to show your teacher that you can use language accurately and well.

7 This can be done with the whole class straightaway as it follows on naturally from the last activity. Again elicit why these are the correct answers, i.e. the person in government will not take your letter seriously if it is not written formally; people in the street need to be instantly persuaded and involved so do not want to read unnecessary language; your friend would be surprised if you wrote in any other way.

Answers 1 b 2 c 3 a

8 Tell Ss that sometimes the sentences could come from more than one type of text. We are not always very informal to our friends so the differences between a leaflet and an email may not always be distinguishable, eg sentences 1, 3, 9, 10 could be from either type of text and even sentence 6 if the leaflet was very informal in style. There may also be times when the letter to the government representative and the leaflet are similar, eg sentences 4 and 10 could possibly come from either. Do not give them the real answers at this time. After they have completed the next exercise they will be able to see where each sentence came from.

Answers 1 – 2, 2 – 3, 3 – 2, 4 – 1, 5 – 1, 6 – 3, 7 – 3, 8 – 1, 9 – 2, 10 – 1, 11 – 1, 12 – 3

9 Tell Ss that, although there may have been some doubt in the last exercise, this time the context of the letters should make it easy to identify which sentences go where. Ss work alone and then compare in pairs. They can then see who was correct in the previous exercise.

Answers a 1 b 9 c 3 d 5 e 8 f 10 g 4 h 11 i 2 j 6 k 7 l 12

10 When the Ss have written their letters, they should swap them with another person in the group and react to them as if they were the intended recipient. Having read them, the 'politician' gives their opinion on whether the letter is formal enough, the 'friend' gives feedback on whether the email was clear and friendly in tone and the reader of the leaflet comments on how effective the leaflet was in making him/her want to do something to help.

11 It may be worth asking Ss to think of an idea on their own and then trying to find other people with similar ideas to make a group with. If some groups are too large or too small, some Ss would have to move to a different group to even up the numbers.

12 Ss discuss what their aims are and how they would go about achieving them. They should all agree on their ideas so that, when they write their letters, the content of all letters in one group should be the same. Ss write the three letters for homework. When marking them, comment on their effectiveness and style as well as their accuracy.

Coming of age

Read, listen and talk about education, applying for jobs.
Practise inversion.
Focus on appropriacy – inversion in spoken English.
Write a letter of application.

EXAM FOCUS

Topic: Education; Work

Speaking
Roleplay: SB p.44, ex.3
Giving presentations: SB p.44, ex.4

Listening
True/False/No information: SB p.39, ex.4
Multiple matching: SB p.39, ex.5

Reading
Multiple choice: SB p.40, ex.4

Grammar and vocabulary
Wordbuilding: SB p.39, ex.9
Sentence transformations: SB p.43, ex.12

Writing
Job application (covering letter): SB p.47, ex.9

Unit 4 Materials

Success Workbook Unit 4

Photocopiable resources 10, 11, 12

Testing and Evaluation Programme tests

LISTENING AND VOCABULARY

This section introduces a number of useful
idioms through a listening on 'rites of passage'.

Culture notes

The voting age in Britain was reduced from 21 to 18
in 1970. In 1999 a vote was taken in parliament on
whether to reduce the age to 16. It was defeated by 434
votes to 36. A 'Votes at 16' coalition was formed in 2003
but, as yet, the voting age remains 18.

Compulsory National Service existed in Britain from
1916–1918 and from 1939–1960. It lasted for eighteen
months after which people were put on a reserve list
for a further four years during which they could be
called up at any time. The time was increased to two
years in 1950 because of the Korean War. Miners,
farmers and merchant seamen were exempt but
university students still had to do their service after
they had completed their studies.

Warm-up Introduction to the topic of the lesson. *Don't say
the word.* Put Ss into groups of up to six. Each
student gets a piece of paper with one of the
situations from Exercise 2 on it: *I'm going to vote,
I'm getting married, I have started driving, I'm
going to purchase some alcohol, I have finished my
education, I have started work.* Ss cannot show their
sentence to the others. Each person in turn has to tell
the other Ss what is on their piece of paper without
using the words written on it, eg *There's an election
next week. I'm going to go to the town hall and put
an X next to the name of the Green Party candidate.*
The other Ss guess what the sentence is.

1 Tell Ss they should describe the picture for one
minute, saying what they can see and what they
think is happening. Then they have another minute to
discuss the questions in Exercise 1.

Possible answers Ss could mention what they are allowed
to do after the age of 18 (eg vote, drink alcohol, get
married) and whether any other age is more significant
(eg the age they are allowed to drive or leave school).
Celebrations could include parties at home or in a specially
hired room, going out for a meal with close family etc.

2 Ss complete the table in pairs. Then ask Ss if they
think the ages should be changed. Elicit other
important things which are restricted by age, eg
joining the army, smoking, going to prison.

3 When Ss have discussed the questions, elicit ideas
before playing the recording. Tell Ss to note down
any key information while they are listening. Play the
recording once only at this stage.

Tapescript `CD 2 Track 1`

Martha: *[Australian accent]* You're listening to *Have
Your Say* on Talk UK with me, Martha Cook. Well, a
debate has been raging over the past few weeks in Britain
about whether the voting age should be lowered from
eighteen, as it is at present, to sixteen. So we thought
that a good topic for today's programme is 'coming of age'
– when should young people officially become adults? My
guest today is Ted Barnes, a specialist in social history at
Uxbridge University. So, Ted, what does a young person
have to do to become an adult?

Ted: *[Northern English accent]* Well, the answer is,
not very much at all. It's usually enough just to reach
the age of eighteen – and bingo – you're part of the
adult world. You can vote, open a bank account, drink
alcohol, watch an X-rated film or be held personally
responsible for a crime.

Martha: So this is why people's eighteenth birthday parties
are such big occasions? You're now officially an adult?

Ted: Yes, that's right. But what's interesting is that this is really a very modern development. A few generations ago, turning eighteen was really quite meaningless.

Martha: So what's changed?

Ted: Well, up until fairly recently, becoming an adult wasn't about reaching a certain age. It was all about proving that you could do something as well as an adult, which usually meant a job or a profession. So, for example, if your father was a coal miner then you'd do a period of training in a coal-mine – your apprenticeship, in other words. During your apprenticeship, you'd 'learn the ropes' by doing the job and once you'd become as good as anyone else then it meant you had joined the adult world. And because some jobs take longer to learn than others, it meant that some became 'adults' when they were just fourteen or fifteen, and others such as doctors or lawyers were in their twenties.

Martha: But surely there was nothing like apprenticeships before the Industrial Revolution?

Ted: Hmm, I'm afraid I have to disagree with you there. These 'rites of passage', these rituals which prove you've joined the adult world, really go back thousands of years. In prehistoric times, boys were taught the customs and killing skills the tribe had accumulated. And the girls would have to learn to distinguish which fruit or mushrooms were edible or inedible, how to treat wounds or brew beer.

Martha: OK. I'd like to talk about exams, if we may. Between the ages of sixteen and eighteen you have to sit an awful lot of exams. Aren't school-leaving exams an example of a 'rite of passage' too?

Ted: Well, yes and no. Obviously passing exams is proving that you can do something. But most people who leave school at eighteen nowadays then continue into higher education. So they're actually postponing joining the adult world for a few more years!

Martha: And who can blame them! So Ted, do you think it's a good thing that we've lost these rituals connected with becoming an adult?

Ted: That's a good question. I think you could argue that teenagers today don't have a very clear role and because of that many of them feel out of place in society. And this in turn leads to problems such as violence and other crime. There's often a kind of emptiness to your teenage years when you're just waiting for things to change and people to treat you differently. In the past, it was much more obvious when you had become a 'useful' member of society.

Martha: Mmm, I'm not sure if I agree with you, but that's an interesting view, nevertheless. Let's take a break for some music now but if any of you would like to share your opinions on this matter then please give us a ring. The number is 01845 ...

Answers 1 Rites of passage are events that you go through which mark the change from a child to an adult. **2** Being taught to kill animals, celebrating your birthday, doing an apprenticeship, taking exams

4 Before Ss listen to the recording again, in small groups they discuss what they remember from the first listening. Then they look at the nine statements alone. Ss then listen again to the recording to check and complete their answers. Elicit the answers and justifications, i.e. 1 'a debate has been raging'; 2 'a specialist in social history'; 3 'A few generations ago, turning eighteen was really quite meaningless.';

4 'because some jobs take longer to learn than others, it meant that some became 'adults' when they were just 14 or 15, and others such as doctors or lawyers were in their twenties'; 5 no age is given for coal miners becoming adults; 6 'And the girls would have to learn to (...) brew beer.'; 7 'But most people who leave school at eighteen nowadays then continue into higher education. So they're actually postponing joining the adult world'; 8 'In the past, it was much more obvious when you had become a 'useful' member of society.'; 9 'There's often a kind of emptiness to your teenage years when you're just waiting for things to change'.

Answers 1 F **2** T **3** T **4** T **5** NI **6** T **7** F **8** T **9** F

5 With books closed, Ss listen for the first time just making notes about the main idea of what the speaker is saying. Ss compare ideas in pairs, then open their books to look at the statements. Ss do the matching and then listen again to check. Ask for justifications for the answers, eg *What does Nathan disagree about?* (the empty teenage years).

For tapescript see page 207.

Answers 1 d **2** f **3** g **4** e **5** a

6 Give Ss one minute to think about what to say and then one minute each to tell their partners. Nominate Ss to tell the class their experiences.

7 Ss work in pairs, first trying to guess the meanings and then looking the idioms up to check.

Answers 1 learn how to do a task **2** not a part of **3** made me realise **4** thinking hard **5** controversial issue **6** very pleased **7** undecided **8** finish

8 In pairs Ss cover Exercise 7 and try to remember the idioms. Then they uncover Exercise 7 and check their answers and correct them if necessary.

Answers 1 call it a day **2** racking my brains **3** brought home to me **4** out of place **5** over the moon **6** learn the ropes **7** in two minds about **8** a can of worms

9 Before Ss try to complete the gaps, they should think about the type of word needed, eg 1 past participle – passive form; 2 negative adjective etc.

Answers 1 lowered **2** meaningless **3** edible **4** preferably **5** apprenticeship **6** emptiness **7** adulthood

10 Ss work in groups of four. In each group, make one student responsible for each of the four questions. After five minutes change the groups so that eg all the students responsible for the question of anti-social behaviour are now together. Ss now compare their ideas in their new groups and then each group presents their ideas for their question.

READING AND VOCABULARY

This section introduces education vocabulary through a reading on a student's first days at university.

Culture notes

The term **'Fresher'** applies to students in their first few weeks at university. Universities call the first week of term 'Freshers' week' and organise events to make the new students feel at home.

Philip Larkin (1922–1985) was a poet and novelist. He was born in Coventry and studied English at Oxford during the Second World War. He was able to study for the full three years of his degree because poor eyesight meant he could not be called up for the armed forces.

Warm-up Review of idioms from the previous lesson.
Match up. Give 8 Ss beginnings of idioms and 8 other Ss the endings. For classes of more than 16 Ss, some Ss can work in pairs. With fewer than 16 Ss, remove some of the idioms.
The Ss with the beginnings of idioms stand up, the others remain seated. The Ss with the beginnings have to find the Ss with the correct endings. To do this, they go to each sitting student in turn and read out their start. The other student reads out their ending and, if they think their words make a complete phrase, the 'beginning' student sits with their partner. Then they work together to make sure they know the meaning of their idiom. When all Ss are seated, each pair in turn defines their idiom and the other Ss have to say what it is.
Idioms to use:

learn the	*ropes*
feel out of	*place*
brought home	*to me*
rack my	*brains*
a can of	*worms*
over the	*moon*
be in two	*minds about something*
call it a	*day*

1 Put Ss into groups of four. Ss first look at the prompts and make sure they understand them. Elicit meanings and then allow one minute to discuss each pair of choices. Ss then discuss their ideas as a whole class. Ask the Ss if they are planning on studying at university, where they want to study and why. They can also discuss what things they are most worried about and what they are most looking forward to.

2 Ss work in pairs to make sure they understand all the vocabulary items. Elicit which four are associated with secondary education only (some words may be associated with both, eg assignment,

resit exams, seminar) and ask Ss if they have these in their school.

> **Answers** classroom, form-tutor, morning assembly, parents' evening

Optional activity: Ss work in pairs or small groups. One student closes his/her book and the other chooses a word from the previous exercise and defines it. The student with closed book has to remember the word. The Ss swap roles after each word. When they have finished guessing the words they change the activity. This time, the student choosing a word tells their partner what the word is and the partner, with book closed, has to give a definition.

Optional lead-in to Exercise 3: Write some key words from the text on the board: *Second World War, working-class teenager, hard-working, grammar school, shyness, Oxford University, elite* and *conservative.* Ss work in groups to guess what the text will be about. Elicit ideas from each group and then Ss open their books and read the information to see how close their ideas were.

3 Tell Ss to imagine they are John. They are shy, working-class and northern (with a strong accent) and they are going to Oxford University with upper-class, private school students from the south. Which of the idioms from the previous lesson would best describe John, eg *feeling out of place, in two minds about whether to go to/stay at Oxford, having the class divide brought home to him, over the moon at getting this opportunity.*
Set a time limit of three minutes for Ss to read the text quickly to try to find how John felt. Elicit ideas and extracts which helped Ss to decide, i.e. 'blurred [taxi] ride', 'he stammered', 'smiled blindly', 'alien surroundings', 'looked around him in alarm'.

> **Possible answers** He is shy and of a different background to the other students so could feel nervous, shy, out of place, uncertain, confused etc. He is also hard-working and has achieved something unique so he may feel keen to start work, proud of his achievements etc.

4 Tell Ss to find the part of the text where the answer to each question can be found and to read carefully deciding which answer is correct and why the others are wrong. Elicit answers and justifications, i.e. 1 'all the taxis had been taken' so he had to wait, he was 'happy to loiter' so he didn't mind; 2 'It was something he had dreaded' therefore he had worried about it before; 3 'John felt a twinge of distrust' so he is suspicious; 4 'a sense of his alien surroundings came over him' so he realises he does not belong; 5 'it had been a touching little expedition', buying the cups meant 'far more to [his mother] than it did to him' implies that the buying of the cups had been an important event for his mother representing his move away from home to university, an event that was obviously very special for her; 6 they talk about him in the third person and although they ask his name and where he is from, they soon start talking about their own friends, thus not taking a lot of interest in him.

Answers 1 c 2 c 3 d 4 d 5 c 6 b

5 The Ss may have already looked at some of these in order to answer earlier questions. Before they look at the definitions, ask Ss to look at the words and read them in context and try to guess what they might mean, eg '(...) all the taxis had been taken. He stood on the pavement, happy to loiter.' There are no taxis and he has to stand and wait, therefore *loiter* means wait. Ss then look at the definitions and do the matching.

Answers 1 chuckle 2 exclaim 3 stammer 4 snap
5 loiter 6 dread 7 whine 8 creep

Optional activity: Tell Ss to try to make new sentences which illustrate the meaning of the eight verbs in Exercise 5. Nominate Ss to read out sentences and decide as a class whether the meaning is clear from the example sentences given.

6 Before Ss listen to the recording, they discuss in pairs what they think the differences between then and now will be. Elicit ideas and then play the recording. Ss note key information as they listen and compare what they have written with their partner. Then they listen again. Compare ideas as a class. Follow up by asking Ss about universities in their country, the type of student that studies there and what the accommodation is generally like.

Tapescript CD 2 Track 4

Clare: *[neutral English accent]* Hello?
Grandad: *[RP accent]* Hello, Clare. It's only me!
Clare: Grandad!
Grandad: I was just wondering how you're settling in at college.
Clare: Oh, that's nice of you. Well, I've been having the time of my life so far! Oxford's brilliant. And I'm really pleased I chose Exeter College.
Grandad: I knew you'd love it! What's your accommodation like?
Clare: Well, I'm in a brand-new building right next to the college itself. So I really feel as though I'm part of the college community.
Grandad: That's good. I've heard that in some colleges nowadays, students end up in halls of residence quite far from the college. And how are you getting on with your room-mate?
Clare: Room-mate? No, I've actually got my own room. In fact, there seem to be very few students who have to share a room now.
Grandad: Oh, that's very good news. When I was at Oxford, all the undergraduates had to share rooms. Apart from the really well-off ones ...
Clare: The room's quite comfortable as well – it's quite bright and modern. Some of the rooms in the older buildings seem a bit gloomy in comparison.

Grandad: Yes – I remember my own room when I was a student. Big and draughty. Even though there was a servant who used to come round every afternoon to light a fire and make tea, it was still really chilly sometimes.
Clare: You had *servants*?! There's nothing like that now! I'd be embarrassed to have someone *attending* to me.
Grandad: No, I didn't feel comfortable with it either. So have you made any friends yet?
Clare: Yeah, lots! People are basically really friendly, nothing like what I was expecting. I thought everyone would be terribly posh and sophisticated but they're not really – and a lot of them seem to be from ordinary state schools like me.
Grandad: I'm pleased to hear that. In the 1940s by far the majority of students at Oxford were from private schools. And of course, there were no women students at Exeter College, just men. We all found it very frustrating! In fact, there were very, very few women at Oxford at all.
Clare: It's amazing when you think about it. Grandad, I'm going to have to go now. I'm going to see a band at the Apollo with a couple of friends. Can I call you back on Sunday morning?
Grandad: Yes, of course. Well listen, I'm so pleased you're having a good time. Enjoy your concert and make sure you don't ...

Answers Accomodation Claire has her own room, not shared. The room is bright and modern not old and chilly. **Servants** Claire's grandfather had servants, Claire doesn't. **Type of student** In the 1940s there were no women at Exeter College and the students were generally from rich families. A lot of them now are from normal state schools and are very friendly.

7 Put the Ss into pairs. Allow Ss one minute to read through the situations and choose one to talk about. When they are ready, nominate one student in each pair to talk first and tell them they should try to talk for two minutes on the topic. If they are struggling to think of things to say, their partner should try to ask pertinent questions to keep the conversation going. After two minutes, the pairs swap roles. Elicit one or two anecdotes in open class to finish the activity.

ADDITIONAL PRACTICE: Photocopiable resources. Resource 10: *Banned words*. Page 175

GRAMMAR AND SPEAKING

Culture notes

There is an online shop called **Gadget Crazy** which sells all sorts of electronic goods. It is based in Mayfair, London.

Warm-up Review of vocabulary from the previous lesson. *Find ten.* Put the Ss into an even number of groups. Half the groups are given the topic *School* and half the topic *University*. The groups write ten words related to their topic, using words from the Students' Book or their own vocabulary. They also have to write definitions for their words. When they are ready, groups join up so that a 'school' group joins up with a 'university' group. The 'school' group starts by defining their ten words. The other group have two minutes in which to guess all ten. The groups then swap roles and the 'university' group defines their words.

1 Before Ss open their books, write the word *gadget* on the board and make sure Ss know what it means and can give examples. Ss then open their books and discuss the photos. Elicit ideas but do not give the Ss the answers at this stage.

2 Make this an exam style task by telling Ss to discuss the usefulness of all of the gadgets and try to come to an agreement on the best one or two for Ss.

Answers The gadgets are: a microphone that can turn an MP3 player into a dictaphone, a pen that can scan written text and transfer it to a text editor, a slow cooker with free recipe book, a vacuum cleaner that does the cleaning for you, an alarm clock that projects the time onto the wall or ceiling.

3 When Ss have found the collocations they could look for more useful collocations and phrases within the texts, eg introduction: *essential gadgets, little did we realise, academic year, living away from home, imaginative gift ideas, make life bearable.*

Answers **1** dubious delights **2** grim frustration **3** real boon **4** mouth-watering dishes **5** particular care

Work it out

4 Ss find the sentences alone and write both the sentence given in the exercise and the inverted sentences from the text in their notebooks. Then they look carefully at what differences there are between them.

Answers **1** Never again will you face the grim frustration of deciphering your scribbled notes ... **2** So popular was the Lotospen last year that ... **3** Not only does the Zepper avoid stairs (...) but it can even sense dirtier areas ... **4** Such has been the demand for our popular projector alarm clock that we've ... 1, 2 and 3 are similar in form to questions (will you; was the Lotospen; does the Zepper avoid)

5 Ss may have trouble identifying the inverted sentences so it may be worth helping them by telling them where they are (one in the introduction, two in text 3, one in text 4 and one in text 5). Again, it may be worth asking the Ss to write the sentences in their notebooks with the equivalent, non-inverted form.

Answers Little did we realise it would become ... No sooner have you got back from a hard day's lectures than ... Neither will it add much to your electricity bill ... Never before has cleaning been so easy ... No longer will you have any excuse ...

6 Elicit the answer in open class and see if Ss can start sentence (a) with *such* and (b) with *so*, i.e. *Such was the popularity of the Lotospen last year ...*, *So much demand has there been for our clocks that ...*

Answers **1** b **2** a

7 Look at the form of the sentence with the class and elicit that it consists of two inverted clauses, the first of which has an affirmative sentence word order (*you have tried*) and the second a question word order (*will you*). The equivalent non-inverted sentence would be something like: *You will only wonder how you ever survived without it when you have tried it.*

Answers It has two parts

Check it out

Refer Ss to the Check it out section on page 155 and tell them to use this when doing homework and practising the form to make sure they do it correctly.

8 Ss work in pairs. Tell Ss to write the sentences in full in their notebooks, not just number the words in the Students' Book.

Answers 1 Not until they're sixteen can students leave school. 2 Not since the 1980s have business degrees been this popular. 3 So beautiful was the view that it took their breath away. 4 Such was the noise that I was forced to change rooms. 5 Scarcely had I got into the shower when the phone rang. 6 Never before have I been so glad to see you.

Mind the trap!

Refer Ss to the inversion in text 3: *No sooner have you got back from a hard day's lectures than it's time to go out …*
Now look at sentence 5 in Exercise 8. Show Ss the use of *when/than* and tell them to be careful, especially in cloze exercises and transformations.

9 Ss work in pairs and try to complete the gaps without referring back to the previous exercises. When they have finished, they check their answers with the Check it out section on page 155.

Answers 1 Never 2 So 3 Little 4 sooner; than 5 had; when 6 Such; that 7 when 8 until

10 Play the recording once for Ss to answer the questions. Elicit the answers and then play the recording again. Ask Ss to note what Paul and Ewan are doing and why. Ss then discuss whether they think Paul and Ewan are right or wrong to act as they did.

Tapescript CD 2 Track 5

One
Paul: *[neutral English accent]* Well, we've got about forty minutes before the film starts so why don't we grab a quick bite to eat and then get going? Are you happy with a toasted sandwich, Clare?
Clare: *[neutral English accent]* Yeah, whatever … Although I have to say, there's a really delicious smell in this kitchen. Smells like a stew or something …
Paul: Oh, that's Nick's!
Clare: He must be a really good cook!
Paul: Well, not really. He just chops up a load of meat and vegetables before he leaves for lectures in the morning and he just leaves it to cook all day. It's pretty simple.
Clare: What a great idea. Perhaps I should get something like that!
Paul: Well, he never lets the rest of us use it. And he never shares any of the food with us either. In fact, it really gets on our nerves. He's so smug!
Clare: Paul! I do believe you're jealous!
Paul: In fact, I think it's time I taught Nick a little lesson.
Clare: Paul, what are you doing?
Paul: Just adding some of my special, extra hot chili sauce to his 'delicious' stew!
Clare: But you've added half a bottle! It's probably inedible now.
Paul: That was exactly my intention!
Clare: That's really cruel!

Two
Lecturer: *[Northern English accent]* Although there are many sympathetic male characters in the story, the women are much more sketchily drawn. Indeed, one criticism that can be levelled at Hemingway in general is that his female characters tend to be rather one-dimensional. Some feminist critics have gone as far as to er, as far as to, um … Er, excuse me. Can I ask what you're doing? The fair-haired guy in the third row. Yes, you!
Ewan: *[neutral English accent]* Well, I was just checking that my microphone was recording OK.
Lecturer: Microphone?
Ewan: Yes. You see I find it useful to record our lectures and then I listen to them later when I'm revising. Or I sometimes let my friends listen to them when they, er, can't come to your lectures.
Lecturer: What goes on within the walls of this lecture theatre is copyright! Under no circumstances are my lectures to be recorded. Do you understand? And another thing. On no account will you lend any materials from these lectures to friends who are simply too lazy to attend. That applies to all of you. Is that clear?
Shamefaced chorus: Yes.

Answers 1 Nick – slow cooker, Ewan – voice recorder 2 In a halls of residence or student flat; in a lecture theatre 3 Nick has made his flatmates jealous because he won't share his food and now Paul has made his meal inedible; Ewan has been told not to use his voice recorder in lectures.

11 Ss look at the two sentences as a whole class and identify how they are formed.

Answers The inverted phrase is formed by preposition + *no* + noun. This is then followed by a question order inversion (*are my lectures, will you lend*).

12 Ss attempt the transformations alone using their notes and the Check it out section. Elicit the answers and make sure Ss have not only used the correct word order but also that the tense of the second sentence agrees with the original.

Answers 1 Little did I know that the entrance exam was so difficult. 2 So artificial were his examples that nobody was convinced. 3 Seldom does he hand in work on time. 4 Under no circumstances will cheating be tolerated in exams. 5 Only later did I appreciate what a great teacher he was. 6 No sooner had he reached his seat than the lecture began. 7 On no account should you (ever) disclose your credit card details in an email.

13 Put Ss into groups of three or four. Set a time limit of one minute for the Ss to look at the gadgets and choose one. Then they decide on its main advantages and work together to write the entry.

ADDITIONAL PRACTICE: Photocopiable resources. Resource 11: *The exam.* Page 176

SPEAKING AND LISTENING

> This section reviews inversions and shows Ss how to make themselves sound more natural.

Culture notes

Southampton is a major port on the south coast of England with a population of over 200,000. In 1620, the Mayflower sailed to America from Southampton with the Pilgrim Fathers aboard. In 1912, the Titanic set sail from the port. It was also the place where the Spitfire aeroplane was developed.

Warm-up Review of inversions. *Continue the sentence.* Put Ss into four or five groups. Tell Ss that they are going to have to make sentences by adding one word at a time. All the sentences must be inversions. Start by saying *Under no circumstances*. The first group must continue by saying a word that can follow this phrase, eg *will/can/should* etc. Then they pass the sentence to a second group who add another word. This continues until a sentence has been made or someone says a word which is grammatically wrong. To help Ss you can write the words that they say on the board. Repeat with other inversions, eg *Hardly, No sooner, Such* etc.

1 Ss read through the sentences. Explain that they are all grammatically correct but sometimes it is strange to use an inverted sentence. Ss discuss their ideas in pairs and then listen to the recording.

Tapescript `CD 2 Track 6`

One
Employee: *[London accent]* If you really want to know, you're a big-headed, ignorant buffoon and I don't intend working for you a minute longer. I quit!
Boss: *[RP accent]* Never in all my life have I been so insulted by one of my own employees!

Two
Debby: *[Birmingham accent]* What do you think of the tea?
Tom: *[Birmingham accent]* Mmm ... I've never drunk jasmine tea before but I have to say it's really nice.

Three
Mel: *[Yorkshire accent]* I felt so tired this morning that I really struggled to stay awake during the lecture.
Mum: *[neutral English accent]* Well, why don't you have an early night tonight then, dear?

Four
[RP accent] Never before in the field of human conflict was so much owed by so many to so few.
All hearts go out to the fighter pilots, whose brilliant actions we see with our own eyes, day after day, but we must never forget that all the time, night after night, month after month, they ...

Answers 1 and 4. It is a dramatic form used in 1 to show anger and in 4 in a dramatic speech to the nation. The other two are informal chats.

2 Play the recording once while the Ss have their books closed. Ask the Ss who the people are and what kind of conversation it is (two friends chatting in a café). Play the recording again while the Ss read through the text. Ss then work in pairs to rewrite the inversions that sound wrong. Elicit answers by nominating pairs to act out parts of the text.

Answers 1 So crowded was the number 16 bus ... The number 16 bus was so crowded ... **2** And little did I know that it doesn't go up King Street. And I didn't know that it doesn't go up King Street. **3** In fact, not until we went past the hospital did I realise that I had to get off the bus. In fact I didn't realise that I had to get off the bus until we went past the hospital. **4** Not until two o'clock do I have to be back at the office. I don't have to be back at the office until two o'clock. **5** In fact nowhere in the whole of Southampton can you find such great salads. In fact you can't find such great salads anywhere in the whole of Southampton. **6** Yes, seldom is it so quiet. It's seldom this quiet. (*Seldom* itself is quite formal. *It's not often this quiet* sounds better.)

3 Give Ss one minute to look at the situations and plan what they are going to say, including any inversions they feel appropriate. After the roleplays, nominate pairs to act out their conversations in front of the class.

4 It might be best to tell Ss which topic they are going to present, one each in each pair. Allow them two minutes to prepare their speeches and make notes. Tell them not to script it but just jot down ideas to help them. Nominate Ss to present their topic to the class.

VOCABULARY AND READING

> This section introduces phrasal verbs through a reading on exam revision.

Culture notes

A (advanced)-level exams were introduced in 1951. In 2000, the exam was split into two parts, an AS (advanced subsidiary) level taken at the end of year 12 and an A2 exam taken at the end of year 13, the final year of school. A-levels also count as university entrance exams. There are five pass grades from A–E with an E grade starting at a mark of 40 percent. Most school students study three or four subjects at A-level.

Maidenhead is a town in Berkshire, about 40km west of London. It lies in the 'silicon corridor' or towns which are found along the M4 motorway and which are home to a lot of high technology industry. In 1901, 92mm of rain fell on the town in sixty minutes, a record for Britain.

Grammar schools were introduced by the 1944 Butler Education act. They formed part of a tripartite system of education. All students took an exam at eleven years of age (the 11+). Those who passed it went to a grammar school which focused on academic subjects such as Literature and complex Mathematics. Those who failed, went to a secondary modern school which was more practical or a secondary technical school if they were good at scientific subjects. In 1965, comprehensive schools started to replace the tripartite system.

Warm-up Introduction to the topic of the lesson. *Board crossword.* Write the words *Exam revision* down in the middle of the board. Starting with the *E* at the top, write *go to bed Early*. Tell Ss that, for every letter, they should write some advice. If they cannot think of a word starting with the letters on the board, they can use words in which these letters appear, eg for *X – do eXtra work at home*. Ss work in groups of three or four. Elicit ideas when they have finished.

1 Ss read through the exam tips quickly writing a tick or a cross next to each depending on whether they like them or not. Ss then discuss how they usually approach exams as a class.

2 Tell Ss not to look up unknown words yet as there is a vocabulary exercise coming up later. Give Ss a time limit of five minutes to read the text and discuss their ideas in pairs. Elicit ideas in open class.

> **Answers 1** Not very hard-working. She does revision but is a bit disorganised and has missed lessons.
> **2** Sensible: making a timetable, recording quotations onto an MP3 player Reckless: not bothering with George Orwell, listening to the Biotoxin CD so much, staying up all night 'cramming'.

3 Ss find the words in the text and work in pairs to think of what they could mean. Elicit ideas and then either give definitions or tell Ss to look them up in a dictionary.

> **Answers 1** time when there are no lessons and students are free to organise their own study time **2** a hard-working student **3** stay up very late **4** to study a lot in a short time **5** can't understand **6** unable to think quickly

4 Ss again look at the verbs in context and try to work out the meanings without looking at Exercise 4. Ss then look at the choices and do the matching. Point out that *mug up on, chuck out* and *skive off* are very informal.

> **Answers 1** draw up **2** get out of **3** mug up on **4** break up **5** chuck out **6** come up **7** get down to **8** skive off

5 Tell Ss to work out the correct phrasal verbs for each sentence first and then to write them in using the correct form.

> **Answers 1** get out of **2** drawn up **3** break up **4** skive off **5** chuck out **6** mug up on **7** come up **8** get down to

6 Ss should treat this as an oral exam type question. They should try to agree on how to approach the revision and which tips to use with reasons. Allow three minutes for the discussion and then elicit answers in open class.

WRITING

> This section looks at writing job applications.

Culture notes

Perivale is a suburb of London situated about 16km west of the centre. It is mainly residential but also houses the famous art deco Hoover building.

Eastbourne is a seaside resort on the south coast just east of Brighton. It has a population of almost 100,000, many of whom are pensioners who have moved here to retire. The South Down hills join the coast here at the famous Beachy Head cliff, a popular suicide spot.

Warm-up Review of phrasal verbs. *Spot the error.* Tell Ss you are going to read out some sentences. Some are correct and some have a mistake in them. Ss have to decide if they think they are right or wrong and, if wrong, have to say what the mistake is. Put the Ss into four groups. Each group has two pieces of paper, one with a tick on it and one with a cross. When you read out the sentence, the Ss hold up one of the pieces of paper. Those who are correct get a point.
Sentences:
I came on with a really good idea. (✗ came up with)
Our school breaks up for Christmas on December 21st. (✓)
I must go down to some revision soon. (✗ get down to)
I wonder if conditionals will get up on our test. (✗ come up on)
I have to mug up on my History. (✓)
My friends sometimes skive off Maths but I never do. (✓)
I think we should draw off a plan for the weekend. (✗ draw up)
Don't chuck those books away. (✗ chuck out)

1 Tell Ss that the texts are about gap years. Explain that, in Britain, it is quite popular to take a year out between school and university to travel or do voluntary work. Universities often offer students a place for the following year so their studies are guaranteed before they leave.
Ss then answer the questions in pairs and as a class.

Suggested answers 2 teaching, waiting, kitchen assistants, cleaners etc; often in third world countries or resorts **3** Life experience, discovering yourself, having to do without normal western 'luxuries'.

2 Ss again discuss the ideas in pairs. They could alternatively read one advert each and then try to 'sell' it to their partner, stressing the advantages of it and making it sound as interesting as possible.

3 Ss do the matching alone and then check in pairs. Elicit the answers and ask follow-up questions to check the answers, eg 1 *When is he available for interview?* 2 *What is his reason for writing?* 3 *What personal qualities does he have?* 4 *What education has he completed and is he planning on doing in the future?* 5 *What skills and experience has he had?*

Answers 1 E **2** A **3** D **4** B **5** C

4 When Ss have matched the words, tell Ss that both sets of words, in the letter and in the exercise, are equally as good. This is one area where it is probably best for Ss to learn just one of the alternatives and always use the same phrases so that they are able to remember them easily during an exam.

Answers 1 gain **2** In addition to this **3** I am planning to **4** I believe I am well suited for this position **5** I consider myself to be **6** the latest edition of **7** in connection with

5 Ss work in pairs to match the words. Go through the answers and elicit what they mean, eg a clean driving licence is without points deducted for offences; a full licence means you are not a learner; a working knowledge of German is enough to get by but probably not fluent.

Answers 1 d **2** g **3** a **4** f **5** b **6** c **7** e

6 Set a time limit of three minutes for Ss to discuss the ten qualities. Elicit ideas in open class. If Ss disagree, ask them to justify their opinions, eg 2 most jobs require some communication skills and interaction; 3 this could be useful in certain circumstances but not for most jobs; 4 too vague, should say: *I am always reliable*; 5 this sort of character can cause conflict in the work place; 8 it is not a quality; 9 like (5) this can cause problems; 10 a negative characteristic not a quality.

Answers 1 Yes **2** No **3** No **4** No **5** No **6** Yes **7** Yes **8** No **9** No **10** No

TRAIN YOUR BRAIN

7 Tell Ss to cover Exercise 7 and to look at the Train Your Brain box only. Ss work in pairs to try to think of what the missing information is and, when they have looked at all the gaps, they uncover the exercise and complete the gaps.

Answers 1 b **2** a **3** d **4** e **5** c

8 Ss should make a detailed plan of all the information they are going to write in the five paragraphs. Allow ten minutes for this. When Ss have finished, ask different Ss questions about their notes, eg *Which advert are you responding to? What field are you most interested in? What are your future education plans? What skills and experience do you have which would be useful for this position? What personal qualities do you have? When are you available for an interview? What are you enclosing with the application?*

9 Before Ss start writing, look at the example letter on page 46. Tell Ss that quite a lot of this letter can be used in other job application letters and only the details need to be changed to suit the individual task. Elicit phrases which the Ss could use in their work. They can underline these to help them later.

Dear Sir/Madam

I am writing in connection with your job advert for ... which appeared in ... I am particularly interested in working in the field of ...

I am an ... -year-old ... I am planning to ... In the meantime, I am keen to ... but would welcome the opportunity to also gain some work experience.

I believe I am well suited for this position for a number of reasons. (...) I am also extremely interested in ...

In addition to this, I believe I am ... and ... Moreover, I consider myself to be ... and ...

I would be delighted to attend an interview at your earliest convenience. As requested, I enclose ...

Yours faithfully,

Ss can now write the letter either in class or at home. When marking the letters, try to react to them as an employer, deciding whether the person would be given an interview and, if not, why not.

ADDITIONAL PRACTICE: Photocopiable resources. Resource 12: *Complete the job application.* Page 177

THINK FORWARD TO EXAMS REVISION 2
UNITS 3–4

VOCABULARY AND GRAMMAR

1 Ss look through the exercise quickly to decide what is needed. Elicit what the exercise is testing (collocations). When Ss have finished the exercise, elicit the correct answers.

As a follow-up, Ss work in pairs to try to write new sentences in which one of the other words given as choices would be correct. Where there is a phrasal verb, Ss must use the preposition given in the sentence in their examples – 3 *stand up* or *blow up*; 4 *play down* or *turn down*; 6 *draw up* or *mug up*. Then they test a second pair and are tested by the second pair, eg 1 *The government has (raised) taxes from 20 percent to 22 percent. I'm going to buy some clothes here. Prices have been (slashed) by over 50 percent.*

> **Answers** 1 risen 2 slump 3 make 4 cut 5 harness 6 come 7 out of place 8 loitering

2 Tell Ss that, sometimes, more than one word is possible but that they should try to remember the collocations and phrases that came up in the previous two units. Ss work in pairs. Elicit answers and what some of the vocabulary items mean, eg *global warming; to bring something home to you; carbon footprints; renewable energy; skive off classes; gap year.*

> **Answers** 1 hard 2 disastrous 3 warming 4 home 5 footprint 6 measures 7 renewable 8 skiving 9 hand 10 lectures 11 resit/retake 12 gap

3 Tell Ss to cover the root words given on the right and to look at the sentences. In pairs they decide what kind of word is needed in as much detail as possible. Elicit ideas in open class and what the missing word could be: 1 positive adjective – it describes the job and contrasts with the negative fact about the money, eg *good*; 2 noun – a thing or place in which you learn, eg *lesson*; 3 a plural noun – people who attend university, eg *students*; 4 noun, negative meaning, eg *rubbish*; 5 noun, must start with a vowel – a place to live, eg *attic*; 6 adjective or noun – a kind of organisation, eg *profit*; 7 noun – a kind of job, doesn't start with a vowel, woman speaking, eg *secretary*; 8 adjective to describe an experience, starts with a vowel, could be negative or positive, eg *unbelievable*.

Ss then uncover the words and complete the activity in pairs.

> **Answers** 1 prestigious 2 tutorial 3 undergraduates 4 meaningless 5 orphanage 6 governmental 7 receptionist 8 unforgettable

4 Tell Ss to look through the sentences in pairs and discuss which can be rewritten in the passive. Ss should not write anything at this time. Elicit which sentences cannot or should not be rewritten in the passive and why, i.e. 1 possible but would sound very strange to emphasise the bike over oneself; 4 possible but, because the subject is *she*, it would sound strange to emphasise the air-conditioning. Ss then work alone to rewrite the other five sentences.

> **Answers** 2 A tax on airline fuel is going to be brought in. 3 The invention is being tested at a secret laboratory. 5 Less energy will almost certainly be required by the new engine. 6 The process of nuclear fusion was explained to us by the engineers. We were given an explanation of the process of nuclear fusion by the engineers. 7 I have been concerned about the consequences of global warming on the future of our civilisation for years.

5 Ss look through the sentences to see what is being tested (inversions). Ss work in pairs trying to complete the sentences without looking back in their books. Tell Ss to write the sentences in full in their notebooks, both Ss writing even though they are working together. When they have finished, they should check their sentences. Elicit the answers making sure Ss have used inversion correctly and that the tenses used in their sentences agree with the originals.

> **Answers** 1 So determined is he to pass the exam that he's going to study all night. 2 Little had he realised that it would take him so long to revise his notes. 3 Such was its (level of) difficulty that nobody passed the exam. 4 No sooner had he closed his eyes than the alarm went off. 5 Under no circumstances may/can you talk during the exam. 6 Only when he had written everything he could did he put his pen down. 7 Not only have I failed the exam but I've also been given the lowest mark in the class. 8 Never again would he stay up studying all night.

READING SKILLS

1 Ss read through the text quickly to get a general understanding of its contents (German studies have found that bees may be affected by radiation from mobile phones and power lines). Tell Ss to concentrate on the text insertion exercise first. Look at the first gap with the class and ask Ss which bit of text gives the biggest clue to what might be in the missing sentence ('to hit the UK as well' – this indicates that the missing sentence may mention other countries in which bees have disappeared). Ss find the correct extract (f mentions the USA and Europe). Tell Ss that this type of exercise is never about guesswork. The clues are either the topic or references in the text or sentences to insert. Ss work together in pairs. Elicit the answers and the clues that helped them: 1 the mention of the USA and Europe; 2 the inserted sentence says there is evidence to back the theory up and the next section of the text tells us what this evidence is; 3 'who carried it out' in the sentence to insert refers to the German research mentioned in the text; 4 the text beforehand says that the bees disappear, the sentence continues the topic talking about the vanished bees; 5 the reference to half the American states in the sentence to insert is followed up by the mention of the West and East Coasts in the text; 6 the sentence gives a reason why the implications mentioned in the text are alarming; 7 the text follows up the idea of no one knowing why it is happening with some possible theories.

Ss now look at the two multiple choice questions. Tell them to look at every statement as if it were a true/false question. Elicit whether each is T or F (or if there is no information). If the Ss are correct, one statement in 8 and 9 should be true while the others are false or not known. 8 The summary says the implications are alarming and that all theories need further investigation. Therefore 8a is wrong as there is something to worry about, 8c is wrong as these are still theories and none has been proved as yet, 8d is wrong as there has been research to suggest that it might be mobile phones causing the problem. 9b The East Coast has suffered more than the West Coast so far but there is no information to say that it would suffer more than other areas; 9c the quote from Einstein suggests that it would be deadly for humans as well; 9d this is not mentioned at all.

Answers 1 f 2 e 3 i 4 g 5 h 6 d 7 b 8 b 9 a

SPEAKING SKILLS

1 As in the previous review section, Ss should avoid scripting a presentation. They will not be able to do this in an exam and a presentation that is read out word for word is never as interesting as the student's main focus is on the written word rather than the audience. Set a time limit of ten minutes for Ss to plan their presentation, noting ideas and useful vocabulary to use. Nominate Ss to present their topic to the class and then discuss both topics as a whole class.

Live to eat?

Read, listen and talk about food and eating.
Practise conditionals; *I wish/If only, It's time, I'd rather, as if/though.*
Focus on problem solving and staging (two-way conversation between candidates).
Writing subskill register (written formal English).

EXAM FOCUS

Topic: Food and eating

Speaking
Problem solving: SB p.56, ex.4

Listening
True/False: SB p.51, ex.5
Multiple choice: SB p.54, ex.3

Reading
Multiple matching: SB p.52, ex.4

Grammar and vocabulary
Sentence transformations: SB p.55, ex.8, p.57, ex.6
Verbs in brackets: SB p.55, ex.7
Wordbuilding: SB p.53, ex.6

Writing
Formal register in for and against essay: SB p.59, ex.8

Unit 5 Materials
....
Success Workbook Unit 5
....
Photocopiable resources 13, 14, 15
....
Testing and Evaluation Programme tests

VOCABULARY AND SPEAKING

This section extends the Ss' knowledge of food- related vocabulary and introduces food-based metaphors and proverbs.

Culture notes

Louis Simpson (born 1923) is a Jamaican poet. He won the Pulitzer Prize in 1964. His father was of Scottish descent and his mother was from Russia. *Chocolates* is one of two poems which reference Chekhov, the other being *Caviar at the Funeral*.

Anton Chekhov (1860–1904) was a Russian writer, often considered to be the greatest short story writer in history.

Warm-up Introduction to the topic of the lesson. *Gapped phrase.* Write on the board the following gaps:
_ _ _ _ _ _ _ _ _ _ _ _ _ _ _ _ _ _ _ _?

Nominate Ss to guess letters for the words and, when the phrase is complete (*Eat to live or live to eat?*) Ss discuss what they think it means and decide which is true for them, eg *If you eat to live you use food for survival. If you live to eat, eating is an important part of your enjoyment of life.*

1 Set a time limit of two minutes for Ss to discuss their ideas and then elicit them in open class.

2 Ask Ss if they know who Chekhov was. Ss then discuss the questions. Elicit answers and justifications for them from the poem, i.e. 1d is wrong because he asked questions to continue the conversation. All the other answers are possible.

Answers 1 a, b, c **2** a, b, c, d

3 Ss work in groups of four to share knowledge and reduce the need for dictionaries. Ss then add other words they know as a class. Put these on the board and allow all Ss to make a written record of them.

Answers adjectives for food/drink appetising, bitter, creamy, juicy, savoury, sour, stomach-turning, sweet (delicious, tasty, spicy, raw, fizzy etc) **adjectives for hunger/thirst** famished, parched, peckish, ravenous (starving) **verbs of eating/drinking** chew, gobble, guzzle, nibble, sip, slurp, swallow (bite, taste, etc) **verbs of food preparation** bake, chop, roast, slice, stew (fry, boil, cut, grill etc)

4 Set a time limit of three minutes, then discuss ideas in open class. A *sweet tooth* means you like sweet foods. An *acquired taste* is something that you may, at first, not like but you later do.

5 Ss read through the sentences and decide which they would do if they were going to someone's house for a meal. Tell Ss they are now going to listen to people discussing good manners in the UK. Ss listen to the recording twice.

Tapescript CD 2 Track 8

Tom: *[Newcastle accent]* What about the first one? 'Make sure you are dressed up for the occasion.'
Amy: *[Newcastle accent]* Mmm, I think most British people are quite relaxed about that sort of thing. When you invite someone to your home you want to make things as informal as possible for your guests. So I think the guests and the hosts would tend to wear fairly ordinary clothes, don't you?
Tom: Yes, I think you're right. In fact, you shouldn't be surprised if your hosts are wearing scruffy jeans and an old pair of slippers.

Amy: So we'll put 'false' then. What about starting to eat as soon as you get your plate? That would be quite rude, wouldn't it?

Tom: Yes. Even with friends, you'd probably wait until everyone had their plate and then the host will say, 'Tuck in, everyone' or 'Please just start'.

Amy: OK, so that's 'false'. Just looking down the list, I think the next three are all true.

Tom: Yeah, I think everyone's taught that it's good manners not to chew with your mouth open and stuff like that. Although, to be honest, when I'm eating with friends my age I don't even think about it.

Amy: True. Slurping your soup? That would be quite irritating.

Tom: Yeah, it's not really good manners, is it? Although, in some countries I think it can be a sign that something's really tasty.

Amy: What about not picking at your food? That's a tricky one, isn't it?

Tom: Yeah. I mean if someone's gone to loads of trouble to prepare something and it's pretty clear that you're not enjoying it – you do run the risk of offending them. It depends on what kind of person the cook is, really!

Amy: Yeah, sometimes it's best to come out with a white lie like you're not feeling very hungry. What about leaving food on your plate to show you were given enough? I've never heard of something like that before.

Tom: Again, I think the British are quite relaxed about that sort of thing. I don't think it matters if you eat it all up or leave a little food. And the same goes for asking for second helpings. I think most people would take that as a compliment.

Amy: Yes, I agree. OK, one more – offering to do the washing-up. I do quite often if I'm visiting friends or relatives. It just seems a friendly thing to do.

Tom: Yes, me too. Even if you know your host will say 'No, it's OK. I'll do it later', it's quite nice to offer.

Amy: Although I think in some countries it would be a very strange thing for a guest to do. I remember offering to wash up at my friends in Budapest and they seemed mortified!

Tom: Maybe it's just the British who are mad enough to offer?

Answers 1 F 2 F 3 T 4 T 5 T 6 F 7 D 8 F 9 F 10 T

6 Read through the three examples with the whole class: *I'll make him ...* means that I will show him that he is wrong; a *sugary tone* is over sweet and annoying; *a recipe for disaster* means that the ideas or plans will lead to problems in the future. Show Ss that other words in the sentences can help to understand the meaning, eg 2 *I hate*. Ss then work in pairs.

Answers 1 hard to believe 2 turned bad 3 Let him suffer from his own mistakes. 4 uses a lot (of) 5 interesting/exciting 6 get very hot 7 sickening

7 Ss discuss their ideas in pairs, then look up the metaphors in dictionaries and make new sentences using the alternative metaphors.

Answers 1 b (Your idea is completely impractical. It's just a pie in the sky.) 2 a (Ken is the salt of the earth.

You can rely on him totally.) 3 a (Good teachers use a carrot and stick approach – reward the good students and punish the bad!)

8 Allow Ss two minutes to discuss the four proverbs. Elicit ideas and then play the recording.

Tapescript CD 2 Track 9

One

Mum: *[English Midlands accent]* You know, I just don't understand my Steven. He's always saying that he wishes he had some money so he can upgrade his computer. But when I say to him that he should get a job for the holidays he says that he deserves a rest and he doesn't see why he should work all summer.

Friend: *[English Midlands accent]* Typical. My Sandra's the same. I said to her, 'Sandra, you can't have your cake and eat it!'

Two

Rich: *[English Midlands accent]* Apparently Karl's dropped out of his accountancy course. He says he hated having to learn things by heart all the time.

Keiron: *[English Midlands accent]* Yeah, I heard. He's decided to study law instead.

Rich: But surely that's even worse?

Keiron: Yeah, that's what I thought. Out of the frying pan, into the fire, if you ask me!

Three

Kate: *[neutral English accent]* I've just had offers from two universities this morning.

Dad: *[neutral English accent]* Great! Which ones?

Kate: Well, I got an offer from Kent University and one from Exeter University.

Dad: Fantastic! I'm really pleased for you. Have you decided what you're going to do?

Kate: Oh, well, I'm going to reject both of them. I mean I'm only interested in going to Bristol University really and hopefully they'll make me an offer too.

Dad: Is that wise, Kate? You never know what might happen. You shouldn't put all your eggs in one basket, you know.

Four

Reporter: *[London accent]* Your team's lost the last three games and your captain's out of Saturday's match because of injury. Don't you think it's a big risk to have so many new players in the team for the game against Portugal? You haven't won a game in Lisbon since 2004.

Manager: *[Scottish accent]* I'm confident that I've made the right decision. But let's wait until we see what the result is on Saturday. As I always say, 'the proof of the pudding is in the eating'.

Answers 1 You want the best of both worlds (which is impossible). 2 You get yourself out of one bad situation by getting into a worse one. 3 You should have more than one option. 4 You won't know how good something is until you try it.

9 Give Ss four minutes to discuss their topics.

ADDITIONAL PRACTICE: Photocopiable resource. Resource 13: *The proof of the pudding ...* Pages 178–179

READING AND VOCABULARY

This section extends the Ss' range of food-related vocabulary through a series of literary extracts.

Culture notes

Laurie Lee (1914–1997) was an English novelist and poet. In the 1930s he travelled to Spain and fought in the Civil War there. He is most famous for his trilogy of autobiographies, the first of which was *Cider with Rosie* which sold six million copies.

A.A. Milne (1882–1956) is most famous as the writer of the Winnie the Pooh stories. He was born in London and studied Mathematics at Cambridge University. The first Winnie the Pooh book was published in 1926. The character Christopher Robin was named after his son who was born in 1920.

Aristotle (384–322BC) was a Greek philosopher. He was a student of Plato and taught Alexander the Great. He was the first philosopher to create a comprehensive system of Western philosophy which included morality, aesthetics, logic, science and political thought.

Helen Fielding (born 1958) is an English writer. She is best known for *Bridget Jones' Diary*. She studied English at Oxford University and worked as a researcher for television programmes before starting to write.

Isabella Beeton (1836–1865) wrote *Mrs Beeton's Book of Household Management*. The book contained 900 recipes as well as advice on money, children, husbands and servants and was published in 1861. The book is still available today although new additions are very different to the original.

George Orwell, real name Eric Blair (1903–1950) is best known for his novels *Animal Farm* and *1984*. He also wrote about real people's lives, noticeably in *The Road to Wigan Pier* and *Down and Out in Paris and London*. He also fought in the Spanish Civil War and wrote about the experience in *Homage to Catalonia*.

Warm-up Review of food vocabulary. *What is it?* Ss work in pairs and think of a meal and choose adjectives and verbs to describe it. Give them an example first: *It's hot and spicy. It's an acquired taste. It can be creamy, it can be greasy. It can be meaty or vegetarian. The aroma is appetising. It is usually fried.* (curry) When Ss are ready, they join up with other pairs in groups of four or six and describe their meal for the others to guess.

1 Set a time limit of three minutes to discuss the three quotations. Ss may have discussed the third already in the warm-up to the previous lesson but they can still remind themselves of what it means and what they think of it. Elicit ideas in open class.

Answers 1 If a woman wants a man to love her, she should feed him well. 2 English food isn't very good so it's not a pleasure to eat it, just a biological necessity. 3 Eating should be like breathing, a necessity, not an enjoyment.

2 Set a strict time limit so that Ss cannot read more than the first two sentences of each text. Ss discuss their answers in pairs and identify words or phrases that helped them to decide, i.e. A *would* is often used to talk about childhood memories; B although personalised, the description of the courtyard is like a travel guide; C a talking rabbit indicates a children's story; D the text starts with a date as a diary entry; E it starts with a rhetorical question which is one way of making an article interesting and making people read on.

Answers 1 B 2 – 3 E 4 C 5 A 6 D

3 In order to keep Ss reading at the same speed, play the recording for them to read along to. When it has finished, Ss work in pairs and tell each other which extract they liked best and why. Ask who liked A the best and why, and repeat for the other texts.

4 Tell Ss that, when deciding the answers, they should underline or note down the information in the text which justifies them. Elicit answers and justifications in open class, i.e. 1 calories, diets; 2 'natural reserve (...) and distrust of spontaneity'; 3 'the Party leader (...) disappeared'; 4 'could be worse/mustn't grumble'; 5 'my tongue tingled pleasantly'; 'I felt at home'; 'shook Rabbit lovingly'.

Answers 1 D 2 E 3 A 4 E 5 A, B, C

5 Ss work in pairs. Elicit answers and exact definitions of the words. Give other forms of the words where useful, eg *to pickle*, peel (v) / noun (uncountable).

Answers 1 pickled 2 acrid 3 herbs 4 choked 5 calorie 6 peel 7 staple

6 Tell Ss to look at the gaps first and decide the kind of word needed. Elicit ideas and then Ss look through the texts to find the words. Elicit the answers and which texts they are in, i.e. 1 negative adjective (A); 2 negative adjective (A); 3 noun (B); 4 adverb (C); 5 noun (D); 6 negative adverb (E); 7 noun (E); 8 noun (E).

Answers 1 disillusioned 2 restless 3 idiocy 4 lovingly 5 consciousness 6 unfavourably 7 spontaneity 8 extravagance

7 Give Ss two minutes to read through the questions alone and think about their answers. Then they discuss together each question for one minute. Nominate Ss to answer the questions in open class.

Students' Book ➡ pages 52–54

LISTENING AND GRAMMAR

This section extends Ss' knowledge of conditional structures through a listening on the history of certain foodstuffs.

Special difficulties: Ss may still have some problems with basic conditional forms so it is important to remind them of the four conditionals (zero, first, second and third) before they start looking at mixed conditionals and inversions.

Culture notes

The Irish potato famine started in 1845 and lasted until 1850. Approximately one million people died and another million emigrated, reducing the population by about 25 percent. The cause was a disease called late blight which affected potatoes in the USA in 1843 and was brought to Ireland in a shipment of seed potatoes.

Warm-up **Lead-in to the topic of the lesson.** *Conditional review.* Put the Ss into four groups. Tell the groups that they are going to present a conditional form to the class. One group has to think of the zero conditional, another the first conditional, one the second and one the third. When they are ready, they will come to the front of the class and write the form of the structure on the board, what it is used for and three example sentences (a positive, a negative and a question). Allow the groups to plan their presentation for three minutes and then each in turn comes to the front to talk to the class.

1 Ss may know some of these so, when they have discussed their ideas in pairs, ask if anyone knows the real connections and ask them to explain to the class. Do not give any answers at this point.

2 Tell Ss to make notes in their notebooks while they listen to the recording. After it has finished, Ss compare what they heard in small groups.

Tapescript CD 2 Track 11

Voiceover: The Seeds of Change
Narrator: [*neutral English accent*] Did a love of sweet wine lead to the decline of the Roman Empire? Would the Industrial Revolution have happened if Europeans hadn't started eating potatoes? Would America still be a British colony if Americans hadn't been so fond of tea? Historians have sometimes been shy to acknowledge the impact of food and drink on world history, but many commonplace crops have had the power to fuel revolutions and destroy empires. Let's start with the humble potato. This crop, originally grown in the Andes Mountains of South America, was unknown to the rest of the world until potatoes reached Spain in the 1550s, from where they were introduced to other European countries and then eventually to Asia and Africa. However, it took over 200 years for the potato

to finally take off as a food in Europe. The potato is a member of the poisonous nightshade family and for a long time people believed that the whole plant was harmful to health. Indeed, when an English landowner introduced one potato plant as an ornamental plant onto his estate in Ireland, he was lucky to escape with his life.

Angry neighbour 1: If he cared more about his neighbours, he wouldn't have planted it. I mean, if the potato spreads it'll poison everyone in the village!
Angry neighbour 2: He wants to kill us all. Let's find his potato plant and destroy it!
Angry neighbour 3: I've got a better suggestion. Let's burn his house down!
Narrator: Nevertheless, Europeans gradually realised that the plant was easy to grow, could tolerate cool, moist conditions and, more importantly, was rich in vitamins and other nutrients. Their impact was enormous. Because potatoes can yield twice the amount of high-quality protein per hectare as wheat, it meant the land could suddenly support many more people. For example in Ireland the population grew by an incredible 300% between 1770 and 1840. And as potatoes required relatively little attention after planting, it meant that large numbers of the rural population were no longer required to work on the land. For a time in Ireland, this led to a flowering of the arts in rural areas. As people no longer had to spend all day in the fields, they had more time to indulge their other interests such as music-making and story-telling – traditions for which Ireland is famous even today.

Meanwhile, in countries such as Britain and Germany, the rapidly growing number of the rural unemployed were forced to look for work in the new factories in the cities, helping to fuel the emerging Industrial Revolution. However, this dependence on the potato was to have other, more tragic consequences – when the potato harvest repeatedly failed in Ireland between 1845 and 1849, a million people were forced to emigrate to the US and Canada and over a million more died. The tragedy sparked off the struggle for Irish independence from Britain – indeed, had the British reacted to the Irish famine more sympathetically, the independence movement might never have gained momentum so quickly.

Drinks too have played a major role in shaping history. Let's take for example wine. Wine has been drunk for at least 7,000 years and it quickly became a status symbol. This meant that regions (such as Rome or southern Greece) that had a reputation for producing quality wine received an important economic boost. In this way wine helped lead to the expansion of the Greek and Roman Empires.

However, storing wine was a significant problem – great care was needed to stop fermenting grape juice from turning into vinegar. Because of this, the Romans often added seawater to wine to preserve it. An even more common way of correcting soured wine was lead and the Romans slowly became addicted to lead's sweet taste. What they didn't realise, of course, was that lead is highly poisonous – were you to drink leaded wine over a long period, the chances are that you would end up with serious health problems such as sterility or dementia. Many historians have suggested that the general decline in health of the Romans, caused by endemic lead poisoning, contributed to the gradual decline of Roman civilisation itself.

Another drink that helped to shape history was coffee. Coffee reached Europe from the Arab world at the end of the seventeenth century. However, it was not without controversy and many Puritans in England regarded coffee as harmful and decadent. Nevertheless, London coffee houses soon became part of the daily routine of politicians, writers, businessmen and lawyers. Because of their clientele, they became places of political gossip and business deals – it was no accident that the growth of the coffee houses led to the appearance of the first newspapers and that several famous insurance companies (and indeed the London Stock Exchange itself) began as coffee houses.

Gentleman 1: Greetings, Mr Thomas!

Gentleman 2: Ah, Mr Lloyd, good afternoon. I'd have a look at today's newspaper, if I were you!

Gentleman 1: Why? Not bad news, I pray?

Gentleman 2: Well, the King has been seen giving orders to the trees in Windsor Great Park.

Gentleman 1: Ha! Were it ever so!

Gentleman 2: But more to the point – the price of pepper has risen to five pounds and five shillings a sack!

Gentleman 1: Good Lord! I shall require another coffee forthwith!

Narrator: Whereas in England coffee fuelled commerce and politics, elsewhere in Europe it helped to fuel new, often revolutionary ideas. Coffee houses in France and Germany became the favoured haunts of radical thinkers and intellectuals where they would exchange ideas and argue about the great issues of the day – this was the time of the Enlightenment, the Age of Reason, and coffee, a drink which 'sharpened the mind', was the perfect accompaniment. Indeed, the seeds of the French Revolution are often said to have been sown in the Parisian coffee houses.

Gentleman 1: Remember, my friends – we may acquire liberty but it is never recovered if it is once lost!

Gentleman 2: I fear that is just the coffee talking.

Narrator: At the same time, tea helped factory workers to stay alert during gruelling, monotonous shifts. It also had unintended but beneficial effects on the health of people in rapidly-growing industrial towns – the fact that tea required boiling in order to brew it meant that people were less susceptible to diseases caused by contaminated drinking water. Tea was also extremely popular in the American colonies, then governed by Britain, and in fact it was a protest by New Englanders in 1773 against high British taxes on tea that sparked off the struggle that eventually led to American independence.

What of the future? At present, for the first time in 10,000 years of world history, the amount of land devoted to growing wheat is gradually shrinking. In fact, in terms of tonnage, the most commonly-grown crop is now sugar cane. Meanwhile, many Asian countries are developing a real taste for chocolate for the first time and prices of cocoa are already beginning to rise significantly. Should these trends continue, there may be major consequences not only for our health and diet but perhaps the outcome of history itself.

Answers 1 The potato was easy to grow and so relied upon to provide food. When the crop failed, the people had nothing to eat so had to emigrate to survive. **2** The wine gave the economy a boost but, to stop it fermenting, the Romans added lead to the wine, which poisoned them. **3** Coffee houses were popular meeting places for writers, politicians and business people, which led to the formation of newspapers. **4** Because tea required boiling water, people drank less contaminated, uncooked water.

3 Allow Ss two minutes to read through the questions to see if they know any of the answers already from their notes and to prepare themselves for what they need to listen out for. Elicit the answers and Ss' justifications for them, i.e. 1 they grew in the Andes; 2 'more importantly' were 'rich in vitamins and nutrients'; 3 A and B made the effects worse and D was a result not a cause; 4 it corrected the sour taste and had an addictive sweet flavour; 5 it was no accident; 6 'haunts of radical thinkers and intellectuals'; 7 'had unintended but beneficial effects on the health of people'; 8 A gradually shrinking not sudden, B more tonnage of sugar cane but does not mention the amount of land, C sudden taste for chocolate but they may have had a sweet tooth before now, D 'prices of cocoa are already **beginning to rise** significantly' implies they will continue to do so.

Answers 1 C **2** B **3** C **4** C **5** C **6** B **7** D **8** D

4 Think Back! Remind Ss of their presentations at the start of the lesson and elicit the conditionals used in the two sentences. Ss then look at the uses in pairs and match them to the correct sentences.

Answers 1 (second/third) b **2** (second/third) a

Work it out

5 Look at the sentences with the whole class. Elicit ideas and tell Ss the correct answers. Elicit or give more examples, eg *If I'm late/If I should be late, please start the meeting without me. If your son worked harder/were to work harder, he would do well in his exams.*

Answers 1 b **2** b

6 Ss look at the sentences in pairs and discuss the questions. Elicit the answers and ask Ss to rewrite them using *If*, i.e. 1 *If you drank* … 2 *If the British had reacted,* … 3 *If these trends continue* …

Answers 1 If **2** a and b change the sentence order, reversing the verb and subject, c keeps the same sentence order **3** first conditional c, second conditional a, third conditional b

64   Students' Book ➡ pages 54–55

Check it out

Tell Ss that they should refer to the Check it out section on page 155 if they are having problems with the different forms.

7 Ss decide in pairs what conditional is used in each sentence and then choose the correct form of the verbs. Elicit the answers and give extra practice by asking Ss to rewrite sentences 1 and 5 starting *He always* and *I won't*, i.e. *He always eats breakfast if his mother makes it for him. I won't make supper unless you (if you don't) help me wash up afterwards.*

Answers 1 makes **2** hadn't eaten **3** wouldn't get **4** would sleep **5** help **6** had added

Mind the trap!

Look at the Mind the trap! box with the Ss and ask them to rewrite sentence 2 from Exercise 7 starting with *Had*, i.e. *Had they not eaten all the chicken, I would have made a curry.*

8 Ss work alone to transform the sentences. Make sure that the Ss write the sentences out in full, even where the second half of the sentence is exactly the same as the original. Allow Ss to compare answers before nominating Ss to read out their sentences in open class.

Answers 1 Had I known you were allergic to fish, I would have cooked something different. **2** Were we to buy a sandwich-toaster, it would make our lives easier. **3** Had you gone to bed earlier, you wouldn't feel so drowsy now. **4** Should you need further advice about this product, please contact our customer services helpline. **5** Had he learnt to cook, he wouldn't waste so much money on takeaways. **6** Had explorers not brought back tomatoes to Italy, Italian cuisine might have turned out very differently.

9 Look at the example sentence with the Ss. Ask what the situation now is (he doesn't understand). Ask why he does not understand (he didn't listen). Ask: *How would the situation be different now if he had listened?* (he would understand). Tell Ss that, if they look at the other sentences like this, the conditionals will be easy to write. It may also be easier to start them all with *If*, eg *If Peter had paid attention during the lesson, he would understand mixed conditionals.* Ss work in pairs. You could give Ss further practice by asking them to reformulate the sentences so that they all start with *Had*, eg 1 *Had Peter paid attention during the lesson, he would understand mixed conditionals.*

Answers 2 If Tim hadn't eaten so/too much chocolate, he wouldn't feel sick. **3** If Tonia wasn't a very fussy eater, she wouldn't have been hungry all the time on holiday. **4** If Marcus didn't eat like a horse, he wouldn't have put on a lot of weight last year. **5** If Milly ate properly, she would have been able to shake/could have shaken off her cold last year. **6** If Kurt hadn't forgotten to put the milk back in the fridge, it wouldn't be sour.

10 Ss could also think of a third conditional sentence for each situation as well as a mixed conditional. Allow five minutes for Ss to discuss ideas in pairs and write the sentences. Elicit sentences in open class.

ADDITIONAL PRACTICE: Photocopiable resources. Resource 14: *On condition ...* Page 180

SPEAKING

This section introduces useful phrases for problem solving.

Warm-up Review of conditional forms. *Alphabet race.* Write a sentence on the board and tell Ss that, to complete it, they have to use every letter of the alphabet once. Nominate Ss to say a letter and where it should go in the sentence.

_ _ _ you _ _ _ told me a _o_e d_r_n_ the _h_si_s e_a_, I _ou_d ha_ _ heard the _uestion, I wouldn't have _ailed with a _core of _e_o and I wouldn't _e in trouble now!

(Had you not told me a joke during the Physics exam, I would have heard the question, I wouldn't have failed with a score of zero and I wouldn't be in trouble now.)

1 Tell Ss to look through the vocabulary first and make sure they understand all the words. Then set a time limit of one minute each for the Ss to describe what they can see in two of the four photos and then three minutes for Ss to answer question 2 together. Nominate two Ss to act out the conversation in front of the class and, as they are speaking, note down any good phrases they use for giving opinions, agreeing and disagreeing. Write these on the board and then tell Ss that they are going to listen to other people doing the same task.

2 Tell Ss to make notes as they listen and to compare what they understood in pairs.

For tapescript see page 207.

Answers 1 Yes **2** The expensive, posh restaurant **3** Yes **4** Ss' own answers

SPEAK OUT

3 When Ss have completed the Speak Out box, ask which of these phrases they have used before and which are new to them. Remind Ss that any discussion during lessons is a good chance to get exam speaking practice, it does not have to be a specific exam style task.

Answers 1 way **2** idea **3** convinced **4** What **5** do **6** consideration **7** go **8** safe **9** settled

Optional activity: Before doing Exercise 4, Ss could answer question 2 from Exercise 1 again, this time in groups of four. One pair starts by answering the question while the other pair note which phrases from Speak Out they use. Then Ss swap roles. Finally, they report to each other on how many of the phrases, and which other phrases, they used.

4 Set a time limit of two minutes for Ss to read the instructions and prepare themselves. Ss then carry out the task in pairs. Nominate one or two pairs to act out their conversation in open class.

ADDITIONAL PRACTICE: Photocopiable resources. Resource 15: *Solve it together.* Page 181

GRAMMAR AND LISTENING

This section introduces structures which take the past form for present meaning: *I wish, If only, I'd rather, I'd prefer, as if/though.*

Special difficulties: Although Ss should have seen these structures before, they may still have problems with the tense forms, especially if L1 uses a present tense for the same structure. Where mistakes are made, try to elicit self-correction if possible.

Warm-up Review of problem solving vocabulary. *The genie.* Put Ss into pairs. Tell Ss that they have found a magic lamp containing a genie. He can grant three wishes but cannot give you money. The only problem is that the three wishes have to be shared between you so you have to agree on the best three things to wish for. Give the Ss two minutes to try to come to an agreement using the phrases they learnt in the last lesson. Elicit ideas and write them on the board, eg *live for ever, a new house, a good job, be tall and strong* etc. Leave the ideas there until later.

1 Remind Ss that this is another chance for them to use some of the expressions learned in the previous lesson, especially for agreeing and disagreeing with their partner's opinions. Elicit ideas in open class.

Possible answers 1 A boyfriend and girlfriend having a meal together. It doesn't look as if it is a special occasion because he isn't dressed very smartly. It could be lunch. **2** The waiter looks upset or fed up. The man and woman look unhappy. **3** Maybe they are awkward customers and they have upset the waiter. The man is looking at his food as if there is something wrong with it. Maybe the food isn't very good.

2 Tell Ss that, when they listen to the recording the first time, they should only note down the complaints, not worry about the expressions in the exercise. They could do this with their books closed so they are not distracted. Elicit the answers and then Ss open their books and complete the exercise.

Tapescript CD 2 Track 13

Sylvia: *[neutral English accent]* Have you decided what you gonna have yet?

Simon: *[neutral English accent]* Nothing really grabs me. It's about time they changed the menu in here. Same old uninspired dishes.

Sylvia: Would you rather we went somewhere else?

Simon: Oh, no – it's OK. The best of a bad bunch.

Sylvia: I'll have the goose liver pâté, followed by the beef fajitas, please.

Waiter: [London accent] Mmm, hmm. And for you, Sir?

Simon: The salmon, followed by the lamb.

Waiter: The lamb's off, I'm afraid.

Simon: If only you'd told me that earlier! In that case I'll have the beef fricasee, then.

Waiter: Thank you. And to drink?

Simon: Will you join me in a bottle of wine, Sylve?

Sylvia: Mmm!

Waiter: I'd recommend a dry red with the beef.

Simon: Yes, that had crossed my mind, thank you. Erm, a bottle of the house red.

Waiter: Thank you.

Simon: Honestly. They treat us as though we were idiots! ... How's the pâté?

Sylvia: Mmm. It's out of this world!

Simon: Have I ever told you how they make that stuff? Well, just two weeks before it's time to kill the geese, they change the diet so the amount of ... so that the birds die a really painful death.

Sylvia: You know, I'd rather you hadn't told me all that!

Simon: Aren't you going to eat it?

Sylvia: Help yourself!

Simon: Mmm, it's not bad, actually. I wish I'd ordered it myself! ... Are you alright? Can I top you up, perhaps?

Sylvia: Yes, perhaps you'd better.

Simon: Say when! ... Oh, I wish they didn't serve boiled potatoes with everything!

Waiter: Is anything, er, everything OK?

Sylvia: Yes, lovely, thank you.

Simon: Disgusting coffee. It tastes as though it had been squeezed from a wet shirt-sleeve.

Sylvia: I think it's time we asked for the bill! Actually, I'd prefer it if you didn't pay for the meal. I mean you haven't enjoyed it at all.

Simon: Nope, I insist. It's on me!

Sylvia: You know something, Simon? Ever since you got that job on the newspaper it's become a nightmare going out with you. It's no pleasure eating out with you at all. I really wish you had never become a restaurant critic.

Simon: I don't know what you're talking about. For the price range, this is one of the most enjoyable eating experiences in the neighbourhood! Isn't it?

Answers Complaints: menu hasn't changed, no lamb, being treated like idiots, boiled potatoes with everything, disgusting coffee
1 d **2** f **3** c **4** h **5** g **6** a **7** e **8** b

3 Ss look through the sentences before they listen again. In pairs, they try to guess the correct form. Elicit ideas but do not tell Ss if they are right or wrong. Let them listen and find out for themselves.

Answers 1 changed **2** went **3** had told **4** were **5** hadn't told **6** had ordered **7** didn't serve **8** had been squeezed **9** asked **10** didn't pay **11** had never become

Work it out

4 When Ss have looked at the sentences, look at the similarities between them and the second and third conditionals. In the first sentence we are talking about a hypothetical present situation: *as if we were idiots* although in reality we are not idiots. In the second, we are talking about a hypothetical past situation: *If only you had told me that* but you did not tell me that.

Answers 2 But we aren't idiots! **2** It's a pity you didn't tell me!

5 Ss find all the examples of sentences referring to the present (1, 2, 4, 7, 9, 10) and all those that refer to the past (3, 5, 6, 8, 11).

Answers 1 the Past Simple **2** the Past Perfect

Check it out

Refer Ss to the Check it out section on page 156. As an optional activity, if the ideas from the warm-up activity are still on the board, elicit how we say these wishes, i.e. *I wish/If only I could live for ever, I wish/If only I had a new house, I wish/If only I had a good job, I wish/If only I was tall and strong.*

> **Mind the trap!**
>
> Go through the notes in the box with Ss and ask them which sentence from Exercise 3 could be rewritten with *would*. Ss work in pairs and, as soon as someone thinks they have the answer, they tell you the sentence (7 *I wish they wouldn't serve boiled potatoes with everything.*).

6 Remind Ss about the tenses used to talk about present and past situations. Ss work alone and compare answers in pairs.

Answers 1 He acts as if (though) he owned this place. **2** If only he could be with us today. **3** I wish he would listen to me. **4** It's time I did some revision. **5** He looked as if/though he hadn't eaten a square meal for days. **6** She wishes she had learnt to cook. **7** We'd rather you didn't go to too much trouble. **8** I'd rather you hadn't told everyone about my diet.

7 Ss write their sentences alone and then read them to their partner. As an alternative, ask the Ss to write the sentences on pieces of paper and redistribute them around the class. When Ss get a new set of sentences, they have to check that they are written correctly and guess who wrote them.

WRITING

This section introduces ways of making written work more formal.

Warm-up Review of regrets and conditionals. *Why?* Ss write two sentences starting: *If only* and *I wish*. One must be about a past situation and one a present situation. Give two examples on the board: *If only I'd gone to bed earlier last night. I wish I had a watch.* When Ss have written their two sentences put them into groups of four. Tell Ss that they are going to say why they wrote these sentences. Again, give them examples: *If I'd gone to bed earlier, I wouldn't be so tired now. If I had a watch, I would know what the time was.* Ss get into their groups. The first student reads out a sentence and the others ask *Why?* The student answers using a conditional and the process is repeated for the other students.

1 Set a time limit of three minutes for the Ss to read the fact boxes and the article. Discuss with the class what they are about (problems associated with supermarkets – importing food unnecessarily, paying low wages to overseas workers). Ss then complete the questionnaire alone and discuss their answers with their partner. Elicit answers in open class.

2 Ss read the paragraph alone and write the question they think it was answering. Ss then work in groups of four to compare questions and choose the best one. Elicit one question from each group.

Possible answer Supermarkets have made our lives much better.

3 Ss read the paragraph carefully, underlining the key vocabulary that answers the questions. Elicit the answers and write these on the board under the headings:
Arguments in favour
Linkers
Most important point

Answers 1 Three – cheaper, save time, provide variety 2 First and foremost, Secondly, Last of all 3 First and foremost

4 Ss look at the paragraph in pairs to find examples where the structures can be used. Elicit the original sentences and write them on the board. Nominate Ss to come to the front of the class and write the transformed sentences below the original ones. If there are any errors, ask other Ss to come to the front to try to correct them.

Answers 1 Secondly, were we to visit many different shops ... 2 Not only do they save us time but ... Never have we had such a tempting array of fresh produce (...) to choose from. 3 Last of all, it is said that ...

5 Ss do the same as they did in Exercise 3. When they have finished, again write the words on the board under the same headings as before (only *Arguments against* rather than *Arguments in favour*). Linkers used are: *on the other hand, one bad thing, also, another bad thing, last but not least.*

Answers 1 Three – transporting food and contributing to carbon emissions, encouraging people to grow unsuitable crops, paying low wages. 2 Last but not least 3 Ss' own ideas and justifications. The against paragraph is concerned with more global issues regarding supermarkets rather than possibly selfish benefits for ourselves. However, some of the language is simpler than in paragraph 1.

Optional activity: Refer Ss to the Train Your Brain box on page 47. Tell Ss that, as there is no Train Your Brain box on this page, they should use the information from Exercises 3, 4 and 5 to write their own. They can do this in any way they wish. Ss work in groups of four and, when they have finished, present their ideas to the class in turn.

The box should include some or all of the following:
• A for and against essay should consist of a brief introduction and conclusion and two other paragraphs.
• The two middle paragraphs should consist of about three arguments for and against the statement given in the question.
• Each argument for and against should be introduced by linkers such as:
Firstly, secondly, lastly, Also, Another good/bad thing ...
• The most important arguments can come at the beginning or the end of the paragraph. They should be introduced by phrases such as *First and foremost* or *Last but not least.*
• The arguments against should be contrasted with the arguments for by a linking phrase such as *On the other hand.*
• In order to make the essay more formal, we can use inversions, inverted conditionals and impersonal passive forms.

6 Ss work in pairs to match the phrases with the ones they could replace. In order to give the Ss more practice and to make the activity more memorable, they could rewrite the entire paragraph, using the phrases in Exercise 6 in place of those underlined in the text.

Answers 1 f 2 k 3 d 4 g 5 e 6 c 7 l 8 b 9 i 10 j 11 a 12 h

7 As an alternative, you could tell the Ss which essay they have to look at to ensure that half the class are writing one and half the other. When they have written their arguments, elicit them and write them on the board. This will ensure that all the Ss have the same ideas to work with.

Possible answers 1 Advantages: No factory farming and cruelty to animals, need less land, less heart disease and obesity, less methane which contributes to global warming. Disadvantages: Less choice of meals, possible unbalanced diet, recipe books would have to be rewritten and traditional recipes couldn't be handed down from one generation to another. 2 Advantages: It would give smaller shops a chance to compete, shop assistants wouldn't have to work unsocial hours, evenings and Sundays could become family time. Disadvantages: Less overtime for shop workers, people who work strange hours would find it more difficult to do their shopping, shops would be more crowded if opening hours were limited.

8 Before Ss start writing, they should decide on the linking expressions and other words they are going to use. They should also try to use at least one inversion and one inverted conditional as well as an impersonal passive form. Ss can then write the essay in class alone or at home.

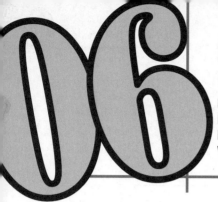# Sounds around us

Read, listen and talk about the sounds around us, music.
Practise infinitives and *-ing* forms.
Focus on describing similarities and differences.
Writing a review of a music CD.

Unit 6 Materials
....
Success Workbook Unit 6
....
Photocopiable resources 16, 17, 18
....
Testing and Evaluation Programme tests

VOCABULARY AND GRAMMAR

This section introduces vocabulary items for different kinds of noises as well as looking at when to use infinitives after verbs of perception and when to use the *-ing* form.

Warm-up Introduction to the topic of the lesson. *Open your ears.* Tell Ss that they must sit in absolute silence for one minute and, while they are sitting, they should note down every noise they hear – it could be things happening outside, things in the corridor, other Ss in the class moving or coughing etc. Then Ss get into groups of four to compare lists and add each other's words to their lists. Ask the groups how many words they have altogether and elicit all in open class, eg *footsteps, talking, sniffing, coughing, chairs scraping on the floor, car horns, car engines, birds singing, doors opening and closing, bells ringing* etc.

1 Ss read the text quickly. Ask: *What was Kirsty trying to do?* (relax) *Why couldn't she?* (she noticed all the sounds) *What happened when she opened the window?* (she heard more sounds, then a strange sound, then nothing). Tell Ss to cover Exercise 2. Ss now work in pairs to look at the picture and think of

the noises that Kirsty could hear and what the strange noise might have been and why it stopped all the other noises. Elicit ideas and then Ss uncover Exercise 2 to look at the noises listed.

2 Go through the noises before Ss listen, eliciting what each might sound like. Do not give definitions of the words in bold yet. Tell the Ss that, when they listen, the meaning of the words should become clear. Play the recording twice and elicit the order and the meanings of the words.

> **Answers** 1 b 2 e 3 g 4 i 5 h 6 k 7 f 8 d 9 j 10 l
> 11 a 12 c

Work it out

3 Ss look at the two sentences but not the rules. Ask what the difference between *a door slam* and *a heart beating* is. Accept all ideas, eg *a heart beat is quiet, a door slamming is loud*, but try to elicit that the door slams once but a heart continues to beat. Ss then complete the rules.

> **Answers** 1 b 2 a

Check it out

Refer Ss to the Check it out box and elicit that sometimes both forms can be used. Eg in films, they may show a car crash in slow motion to emphasise the impact and change the idea from seeing a car crash to seeing a car crashing.

4 If there are any answers that Ss disagree with, they should say why because they may also be correct, eg 4 the girl may have shrieked once only so *I heard her shriek* would be correct.

> **Answers** 1 crash 2 crashing 3 rumbling; flash 4 cut; shrieking 5 fire; running 6 creaking; rustling; rushing

Optional activity: To give Ss a short break in the lesson, play *Hangman* with them using the word *onomatopoeia* (on-uh-mat-uh-pee-uh). When the Ss have either guessed the word or lost the game, tell them what it means (words which sound similar to the noises they describe) and look at examples from Exercise 2, eg *tick, hum, crash.*

5 Ss read through the things making the noises to make sure they understand them. Look at the first sentence with the whole class. Ask what kind of noise a church bell makes. Then read the sentence twice, stressing the underlined words each time. Ss should be able to say that *chime* sounds more like the noise a church bell makes than *click*. Then they do the same in pairs, reading out the sentence using the two choices and seeing which sounds better. Play the recording and elicit the correct sentences.

Tapescript `CD 2 Track 15`

Paula: *[slight West Indian accent]* Oh, listen to that. I love that sound.
Simone: *[neutral English accent]* What sound?
Paula: Simone! Listen! The chime of church bells. It's wonderful.
Simone: Yeah, I suppose ... Not really my cup of tea, though.
Paula: So what's your favourite sound then?
Simone: My favourite sound is definitely the sweet click of a computer mouse.
Paula: Oh, come on, be serious!
Simone: OK, well, apart from that, I adore the crunch of footsteps in new snow in winter.
Paula: Yeah, so do I.
Simone: Or my boyfriend whispering the words 'I love you'.
Paula: Hmm, oh yeah, that's great ... I just love the sound of a little baby babbling to itself!
Simone: Paula! I didn't know you had maternal instincts!
Paula: Oh, yeah ... But don't tell me you don't like the sound of babies babbling!
Simone: Not really, no ... What kind of sounds you really hate?
Paula: Oh, I really hate it when Arthur cracks his knuckles. He does it all the time without even thinking about it. Awful!
Simone: I hate the banging of pots and pans in the kitchen.
Paula: Yeah, but you love it when my spaghetti sauce is bubbling away, don't you?
Simone: Well, you're such a great cook, Paula ...
Paula: You know what I hate? The screech of chalk on a blackboard.
Simone: Ah, stop it! Just thinking about it drives me nuts.
Paula: But you know what the worst sound of all has to be, don't you?
Simone: What?
Paula: The high-pitched whine of the dentist's drill!
Simone: Ow! Don't even go there, girl!

Answers 1 chime **2** click **3** crunch **4** whispering **5** babbling **6** cracking **7** banging **8** bubbling **9** screech **10** whine

6 Before Ss listen again, ask which of the sounds they like or do not like. Elicit ideas and then Ss listen and complete the table.

Answers Paula loves: the chime of church bells, a baby babbling **Paula hates:** someone cracking their knuckles **Simone loves:** the click of a computer mouse, sauce bubbling in a pot **Simone hates:** the banging of pots and pans **They both love:** the crunch of footsteps in the snow, someone whispering the words 'I love you' **They both hate:** the screech of chalk on a blackboard, the whine of a dentist's drill

7 Tell Ss to cover Exercises 5 and 6. As they listen to the recording they should write just the object making the noise, eg a church bell. Then they listen a second time to check their answers. Then, in pairs, without looking at the words in the exercises, they should try to write down what they heard in full sentences, using the correct vocabulary for the noises. Finally, they check their answers by looking at Exercise 5.

Answers 1 church bells chiming **2** sauce bubbling in a pot **3** a little baby babbling **4** the banging of pots and pans in a kitchen **5** someone walking in thick snow **6** someone clicking a computer mouse **7** a young man whispering the words 'I love you too' **8** the high-pitched whine of a dentist's drill **9** the screech of chalk on a blackboard

8 Ss first of all read the seven words so they can hear the noise they represent. Ss work in pairs to do the matching. Elicit the answers and the sort of noise each word represents, eg *A tinkle is a sound of pieces of glass or metal lightly banging into each other in the wind or when shaken. It's a gentle, pleasant sound. A creak is a long, strange sound, often scary, made when you walk on certain wooden floorboards or when you open an old door that needs oiling.*

Answers 1 tinkle **2** creak **3** roar **4** crunch **5** rustle **6** click **7** bang

9 Ss take it in turns to read out a clue to their partners. When they have finished, read out clues in a random order and the groups race to be the first to put their hands up to give the correct noise.

10 Ss work alone listing their favourite sounds and worst sounds. Then they get into pairs to see if any of their ideas were the same or, if not, whether they can agree on any of the ideas that they wrote. Elicit ideas and ask why Ss love or hate them.

11 Remind Ss of the story in Exercise 1 and 2 and ask Ss what they think is going to happen next. Allow Ss to discuss their ideas in pairs for two minutes and then elicit ideas. Ss then listen to the recording and note the sounds they hear. Tell Ss they now have to write this section of the story in a paragraph of a similar length to the one on page 60. Set a time limit of fifteen minutes to write the story. Nominate Ss to read their stories out to the class making them sound as interesting as possible.

For tapescript see page 208.

ADDITIONAL PRACTICE: Photocopiable resources. Resource 16: *Noise bingo*. Pages 182–183

READING AND VOCABULARY

> This section introduces new collocations and phrasal verbs on the topic of noise and music.

Culture notes

Samuel Johnson (1709–1784) was a writer and journalist. He is perhaps best known for his *Dictionary of the English Language* which was published in 1755 after nine years of work. He was also the subject of one of the most famous biographies ever written, *The Life of Samuel Johnson* by James Boswell.

YMCA was a disco hit by the group the Village People. It reached #1 in England and #2 in the USA. There is a dance that goes with the song in which you spell out the letters of the title.

Macarena is about a woman from the La Macarena district of Seville. It was sung by Los del Rio and six versions have been released by the band. The first, in 1993, was a rumba but it was not a hit until 1996.

Valentino Rossi (born 1979) is an Italian motorbike racer. He is one of the most successful racers ever with 7 grand prix wins and he earned an estimated $34 million in 2007. Rossi is also interested in rallying and Formula 1 and it is rumoured that he may switch to four wheels in the future.

La Marseillaise became the French national anthem in 1795 having been written in 1792. It was banned by Napoleon I and did not become the anthem permanently until 1879. It has been used many times in film, notably in *The Simpsons* movie and in the film *Casablanca* when the French drowned out the Germans who were singing their own anthem.

Warm-up Review of noise vocabulary form the previous lesson. *Random comparison.* Write the vocabulary items from the previous lesson on separate pieces of paper, eg *slam, tick, beat, creak, crackle, roar, tinkle, rumble, hum, crash, rustle, shriek, chime, click, whisper, crunch, babble, crack, bubble, bang, screech, whine.* Put Ss into pairs or groups of three (a maximum of eleven groups) and give each two of the words. They have to compare them in some way that shows they know what they mean and what sort of objects make those noises, eg *The tinkle of a chandelier is more musical than the hum of a computer.* When the Ss have finished, elicit the sentences in open class.

1 Remind Ss that this is a chance to use their problem solving vocabulary and set a time limit of three minutes for Ss to discuss what the quotations mean, whether or not they agree with them and justifications for their answers. Follow up by telling the Ss that Johnson's quote is an example of 'damning with faint praise', i.e. that, although at first

the sentence may seem positive, when you look at it carefully, it is actually negative. The Chinese saying has an English equivalent: *Empty vessels make the most noise* which has the same meaning.

2 Allow Ss two minutes to discuss the questions. Elicit ideas in open class with reasons for them. Do not comment on the Ss' answers and, if there is any disagreement, tell the Ss they will find out later.

3 Set a strict time limit and tell Ss that they are not trying to find the answers to Exercise 2, just where the answers can be found. As soon as someone has finished, stop the activity and elicit the answers.

Answers a 3 b 6 c 1 d 4 e 2 f 5 g 7

4 Ss work alone and note down words and phrases from the text which help them to choose the correct answers. Elicit the answers and justifications for them in open class, i.e. 1 women and musicians are more susceptible but 97–99% of all people have suffered so men and non-musicians must suffer, just slightly less; 2 eg taste sounds, smell shapes, see music, feel flavour etc; 3 'could be responsible'; 4 'not everyone who has looked for the 'Mozart effect' has found it'; 5 this is a use of sarcasm – the information following the word 'friendly' shows that the writer doesn't think this at all; 6 children spelt three or four more words wrong than when it was quiet, and special needs children did worse than normal children but we don't know how much worse; 7 filled with 'a trivial or pointless comment'.

Answers 1 F 2 T 3 F 4 T 5 F 6 F 7 T

5 Tell Ss that there may be more than one word which could go into the gaps (eg 1 baffling six-year-olds, barking six-year-olds, babbling six-year-olds) but that one word will make more sense than the others. If Ss are having problems finding the words, help them by telling them in which paragraph they can find them (1 – introduction; 2, 3 – paragraph one; 4, 5, 6, 7 – paragraph two; 8 – paragraph three; 9 – paragraph five; 10 – paragraph seven). Elicit the answers and what the adjectives mean.

Answers 1 boisterous 2 catchy 3 susceptible
4 baffling 5 distinct 6 involuntary 7 hereditary
8 excessive 9 rowdy 10 pointless

Optional activity: Tell Ss to close their books. Ask the class the questions from Exercise 2 and see how many the Ss can answer having read the text. Ask them how many of their guesses were correct and what new information they have learnt.

6 Ss try to work out the collocations themselves, then look in dictionaries to check. Elicit sentences in open class and check that Ss really do understand the vocabulary.

Answers 1 f 2 a 3 d 4 b 5 c 6 e

7 Tell Ss to first find the phrasal verbs in the text and try to work out their meaning from the context. Ss then complete the questions and answer them in pairs. To check that Ss have done the activity correctly, ask one student to ask another the first question. When the second student has answered, he/she asks a different student the next question and so on.

Answers 1 put up with **2** set off **3** take on **4** mix (things) up **5** showing off **6** getting rid of

8 Ss work in pairs to complete and discuss the questions. Elicit ideas in open class and then play the recording. Elicit the answers from the recording and ask Ss whether they agree with them.

Tapescript `CD 2 Track 19`

Didi: *[RP accent]* Hi Damian. Didi here.
Damian: *[neutral English accent]* Oh, hi Didi.
Didi: Look, I hope I'm not bothering you, but we've been getting some emails with questions about your article on noise and I've been asked to write replies to them, so do you think you could help me?
Damian: Sure.
Didi: Thanks. Someone wants to know if synaes... synaes... synaesthesia only happens when one sense gets mixed up with another.
Damian: Well, that's the traditional type of synaesthesia, you know you hear smoke or you taste music, but there appears to be another type, which is conceptual synaesthesia.
Didi: Conceptual synaesthesia?
Damian: Yeah, it's where a sense like sight or taste triggers not another sense, but a concept – an idea in your mind. There's a case of one woman for whom the letters of the alphabet, you know, their shapes have a conceptual meaning, every letter has a distinct human personality. 'A' is a mother-type, very sensible. 'I' is a little guy, 'H' and 'G' are always fussing over him. 'M' and 'N' are two old ladies who spend all their time together and chat a lot and so on.
Didi: Right, thanks. Another question ... Someone wants to know if it can cause heart disease and kill us, why there aren't stricter laws to control noise pollution.
Damian: Well, it's because the scientific evidence is quite recent. But if it's confirmed, then governments will have to bring in new laws to control noise pollution, the same way they had to with anti-smoking laws. Even if industries and our music-loving neighbours are not happy about it.
Didi: About the 'Mozart effect' ... is there any particular type of intelligence which is improved by children taking music lessons?
Damian: Yes, spatial reasoning, you know the ability to think about shape and size and where objects are, the ability to picture things in your mind. It's the type of intelligence which is important in mathematics and computer science. We're not sure why music lessons can help develop this intelligence, but perhaps it's because they help you exercise your memory, and because you need to use precise finger movements, and to listen for pitch and rhythm too.

Didi: OK, last question ... Which are the quietest societies in the world?
Damian: It's hard to answer that. As far as I know there are no definitive studies, but certainly it appears to be the case that silence is appreciated more in eastern countries. As the Chinese saying goes: 'Those who know do not speak; those who speak do not know.' However, having said that, Japan is widely recognised to be the noisiest country in the world.
Didi: OK, thanks a lot Damian. I'll ...

Answers 1 synaesthesia; sense   No, sometimes a sense can trigger a concept. **2** heart disease; noise pollution Because evidence is quite new and not yet confirmed so laws haven't been brought in yet. **3** intelligence; music lessons   Spatial reasoning – the ability to think about shape and size and to picture things in your mind. **4** societies   Eastern societies but not Japan.

9 Put the Ss into six groups. Tell Ss to discuss each question for two minutes, giving personal experiences where possible. Each group presents their ideas on one of the questions and then the class comments and give their own opinions.

GRAMMAR AND SPEAKING

This section extends Ss' understanding of verb patterns.

Special difficulties: Ss may be overwhelmed by the number of different structures, especially where verbs can take different forms with a change of meaning. Correct thoroughly and encourage peer and self-correction where possible.

Culture notes

Green Day are a rock trio from the USA. They formed in 1987. Originally they were an underground punk band but they signed to a major label and their debut album for them, *Dookie*, sold 15 million copies.

Can't Help Falling in Love was written for the 1961 film *Blue Hawaii*. It is based on *Plaisir D'amour* by Jean-Paul Egide Martini. The song reached #2 in the US charts and was often used by Elvis Presley as the last song in his live performances.

Warm-up Introduction to the topic of the lesson. *What do you know about …?* Put Ss into four groups. Each group is given one topic that is mentioned in the lesson. The groups discuss what they know, if anything, about their topic and present them to the class. If they do not know anything, they have to make up some 'facts'. As they present them, the other Ss have to decide whether the information is true or made up.

Things to discuss:

1 Elvis Presley
2 Vienna
3 The Rolling Stones
4 Green Day

1 Ask Ss what the difference between classical music and pop music is. Accept any answers, eg one is interesting, one is boring, one you can dance to, the other you cannot, one is modern, one is old etc. Then Ss do Exercise 1 in pairs. Elicit the answers and meanings of the words. Some of them the Ss may disagree with, eg an orchestra could be used on a pop song. As long as the Ss understand what the words mean and can justify their answers, accept answers differently to those suggested. Nominate Ss to talk about a concert they have been to.

Answers classical music: conductor, orchestra, recital, string quartet, symphony **pop music:** four-piece band, gig, group, lead guitarist, lip-synching, lyrics, tour **both:** chords, composer, concert, tune, live music, melody, rhythm, solo

2 Ss work in pairs, giving and justifying their opinions. Set a time limit of three minutes for Ss to fill with discussion and then elicit ideas in open class.

Answers Jack Probably old rock music. He is pretending to play the guitar and there is a poster of Jimi Hendrix behind him (popular guitarist from the late 1960s). **Yuki** Probably pop music. The way she is dressed and her make-up and hair look as if she likes Kylie Minogue or similar artists. **Vincent** He looks quite old. He could be an old metal fan or rocker. **Audrey** She might like classical music or she could like someone like Elton John who plays the piano.

3 Think Back! Ss work in groups of three or four to try to think of at least one more verb for each rule. Elicit all and write them on the board in the form of a table to allow all Ss to make a written record.

Possible answers 1a should, will, can etc **1b** 'd rather **2a** hope, 'd like **2b** chance, plan **2c** nice, interesting **2d** anywhere, no one **3** help **4a** enjoy, don't mind **4b** apologise for, congratulate on, no chance of, little time for, interested in, worried about

4 Ss work in pairs. Set a time limit of five to ten minutes for Ss to read all four texts and complete as many of the gaps as possible. After the listening, elicit the correct form of the verbs and which group from Exercise 3 each belongs to. Ss then write them all into their tables in their exercise books. Go through possible problem areas with the Ss, i.e. *make* and *let* are both followed by an object before the verb; *made* can be used in the passive *I was made to …* whereas *let* cannot – we have to use *allowed to*; *look forward* is unusual in that it is followed by *to + -ing*.

Answers 1 to play **2** changing **3** be **4** to be (*It must be great being …* may often be used by native speakers as well.) **5** asking **6** to go **7** stick **8** listening **9** appreciate **10** to have **11** to invite **12** to bother **13** to try **14** (to) do **15** singing **16** thinking **17** go **18** to make **19** feel **20** trying **21** doing **22** trying **23** applying **24** losing **25** going **26** to be **27** living **28** changing **29** rocking **30** falling **31** getting **32** feel **33** crying **34** to be **35** performing **36** to join **37** to turn **38** to gain **39** to lose **40** going **41** becoming **42** to study **43** to choose

5 Tell Ss to discuss all four people and their attitude to music and what they like or do not like about it. Ss then tell each other which one they would prefer to talk to and why.

Work it out

6 Ss work together in pairs to quickly find examples of the five verbs in the texts. Elicit where they are, i.e. Jack: *tried to learn, remember to buy*; Yuki: *try singing, try to get on, mean going to, try to discourage*; Vincent: *mean to go on, go on living, remember buying, forgot to pay, I'll never forget playing it*; Audrey: *went on to study*. Then Ss do the matching.

Answers 1a try to do **1b** try doing **2a** mean doing **2b** mean to do **3a** remember doing **3b** remember to do **4a** forget doing **4b** forget to do **5a** go on doing **5b** go on to do

7 Ss decide on the correct form in pairs and then work together to make sentences using the other form of the verb. Elicit answers and point out that the two meanings of *try* can sometimes be quite similar as in the example in sentence 1. If you were talking to someone who knows a lot about guitars, you would use *tuning* but, if you were giving someone their first ever guitar lesson, you may say *try to tune it* meaning *to see if you are able.*

Answers 1 tuning **2** seeing **3** to take **4** leaving **5** to form

8 When Ss have completed the song lyrics, ask them to try to work out who is singing to whom and what the song is generally about, eg a man to his ex-girlfriend. He has just split up with her and she is very upset. He is trying to explain that it is for the best and he is not going to change his mind. Sometimes more than one answer may be possible. Ss should justify why they have chosen the form they have.
Note: 10 Although *problems to believe* seems to follow the rule that nouns are followed by the infinitive, this is an example of a gerund following a preposition which is then dropped. Tell Ss they will look at this in more detail in the Mind the trap! section. 11 This could mean both *make an effort to do something* or *to do something to see what it's like.*

Answers 1 crying **2** talking **3** to say **4** to find **5** to see **6** living **7** accept **8** losing **9** to live **10** believing **11** to live/living

Mind the trap!

Go through the Mind the trap! box with the Ss and elicit more example sentences using the noun phrases mentioned, eg *I'm having some difficulty (in) understanding this lesson. I've got a few problems (with) organising my time.*

Check it out

Tell Ss to refer to the Check it out section on page 156 if they are still having difficulties or are unsure.

9 Look at the first sentence with the whole class. Play the first part of the recording and ask the class how they could use the words given to respond. Elicit ideas and then play the second part of the recording. Now that Ss have a clear idea of what they need to do, play the whole of the recording while Ss think about the responses and then listen. Now play it a second time, this time nominating Ss to respond each time.

Tapescript CD 2 Track 21

1 A: *[English Midland accent]* Do you know why the concert was called off?
B: *[English Midland accent]* Apparently, there was some difficulty obtaining permission from the Town Hall.
2 C: *[Scottish accent]* Tell me again why you need me to come round and help you with your computer.
D: *[Scottish accent]* Yeah, I've been having a few problems installing the Media Player.
3 E: *[Bristol accent]* It must have been hard to get her to give you her autograph.
F: *[Bristol accent]* No, I had no trouble persuading her to give it to me.
4 G: *[Manchester accent]* Do you think we should get this guitar for Kevin's birthday?
H: *[Manchester accent]* No, there's no point paying so much if he can't play.
5 I: *[Welsh accent]* We need a singer for the gig tonight. We're desperate!
J: *[Irish accent]* It's no good asking me. I can't sing in tune.
6 K: *[New York accent]* I wish Green Day would ask me to go on tour with them.
L: *[New York accent]* It's no use dreaming. Keep on studying!
7 M: *[Australian accent]* Hey the *Great Rock'n'Roll Swindle* is on TV tonight.
N: *[Australian accent]* It's not worth watching. I'd rather go out.

Answers 1 There was some difficulty obtaining permission from the Town Hall. **2** I've been having a few problems installing the Media Player. **3** I had no trouble persuading her to give it to me. **4** There's no point paying so much if he can't play. **5** It's no good asking me. I can't sing in tune. **6** It's no use dreaming. Keep on studying! **7** It's not worth watching. I'd rather go out.

10 When Ss do the exercise, they should bookmark the page on which their questions are written and, while their partner is asking a question, they should keep their book closed. This will stop them looking in advance at the questions they have to ask and thinking about them rather than what their partner is asking them.

ADDITIONAL PRACTICE: Photocopiable resources. Resource 17: *Ask your friends.* Page 184

SPEAKING AND LISTENING

This section introduces ways of comparing things – showing big differences, small differences and similarities between them.

Warm-up Review of verb patterns. *What is it?* Tell Ss to think of an activity, eg playing the guitar. They have to make five sentences about the activity using five of the verbs from the previous lesson, eg *When I first* **tried to do** *this I found it very difficult. I couldn't get my fingers on the right strings. My mum didn't* **let me do** *this in the house because of the noise. I'm* **thinking of doing** *this in a band next year. It's a rock band and I want to be a star! My friend told me* **to keep on trying to do** *it because one day I've got a* **chance of becoming** *famous like Kirk Hammett of Metallica.* Ss do the same and then tell their partner their sentences. The partner guesses the activity. Nominate two or three Ss to read out their sentences to the class.

1 Ss read through the adjectives and descriptions before listening. Then they listen to the recording twice and try to match all the words. Finally, Ss check their answers in dictionaries.

Tapescript `CD 2 Track 22`
....
1 *[RP accent]* Hello, my name's Victor and I've got a velvety voice.
2 *[London accent]* Hello, my name's Cindy and I've got a squeaky voice.
3 *[London accent]* Hello, my name's Horace and I've got a hoarse voice.
4 *[RP accent]* Hello, my name's Heather and I've got a husky voice.
5 *[London accent]* Hello, my name's Harry and I've got a harsh voice.
6 *[RP accent]* Hello, my name's Sharon and I've got a shrill voice.

Answers 1 f **2** e **3** c **4** a **5** b **6** d

2 As an optional follow-up, read out some of the Ss' descriptions of their voices to the class without saying who wrote them. See if the class can guess who wrote them.

3 Put Ss into groups of three. One student listens to the two Ss who are answering the questions and notes down good vocabulary and ideas used. Ss then listen to the recording. Elicit the answers.

For tapescript see page 208.

Answers 1 The people are two actors and a director. They're making an advert for the SoundSnake music player. **2** They don't sound natural or as the director would like them to sound. **3** A music and video player similar to an iPod or MP3 player but much better.

SPEAK OUT

4 Go through the Speak Out box with the whole class and elicit full sentences which could contain the phrases given, eg *Brad Pitt is not quite as cool as George Clooney. Punk rock is far better than hip-hop.* Ss then work in pairs to complete the sentences with the correct words in brackets. More than one answer may be possible.

Possible answers 1 quite similar to **2** fairly similar to; totally different from **3** nearly as good as; by far the worst **4** nearly as noisy as **5** a lot angrier/more angry than **6** slightly louder than

5 Look at the information in the advertisement and ask Ss what it represents and what adjectives could describe it, eg storage – size of memory (*big* or *small*), price – *high* or *low*, screen – *big* or *small*, ease of use – *easy/simple* or *difficult/complicated*; appearance – *nice/beautiful* or *ugly/horrible*; value for money – *good value* or *bad/poor value*. Ss then look up their information and tell each other about their music player compared to the SoundSnake, finally using the information to compare all three players.

Possible answers storage SoundSnake has a slightly bigger storage capacity than Songvault. Earblaster has by far the smallest storage capacity.
price SoundSnake and Songvault are exactly the same price. Earblaster is a lot cheaper.
screen Earblaster's screen is a bit bigger than SoundSnake's screen. Songvault has a much smaller screen.
ease of use Earblaster is marginally more easy to use than SoundSnake. Songvault is by far the most complicated to use.
appearance Songvault and SoundSnake are fairly similar in terms of appearance although SoundSnake is marginally more attractive. Earblaster is by far the least attractive.
value for money SoundSnake is slightly better value for money than the other two. Songvault's value for money is just the same as Earblaster's.

6 Look at the example given and elicit how else this could be said, i.e. *The second speaker sounds much more excited than the first speaker.* Tell Ss to try to use a different expression for each situation.

Tapescript `CD 3 Track 1`
....
1 A: Fred: *[sounding really unexcited]* We've just won £10 million pounds on the lottery!
1 B: Kelly: *[sounding really excited]* We've just won £10 million pounds on the lottery!
2 A: *[sound of a really loud motorbike roaring down the road, its horn blaring]*
2 B: *[sound of a slightly squeaky bike trundling down the road, its bell ringing]*
3 A: Kelly: *[sounding convinced]* I love you with all my heart.

3 B: Fred: *[sounding less convinced]* I love you too, darling.
4 A: *[sound of a really fierce dog barking]*
4 B: *[sound of a friendly dog barking playfully]*
5 A: Fred: *[sounding very cold and harsh]* Your dog is very ill. It's going to die.
5 B: Fred: *[sounding warm and reassuring]* Your dog is very ill. It's going to die.
6 A: *[jolly happy soundtrack music]*
6 B: *[creepy soundtrack music]*
7 A: *[evil laugh]*
7 B: *[silly giggle]*

Possible answers 2 The motorbike is far louder than the bike. **3** The man isn't nearly as romantic as the woman. **4** The second dog is much friendlier than the first. **5** The words spoken by the first person were absolutely identical to the words spoken by the second speaker but the tone was totally different. **6** The first music was totally different from the second music. **7** The first laugh was much scarier than the second.

7 Give each student a number: 1, 2 or 3. The students look at their topic and make sentences alone. Then they tell their group their ideas and the other two agree or disagree. Elicit ideas from the whole class.

ADDITIONAL PRACTICE: Photocopiable resources. Resource 18: *Just our opinions.* Page 185

LISTENING AND PRONUNCIATION

This section introduces different stress patterns on verbs and nouns which are identical in spelling.

Culture notes

Emile Berliner (1851–1929) was a German inventor. He moved to the USA in 1870 and was granted a patent for his gramophone in 1887. In 1895, he started the Berliner Gramophone Company. He also helped to develop an early helicopter.

Thomas Edison (1847–1931) was an American inventor best remembered for inventing the phonograph and the electric light bulb. He held a total of 1,093 patents in the USA as well as others in Europe.

Warm-up Review of making comparisons. *Who am I thinking of?* Tell Ss to write down the name of a famous person, dead or alive. Tell the group why your person is famous, eg *He's a singer.* A student gives the name of a singer, eg Robbie Williams and you compare your person with the person guessed: *Oh no, my person is much older than Robbie Williams.* Then a second student guesses another, older singer

and the process is repeated until the singer (eg Paul McCartney) has been guessed. Ss then do the same in groups of four.

1 Ask Ss if they have got any of these things in their homes. In pairs Ss try to date the different devices. Play the recording to check the dates.

For tapescript see page 208.

Answers A 1979 **B** 2001 **C** 1930s **D** 1877 **E** 1948 **F** 1888 **G** 1963

2 Ss read through the text and try to remember or guess what the missing words could be. Play the recording again and elicit the answers in open class.

Answers 1 history **2** sound **3** sound waves **4** human voice/nursery rhyme **5** historical recordings **6** cylinders **7** mass-produced **8** electronic amplifiers **9** singles **10** personal music listening

3 Ask Ss to read the sentences out loud in pairs. Before they listen to the recording, they try to come up with a rule for the stress of the underlined words. Elicit ideas but do not tell Ss the answers until after they have listened to the recording.

Answers 1a record **1b** record **2a** progress **2b** progress **3a** rebel **3b** rebel The nouns have the stress on the first syllable. The verbs have the stress on the second syllable.

4 Ss work in pairs deciding whether the words are verbs or nouns and how to pronounce them. Elicit ideas of who is speaking in each case and how they feel, and then play the recording.

Answers 1 A rapper and a politician – permit, permit **2** A father and daughter – perfect, perfect **3** A musician and her manager – insult, insult **4** The same two as in # 3 – desert, desert, desert **5** A rebellious student and a teacher – conduct, conduct, conducting **6** A businesswoman or politician, a musician – present, present, present, present, presents

5 Play the recording again so Ss can note down how the people feel and their tone of voice. Ss practise in pairs. Nominate pairs to act out dialogues in open class.

6 Put Ss into groups of five. The groups discuss the questions and then each student is given a number 1–5. The number ones have to summarise what their group said about question 1 and so on.

WRITING

This section looks at how to write a review of a music CD.

Culture notes

The Sound of Silence was written by Paul Simon in 1964. It attempted to show the feelings of people in the USA over the murder of John Kennedy. It was released in 1965 and finally reached #1 in the USA in January 1966. It was originally called *The Sounds of Silence* and both singular and plural form appear in the song's lyrics.

Chuck Berry (born 1926) is a singer, song writer and guitarist. He was one of the pioneers of rock'n'roll in the 1950s and influenced bands like The Beatles and Rolling Stones. *School Days* was released in 1957.

Lose Yourself was released in 2002 and appeared in the film *Green Mile*. It reached #1 around the world, won an Oscar for the Best Original Song and two Grammys. The song's lyrics are about the character Eminem plays in the film and the plot of the film.

Like a Rolling Stone was released by Bob Dylan in 1965. It reached #2 in the USA but was criticised by many of Dylan's fans at the time as it changed his sound from an acoustic, folk one to an electronic rock sound.

Heartbreak Hotel was released by Elvis Presley in 1956. It was his first #1 hit and the highest-selling single of the year. It was the first record Elvis recorded for RCA Victor, having moved from the Sun label, and most people at the record company thought it was a mistake as the style was so different.

Warm-up Review of word stress. *Missing words.* Have words written on slips of paper and give one to each student or pair of students. They have to make a sentence using their word, using the sentence stress to show them whether it is a verb or a noun. Then they read out their sentence but do not say the word they were given. The other Ss have to say what the word was with the correct stress.

Words to use: *record, record, progress, progress, rebel, rebel, permit, permit, perfect, perfect, insult, insult, desert, desert, conduct, conduct, present, present, protest, protest*

1 Set a time limit of five minutes for Ss to discuss the questions. Elicit ideas in open class and encourage Ss to use the language of comparisons and giving opinions that they have learnt recently to argue with each other effectively.

Possible answers **1** Advantages: you get the most famous songs all together on one album; it's a cheap way to get a selection of songs by one band. Disadvantages: some of the more obscure songs may be better than the commercial ones. The idea is outdated with downloads meaning you can make your own compilations. **2** Famous cover versions include Sid Vicious covering Frank Sinatra's *My Way* and rap band Run DMC covering Aerosmith's *Walk This Way* (with Aerosmith). Nirvana covered *The Man Who Sold the World* by David Bowie. Early Beatles albums had many covers and their song *Yesterday* has been covered several hundred times. **3** Magazines, newspapers, online **4** Ss' own answers

2 Give Ss about five minutes to complete as much of the song as possible and then play the recording. Nominate Ss to read out lines from the song.

Answers **1** friend **2** again **3** creeping **4** sleeping **5** brain **6** remains **7** alone **8** cobblestone **9** lamp **10** damp **11** light **12** night **13** saw **14** more **15** speaking **16** listening **17** share **18** dare **19** know **20** grows **21** teach **22** reach **23** fell **24** wells **25** prayed **26** made **27** warning **28** forming **29** walls **30** halls

3 Tell Ss that there are clues in the song to help them answer the first question but the other two questions are for them to think about between them. Allow Ss five minutes to discuss their ideas and then elicit answers in open class.

Answers **1** No – 'like a cancer grows', 'hear my words that I might teach you' **2** It's almost impossible to answer because there is never true silence, there's always something we can hear in the background. **3** eg when sad, when working/concentrating etc

Optional activity: Ss work alone to write things they like about the song they just heard (voice, guitar, lyrics etc) and things they dislike (speed, ending etc). Then they write adjectives for each of the things they have listed, eg *nice voice, exciting guitar, intelligent lyrics* etc. Then they get into groups of three to compare what they have written and why. This activity concludes the work on the song and leads on nicely to the idea of writing reviews.

TRAIN YOUR BRAIN

4 Tell Ss to imagine they were going to write a review of the song they have just listened to and that they knew something about the band who sang it. Their review would include the six things in the Train Your Brain box but in a different order. Ss discuss what order they would put the information in and then read the review of the CD on page 69. Elicit what order was used in the review and why this is a good order to use, i.e. the opening sentence makes us want to read on, the background information helps us to imagine what the group are like if we do

Students' Book ➡ pages 68–69

not already know. The description of the contents of the CD also helps us to understand what kind of music it is. If we do not like the sound of the band or the contents, we do not have to read what the reviewer likes and dislikes or whether we should buy it.

Answers **1** opening sentence **2** background information **3** description of contents **4** what you like **5** what you dislike **6** recommendation

5 Ss work in pairs to identify words and phrases which show the writer's opinion. Elicit these and write them on the board under headings: *opinion adjectives* (eg *brilliant, stunning*), *descriptive adjectives* (eg *crashing, roaring*) and *other phrases* (eg *In my humble opinion ...*).

Answers **words and phrases** you've got nothing to worry about, stunning, finest, one of the best, fantastic, catchy, witty, great, classic, firing on all cylinders, husky, crashing, contrast exquisitely, subtle, unforgettable, brilliant, isn't quite as good, roaring, thundering, I can't remember hearing a better version, In my humble opinion, the only mistake, mellow, sweet, there's no point trying, I'd rather listen to, genuinely worth buying, I'm really looking forward to seeing **writer's opinion** The reviewer is very positive.

6 Check that Ss understand *synonym* and *antonym* (opposite). Ss work in pairs to find the words and phrases in the text. Tell Ss that all the phrases are good to use in reviews and this exercise is not intended to replace words with better ones, just to extend the Ss' vocabulary.

Answers **1** run out of ideas **2** worry about **3** stunning **4** fantastic **5** witty **6** exquisitely **7** unforgettable **8** brilliant **9** In my humble opinion **10** worth buying **11** looking forward to seeing

7 Ss work in pairs. First they must recognise where the phrases could go in the text and whether any other changes need to be made. Then they work together to rewrite the review negatively. Nominate Ss to read out sentences from the new review in open class before they check the version on page 147.

8 Think Back! Try to elicit which adverbs can go with base and strong adjectives before Ss look at page 17. When they have re-read the rules, look at the first adjective in the original review – *stunning* – and elicit that it is a strong adjective meaning 'very good'. Elicit that Ss could say *absolutely stunning, simply stunning, totally stunning, utterly stunning, really stunning* and *pretty stunning* but could not use the other four adverbs. Tell Ss that *slightly* and *pretty* need to be used carefully because they can change the meaning of the review and make it sound strange. Although *pretty stunning* is grammatically correct, it probably would not be used here. *Slightly* is more likely to be used in the negative review

(to make it sound less negative) than in a positive review where the reviewer will want to make things more positive.

When Ss have compared ideas with their partners, elicit adverbs and adjectives and correct where necessary.

Answers *Absolutely, utterly, simply, totally* can be used with extreme adjectives.
Terribly, extremely, slightly, very can be used with base adjectives.
Really, pretty can be used with all adjectives.

Positive version
Extremely/terribly/very/really: catchy tunes; witty lyrics; subtle tinkling keyboard; (+ pretty) mellow and sweet
Absolutely/simply/totally/utterly/really: stunning debut; fantastic songs; classic songs; great lyrics; (+ pretty) unforgettable; brilliant; roaring version, thundering drum solo;

Negative version
Extremely/terribly/very/really/pretty/slightly uninspired; hoarse voice, muddy guitar chords; bland tinkling; shrill, squeaky version
Absolutely/simply/totally/utterly/really/pretty dreadful compilation

9 Tell Ss to plan their review before they start writing it. First they should note down a few facts about the band and the CD. Then they should list what they like and do not like and then write some good adverbs and adjectives that could be used in the review. Once they have done this, Ss either write the review in class or at home.

10 When Ss swap reviews, they note all the adjectives and opinion words that their partner has used. Then they think about how these could be rewritten with antonyms and write the review with the opposite meaning. Ss read each other their alternative review.

VOCABULARY AND GRAMMAR

1 Ss work in pairs to choose the correct words and explain what the sentence means. Then they decide what the other two words mean and how they could be used in a sentence.

As before, as a follow-up, Ss can work in pairs to try to write new sentences in which one of the other words given as choices would be correct. Ss then read out one of their sentences without saying the word from the exercise. The other Ss have to try to guess which word should be used. This is more challenging as Ss do not just have a choice of three but of any of the unused words from the exercise.

Answers 1 nibbled 2 parched 3 slice 4 beneficial 5 rustling 6 creaked 7 rowdy 8 velvety 9 boisterous 10 choked

2 Before Ss start the exercise, look at the first two gaps with the whole class. Point out that in the first gap, there is only one possible answer because it is part of a phrase *to put all your e… in one basket*. In the second gap, it looks as if many words are possible, eg *cool, clever, crazy, classic*, but Ss should try to use an adjective that they have learnt collocates with *tune*. Ss complete the activity in pairs. Elicit the answers and then ask Ss for examples of the following: *a catchy tune, clever lyrics, a cover version, a compilation album*.

Answers 1 eggs 2 catchy 3 lyrics 4 musician 5 string 6 cover 7 album 8 appetising 9 Help 10 topped 11 screaming/screeching/shrieking 12 shrill 13 ticking 14 beating 15 silence

3 Remind Ss that the tense of the second sentence must agree with the tense of the original. Ss work in pairs. As soon as a pair have finished, ask them to write their answers on the board (the missing words only). When the other Ss have finished, if they have different answers, they write them on the board next to the one they think is wrong. Finally, go through the correct answers with the whole class.

Answers 1 wish you wouldn't always but in 2 no good crying 3 If only I hadn't 4 as though his mouth were/was 5 it's high time we were 6 I wish they enjoyed/would enjoy

4 Look at the first sentence with the Ss. Ask: *What tense is it?* (past) Ss now look at the sentence they have to write. Ask: *What kind of sentence will it be?* (conditional – it starts with *If*) *What conditional do we use to talk about an imaginary past?* (third) Tell Ss to do the same with the other sentences so that they know exactly what is needed each time. Elicit ideas and then Ss do the exercise alone: 2 mixed conditional – imaginary past action with present

result; 3 mixed conditional – imaginary present situation with past result; 4 second conditional with inversion; 5 third conditional with inversion; 6 first conditional using *Should* instead of *If*; 7 *It's about time* + past form.

Answers 1 If I'd known you were a vegetarian, I wouldn't have made steak pie. 2 If he hadn't eaten so much last night, he wouldn't be suffering from stomachache. 3 If she was Italian, she wouldn't have made risotto with long-grained rice. 4 Were food prices to rise by 10 percent, millions of people could starve. 5 Had food not been so scarce, French cuisine wouldn't have become so inventive. 6 Should you require more nutritional information, visit our website. 7 It's about time we had something else for lunch.

5 Ss work alone to put the verbs in the correct form. When they have finished, Ss get into pairs and compare ideas. Elicit the answers in open class. Where two verb forms are possible grammatically, elicit why the choice below is correct: 2 *went on to compose* means *to start to compose*. *Went on composing* means *to continue composing*. It is fairly obvious that composing film music was a new thing for him. 7 He is trying to do something difficult so this needs *to* + infinitive after *try*, not the *-ing* form.

Answers 1 honking 2 to compose 3 rushing 4 stir 5 to pay 6 (in) swallowing 7 to shake off

LISTENING SKILLS

1 Tell Ss to read through the questions and choices carefully before they listen to the recording. Ss then listen and take notes of what is said. Before they listen to the recording a second time, they choose the correct answer for each question and then listen again to check their answers and change if necessary. Elicit the answers and the reasons for them: 1 'the earphones on his iPod conducted the electricity through his head, deafening him and breaking his jaw' – point out that when Tessa says that it was lucky he wasn't listening to heavy metal she was joking; 2 'Sorry, it starts next Friday, the fourth of May. You'll be able to see all sorts of devices for recording and playing music, you know gramophones, the first cassette players and so on, and also take a look at how the process of recording sounds might change in days to come. It's only on for one week, so get your skates on.' 3 'so he has to use a specially built artificial arm with a guitar pick stuck on the end'; 4 'A diet like that is deficient in fibre and is almost certain to cause serious health problems.' 5 'Despite assurances from current champion Dan Despateer that he definitely wasn't going to defend his title this year, it now seems he will be tucking in after all.' 6 'started fighting over who should get the last cake'.

Tapescript `CD 3 Track 6`

Tessa: *[neutral English accent]* You're listening to *Morning Madness* with Phil Duffy and me Tessa di Matteo. Good morning, Phil.

Phil: *[Northern English accent]* Morning, Tessa. Now, if you like listening to music while you're jogging, then you'd better be careful if the weather's bad.

Tessa: Why's that, Phil?

Phil: Well, there's this story in the papers today about an unfortunate young lad in Canada who was in the park jogging and listening to music when he was struck by lightning and thrown over three metres. Fortunately, he survived but the earphones on his iPod conducted the electricity through his head, deafening him and breaking his jaw.

Tessa: Ouch!

Phil: And he also got burns on his chest and face from the cables.

Tessa: Do they know what he was listening to at the time?

Phil: Uh ... yeah ... a Mozart piano concerto.

Tessa: Just as well he wasn't listening to heavy metal.

Phil: You think that would have been worse, do you?

Tessa: Oh of course!

Phil: Speaking of music, you shouldn't forget to go to the music exhibition, the History of Recordings, that starts next Friday, that's the third of May in the Stewart's Art Centre. It's ...

Tessa: Phil? Get it right. Next Friday is the fourth.

Phil: Oh, is it? Sorry, it starts next Friday, the fourth of May. You'll be able to see all sorts of devices for recording and playing music, you know gramophones, the first cassette players and so on, and also take a look at how the process of recording sounds might change in days to come. It's only on for one week, so get your skates on.

Tessa: Staying on a musical theme, here's a great story. Marc Playle, a one-armed guitarist has reached the final of an international music competition beating 750 two-armed guitarists to get there. Marc was born without the lower part of his left arm so he has to use a specially built artificial arm with a guitar pick stuck on the end. He's been playing since he was 14 and he's got a group that plays heavy rock with a touch of grunge.

Phil: Where's he from?

Tessa: He's one of yours, Phil. He's from Durham.

Phil: Doesn't surprise me. We're special, we are.

Tessa: And so are the people from Liverpool, or at least one of them is. A 37-year-old Liverpool man claims he has eaten nothing but Mars Bars for the last 17 years.

Phil: No way!

Tessa: That's what he says. Apparently he eats a dozen bars every day for breakfast, lunch and dinner, and at weekends he might treat himself to one or two more.

Phil: It must be terrible for his health.

Tessa: He says he drinks a lot of orange juice and takes vitamin supplements, so he should be getting enough calories and vitamins and proteins and so on. Now, should any of you out there be thinking of following his example remember that any nutritionist will tell you, it's definitely not a good idea. A diet like that is deficient in fibre and is almost certain to cause serious health problems.

Phil: I'm not surprised.

Tessa: While we're on the subject, how's yours coming along, Phil?

Phil: Hmm. I might not have actually lost any weight to speak of yet, and I still feel like guzzling cakes and sweets and well, everything basically, but if I hadn't started it, I wouldn't be feeling as healthy as I do now.

Tessa: Well, you'd better steer clear of Peel Park this weekend.

Phil: How come?

Tessa: It's the third annual pie eating competition.

Phil: Tell me more.

Tessa: Despite assurances from current champion Dan Despateer that he definitely wasn't going to defend his title this year, it now seems he will be tucking in after all. The organisers are expecting twice as many as the 25 competitors that took part last year.

Phil: I hope they've ordered enough pies so they don't end up fighting over who gets the last one. That's what happened recently at a restaurant in Plymouth. Two pensioners – both of them in their seventies – started fighting over who should get the last cake at one of those all-you-can-eat buffet restaurants. And one of them picked up a knife and stabbed the other one!

Tessa: Oh dear.

Phil: The victim wasn't badly hurt, but the attacker was so scared by what he'd done, he tried to run away.

Tessa: Run?

Phil: Well, walk quickly away – he had a walking stick. But the police caught up with him later.

Tessa: It just goes to show you, doesn't it?

Phil: What?

Tessa: You can't have your cake and eat it too!

Phil: Oh!

Answers 1 b 2 b 3 c 4 d 5 c 6 b

SPEAKING SKILLS

1 Put the Ss into two groups: A and B. As look at the first topic and discuss together in small groups ideas that they could use in a presentation. Bs do the same with the second topic. Allow three minutes, then give Ss a further five minutes to think alone about what to say and how to say it. Ss then get into pairs, A and B, and present their topic to each other. Nominate one or two Ss to present each topic to the whole class.

2 Tell Ss to cover the task but leave the photos showing. Put Ss into pairs and give them a role, A or B. Give A their task and tell them to speak for one minute. When they have finished, tell B their task and again tell them to keep talking for one minute. Now tell Ss to talk together and give them the final task. This will prevent student B from planning what to say while A is speaking.

Students' Book ➡ pages 70–71 **81**

Calm down!

Read, listen and talk about conflicts and aggression, stress and health, assertiveness.
Practise impersonal reporting structures.
Focus on being assertive.
Write an information sheet.

Unit 7 Materials

Success Workbook Unit 7

Photocopiable resources 19, 20, 21

Testing and Evaluation Programme tests

LISTENING AND VOCABULARY

This section introduces some useful informal phrases to describe anger, annoyance and other feelings.

Culture notes

Nemesis is used to describe one's worst enemy, someone the complete opposite of oneself. The word comes from the ancient Greek goddess of retribution.

Warm-up Lead-in to the topic of the lesson. *Mime the feeling.* Have some feelings written on pieces of paper. Nominate one or two Ss to come to the front of the class and show them one of the feelings. Without speaking, they must show this feeling to the class. After each act, ask Ss how the Ss showed the feeling (eyes, mouth, body position, hands etc). Repeat with other Ss as many times as required.

Feelings to use:
worried, unhappy, crazy, angry, tired, embarrassed

1 Having done the warmer, the Ss will know what clues to look out for in the photo. Set a time limit of two minutes for Ss to discuss the questions. Elicit ideas and ask for definitions of the forms of body language and feelings given in the exercise.

Answers 1 The man on the left is pointing to his watch so the boy on the right is probably late for work. **2** The man pointing at his watch is aggressive, dominant and admonishing. The boy is holding his palm up showing possibly that he is resentful and bewildered.

2 Ss read through questions 1–3 and predict possible answers in pairs. Play the recording and elicit the answers. Then give Ss two more minutes to discuss questions 4 and 5.

Tapescript `CD 3 Track 7`

Barnes: *[Northern English accent]* I've been looking for you, Alex. But I might have guessed you'd be taking yet another break. Are you aware of the fact that there was no one around to serve customers for a good ten minutes?
Alex: *[London accent]* But, Mr Barnes, I've been on my lunch-break for the past half an hour.
Barnes: I've had to warn you before about leaving the sales counter unattended.
Alex: But according to the staff rota Gareth and Roweeta were supposed to be here between one thirty and two o'clock.
Barnes: You know perfectly well that Roweeta is off sick today.
Alex: But surely it's not my responsibility to sort out alternative arrangements when people are …
Barnes: Look, I've had to warn you already about your attitude problem. And what did we agree last time we spoke?
Alex: Look, you've obviously got some sort of a problem with me. Why don't you just come out and tell me exactly what you …
Barnes: We agreed last time that if you left the sales counter unattended you'd be out on your ear. Listen, mate. You might think the fact that you're studying for a business degree means you know better than anyone else. But as far as I'm concerned you've proved yet again that you're obviously not up to the job. Any normal person would have taken the trouble to consult with me personally before taking their lunch break today.
Alex: Why are you always belittling me in front of everyone?
Gareth: *[London accent]* Er, Mr Barnes. Can I just say that …

Barnes: You can see that this isn't a good moment, Gareth. Alex – you can clear up that mess by the DVD display and when you've finished we'll continue our little chat in my office.

Answers 1 He left the sales counter unattended to have a break. **2** No – 'taking yet another break'; 'I've had to warn you before'; 'I've had to warn you already about your attitude problem'; 'We agreed last time'; 'Why are you always belittling me' **3** Maybe he's a bad boss; he wants everyone to know that he's in charge; he feels insecure, he thinks that humiliation may stop Alex's behaviour etc. **4** Bullying is physical or verbal abuse of someone weaker or less socially powerful than you. Yes – he knows Alex can't shout back without losing his job. No – he's only acting like this because he is responsible for the running of the store.

3 Ss read through the statements before listening and predict the answers. Play the recording and tell the Ss to note any information that helps them to answer the questions, i.e.: 1 'Don't tell me – you've had another row with Mr Barnes. What was it this time?' 2 'I was having half-an-hour lunch break, just like I do any other day.' 3 'It's just because you're a threat to him. He knows you could probably do his job better than he does.' 4 'I need to keep my head down and finish the six months for my work experience.' 5 'Gareth stuck up for me and explained that it was actually his fault that there was no one around.' 6 'I've tried to be friendly to him.' 7 'He was so cool about it.' 8 'I think he was trying to clear the air and tell me that he'd got over it, that he'd forgiven me.' Then play the recording a second time to allow them to check and complete their answers.

For tapescript see page 209.

Answers 1 F **2** F **3** T **4** T **5** T **6** F **7** T **8** T

4 Ss work in pairs to try to do the matching. Ask Ss who they think said each of the sentences (1 M, 2 A, 3 M, 4 A, 5 A, 6 A, 7 A, 8 A, 9 A). Play the recording again and elicit the answers.

Answers 1 cheesed off **2** rant and rave **3** stick up for **4** jumped down my throat **5** keep my head down **6** at the end of my tether; gets my back up **7** pick on him **8** wind him up; lose his temper **9** clear the air

Optional activity: In pairs Ss choose three of the expressions and write sentences in which they appear and their meanings are clearly shown. Then in groups of four Ss take turns reading out their sentences but not saying the expression. The other pair has to guess which expression is being used.

5 Recap on the history between Gareth and Alex (Alex bullied Gareth at school but it seems that Gareth has forgiven him and has helped him in his argument with the boss). Now look at sentence 1 with the Ss. Ask: *Did Alex come back late from*

lunch? (He said to Megan that he didn't but Gareth says he came back ten minutes late.) Ask the Ss what is going to happen next. Elicit ideas, then Ss summarise Gareth's blog. Finally, Ss write the alternative sentences. These do not have to have a completely opposite meaning to those in the exercise (eg 3 does not mention sacking at all).

Answers 2 Alex, as usual, was perfectly happy to make out it was my fault. **3** They're always at each other's throats. **4** For the first time since we started working he was forced to actually acknowledge me. **5** You've no idea how satisfying it was proving to him that I have always been a lot stronger than he is.

6 Ss write out the phrases in their notebooks. Tell them to write in the form of a dictionary entry, eg *make someone's life a misery*. They discuss what they think they mean. Elicit ideas and give definitions for Ss to make a written record.

Answers to make someone's life a misery – to be cruel to someone and make them unhappy over a period of time **there's a lot of bad blood between them** – they both have negative feelings about each other **at each other's throats** – arguing **livid** – very angry **land someone in trouble** – blame someone, act in such a way that the blame falls on someone **save one's own skin** – stop oneself from getting into trouble

7 Give Ss two minutes to discuss their views, using clues from the dialogue and from Gareth's blog. Elicit answers and justifications and allow Ss to disagree in open class if necessary.

Possible answers From what Alex says, he is sorry about bullying Gareth but from Gareth's blog it seems as if Alex is still the same, blaming Gareth unfairly and getting him into trouble. Gareth seems to be stronger, either able to forgive and forget as Alex thinks or determined to fight back as he says in his blog.

8 Ask: *What is an argument?* Elicit that it is when two or more people disagree about something and tell each other their views. It can be a very civilised debate or a loud shouting match. Tell Ss they are going to read about five different kinds of argument. Ss then read the definitions and do the matching.

Answers a 5 **b** 4 **c** 3 **d** 2 **e** 1

9 Give Ss one minute to think quietly alone about their anecdote and then put them into groups of three or four to tell each other their stories.

10 Ss read the text alone. Then in small groups they discuss what an ASBO might be. Ss then discuss the questions, guessing where they are not sure. Elicit ideas and then give Ss the correct answers if necessary.

Possible answers 1 Bullying Cheryl Martin in some way, eg sending texts repeatedly, following her, threatening her, threatening people she meets etc.

READING AND VOCABULARY

This section extends Ss' knowledge of vocabulary related to illnesses and ailments through a reading on stress.

Warm-up Review of vocabulary from the previous lesson. *Finish them.* Put the Ss into groups of three or four. Each group gets the six incomplete phrases from the previous lesson listed below. Write the 18 missing words on the board in random order and the Ss try to complete their six phrases the quickest without looking in their books. The first group who finish, shout out. They read out their phrases. If correct, the activity finishes. If they are wrong, the teacher does not say which mistakes or how many mistakes there were, the activity continues until a second group finishes.

1 *I'm _____ the _____ of my _____. (at, end, tether)*
2 *I need to _____ _____ head _____. (keep, my, down)*
3 *My boss suddenly jumped _____ _____ _____. (down, my, throat)*
4 *There's a _____ of bad _____ _____ my brother and me. (lot, blood, between)*
5 *You just wanted to save _____ _____ _____. (your, own, skin)*
6 *My mum and my sister are always _____ each _____ _____. (at, other's, throats)*

1 Put the Ss into groups of three to discuss their ideas. Tell them to write three things each on their own and then to agree on the top three as a group. When Ss get together with a second group, they each tell the other group about one of the things that makes them stressed and why it is stressful.

2 Ask Ss when they usually do quizzes such as this (they are often in magazines). Tell them to pretend they are reading a magazine. One of them finds the quiz and reads out the questions. The partner answers the questions and then the person reading the quiz agrees or disagrees and gives their answers. When Ss have found out what it means, ask who is now worried about their life and who feels more relaxed having done the quiz.

3 Put the Ss into groups of four. Ss look through the words and tell each other any that they know. Then they look up the words that no one knows. Ss predict which are connected with stress, then listen to check. After listening to the recording, Ss go back to their groups of four to discuss which of the problems they have suffered from and give any details they can.

Tapescript | CD 3 Track 9

Marina: *[Ulster accent]* Well today on *Health Matters* we're talking about stress – how to recognise it and how to beat it. I'm joined now by Dr Kate Stanley from Thamesdown University. Kate has been studying the effects of stress for the last ten years. Welcome to the programme, Kate.
Kate: *[neutral English accent]* Good afternoon.
Marina: So tell me, what are the major warning signs that someone is suffering from stress?
Kate: Well, Marina, the first thing to look at is sleeping patterns. If you're oversleeping or suffering from insomnia then it's very likely that this is caused by stress. But there are a lot of everyday ailments which may be a result of ongoing stress. I'm talking about things like headaches, mouth ulcers and back or stomach pains.
Marina: OK but things like headaches and stomachaches are very common – surely they're not always caused by stress?
Kate: No, you're right. But if you frequently have headaches or mouth ulcers then this does suggest long-term stress. Certain skin complaints like acne or eczema are also often triggered by stress. The other thing to remember is that stress produces hormones which shut down the body's immune system so a lot of stress increases the risk of various infections.
Marina: So we're more prone to suffer from things like colds or chest infections?
Kate: That's right.
Marina: What about the emotional cost of stress?
Kate: Yes, stress obviously has a huge impact on our emotional well-being. Mood swings are a classic symptom of stress as well as feeling irritable, overreacting to situations or failing to see the funny side of things. Stress also affects our ability to concentrate or retain information. What's interesting is that many people get used to these emotional symptoms without ever suspecting that something is wrong.
Marina: OK. Well let's take a break for some of your calls now. I believe we have Tonia from Tewkesbury on the line. Good morning, Tonia – what do you want to …

84 Students' Book ➡ pages 74–76

Answers acne, backache, chest infections, colds, eczema, headaches, insomnia, mood swings, mouth ulcers, oversleeping, stomachaches

Optional activity: Tell Ss that, at the beginning of the recording, the presenter said they were going to look at how to recognise stress and how to beat it. They heard how to recognise it. What ideas do the Ss think the expert will give for beating stress. Ss work in groups of four to brainstorm ideas for reducing stress and then choose two of their group to roleplay the parts of presenter and expert. They continue the discussion, the presenter asking questions and the expert answering them. The other two Ss play the parts of people phoning into the show to give their ideas for how to beat stress. Nominate one pair to act out their roleplay in front of the class and allow Ss from other groups to 'phone-in' to the show.

4 Ss can read while a recording of the text is played. However, as this is quite a lengthy text, an alternative way to do this would be to put Ss into groups of three. One student in each group reads paragraphs A and D, one B and E and one C and F. When they have finished, they summarise what they read to the other two Ss in their group. They then discuss together which of the six tips they think is the most useful and which the least useful. Elicit what tips are mentioned and ideas about the best ones as a class (tips: deep breathing; drink more water, less coffee and more tea; eat a good breakfast; listen to slower music, Baroque music is good; take exercise).

5 Tell Ss that they should first of all try to match sentences to paragraphs where possible, i.e. a is about exercise so matches with F, b and c look as if they match with E (c does not actually match here; it is about exercise (F) not music but it is good to show that this method is not infallible and that Ss still need to check carefully), d with A, e with D, f with A, g with C and h with B.

Once Ss have done that, they insert the sentences where they think they should go and then, to make sure they are correct, they should look at linguistic and grammatical clues in the sentence and the text before and after where it fits in to make sure it fits logically and grammatically.

Elicit the answers and ask how Ss can be sure that they are correct, i.e. 1 'this may be due' – *this* refers to the fact that some people thrive on stress; 2 *also* – refers to the fact that one problem with not breathing well is that you have less energy and the second problem is listed in the sentence 'your body can't deal with toxins'; 3 *instead* – refers to finding an alternative to coffee; 4 'These sugar crashes' – refers to the sudden dips in energy after eating sugary foods; 5 the inserted sentence is about people who like fast, loud music and it is followed by a contrast *However*, slower music is even more effective; 6 there is no contrast with people who do not like exercise so d does not work. Many people do one thing – *others* do something else.

Answers 1 f 2 h 3 g 4 e 5 b 6 c

6 Ss work alone with a time limit of ten minutes to complete the exercise. When they have finished, put the Ss into pairs or small groups to compare their answers and justify them if there are disagreements. Elicit answers in open class and ask why the Ss think theirs is the correct answer. If others disagree, ask them why the answer is wrong. It is important to show Ss that, in a multiple choice, it should always be possible to find why an answer is wrong, either because the text contradicts it or the information is not explicitly stated.

Justifications: 1 'stress is good for us as it keeps us on our toes' – this means we do not become complacent. Although b, c and d may all be true for some people these facts do not mean that stress is good for us. 2 'Being a student is no exception' i.e. it is the same as other times in life. Illness may be caused by stress but there is no information about students becoming ill. b is definitely wrong and d is not stated. 3 a It does not say that babies tend to sleep on their backs, just that this is when to look at them; b is not mentioned at all and, although we can see their stomachs rising, it does not say they are taking deep breaths. 4 b Sugary, fizzy drinks are bad for us but it does not say avoid all sugar; c it warns against too much coffee in the morning; d black tea helps recover from stress not concentrate. 5 a The snack replaces breakfast but is not the reason why people avoid breakfast; b not mentioned; c this is not the main problem as the level reduces again. 6 a Not mentioned; b some techno and hip-hop is also slow; c not mentioned; d 'provoke a feeling of calmness whilst boosting learning and creativity'.

Answers 1 a 2 c 3 c 4 a 5 d 6 d

7 Tell Ss to look at the highlighted words without looking at the synonyms in Exercise 7. Ss work in pairs to try to guess the meaning from context and then look at the synonyms to do the matching.

Answers 1 conducive to 2 adage 3 thrive 4 prolonged 5 sustenance 6 well-being 7 alleviate 8 self-esteem

8 Before Ss look at the exercise, read out the first heading: *Lacking energy or enthusiasm.* Ask half the Ss to mime this feeling and then elicit other adjectives from the watching Ss that could also describe the students who were miming, eg *bored, fed-up, slow, lazy* etc. Repeat with *Anxious* and elicit, eg *nervous, worried*. Then tell the Ss to imagine you are going to play some baroque music to calm them down. They think of more adjectives for the music, eg *boring, relaxing, quiet*. Finally, tell them to imagine they are drinking an energy drink. How could they describe what it does to them, eg *livens them up, wakes them up* etc. Ss then look at the words in pairs and do the matching, using the text if necessary.

9 Tell Ss to try to talk on each topic for thirty seconds so that they do not just give one word answers. Nominate Ss to answer questions in open class.

10 Ss try to work out the words in pairs without looking at the text. They then find the collocations to check. Elicit the answers and what the words mean: a *recurring nightmare* is a bad dream you have more than once, *common knowledge* is something known by most people, a *detrimental effect* means it causes harm, *under pressure* means that Ss have pressure on them, *red alert* means it is an emergency situation, *skip lunch* means go without it, *speaks volumes* means it tells us a lot.

11 One way to do this would be to continue the roleplay idea suggested after Exercise 3. Tell the Ss that they are now themselves and have been invited onto a radio show to talk about how they deal with stress. The students take it in turns to play the role of presenter asking their partner their tips for coping with stress.

ADDITIONAL PRACTICE: Photocopiable resources. Resource 19: *Stop stress.* Page 186

GRAMMAR

This section introduces impersonal reporting structures.

Special difficulties: The students should know these structures but there may be some confusion with different combinations of tenses, eg *It **has been said** that **there was** more violence in society twenty years ago. It **is believed** that society **has changed** over the last thirty years.* It is important that Ss understand exactly what each part of the sentence is referring to and why that tense is needed.

Culture notes

UCL (University College, London) was founded in 1826 and is ranked in the top ten universities worldwide. There are about 25,000 students at the university which has colleges throughout London. Its alumni include Gandhi, Alexander Graham Bell, comedian Ricky Gervais and several members of the band Coldplay.

Amy Winehouse (born 1983) is an English singer most famous for her problems with drugs. She has suffered from depression, self-harm and eating disorders. Her debut album was released in 2003 and her second album, *Back to Black*, was the best-selling album in Britain in 2007.

Warm-up Review of vocabulary from the previous lesson.
Spot the error. Tell the Ss that you are going to write ten words from the previous lesson on the board. Six of them will be spelt incorrectly. The Ss work in groups of four and try to identify which are correct and which are wrong and rewrite the incorrect words. When Ss have finished, elicit the correct spellings and the meanings of each word.
Words to use:
  1 *anarexia (anorexia)*
  2 *eczema* ✓
  3 *condusive (conducive)*
  4 *sustinance (sustenance)*
  5 *sluggish* ✓
  6 *lethargic* ✓
  7 *invigerating (invigorating)*
  8 *recuring (recurring)*
  9 *detrimental* ✓
  10 *aleviate (alleviate)*

1 Before Ss look at the exercise, ask them why we use the passive form. Elicit ideas, eg because the agent is unknown or unimportant, because we want to emphasise the action not the agent. Ss then look at the sentences and answer the questions.

Work it out

2 When Ss have completed the gaps, look at the different tenses that could be used and why.

It is said (regularly)
It has been said (at some time in the past)
It was said (at a specific time in the past)

Black tea is found to (general fact)
Black tea has been found to (at some time in the past)
Black tea was found to (at a specific time in the past)

Answers 1 *that*-clause **2** infinitive clause

3 It may be a good idea for Ss not only to list just the reporting verbs used but the whole of the structure so they can see the different tenses used. **Note:** *The Chinese are thought to have known about* ... This is a slightly different form which will be looked at in Exercise 4.

Answers patterns It is often said that ..., it is estimated that ..., this is believed to be ..., It is generally recommended that ..., fizzy drinks are understood to leach minerals from your body, research has shown that ..., The Chinese are thought to have known ..., studies have suggested that ..., Black tea has been found to ..., young people are thought to be ..., It has been demonstrated that ..., Music with repetitive melodies or rhythms is also supposed to ..., Listening to music that has 60 beats per minute has been shown to ..., endorphins are thought to be produced ...
reporting verbs believe, recommend, understand, suggest, find, think, demonstrate, suppose, show

4 Remind Ss what was said earlier about different tenses being possible. Look at the examples and ask Ss to write the two sentences in active forms: *People think that the Chinese knew about tea ... People think that more and more young people are skipping breakfast.*
Point out that, in the first half of the sentences, the verb *think* is in the Present Simple but the second parts are in the Past Simple and the Present Continuous. Elicit the answers to the questions in the exercise.

Answers 1 The first half follows the same pattern but the infinitive clause changes: in the Past Simple it is *to + have* + past participle; in the continuous form it is *to + be + -ing* form. **2** before: *to + have* + past participle; continuing: *to + be + -ing* form

Check it out

Refer Ss to the Check it out section on page 157 and tell them to use this if they have any problems with the next two exercises.

5 Ss work in pairs. Tell them to first identify the tense(s) used in the original sentences and make sure the transformation sentence agrees with these. Go through the answers and the reasons for the tenses used: 1 the Present Simple is used twice; 2 the belief is true now but the identification was in the past; 3 the finding was in the past but the finding is still true today – the Present Simple sounds better but a past form may also be acceptable; 4 both the feeling and the pressure were in the past; 5 the showing is in the Present Perfect, the result of it, the unwinding, is generally true.

Answers 1 Stress is often said to be a fact of life. **2** Stress is believed to have been first identified as a medical condition in 1936. **3** It was found that brisk exercise speeds up (sped up) recovery from stress. **4** Many students were felt to have been under pressure. **5** It has been shown that baroque music helps you unwind.

6 Look at the example sentences about Amy Winehouse and elicit why these tenses have been used. Ss should now be able to work alone and then to compare answers in pairs.

Answers 2 The government is expected to lose the next election. It is likely that the government will lose the next election. **3** They are thought to be getting married. It is thought that they are getting married. **4** He's said to have resigned. It is said that he has resigned. **5** They are rumoured to be living in London now. It is rumoured that they are living in London now. **6** Chamomile tea is claimed to help you (to) get to sleep. It is claimed that chamomile tea helps you (to) get to sleep. **7** A stressful classroom atmosphere was believed to have been conducive to learning. It was believed that a stressful classroom atmosphere was conducive to learning. **8** They are reported to have survived the accident. It is reported that they (have) survived the accident.

7 Give Ss thirty seconds to quickly read through the text and find out what it is about. Elicit ideas (it is about the part of the brain which enables us to enjoy activities which are frightening). Ss then complete the text alone.

Answers 1 is **2** to have benefited **3** have identified **4** to be **5** will bring

8 Set a time limit of two minutes per question for the Ss to discuss their answers. Elicit ideas in open class.

ADDITIONAL PRACTICE: Photocopiable resources. Resource 20: *Rumours and lies.* Pages 187–188

LISTENING AND SPEAKING

This section introduces ways of being assertive but sensitive when talking to people in difficult situations.

Warm-up Review of impersonal reporting structures. *It is believed …* Tell Ss to write down on a slip of paper an opinion that they hold on any subject, eg *I think that reality TV is rubbish.* Collect them in and put Ss into pairs. Hand out two opinions to each pair. The Ss now have to rewrite the opinions in impersonal form: one starting with *It …* (*It is thought that reality TV is rubbish.*) and the other starting with the subject (*Reality TV is thought to be rubbish.*). Elicit opinions and allow other Ss to disagree with them if they wish.

1 Check the meaning of *to nick* (steal), *blaring* (very loud) and then allow two minutes for Ss to discuss the irritating habits and try to order them from most to least annoying. Elicit ideas and discuss when you may have to share a flat (eg students) and any examples they may know (eg on holidays with friends or stories their older brothers or sisters have told them about student life).

2 Ss again work in pairs to discuss the questions. Elicit ideas in open class.

> **Answers 1** Chrissy and the people the email was sent to all share a flat. Chrissy is obviously upset because there are often dirty dishes left unwashed. **3** eg talking face to face, organising a cleaning rota

3 Give Ss two minutes to discuss the questions in pairs and elicit ideas before Ss listen to the recording. Tell Ss to note key words while they listen the first time, eg *pathetic, laziest* etc. Ss may note down words which come up in Exercise 4. If so, try to avoid giving definitions at this stage. After the recording, Ss compare words and discuss the answers. Then they listen a second time to check their ideas.

Tapescript CD 3 Track 11

Susan: *[neutral English accent]* Come in! Hi, Justine. Nice to see you again. Take a seat. Did you manage to sort out your problems with your lecturers?

Justine: *[Yorkshire accent]* Yes, I did, thanks. I'm really glad I listened to your advice actually.

Susan: So things are looking up, then?

Justine: Well, not entirely … Well, you see it's my flatmate, Chrissy, again. I was sitting studying in my room the other night and suddenly I got an email. Chrissy had just sent it to everyone else in the flat, although she was sitting in her room next door, just a few metres away!

Susan: And what was the email about?

Justine: It was full of patronising instructions about how to 'wash up'. It was her way of telling us to keep

---

the kitchen tidy. But why couldn't she have just spoken to us in person – we were all at the flat at the time? Why did she have to beat around the bush with her pathetic email about how to wash up? She's been doing this sort of thing for ages. Every time I get home from college I come across Chrissy's little whinging notes all over the flat. 'In future, please don't leave your things on the sofa.' 'It was Justine's turn to buy toilet roll (that's why there isn't any!).' I know it sounds really trivial but it just makes my blood boil! The thing is – she's probably the laziest person in the flat. She's got no right to nag us about the washing-up! It was just a few plates, for God's sake!

Susan: It isn't trivial at all. It's one of the most difficult things about being a student away from home. Not being able to rub along with the people you live with can be extremely stressful. And did you talk to Chrissy about how her notes were making you feel?

Justine: No, I didn't. What I actually did was make about twenty little notes of my own and I stuck them everywhere in the kitchen – on the cupboard doors, on the microwave, on the fridge, even on the communal jar of coffee! I suppose I was just trying to get my own back! I have to say I really enjoyed doing it!

Susan: What Chrissy is doing in her notes and emails is what we psychologists call passive-aggressive behaviour.

Justine: It's funny – Carol, the girl in the flat who's studying psychology, is always saying that Chrissy is passive-aggressive.

Susan: Yes, it's very common. And people like that can be notoriously difficult to deal with. But I'm afraid to say what you did, putting up even more messages in the kitchen, is also a very passive-aggressive response.

Justine: Oh!

> **Answers 1** She's angry. **2** No. It's very important to be able to get along together and one of the most stressful situations for people living away from home for the first time. **3** By putting up notes of her own to get her own back.

4 Ss discuss their ideas in pairs. Tell them to guess the most likely meaning if they do not know. Elicit ideas in open class.

> **Answers** 1 f 2 b 3 g 4 e 5 a 6 d 7 c

5 Set a time limit of five minutes for Ss to discuss the questions. Elicit answers in open class and point out that *to rub along with* and *to beat around the bush* are less common than the other expressions.

6 Before Ss look at the exercise, write the four personality types on the board. Elicit which type Chrissy and Justine are (passive-aggressive) and how this is shown (they do not confront each other face to face but send each other emails and notes). Ss then discuss what they think the other three personality types are like. Give Ss two minutes to read through the notes and predict the missing words. Then play the recording.

Students' Book ➡ pages 78–79

Tapescript CD 3 Track 12

Susan: Before you can start understanding your relationship with Chrissy, I think you need to realise what your behaviour looks like to others. As I said, you both have a tendency to be passive-aggressive which, as the name suggests, means you behave as both a victim and an aggressive person at the same time.

Justine: I'd hate to think of myself as aggressive! My Mum's really aggressive and I go out of my way to avoid copying what she does!

Susan: You know, you don't have to shout at people or threaten them or even hit them to be aggressive – an aggressive person will often use tactless comments and also gossip and sarcasm to attack people. If you're aggressive, your own reputation is the most important thing. You want to win in every situation and that means that someone else has got to lose. An aggressive person does this by simply ignoring other people's feelings and wishes.

Justine: Hmm. And what's the typical behaviour for a victim?

Susan: Well, this is what we call the passive personality. Someone who is always negative and full of self-pity, who tends to feel they've been unlucky in life – but because of other people or even fate and not because of their own bad choices. They tend to accept being treated badly and don't complain.

Justine: In other words, a bit of a doormat!

Susan: Yes, exactly. And aggressive people often enjoy dealing with people like this because they're guaranteed an easy win.

Justine: It's all very depressing! So you're saying that Chrissy and I are both acting like these types of people at once?

Susan: In a sense, yes. You're both very aggressive with each other but you do it in quite a passive, indirect way. Chrissy chose to write that email and leave notes around the flat rather than speak to you directly. And she's using the notes to defend her reputation as someone who's sensible and reliable but also suggesting that she's a victim – that poor Chrissy had to clean up everyone's mess. And this made you very angry – but instead of telling her, you got your revenge indirectly by parodying her notes.

Justine: I see.

Susan: Responding to someone's anger or criticism by lightly making fun of them is a very passive-aggressive thing to do and sometimes this sort of joke works really well. But it probably didn't in this case.

Justine: Well, everyone else in the flat thought it was hilarious! To be honest, Susan, I thought I came here today to try and sort out my problems with my flatmate and not to find out I've got a deeply-flawed personality.

Susan: Justine, you aren't 'deeply-flawed' in the slightest. This behaviour we've been talking about is very common. You can probably think of several people you know who never tell you what they're thinking, who reject good advice or never return phone calls. It's all passive-aggressive behaviour. The good news is that once you're aware of it, it's quite easy to change it.

Justine: Yeah?

Susan: Yes. You need to learn to be more assertive. In other words, your priority is to make sure that people understand what you want from them, but you don't hurt their feelings.

Answers 1 gossip 2 reputation 3 ignore 4 their own 5 complains 6 rather than 7 to reject 8 return 9 doesn't

7 In order not to hurt people's feelings, it may be a good idea to tell Ss before they start not to use people in the class as examples. Ss think alone for a minute about two different people and then share their ideas.

SPEAK OUT

8 Go through the Speak Out box with the Ss. Give an example: a new employee in an office has decided to try to help the manager by collecting all his papers on his desk and has then tripped over and dropped them all. The manager could shout: *You stupid idiot!* Or he could say: *I realise you were only trying to help but I really do think that it would be better if you sat down and let me sort my own papers out.*

For tapescript see page 209.

Answers I really appreciate that she; You've got every right to be annoyed about; I realise you're the kind of person who prefers to; I really do think you; Don't you agree it would be better if; I was wondering whether; I was really hoping

9 Tell student A to look at situations 1 and 3 and think about how to express them assertively and B to look at situations 2 and 4. Ss roleplay the situations and then listen to the recording.

Tapescript CD 3 Track 14

1 *[Manchester accent]* I realise you're having a hard time at the moment and this might not be a good moment to mention this, but when will you be paying me back that £30 I lent you?

2 *[Ulster accent]* I appreciate that music is really important to you. But I really do think you should turn the volume down a bit in the evenings.

3 *[Southern English accent]* I realise you have my best interests at heart but I was really hoping you'd let me stay out later tonight. All my friends are allowed to.

4 *[neutral English accent]* I appreciate you're trying your best at the moment but I couldn't help but notice that the standard of your work seems to have declined a bit recently. Is everything OK?

10 Give Ss two minutes to look through the situations and decide what they are going to say and then they roleplay them. Nominate one or two pairs to act out their roleplays in open class.

ADDITIONAL PRACTICE: Photocopiable resources. Resource 21: *A talk with Tom.* Page 189

WRITING

This section gives tips on how to write an information sheet looking at the style and organisation necessary.

Culture notes

The earliest known example of the word **troll** in Internet use was in 1991. It could come from the Swedish mythological characters who were obnoxious and wicked. The verb *troller* in French means *to hunt* and this could also be where the word originates as it was used *to troll for newbies*, i.e. new users of an Internet site.

The first newspaper article to ever use the phrase **'happy slapping'** was 'Bullies film fights by phone', published in *The Times Educational Supplement* in 2005. At first, the attacks were seen as fun, surprises but they have become increasingly violent and occasionally have caused death.

Lubelszczyzna is an area of Eastern Poland around the city of Lublin. It includes the famous tourist town of Kazimierz Dolny situated on the River Wisła.

Warm-up Lead-in to the topic of the lesson. *The web and us.* Elicit ways of receiving and sending electronic information, eg texts, phone calls, email, website, blog, photo albums, school reunion sites (eg Friends Reunited), personal information sites (eg Facebook, My Space), webcams, forums etc. Ss write down which they have got and which they look at. Ss then work in groups to discuss any problems there can be with any of these, eg receiving texts from people you do not like, negative comments on your blog site etc. Ss discuss these for two or three minutes and then talk about things they have heard about or experienced.

1 Set a time limit of three minutes for Ss to read through the text and make sure they understand it. Then they discuss the questions in pairs. Elicit answers in open class and discuss what things that they discussed in the warm-up may be called cyberbullying.

Answers 1 Cyberbullying is bullying someone through the Internet or mobile phone.

2 Ss work alone to complete the multiple choice task and then compare answers in pairs. Ss then make a written record of the useful vocabulary:
a proportion – *one **in** three/one **in** four* etc
The study reveals (shows) that ...
*abuse/photos/information **on** websites/forums/blogs* etc
make something available online.

Answers 1 c **2** b **3** d **4** b **5** b **6** a **7** c **8** d

3 Ss listen to the recording and make notes about the two problems and the responses. Then they compare answers and listen again to check.

Tapescript `CD 3 Track 15`

One – Dan

Dan: *[neutral English accent]* I was a huge fan of The Beatles and I came across a great website with a message board for Beatles fans. There were people of all ages – my age, or even younger, as well as people in their 50s and 60s – and from all over the world too. People just shared their love of the music and how old you were and where you were from just didn't seem to matter. For several months I was completely hooked and made loads of online friends. Then suddenly out of the blue a guy kept on attacking me on the message board for no apparent reason – he'd write abusive comments, ridicule me – in other words, he was what you'd call an Internet troll and it all started to get a bit personal. He got hold of my email address and started sending me abusive emails as well. People told me just to ignore the troll and he'd go away but to be honest I just deleted all the emails and basically stopped visiting the message board altogether. In fact, it sort of put me off the Internet a bit and I suppose I've gone off The Beatles as well. A shame, although I was spending too much time on there anyway!

Two – Emily

Emily: *[neutral English accent]* It all started a couple of years ago, just after Christmas. Everyone in my class seemed to have got camera phones for Christmas so when we went back to school everyone was suddenly really into filming everything – you know, mucking around with your friends, sitting on the school bus, waiting for classes to start, that kind of thing. Then a group of girls that I wasn't particularly friendly with started picking on me in the school cloakrooms and one of them filmed it with her phone. Well, that was pretty horrible but worse was to come. They put the film up on one of those video-hosting sites on the Internet and invited everyone to write nasty comments. I was pretty distraught. My friends told me to contact the web page administrator and ask them to remove the film and the comments. They did eventually, but it took several weeks, and by then the damage had been done.

Answers Dan A troll. Attacked him on a message board and by email. He deleted the emails and stopped visiting the message board. He ignored the messages which was good but he shouldn't have deleted them as he might have needed them for evidence.
Emily A mobile phone film posted on the Internet. She contacted the web administrator and got the film removed eventually. Yes, she was right to contact the web administrator.

4 Tell Ss to cover the Train Your Brain box. Ss work in pairs and justify their answers by finding examples in the text. Elicit answers and reasons for them in open class. Do not give any answers at this point as Ss will check them in the Train Your Brain box.

TRAIN YOUR BRAIN

5 Go through the Train Your Brain box with the Ss. Elicit examples for each of the points: 1 The title is 'Alarming Rise in Cyberbullying'. 2 Eg 'don't be tempted to drop your guard'; 'You may later need them as evidence'. 3 'It is generally agreed that ...'; 'give out details'; 'take down offensive material'; 'That can be fun too!'. 4 The first paragraph which tells us how many people suffer (one in three), examples of the problems (abuse on personal websites, forums, bullies using mobile phones etc). 5 Introduction – 'How to deal with cyberbullying', 'Prevention is better than cure'; 'If you have been a victim of cyberbullying'. 6 The fact that resting from the Internet can be fun.

Answers 1 a leaflet 2 neutral but friendly 3 the purpose of the information sheet 4 the opening sentence 5 optimistic

6 Ss underline key words and clues in the texts which help them to answer the questions, then discuss them in pairs. Elicit ideas and how the Ss know, i.e. A has been produced by people within the Lubelszczyzna region as it is referred to as 'our region'. B has probably been written by a students' organisation at one specific university. Tips about accommodation and a city are too specific for general information for students and the tone is too informal for it to have been produced by the university itself. A is giving recommendations about the main attractions of the region. This may include advice but not reassurance as that would imply there was something off-putting about the area in the first place. B does give practical ideas and suggestions about making friends, accommodation and the city and also tries to reassure nervous new students.

Answers 1 A – local government or tourist board; B – a student organisation at a university 2 A – tourists; B – students 3 A – practical ideas and suggestions; B – advice and reassurance and practical ideas and suggestions

7 Set a time limit of ten minutes for Ss to discuss and plan the information required. Tell each student to make their own notes as they will be working on their own later. When they have finished, ask each group what they have decided. Each group presents their ideas to the class giving reasons for their choices of headings and the information they want to include. When all the groups have finished, allow a further two minutes for Ss to add or change ideas based on what they heard from the other groups in the class.

8 Ss now work alone to write their information sheet, either in class or at home.

Optional activity: When Ss have finished their information essays, they get back together into their planning groups and swap essays with a second group. Each person reads one of the essays and then tells the people in their group their views on how well it was written, the information contained, the style of the language and the organisation. The Ss then work together to say which they think is the best essay and why.

Getting around

Read, listen and talk about travel, tourism, money.
Practise participle clauses; words and expressions connected with travelling.
Focus on using clichés.
Write a report.

EXAM FOCUS

Topic: Travel, tourism and money

Speaking
Problem solving: SB p.83, ex.9

Listening
True/False: SB p.84, ex.4

Reading
Multiple choice: SB p.87, ex.3

Grammar and vocabulary
Sentence transformations: SB p.85, ex.7
Verbs in brackets: SB p.85, ex.6

Writing
A report: SB p.91, ex.8

Unit 8 Materials

Success Workbook Unit 8

Photocopiable resources 22, 23, 24

Testing and Evaluation Programme tests

VOCABULARY AND SPEAKING

This section introduces collocations and idioms on the topic of travel.

Culture notes

The Avenue des Champs Élysées is a 2km long road in Paris which runs from the Place de la Concord to the Arc du Triomphe.

Leicester Square is an area of central London. It contains the cinema with the most seats in Britain (1,600) and with the largest screen.

The CouchSurfing network is the largest hospitality network on the Internet. It was launched on 1 January 2004 and by August 2008 had 700,000 members in 232 countries. Membership is free and there is no payment for accommodation swaps between members.

Warm-up Lead-in to the topic of the lesson. *Best holiday advice.* Put Ss into groups of three or four. Tell Ss that they want to go on holiday to a big city like London or Paris but haven't got much money. You are going to give them one word and they must think of some advice about the holiday. Give an example to start, eg *travel* could give the following advice: *travel by bus, don't travel at the weekend, book your travel in advance* etc.
Words to give: *coffee, theatre, restaurants, passport, trains, backpack, museums, discounts*

1 Tell Ss to cover the travel tips to stop them reading ahead. Set a time limit of one minute for Ss to quickly read the introduction and discuss the heading. Elicit ideas and clues in the paragraph but do not give the meaning of the highlighted or underlined words yet.

> **Answers** To live on very little money.

2 Set a time limit of five minutes for Ss to read and discuss the tips. Ss try to agree as a class on the five most useful tips.

3 Ss read the sentences containing the underlined phrasal verbs in the text and try to work out what they mean and what word they could be replaced by. Then they look at Exercise 3 to see what words are given. Finally, they rewrite the sentences in Exercise 3 using the phrasal verbs.

> **Answers** 1 rip you off 2 get by 3 put someone up; check out 4 messed up 5 show you around 6 come across

4 Look at the first two highlighted phrases with the whole class: *cost the earth* and *money to burn*. Elicit what these mean, using the context of the sentences to help: *cost the earth* – be very expensive; *money to burn* – a lot of money, more than you need. Ss then do the same for the other phrases: *get a much better deal* – find cheaper prices; *cost an arm and a leg* – be very expensive; *made of money* – rich; *save a fortune* – save a lot of money; *book in advance* – buy tickets a long time before your holiday; *good value for money* – cheap for the benefits it can bring; *entitles you to discounts* – gives you money off. Then Ss do Exercise 4.

> **Answers** 1 cost an arm and a leg/cost the earth 2 entitles you to discounts 3 save a fortune/get a much better deal 4 money to burn 5 get a much better deal/save a fortune 6 cost the earth/cost an arm and a leg 7 book in advance 8 made of money 9 good value for money

5 Ss work in pairs to guess the odd one out in each group. Elicit the answers and the meanings of all the

---

collocations, eg *airport taxes* – money added to the cost of your plane ticket to pay for the airport.

Answers 1 budget 2 bargain 3 income 4 coin
5 interest 6 off-peak

6 Ss look through the questions. Check: *dilemma* (a problem; choice of alternative actions to take). Ask further questions, eg *Where did she start her journey from?* (Sheffield) *When did she start work?* (May) *What is her mum worrying about?* (Claire is travelling alone) etc.

Tapescript CD 3 Track 16

[Yorkshire accent] Hi, this is Claire speaking. I'm in Sheffield bus station and it's the twelfth of July. I'm fed up with the drizzle and the gusty winds of a Yorkshire summer so I'm heading for the blue skies and scorching sunshine of southern France. I only started working in May, so I can't afford one of those package holidays at exorbitant prices. But I booked my flight well in advance so I got a much better deal and thanks to CouchSurfing my accommodation won't cost the earth – in fact, if everything goes to plan, it won't cost me a thing. My Mum's worried about me travelling alone, but I know I'll be fine as long as I keep my eyes peeled. I'm travelling light – just one small rucksack that weighs only 9 kilos. It's a pity I've only got a week off, I'm sure I'm going to have a great time.

During the flight: July 12th

I'm furious 'cause I got ripped off at the airport. At the check-in, I had to pay a supplement because of the airport taxes. That's typical of budget airlines. You can get really great bargain rates on the net, but then you have to pay all sorts of extras.

At Yvette's in Nimes, Southern France: July 13th
My CouchSurfing host is called Yvette and she's lovely and so are her family. They're like friends already. It's so nice of them to put me up. They're not made of money, but they're not hard-up either, and they've got a big flat in the city centre. Yvette showed me round town this morning. It's just as well I brought my student card because it entitled me to a discount on the admission fee to all the Roman ruins. They're amazing. There's nothing like that in Sheffield!

Nimes: July 15th

Yvette's like me. We're both very careful with our money – when we have a drink, we always sit at the counter of the café 'cause it's cheaper. You can save a fortune that way. But last night Yvette's cousin, Luc took us out to a really pricey restaurant. When we saw the menu, we didn't want to go in, but Luc insisted. He must have money to burn, because it cost an arm and a leg, but he wouldn't let me pay my share, not even the service charge! I'm supposed to be going to Marseilles tomorrow to stay with my next CouchSurfing host and I've got my flight back home next Sunday. But Yvette and Luc want me to stay until the end of the summer! Luc says he can get me a job. I don't know what to do.

Suggested answers 1 To the south of France. To get some good weather. 2 She had to pay airport taxes which she didn't know about. 3 Lovely, like friends, not very rich. 4 Whether to go home as she had planned or to stay in the south of France for the summer and get a job there.

7 Ss work in pairs to think of what words could go into the gaps. Elicit ideas and then play the recording again for Ss to check their answers.

Answers 1 exorbitant prices; better deal; cost the earth 2 airport taxes; budget airlines; bargain rates 3 made of money 4 to a discount; admission fee 5 save a fortune 6 money to burn; arm and a leg; service charge

8 Tell Ss to make a list of advantages and disadvantages of staying in France (eg she improves her French) or going home (eg she still has a job). After playing the recording, ask Ss if they think she has made the correct choice.

Tapescript CD 3 Track 17

Claire: ... and this guy, Luc, he ...
Mum: *[Yorkshire accent]* Her cousin?
Claire: Yes, he's got tons of money and he says he's got a friend who can get me a job.
Mum: What kind of job?
Claire: Working in a sea-life centre. It sounds like a lot of fun and the working hours are ...
Mum: What's the money like?
Claire: About the same as I'm getting at home.
Mum: Oh!
Claire: What do you think I should do, Mum?
Mum: Well, if it's just for the summer, and ...
Claire: It is.
Mum: ... you're coming back in September, then why not?
Claire: Oh Mum, that's just what I wanted to hear! Hey, maybe you and Dad could come ...

Answers She decides to stay in France for the summer.

9 Set a time limit of about five minutes for Ss to find the information and answer the questions. Ss then discuss the advantages and disadvantages of CouchSurfing and whether they would use it.

Answers 1 An organisation that lets travellers find people who can give them a room to sleep in. 2 Casey Fenton sent messages to students in Iceland and had a great holiday there sleeping in someone's garage. 3 You offer a place in your home and search for places you want to go to. 4 It's free. 5 Usually young and single but not always. 6 They meet interesting people. 7 No. Also advice and friendship. 8 Checks of names and addresses, descriptions, reviews of people and recommendations to meet and get to know people before staying with them.

10 Elicit some general ideas for advice, eg cheap places to eat and stay, free museums or other attractions etc. Ss then make a list of advice and discuss their ideas as a class.

ADDITIONAL PRACTICE: Photocopiable resources. Resource 22: *Travellers' forum.* Page 190

GRAMMAR AND LISTENING

This section introduces participle clauses.

Special difficulties: Ss may be confused by the number of different structures but, at this stage, they should not be expected to use them in freer writing but to be able to recognise them and use them in transformations or cloze exercises.

Culture notes

John Harrison (1693–1776) was an English clock maker. The H1, H2, H3 and H4 clocks were rediscovered after the First World War. They were restored and are now on view in the National Maritime Museum in Greenwich.

The Scilly Isles are a group of five inhabited, and numerous uninhabited, islands lying about 45km off the south-western tip of England. They are a popular holiday resort and enjoy a very mild climate, allowing the local flower industry to be able to produce plants earlier than other areas of the country. Only one of the five islands, St Mary's, allows cars. The total population of the islands is about 2,100.

Sir Edmond Halley (1656–1742) was an English astronomer, mathematician and physicist. He studied at Oxford and produced papers on the solar system and sunspots. He is best remembered because of the comet which takes his name which appears in the sky approximately every 75 years.

Greenwich is a district on the south bank of the River Thames in London. It is most famous as being the site of the Greenwich Meridian, the place which has a longitude of 0. This was established in 1851 and also led to the use of Greenwich Mean Time. Other sites in Greenwich are the National Maritime Museum and the Royal Observatory.

Warm-up Review of idioms and collocations from the previous lesson. *Find your partner.* Give each student (up to a maximum of 20) one of the words or phrases listed below. Tell Ss that they have to find someone with words or phrases with the same meaning as theirs. Ss all get up and mingle, telling others their words. When they have found their partner, they sit down. Elicit all the phrases and make sure Ss have the correct partners.

Words to use:
service charge – tip
cost a fortune – expensive
mess up – spoil
ripped off – charged too much
get by – survive
put up – offer a room to sleep in
off-peak – not the busiest time of day
bargain rates – cheap prices
check out – verify
find by accident – come across

1 Elicit the answers and ask Ss what the words are in L1. Ask Ss if anyone knows their own city's map reference in terms of longitude and latitude.

Answers 1 b **2** a

2 Set a time limit of two minutes for Ss to find the answers. Elicit the answers and ask Ss if they know anything else about longitude and latitude, eg that Greenwich in London is on the line of zero longitude and the Equator is the line of zero latitude.

Answers 1 Because clocks weren't able to keep true time at sea. To know the degree of longitude, sailors needed to know the time where they were and in the port of departure. **2** Four ships sailed onto rocks and 2,000 sailors were drowned. **3** They offered a prize of £20,000 for a way to calculate longitude.

3 Ss look at the three questions. Elicit the information they are listening out for and how difficult or easy it may be, eg 1 a number, should be straightforward; 2 they have to listen out for reports on all the clocks and what is said about them or it may just give a number; 3 probably, after hearing about his inventions, there will be a final summing up which may use linkers such as *However* or *Although* to show that he did not really solve the problem or it may say something like *Therefore* or *Due to this* to show that he did. Ss listen and note the clues which helped them.

For tapescript see page 210.

Answers 1 Four **2** Two (H1 and H4) **3** Yes

4 Allow Ss time to read the statements and try to remember what they heard. Ss discuss their ideas in pairs, then listen to the recording again. Ss make notes while they listen and compare notes with their partner after listening. Elicit answers and justifications: 1 'But I believe that I can make a clock that will keep time on board ship.'; 2 'My clock works and it works well (...). But it lost 5 to 10 seconds a day, which is not good enough.'; 3 'thought the problem of longitude could only be solved by careful study of the moon and the stars'; 4 'to their surprise, the astronomers were not convinced. They ordered another trial to the West Indies.'; 5 'feeling sure they had won the prize'; 6 'convinced that his own method of calculating longitude through observations of the moon should win the prize'; 7 'it is thirty years since I first appeared in front of this board and in all that time I have never spoken to one man who had the slightest understanding of my clocks'; 8 'Finally, in 1773, thanks to the insistence of the King, John Harrison received the full £20,000.'

Answers 1 F **2** F **3** T **4** F **5** T **6** F **7** F **8** F

Work it out

5 When Ss have completed the matching, go through the different types of clauses and elicit further examples, eg reduced relative clause: *I saw a man who was breaking into our house.* Present participle clause: *When he looked Looking at the clock, he realised he was late.* Participle clause with a preposition: *Because he worked hard By working hard, he was able to pass his exams.* etc.

Answers 1 a 2 b 3 e 4 d 5 c 6 a

6 Look at the first sentence of the text with the Ss and elicit the full form: *The solution which was proposed by the man who was standing in front of Astronomer Royal Sir Edmond Halley involved the 'Powder of Sympathy'.* Elicit that both gaps are examples of reduced relative clauses and that the words: *which was* and *who was* can be removed, and the two verbs in brackets need a past participle and a present participle. Ss then complete the exercise in pairs.

Answers 1 proposed 2 standing 3 cut 4 making 5 knowing 6 Having dismissed 7 seeing 8 telling 9 allowing 10 having listened 11 forced

7 Ss can now work alone to rewrite the sentences. Elicit the answers and what kind of clause each is. Point out that, sometimes, it is difficult to know whether to use a present or a past participle clause. In sentences 2 and 8, either could be used, the present participle clause making the decision sound more immediate than the past participle clause. Types of participle clauses: 1 reduced relative clause, 2 past participle clause, 3 reduced relative clause, 4 present participle clause, 5 present participle clause, 6 present participle clause, 7 past participle clause, 8 present or past participle clause.

Answers 1 The money offered was a vast fortune for most people. 2 Having heard of the prize, many people proposed solutions. 3 Some of the solutions proposed were very strange. 4 Measuring only five inches wide, H4 is the most famous timepiece ever made. 5 Arguing that one trial was insufficient, the Board ordered another trial. 6 Going to the meeting, they felt sure they had won the prize./Feeling sure they had won the prize, they went to the meeting. 7 Having dedicated his whole life to his clocks, Harrison felt cheated. 8 Having heard the story/Hearing the story, the king decided to act.

8 Tell Ss to look at the sentence and decide what the *ticking* refers to. Elicit the answer and, before Ss look at the Mind the trap! box, try to elicit why it is wrong and how it should be written (*Ticking loudly, the clock was admired by the king.*).

Answers It is the clock that is ticking, not the king.

Mind the trap!

Go through the Mind the trap! box with the Ss and elicit what the crossed out sentence would mean (that the ship was looking through a telescope).

Check it out

Refer Ss to the Check it out section on page 157 and tell them to use it if they are having problems with the next exercise.

9 Tell Ss to work in pairs and to read the sentences carefully to see if the participles at the beginning of the sentences have the same subject as the other clauses and, if not, what the sentence would mean, i.e. 1 William was tested by the other astronomer not the watch; 3 Harrison had been made with incredible precision; 4 George III wrote the letter to the King (himself).
Elicit the correct answers in open class.

Suggested answers 1 Tested by another astronomer, the watch worked well and pleased William. 2 ✓ 3 Made with incredible precision, Harrison's clocks made him proud. 4 After writing a letter to the King, William was contacted by George III. 5 ✓

10 Allow Ss one minute to think alone about one invention and the reasons they could not live without it. Ss then get into groups of four or five and work together to discuss their ideas and try to agree as a group on the most important and the reasons why. Elicit from each group the most important invention according to their group.

ADDITIONAL PRACTICE: Photocopiable resources. Resource 23: *What's the story?* Page 191

SPEAKING

This section introduces some common clichés in English.

Warm-up Review of participle and other clauses. *Finish the sentence.* Tell Ss that you are going to begin some sentences and that the students should finish them alone. When they have finished, Ss get into groups to compare ideas and make sure everyone has written their sentences correctly. Elicit sentences in open class.

Possible starts:
Not knowing the answer,
The boy talking to my girlfriend,
Having heard about my friend's problems,
Not concentrating on the lesson,
Having forgotten my PE kit,
Since waking up this morning,

1 Set a time limit of two minutes for the activity and then elicit answers in open class. Ask Ss to think of examples from real life that illustrate these meanings, eg (a) people who reply to email scams which say they have won a lottery without having taken part or that someone has chosen them and wants to transfer millions of dollars into their account; (b) it could be a real book which looks interesting but turns out to be boring (or vice versa) or a celebrity who looks wild but does a lot of charity work (eg Bob Geldof who organised Live Aid); (c) Ss think of a time when three or four bad things happened at once; (d) Ss may have been given a new computer and been really pleased and then found that a friend has one that is even quicker or more powerful.

Answers a Stupid people are easy to rip off, steal from etc because they don't think about what they're doing. (3) **b** You shouldn't make judgements about people or things from first appearances. You should get to know what they are really like. (2) **c** When bad things happen, they are really bad. (4) **d** However well off you are you can always find someone who is better off than you are and you are never satisfied. (1)

2 Tell Ss that they are going to hear three stories. At the end of each story, you are going to pause the recording and the Ss must tell you which proverb they demonstrate. Ss then summarise each story and how they relate to the definitions given in the previous exercise, eg 1 they were not happy with the first room and thought one with a sea view would be better. Having got that, they realised that one without a sea view was quieter. 2 A purse was stolen, someone got ill and a camera went missing from a hotel room all on the same day. 3 David did not look as if he could walk very far or be able to climb a volcano because of how he looked but he turned out to be a good walker.

Tapescript CD 3 Track 19

1 *[London accent]* Our hotel room was really nice, but we wanted to get a room with a sea view. Easier said than done, I'll tell you. The afternoon receptionist told us to talk to the morning receptionist, and she told us to talk to the manager, but the manager wasn't there! We were going round in circles! But at the end of the day, we got a new room with a great view. And it was cheaper too! We were on top of the world! But we should have known it was too good to be true. The thing is the street below our balcony was really noisy – motorbikes, people shouting – and we didn't get a wink of sleep all night. It just goes to show you, doesn't it? ... The grass is always greener on the other side.

2 *[Northern English accent]* When you come down to it I know that it's not the end of the world if you have a bad day, but at the time it felt like it. They'd warned us to keep our eyes peeled if we went to the local market because of all the pickpockets. So I left my camera in the hotel, better safe than sorry, you know what I mean. But Jill had her purse stolen anyway. Then Frank fell ill and the taxi to the hospital cost a fortune. I think the driver ripped us off. Frank was OK in the end, but when we got back to the hotel my camera wasn't there! What a day! It's just like the proverb says ... It never rains, but it pours.

3 *[neutral English accent]* When we found out there was an excursion to the volcano, we jumped at the chance. The next morning everyone was ready to go at the crack of dawn. Except for one guy called David. We had just decided to leave without him, when he strolled in as if he had all the time in the world and said 'Better late than never' in this really dopey voice. His hair was sticking up, his eyes were all gummy with sleep and he was wearing a pair of slippers on his feet! It goes without saying we all thought he wouldn't get very far, but in fact, he was a really good walker. I suppose it's true what they say ... You can't judge a book by its cover.

Answers 1 d 2 c 3 b

SPEAK OUT

3 Ss work in pairs to guess the meanings of the clichés. Elicit answers and which ones were easy or difficult to work out, eg *going round in circles* may give the image of someone lost in the desert thinking they are walking in a straight line so may be easy to visualise. *On top of the world* may give the image of a mountaineer who has conquered Mt Everest.

Answers 1 g 2 c 3 b 4 a 5 i 6 d 7 e 8 h 9 j 10 f

Optional activity: Before Ss look at Exercise 4, ask them to work in pairs to imagine situations in which the different clichés may be used. For example you want to study at Oxford University and a friend says: *So, you just need to get top grades in all your exams and you'll get in.* You reply: *That's easier said than done.*
Elicit ideas from different pairs for each different cliché. This will also help them to do Exercise 4 as some of the ideas may be the same.

4 Ss work in pairs to complete the sentences. Elicit the answers and what the sentences mean using the definitions from Exercise 3.

Answers 1 too good to be true 2 it goes without saying 3 jump at the chance 4 easier said than done 5 going round in circles 6 not the end of the world 7 at the crack of dawn 8 on top of the world 9 It just goes to show 10 At the end of the day

5 Ss try to give the cliché and extra information, eg when student A asks: *What time are you leaving?* B may say: *At the crack of dawn. We want to get as far as possible before the sun comes up and the roads get busy.* When the students have completed the activity, tell them to close their books and then you read out the comments and try to elicit the correct clichés without Ss being able to look in their books.

Answers **A 1** I'm going round in circles. **2** Don't worry. It's not the end of the world. **3** I'd jump at the chance. **4** I knew it was too good to be true. **B 1** At the crack of dawn. **2** On top of the world. **3** It just goes to show that you can't trust anyone. **4** That's easier said than done.

6 Allow Ss one minute to think of a holiday they have been on. They can then think of two clichés that they could use whilst talking about it. Ss then carry out the conversations. At the end of the activity, ask Ss how many clichés they managed to use.

ADDITIONAL PRACTICE: Photocopiable resources. Resource 24: *What are they saying?* Pages 192–193

READING AND VOCABULARY

This section introduces collocations through a reading on tourism.

Culture notes

Bill Bryson (born 1951) is an American writer. He was originally from Iowa in the USA but has spent much of his adult life in England. He has written several humorous travel books as well as books about the English language.

The short story ***The Accidental Tourist*** can be found in his book *Notes From a Big Country*. The stories that make up this book originally appeared as columns in *The Mail on Sunday*, a British newspaper. The story ends up by telling the readers that he never did get the frequent flyer air miles that he had been thinking about when he broke the zip on his bag. He couldn't find the card in time but he never does because the card is in the name W. (William) Bryson whereas his tickets are in the name B. (Bill) Bryson. Even though Bill is well known as being a short version of William, the airline officials won't accept that the two names are the same. His final sentence is that it is probably just as well that he can't get a free flight to Bali like his friends and colleagues do because he couldn't go without food for that long.

Warm-up Review of clichés. *Act it out.* Put Ss into up to ten pairs or groups. Each group is given one of the clichés from the last lesson on a slip of paper. They have to think of a small roleplay which illustrates the cliché without actually using it, eg a school child is told that they have passed all their exams with 100% and they have won a special prize (on top of the world). When they are ready, the groups act out their roleplays and the other groups guess the cliché.

1 Ss read through the list alone and note any that have happened to them. Then they get into groups of four to discuss what happened to them. Ask each group to choose their funniest anecdote and elicit this in open class. The Ss then discuss other problems that can happen as a class, eg *have something stolen, fallen asleep on a bus or train and missed your stop, not understood the ticket system in a different country and not done what you should.*

2 Tell Ss this is a test of their skimming skills. As soon as they find the problems mentioned they should put their hand up and stop the activity. The student who does this then tells the class where the information can be found. Ask that student how they found the information so quickly so the others may learn from them. The information can be found in paragraph 3, paragraph 8 and paragraph 10.

Answers had your things fall out of your bag due to a broken zip; spilt food or drink on yourself or another passenger; got ink all over yourself due to a broken pen

3 Ss work alone to find the answers and the justifications for them. Tell Ss they have ten minutes to read the text carefully and remind them that, in this sort of task, there must be actual information in the text that gives the answer. Ss should not assume anything which is not stated. Elicit the answers and the extracts which gave them the answer, i.e. 1 is an overall understanding of the text; 2 line 88 – 'how much I ache to be suave'; 3 lines 50–51 – 'I can't believe you do this for a living'; 4 lines 56–57 – 'found myself pinned helplessly in the crash position'; 5 lines 59–63 – 'I knocked a soft drink onto the lap of a sweet little lady (...) brought me a replacement drink and instantly I knocked it onto the woman again'; 6 lines 76–78 – 'I was writing important thoughts in a notebook ('buy socks', 'clutch drinks carefully' (...).' Although he says these are important, they are obviously not. This is just his humour. 7 lines 102–103 – 'I just sit very, very quietly'.

Answers 1 d 2 b 3 b 4 d 5 c 6 a 7 d

4 Ss find the underlined words and read the sentences in pairs, trying to work out what was happening without looking at the alternatives in Exercise 4. When Ss have finished, elicit the answers, asking Ss for the base form of the verbs (eg *brush – sweep*), and make sure Ss understand exactly what the verbs in the text mean. Ask: *What other use of 'jam' do you know which means 'stuck'?* (traffic jam). *The man 'pulled and yanked' on the zip. The verb in the exercise is 'pulled' so what is the difference between 'to pull' and 'to yank'?* (to yank is more sudden and forceful) *What shape can roll?* (a circle or sphere) *Is a 'gash' a deep or shallow cut?* (deep) *What can you also shed?* (hair, skin – a snake or lizard can shed their skin) *Where does the verb 'pinned' come from?* (a pin is used to stick things and if you are pinned, you cannot move, as if a pin was stuck in you) *What can you sweep with a brush?* (sweep the floor, sweep the chimney) *When might you become drenched?* (in strong rain).

Answers 1 sweep 2 gash 3 shed 4 yank 5 roll 6 drench 7 be jammed 8 pin

5 Tell Ss that, even if they do not know all the answers, they should try to guess. Ss work in pairs. Elicit the answers and ask follow-up questions to practise the vocabulary, eg *Have you ever been filled with fear? Has a handle ever given way on a bag you have been carrying with shopping in it? Have you ever been drenched in the rain? Did you suck your thumb? Has any liquid ever leaked onto your clothes or in a bag you've been carrying?*

Answers 2 jammed 3 gave way 4 yanked 5 rolled 6 gashed; shed 7 leaned; pinned 8 swept 9 drenched 10 sucked 11 leaked

Optional activity: Before Ss look at Exercise 6, put them into eight groups. Each group needs a piece of paper on which they write one of the following:

1 *I was filled with*
2 *I gashed*
3 *The monster shed*
4 *I leaned*
5 *He knocked*
6 *It was swept*
7 *She was drenched*
8 *He pinned*

The Ss now complete their sentence with one idea. They can use the ideas from Exercise 5 here, eg *I was filled with fear. She was drenched in the rain.* Ss now pass their paper to the group on the left. This group looks at the new sentence stem and the way it has been finished. They now have to try to finish it in a different way. Tell Ss that, if they do not know, they should guess. The process is repeated until the papers return to their original groups so they should now have eight possible endings written on them. Elicit some ideas from the Ss and tell them if they are correct or not. Once they have done Exercise 6, Ss can see if any of the collocations in the exercise were used by other Ss in the activity.

6 Ss work in pairs or small groups. They match the beginnings with the endings and then use the new collocations to talk about themselves. Allow Ss to be as imaginative as possible and tell them the sentences do not have to be true, eg *I am filled with joy when I arrive in my English class. In the boxing match, I knocked the other person down three times.* Elicit sentences in open class.

Answers 1 b 2 g 3 h 4 a 5 c 6 f 7 e 8 d

7 Put Ss into groups of four. Ss try to continue the story for another eight sentences. Nominate one group to say the next sentence. They then nominate another group to follow theirs and so on. If you feel that some groups are being nominated too much whilst others are being left out, you can decide who goes next rather than leaving it to the Ss. Try to ensure that each group has provided two sentences of the eight. Once they have done this, re-elicit the story in open class and make sure the Ss have used the collocations correctly.

Optional activity: Have a story about Emily prepared but with the collocations missed out (the underlined sections can be removed). Put the Ss in groups and give each group a copy of the story. The Ss work together to complete the story with suitable collocations. As more than one alternative may be possible, this still enables the Ss to use their imaginations and you can still elicit ideas from each group without it being repetitive.

98   Students' Book ➡ pages 87–89

The story:

Emily's heart was filled with joy when she heard the knock on the door. She ran to open it but it was <u>jammed shut</u>. 'Wait a minute,' she called out. She ran to get a knife from the kitchen but, when she tried to open the door, she <u>gashed her arm</u> and started <u>shedding blood</u> all over the hall carpet. She suddenly realised that the door was locked and quickly turned the key. Unfortunately, Sam, standing outside, was <u>leaning against it</u> and, as soon as she unlocked it, it swung open. Sam fell inside on top of Emily and <u>pinned her to the floor</u>. He saw a shelf above his head and tried to pull himself up but the shelf <u>gave way</u> and a vase of flowers fell on top of them <u>drenching them with water</u>. When they finally got up, Emily looked at the mess and <u>shed some tears</u> at the sight of her beautiful hall. Then Sam took a present out of his coat pocket and she soon <u>swept the tears</u> away.

8 Set a time limit for Ss to read their anecdote and note the key points. When they are ready, tell the Ss to close their books so that they can only refer to the notes, not back to the anecdote itself. Ss should try to keep talking for three minutes each. After they have finished, the Ss try to guess which information was contained in their partner's anecdote and which was made up spontaneously.

9 Try to make sure that Ss are in different groups to those they were in for Exercise 1 so that they can use the same ideas if they wish. Allow two minutes for Ss to think about their story and make notes of the vocabulary they want to use. Ss take it in turns to tell their stories and the others ask them questions. At the end of each anecdote the rest of the group say whether they think it is true or false and the speaker tells them. This can be done for points. Each student who guesses correctly wins a point and the speaker gets a point for each person who was wrong.

WRITING

This section shows Ss how to write reports using formal language, appropriate linking devices and other useful vocabulary and structures.

Culture notes

The name **Perth** derives from the Pict language meaning 'wood' or 'copse' (a small area of woodland.) The town's original name was St John's Town because of the church of St John the Baptist and the local football team is still called St Johnstone rather than Perth. It is one of only three towns in Britain which have been declassified as cities, losing its city status in the 1990s.

Warm-up Review of collocations. *Which one?* Tell Ss that you are going to read out some situations and they should try to think of an occasion when it happened to them (or they should make up a story). Ss then get together in pairs and tell each other the occasions and their partner has to guess the situation. For example read out: *I was drenched.* The student writes that they were walking home from school and there was a sudden storm. They tell this to their partner who has to guess that the situation was *I was drenched* as opposed to, for example, *I was filled with fear.*

Situations:

I was filled with joy.

I was drenched.

I shed blood.

I was filled with fear.

I was pinned down.

I shed tears.

The blame was pinned on me.

I was knocked to the floor.

1 Set a time limit of three minutes for the discussion in pairs. When they have finished, ask the class who has been to a festival and encourage those who haven't been to one to ask questions to those who have. Those who haven't would then answer the second question and the whole class could debate the third.

2 Tell Ss to read through the exam question and underline the key words which help them to decide what and how to write, i.e. *organisers* – intended audience; *report* – style of writing; *suitability* – aim of writing; *220–260 words* – length of writing; *mention the following* – essential information. Ss then read the text alone and decide if all the information has been included in an appropriate style, finally discussing their thoughts in pairs. Elicit ideas but do not give Ss the answer yet.

Answers Not really. All the essential information has been covered and it is well organised. However, the style is too informal and personal, the title isn't clear enough and there should be paragraph headings and bullet points to make it even clearer.

TRAIN YOUR BRAIN

3 Ss read through the Train Your Bain box before listening to the recording and predict what is good advice and what is not based on what they read on page 90 and their own opinions. After Ss listen, ask them if they still think the report on the Krang music festival is a good one.

Tapescript `CD 3 Track 21`

Bernie: *[Scottish accent]* Hey, Ali, could you do me a favour?

Ali: *[Scottish accent]* Depends what it is, Bernie. I'm not doing the dishes.

Bernie: No, it's my homework. I have to write a report and I don't think I've done it right.

Ali: Did you read the question carefully and underline the key words?

Bernie: Yeah. And I made a plan before I started writing, too.

Ali: Good, you're learning ... Here, let me have a look ... This is the question, then, is it?

Bernie: Yeah.

Ali: OK, a report ... 220–260 words ... is your town a good venue for a music festival? OK, I can see one problem already.

Bernie: What's that?

Ali: Well, it doesn't look like a report. A report's got to be clearer than that. You should be able to read it really quickly, you know skim it and still get all the main points. This looks more like an opinion essay or something. You haven't set it out right.

Bernie: So what should I do?

Ali: Well, set it out with a heading for each paragraph for a start. You know, the first paragraph should be headed 'Introduction', the second 'Getting here' the third ... um ... 'Possible venues'. You understand?

Bernie: Right, and then the fourth 'Where to stay' and then 'Attitudes'.

Ali: Yes, and the last one 'Conclusions'.

Bernie: OK.

Ali: Your title's all wrong.

Bernie: What's wrong with it?

Ali: Reports need clear informative titles, not poetry. I mean, 'a marriage made in Heaven'!

Bernie: So, something like 'Perth: a venue for the Krang music festival'?

Ali: Yes, that's fine. I don't like your introduction either.

Bernie: No?

Ali: No. It's too informal. You need to start with a phrase like 'The purpose of this report' or 'The aim of this report is to ...' not a rhetorical question like that.

Bernie: OK, got that.

Ali: And then don't write 'I tried to find out'. Use an expression like 'This report draws on information' or 'It is based on'.

Bernie: It draws on information provided by the Scottish Tourist Board and ...

Ali: Yeah, that's good. OK, the second paragraph isn't bad ... just remember to put the heading.

Bernie: 'Getting here'.

Ali: Yeah, oh and what you could do is to use bullet points.

Bernie: Bullet points?

Ali: Yeah, you put the key information after each bullet point. Like 'It is' ... then first bullet point ... very well connected, blah, blah, blah, and then another bullet point and the stuff about the airport connections. Got it?

Bernie: Yes, thanks.

Ali: OK, the paragraph about possible venues. The first sentence is fine, but I'd cut the second. All that stuff about sports is irrelevant. Reports have got to be concise. Just the information you need and no more.

Bernie: OK, so I'll cut that.

Ali: Right, the next paragraph ...

Bernie: Heading – where to stay?

Ali: Uh huh. And I think I'd cut 'as for' and use two bullet points here – one for the info on the youth hostel and the b'n'b and the other on the campsite. The 'Attitudes' paragraph is fine ... And it's good to begin your conclusion with 'In conclusion', but the last sentence has to go.

Bernie: Why?

Ali: You don't want to talk about your personal likes in a report. What you need here is a recommendation. Use something like 'I recommend' or 'It is recommended that'.

Bernie: OK.

Ali: So what do you recommend?

Bernie: Um ... I recommend negotiating with the Town Council as soon as possible to secure the North Inch as the venue ...

Ali: And?

Bernie: And ... um ... to seek permission to provide a temporary campsite.

Ali: Great. That's that.

Bernie: OK, thanks, Ali. You're a pal. I owe you one.

Ali: Well, you could do the dishes if you like.

Answers 1 Read the question carefully ✓ 2 Make a clear plan ✓ 3 Think of a clear and simple title 4 State the purpose of the report ✓ 5 Give headings to the paragraphs 6 Subdivide the information ✓ 7 Use a formal, impersonal style 8 Conclude with your recommendations ✓

4 Tell Ss to look at the report on page 90 as they listen and, whenever something is recommended, to make notes within the report as to how to change it. When Ss have finished listening, allow them to compare notes in pairs and then elicit from the class what changes should be made.

Answers 1 Paragraph headings: *Introduction, Getting here, Possible venues, Where to stay, Attitudes, Conclusions* 2 Title: *Perth: a venue for the Krang music festival.* 3 Change the introduction so that the first sentence starts: *The purpose of this report ...* or *The aim of this report is to ...* and the second starts *This report draws on information ...* or *It is based on ...* 4 The second paragraph is fine except the different transport options could be separated by bullet points. 5 Cut the second sentence in the third paragraph. 6 Cut *As for* from the fourth paragraph and use bullet points for different types of accommodation. 7 Keep paragraph five. 8 Cut the last sentence of the final paragraph and replace it with *I recommend negotiating with the Town Council as soon as possible to secure the North Inch as the venue.*

5 Ss work in pairs to rewrite the report. Set a time limit of five to ten minutes as Ss do not have to think much about what they are writing but to combine the advice given in the recording with the information written in the report. When they have finished, Ss could swap reports with a second pair to compare to the model answer on page 148 as they may be more likely to check carefully if it is someone else's work.

6 Ss read through the information box to get an overall understanding of the points and then complete it with the phrases. Ss compare in pairs and then as a class. Point out that, although (c) does use an impersonal style, it matches with 6 because, as stated in Exercise 3, the report should finish with recommendations. So this comes under the heading of drawing conclusions.

Answers 1 d 2 b 3 f 4 e 5 a 6 c

7 Ss work in groups of four. Tell all Ss to make a list of the ideas that their group comes up with. Ss then share ideas as a class. This could be done as a debate with half the class thinking it is a good venue and the other half thinking it is not. Encourage the Ss to use connecting words in the debate.

8 Ss have already underlined the key words in the exam question so tell them to spend five minutes making a plan of what they are going to say, useful vocabulary to use and their recommendations. Ss then work alone to write the report, either in class or for homework.

Optional activity: When Ss have finished their writing, they could carry out a roleplay in pairs based on the recording they listened to earlier. One of them is an expert on report writing and the other shows them their report. The expert gives advice and comments on their report. Then they swap roles.

THINK FORWARD TO EXAMS REVISION 4
UNITS 7–8

VOCABULARY AND GRAMMAR

1 Tell Ss to look at the three choices without looking at the sentences. If this is not possible, Ss should keep their books closed and the words should be written on the board. Elicit the meaning of each word. Ss then complete the exercise alone and compare answers in pairs. Elicit the answers and what the sentences mean: 1 an official disagreement; 2 cheap; 3 complained; 4 a set phrase – took the chance eagerly; 5 nervous; 6 saved a lot of money; 7 reduce/get rid of.

As before, if you want Ss to get further practice of the vocabulary, ask them to make sentences which illustrate the meaning of the other words in the choices.

> **Answers 1** dispute **2** affordable **3** whinged **4** jumped **5** uptight **6** saved **7** alleviate

2 Ss should now be in the habit of looking at the gapped sentences and deciding exactly what kind of word is needed. They discuss ideas in pairs and then decide what the missing word is. Tell Ss that, if they do not know the word, they should guess, eg if they think the word needed is a negative adjective and they do not know how to make a negative adjective from their root, they may use the suffix *un-*. It at least gives them a chance of being correct. Elicit the answers and what kind of word each is: 1 noun, 2 adjective, 3 noun, 4 adjective, 5 verb in the Past Simple, 6 verb in base form.

> **Answers 1** admission **2** repetitive **3** nourishment **4** resentful **5** threatened **6** soothe

3 Look at the first gap with the Ss. Write on the board: *I have a really bad dream in which …* Ask the Ss if *really* can collocate with *bad* (yes). Then ask if the sentence makes sense (not really – the Present Simple is used to talk about habits, routines and facts in which case *I have really bad dreams* would sound better). Therefore they need a different word to show that we are talking about having the same dream often. Try to elicit *recurring* and then tell Ss that, in this exercise, even though it may seem as though more than one word is possible, there will probably be one best answer. Ss work in pairs.

> **Answers 1** recurring **2** speaks **3** crack **4** blood **5** to **6** winds **7** saying **8** arm **9** rip **10** fares/flights **11** desk **12** board **13** clenched

4 Ss read through the text quickly to get an overall understanding. Elicit a short summary of what it is about, eg *Tom worked in a café as a kitchen assistant. He got a skin disease that the doctor couldn't cure. He became obsessed with finding out more about the problem on the Internet and lost his job. Then the problem cleared up.* Elicit that the story is set in the past and tell Ss that they should only use the verb form, not pronouns even if they may at first glance think they do, eg 1 *working*, not *he was working*. Ss complete the activity in pairs.

> **Answers 1** working **2** noticed **3** Having never suffered **4** being **5** suspecting **6** used **7** had described **8** reassuring/having reassured **9** came **10** to get/to be getting **11** Not knowing **12** searching **13** became **14** being given/having been given

5 Ss read through the sentences before starting to rewrite them. They work alone and then compare answers in pairs. If there are any differences, Ss should check that their new sentences are grammatically correct and then decide if they have the same meaning and refer to the same time as the originals. Elicit all sentences in open class.

> **Answers 1** is claimed to be the best medicine **2** was discovered to have been stolen **3** On reaching their destination **4** Instead of jumping down my throat **5** It was thought that she would **6** When he had looked everywhere **7** He is supposed to be **8** is expected to start/be starting

READING SKILLS

1 Tell Ss to read through the five comments and write a very short summary of each person's views. Elicit ideas in open class, eg A *We're selfish – need to change – shouldn't wait for governments – inspired by Barbara.* B *Not just planes use oil – why travel so slowly – very small difference in carbon footprint.* C *Expensive and time consuming – who can do the same – short flights can be stopped – not long flights.* D *Great story – travelled by train when young – views, friendships, culture – love to do the same – when retired?* E *Barbara's principles OK but – bus/train don't reduce carbon footprint – need new technology.* Tell Ss to now look at the questions and see if they can answer them from their summaries. If not, they should go back to the comments to find the correct answers.

Tell Ss that, even if they do not write summaries in a matching activity, they should read the texts first and note key words and ideas so that they do not have to look through all the texts every time they want to answer a question but have a good idea of where to look.

> **Answers** **1** A, D **2** D **3** C **4** C **5** E **6** A **7** B, E

Optional activity: As it was not really necessary for Ss to read Barbara's story to answer the questions, Ss should read the story and write questions about it in pairs eg, *Where did she travel? Why did she do it? How far was the journey? How long did it take?* etc. Ss then cover the text and get into groups of four. Each pair asks the other a question about the text and the other pair have to try to remember the answer. Ss could then write their own comment about her journey giving their own opinions. Again, Ss get into groups of four and compare their opinions and reasons for them.

SPEAKING SKILLS

1 As a change from the previous presentations, Ss work in groups named group 1 or group 2. All Ss in groups 1 look at topic 1. This is going to be their partner's topic and they are going to be the examiners. All the Ss in groups 2 look at topic 2. The Ss decide, as examiners, what sort of things they would like to hear, eg the examiners listening to topic 1 may want to hear a personal anecdote which demonstrates the lesson. The examiners listening to topic B may want to hear why people who do not travel miss out. Give the Ss two minutes to list the things they want to hear. Ss now look at the other topic alone. This is what they are going to present. When Ss have planned their presentation, they get into pairs: a student from a group 1 with a student from a group 2. The student presenting topic 1 starts and the other student looks at their checklist to see which of the things they brainstormed earlier are mentioned. When both Ss have made their presentations, the Ss tell each other if there were any things they were hoping to hear which were not in the presentation.

Media truths

Read, listen and talk about the media and news reporting.
Practise reporting verb patterns; clauses of cause and effect.
Focus on giving news.
Write essay introductions.

READING AND SPEAKING

This section introduces some slang expressions and looks at differences between the style of language used in tabloid and broadsheet newspapers.

Culture notes

The story is based on two true stories. A £4.4 million house in Spain was seriously damaged after a girl's 16th birthday party was advertised on Facebook and Bebo and 400 people turned up. £6,000-worth of jewellery and clothes was taken by party-goers, and the televisions, tables and chairs were thrown into the swimming pool. In England, 2,000 people gatecrashed an 18th birthday party in Devon after it was advertised by a DJ on the radio and news of the party was spread on Facebook and MySpace, although not by the girl whose party it was. Less damage was done here as the police, having heard about the invitation, arrived without being called out.

Selly Oak is a suburb of Birmingham. There is a UK soap opera called *Hollyoaks* which is set in a college near Chester. It has been on TV since 1995 and, because it appeals to older teenagers and people in their early 20s, it has quite controversial storylines.

Amersham is about 40km north-west of London and is a commuter town. It is the last station on the Metropolitan Underground line.

Warm-up Introduce the topic of the lesson. *Anagram race*. Dictate the letters:
o – s – l – a – i – c
r – t – n – w – i – o – g – e – k – n
t – w – e – e – s – i – b – s

Ss work in groups of three or four to try to put the letters in the correct order to make the words (*social networking websites*). When one group has guessed it (help with initial letters if they are having problems) discuss different ones (Facebook, My Space, Bebo, Nasza Klasa, Friends Reunited etc). Ask Ss who uses them and what sort of information they post online (news, photos etc) and if there is any information they would not post (eg address, mobile telephone number).

1 When Ss look at Exercise 1, tell them to think of all occasions when they read newspapers or magazines. They may think they do not read a paper but they may glance at their parents' paper or read them at the dentists, hairdressers, cafés etc. Ss discuss the questions in pairs and then as a whole class.

2 It may be worth doing this with the Ss' books closed. Write up the tabloid headline on the board (*Teenage thugs trash TV star's home*). Ask Ss what they know (the house was trashed, whose house it was, who did the trashing) and what they do not know (why). Now write up the broadsheet headline (*Actress's home 'wrecked' after hundreds show up to daughter's Facebook party*). Again, ask Ss what they know and what they do not know. Ss now look at Exercise 2 and answer the questions in pairs. Elicit answers and reasons (the tabloid headline is short and the first three words start with the same letter).

Answers 1 A grabs the attention and B attempts to explain/summarise. **2** A Tabloid (shorter, more emotive, informal language) B Broadsheet (more factual, no slang) **3** *Elicit ideas but don't give the correct answer*

3 One way to do this is to put Ss into pairs. One student reads text A and the other text B. They compare what facts they found out about the party and the damage.

Answers A girl advertised her birthday party on Facebook and uninvited people came, caused damage to the house and may have stolen items of jewellery and clothes.

4 Ss find the underlined words and read the sentences in which they occur. In pairs they decide what the words mean and then match them to the definitions in Exercise 4.

Answers 1 reveller 2 beforehand 3 mayhem 4 be grounded 5 rowdy 6 descend 7 lured

5 Ss again find the words in the text. Some they will probably already know (eg *cop*) and others may have already been discussed (eg *trash* as it was in the headline). Tell Ss that, even if they can do the matching without looking at the text, it is better to find all the words and make sure their ideas are correct.

Answers 1 e 2 d 3 f 4 h 5 b 6 g 7 i 8 c 9 a 10 j

Optional activity: Ss work in pairs. Each pair chooses three or four of the vocabulary items from Exercise 4 or 5 and write new sentences which include them. Ss then get into groups of four. Each pair in turn reads out a sentence missing out the word from the exercises. The other pair has to guess which word it was.

6 Go through the adjectives and make sure Ss understand what each means. Ss then work in pairs to match them to the two texts. Elicit answers and justifications from the texts. Point out that, although the broadsheet has got dramatic words (*war zone*) and colloquialisms (*grounded*) these are both direct quotes.

Answers article A colloquial (the words highlighted in Exercise 5), dramatic, sensational (rowdy, mayhem, wrecking, furious etc) **article B** sophisticated (causing considerable damage; had reportedly), neutral (party-goers, teenagers, young people), restrained (personal items are reported missing, no arrests were made)

7 Ss read through both texts and highlight sections of the text which give them the answers. Elicit the answers and the justifications for them: 1A 'star of TV soap', 1B 'best known for her role in the soap opera'; 2A 'outside Amersham', 2B Buckinghamshire family home; 3A '$3.5 million', 3B 'eight-bedroom family home'; 4A 'posted an open invitation on the Internet'; 4B 'posted the invitation and directions'; 5A 'Cops had to be called', 5B 'police turned up'; 6A 'Revellers (...) swiped designer togs and jewellery', 6B 'personal items are reported missing';

7A 'expelled from school', 7B 'a first-year student at Durham University'; 8A 'Furious mum', 8B 'Mum's speaking to me again'; 9A 'TV funnyman', 9B no information about the father at all.

Answers 1 both 2 A 3 A 4 B 5 A 6 A 7 B 8 B 9 A

8 Allow Ss three minutes to look through the two texts and find facts which are different in the two texts. Elicit ideas and then Ss discuss Exercise 2 together.

Answers 1 over 500 / almost 500; no mention of the top DJ in the broadsheet; no mention of the swimming pool in the broadsheet; no mention of the photos being posted online in the broadsheet; the 'war zone' quote is attributed to different people; no mention of Melissa's outfit in the broadsheet; no mention of the divorce in the broadsheet; no mention of Caroline Braxton being at the party in the tabloid 2a A 2b A 2c Ss' own answers

9 When Ss have completed the exercise, go through the vocabulary and exactly what it means. As a follow-up, ask Ss which type of newspaper they think is more difficult for a foreign language student to read (probably a tabloid because of the colloquial, slang language and the cultural references).

Answers 1 B 2 B 3 T 4 T 5 B 6 T 7 T 8 T 9 T 10 T 11 B 12 T

10 Give Ss two minutes to discuss the two questions in pairs and then discuss them as a whole class.

ADDITIONAL PRACTICE: Photocopiable resources. Resource 25: *Sort them out.* Page 194

LISTENING AND VOCABULARY

This section extends the Ss' vocabulary, introducing collocations and informal phrases through a listening on how people get the news.

Culture notes

Roger McGough (born 1937) is from Liverpool. In the 1960s he was in the band The Scaffold with Paul McCartney's brother, Mike. He has written poems for adults and children and presents a Radio 4 programme called *Poetry Please*.

Radio podcast. The word *podcast* is a combination of iPod and broadcast. This is because the first podcasts were produced for Apple iPod players. A radio podcast is a radio programme that is made available to download on the Internet after it has been transmitted on the radio. Radio podcasts started to become available in 2004, the BBC making the first British radio programme available for download in November 2004.

Warm-up Review of vocabulary from the previous lesson.
Noughts and crosses. Draw a grid, three squares by three on the board and, in each square write a letter as below:

```
P   C   T
G   S   R
L   M   B
```

Put the Ss into two groups. One group chooses a letter. Give them the clue (below) and they have to say the word. If they are correct, draw an X in that square. If not, it is left as it is. The second group then repeat the process and, if they are correct, draw an O in their square. The aim is for Ss to get three squares in a row with their symbol.

Clues:
This P means exclusive or expensive. (posh)
This C means to throw. (chuck)
This T is a word for clothes. (togs)
This G means to enter a party without an invitation. (gatecrash)
This S means to steal. (swipe)
This R means noisy and possibly violent. (rowdy)
This L means to persuade by offering something exciting. (lure)
This M means chaos or anarchy. (mayhem)
This B means in advance. (beforehand)

1 Set a time limit of five minutes for the Ss to discuss the questions in pairs and then elicit ideas in open class.

Answers 1 It is almost as if the news is entertainment, like a soap opera or reality TV or it could be that because the news is so bad, it makes our own problems seem trivial and unimportant. **2** There is a saying in English that 'No news is good news'. This can

mean two things. If you are worried about someone then, if you haven't heard anything bad, it probably means that nothing is wrong. It can also be used to mean that the only stories that are worth being called 'news' are those involving problems or disasters. Bad news is more interesting and attracts more readers or viewers therefore earning TV stations or newspapers more money.

2 Ss read through the news sources to make sure they understand what they mean, eg rolling TV news means 24-hour-a-day news channels such as CNN. Play the recording once. Ss make notes of key words and compare ideas in pairs. Elicit answers and words which helped, i.e. 1 *buy it, light-hearted, tongue-in-cheek, don't believe half the stories, celebrity gossip*; 2 *start page, online, Internet browser*; 3 *local newspaper, once a week, everyone gets*; 4 *glossy weeklies*; 5 *radio instead, podcasts*.

For tapescript see page 210.

Answers 1 g **2** b **3** e **4** c **5** d

3 Give Ss a minute to look through the eight statements and try to remember whether they heard any of them. Tell Ss to mark the statement which most reflects their views. After Ss listen to the recording, allow them to discuss their answers in pairs and which they think people of their age would most agree with. Then ask Ss which one they marked as reflecting their views to see which are the most common.
Justifications: 1 'undemanding entertainment';
2 'you've got a chance to air your own views as well';
3 'I'm pretty clueless about current affairs'; 4 'I'm so rushed off my feet these days I'm finding it hard to keep up with the news', 'But I do make a point of buying one of the glossy weeklies'; 5 'I was appalled at how superficial the coverage of foreign news was'.

Answers 1 c **2** a **3** b **4** h **5** f

4 Ss work in pairs to try to work out or guess the collocations. If there are any problems, you could play the recording for a third time for Ss to try to hear the phrases being said. Elicit the answers and what each collocation means.

Answers 1 overload **2** avid **3** insatiable **4** bookmark **5** air **6** scant **7** gawp **8** skim **9** junkie **10** keep **11** informed

5 Allow Ss to look at the words in pairs and work out what they mean and whether there are any equivalent phrases in their language. Elicit the meanings and ask Ss which apply to them.

6 Put Ss into pairs. Each student speaks for one minute. Nominate two or three Ss to answer the question in open class.

7 Put Ss into groups of three. Each student looks at one of the questions. Student 1 asks the other two Ss question 1. They have to discuss the answer for two minutes, using appropriate expressions to agree, disagree and ask each other's opinions. The process is repeated for the other two questions with a different student asking the question each time.

SPEAKING AND VOCABULARY

This section introduces useful vocabulary for describing TV programmes through a listening on different types of TV shows.

Culture notes

Andy Warhol (1928–1987) was an artist and filmmaker from New York. He made his '15 minutes of fame' quote in 1968 to show how the media quickly tires of news stories and moves onto the next one, thus giving each person written about only a short time in the public eye.

Warm-up Review of vocabulary from the last lesson.
What's in the news? Elicit a current news item and write this on the board. Put Ss into groups of four. Give each student a phrase from the last lesson on a slip of paper. They don't tell anyone else in their group what it is. The Ss discuss the item of news and, as they do so, they try to change the subject, subtly, and use their phrase in the conversation. After three minutes, stop the activity and ask Ss if they managed to use the phrase. If so, the other Ss try to guess what the phrase was.
Phrases to use: *tongue-in-cheek, news junkie, don't take much in, information overload, skim the headlines, insatiable appetite for.*

1 Tell Ss not to look at the TV listings yet, just the photos. Tell Ss that, even if they hate such programmes, they should try to answer the questions as objectively as possible as if they were in an exam. Set a time limit of three minutes and then discuss the questions as a whole class.

Answers 1 A reality TV show *Big Brother* (A), a talent show like *Pop Idol* or *Britain's Got Talent* (B), and a reality survival programme (C) **3 Reality TV** – a group of people are placed in a certain situation (eg a house) which they are unable to leave. They are filmed going about their normal lives as well as being given tasks to carry out. At regular intervals, people are voted out until one person is left as the winner. **Reality survival programme** – similar to the above but the situation in which the contestants find themselves is more difficult. They may be left on a tropical island and have to find and cook food, build shelter and carry out tasks such as eating insects. **Talent shows** – people perform their act in front of a panel of experts who either allow them to continue

or reject them, usually criticising them rudely. Those that have got through to the final perform again and the winner is voted by viewers.

2 When Ss have completed the task, elicit answers and ideas in open class. Elicit or tell Ss exactly what the programmes are, i.e. sitcom is a comedy show that takes place in the same situation each time, eg an office, a hotel, a family home etc. A soap opera is a series following a group of people over a period of time. The shows follow on from each other, often finishing at an exciting point, viewers having to wait for the next episode to see what happens.

Answers Selly Oak – soap opera, **Just Jodie!** – 'sitcom', **Circus Celebrities** – celebrity talent show, **Pop Star 6** – talent show, **Desert Rats 3** – reality TV (docusoap)

3 Ss look up any unknown vocabulary in dictionaries. Elicit the meanings of: *witty, catchy, canned laughter, clichéd, moralistic, irreverent, catchphrase* and *wooden acting*. Ss then take it in turns to describe a programme they know. Elicit ideas of programmes that Ss like and dislike in open class.

4 Ss should read through the opinions before they listen. It may be a good idea to allow them to give their opinions on the statements before they listen to the recording. When they have discussed them in pairs and as a class, play the recording. Ss compare ideas in pairs, then listen a second time to check their answers.

For tapescript see page 211.

Answers 1 T **2** S **3** – **4** T **5** – **6** T **7** – **8** S

5 Tell Ss to decide alone which topic they would like to talk about. Allow Ss three minutes to think about what they could say. Ss now get into groups of three or four and take it in turns to make their presentations to the other members of their group.

ADDITIONAL PRACTICE: Photocopiable resources. Resource 26: *Differing opinions.* Page 195

READING AND VOCABULARY

> This section introduces vocabulary on the topic of hoaxes, pranks and other jokes using a reading about April Fools' jokes in the media.

Culture notes

Casablanca was a 1942 film starring Humphrey Bogart and Ingrid Bergman. The film being referred to in the review may be *Play It Again, Sam* by Woody Allen. In the film, Woody Allen is visited by Humphrey Bogart who gives him advice about how to be successful with women.

Rembrandt (1606–1669) was a Dutch painter. In 1968 the Rembrandt Research Project was set up to try to determine which paintings attributed to Rembrandt may not have been his. Several were removed from collections as they were thought to have been painted by his students. In 2005, four of these were reclassified as being genuine. The problems arise because Rembrandt encouraged students to copy his paintings. He also changed his style quite often making it more difficult to spot genuine pieces of work.

Auckland is on the north island of New Zealand and is the country's biggest city with a population of nearly 1.5 million. Because most people live in their own homes with gardens, it is almost the size of London despite having only a quarter of the population. It is often referred to as 'The City of Sails' because of the number of yachts in its harbours.

Patrick Moore (born 1923) is an astronomer and television presenter. He has presented the BBC programme *The Sky At Night* since 1957 and has written over 70 books on astronomy.

News of the World is a Sunday paper. It sells about 3.5 million copies every week making it the largest selling English language paper in the world. It started in 1843 and was deliberately priced cheaply with sensational stories to appeal to the newly educated working classes.

The Channel Tunnel (or Chunnel) is 50km long and is considered one of the seven wonders of the modern world. The French and English halves of the tunnel joined together in 1990 and the tunnel was formally opened in 1994.

The Massachusetts Institute of Technology opened in 1861. It consists of five schools (Science, Engineering, Architecture and Planning, Management, and Humanities, Arts, and Social Sciences) and one college (of Health Sciences and Technology). The practice of playing pranks is known as 'MIT hacks'. Famous 'hacks' often involve the great dome. A model of the Wright Brothers' plane appeared on top of the dome to celebrate 100 years since their first flight and, in 2007 a dark mark appeared over it in recognition of the fourth Harry Potter film.

Mark Twain has four famous 'idiots' quotes:
'Once I talked to the inmates of an insane asylum in Hartford. I have talked to idiots a thousand times, but only once to the insane.'
'In the first place God made idiots. This was for practice. Then he made School Boards.'
'In the first place God made idiots. This was for practice. Then he made proofreaders.'
'We are all erring creatures, and mainly idiots, but God made us so and it is dangerous to criticise.'

Warm-up Review of TV programme types. *How quick?* Put Ss into groups of four. Each student is given a type of TV programme (reality show, talent show, sitcom, soap opera). They write down five important words related to that kind of programme, eg *soap opera – life, problems, family, relationships, weekly*. The Ss take it in turns to read out their five words and the other Ss in their group have to guess what kind of programme it is. Ss then have to work together to try to write a description of all four programmes without using any of their five words in the descriptions. Elicit definitions in open class.

1 If newspapers do have April Fools' jokes or similar in the Ss' own country, it would be worth preparing an example to talk about in case Ss do not know of any. Allow two minutes for Ss to discuss the two questions in pairs and then elicit answers in open class.

2 Ss work in pairs and look at the vocabulary together to see if they know any of the words. They then look up the ones they do not know and do the matching. Try to elicit examples of each that Ss know before they look at the next exercise.

Answers 1 prank 2 hoax 3 scam 4 spoof 5 fake

3 Ss do the matching exercise alone. Elicit the answers and the word which has a similar meaning to those in Exercise 2 in open class. Ask Ss which words have a negative connotation (*con, scam, fake, forgery* are all negative; *prank* or *practical joke* can be negative).

Answers 1 prank (practical joke) 2 fake (forgery) 3 scam (con trick) 4 spoof (parody) 5 hoax (fabrication)

4 Tell Ss to read through the introduction to the article and ask questions about the information there, eg *Where does April Fools' Day originate from?* (Roman or pagan times) *By what time had April Fools' Day become popular in Britain?* (the end of the eighteenth century) *When did the habit of putting April Fools' jokes in newspaper become popular?* (the 1970s). Ss then read the hoaxes alone. Ss discuss in pairs what the hoaxes were and which they thought was the funniest and why. Elicit ideas in open class.

5 Ss work alone and underline the extracts from the text which give the information. Elicit the answers and reasons for them: 1 'The story was picked up by other newspapers'; 2 'For many years, a similar joke used to be made about the phone system'; 3 'renowned astronomer'; 4 'severely criticised'; 5 'translation error' / 'metric not imperial measurements'; 6 'an email message'; 7 'Hundreds of people' / 'numerous phone calls'; 8 'We can only guess how many people were taken in'.

Answers 1 C 2 E 3 B 4 A 5 C, D 6 E 7 A, B 8 E

6 Ss work in pairs. They read the sentences in the text which include the underlined phrasal verbs and decide what they think the verbs mean. Ss then complete the sentences in the exercise. Elicit the answers and the meanings of the phrasal verbs, i.e. 1 become popular; 2 have the idea of; 3 grow/increase; 4 fool me.

Answers 1 take off 2 dreamt up 3 built up 4 take in

7 Tell Ss to work in pairs and guess the correct answers. Then they look through the text and find the expressions to check their answers. Elicit the answers and what they mean.

Answers 1 mystery 2 playing 3 take 4 gullible 5 renowned 6 numerous 7 blunder 8 disconnect

8 Put Ss into groups of four. Set a strict time limit of five minutes for them to discuss their ideas so that they all start writing at the same time. When they have finished brainstorming ideas, nominate one person in each group to do the writing so that there are no arguments about who should do this. Again set a time limit for Ss to complete their writing. Stop everyone at the same time and, if some groups have not finished, tell them not to worry but to read out what they have.

GRAMMAR

This section extends the Ss' understanding of reporting verb structures.

Special difficulties: Ss should be aware of how we report most of the verbs here but may still make mistakes. Correct carefully and ensure that Ss get a lot of practice of different verb forms.

Warm-up Introduction to the topic of the lesson. *Memory game.* Put the Ss into five or six groups. Give each group a verb: *complain, refuse, remind, recommend, ask, threaten.* Write the words *suggest* and *warn* on the board. Elicit or give a simple sentence to illustrate your two verbs, eg *suggest – Let's go to the cinema. Warn – If you don't work harder, you may fail your exams.* Now tell each group to write a similar sentence to demonstrate the function they were given. Each group in turn reads out their sentence and the other groups guess their verb.

Work it out

1 When Ss have finished, elicit the actual words that might have been said: *A mile-wide swarm of wasps is heading …; (Please) Take steps to protect yourselves; You should leave jars …*

Answers announce – 1, urge – 6, recommend – 4

2 Ss try to guess which verb goes in which gap in the table before they find them. Elicit answers, the other verbs found and where they appear in the text. Point out that *how* counts as a *wh-* question even though it is not spelt with a *w-*.

Answers 2 remind (6), insist on (8), admit (7), accuse someone of (8), warn (2), describe (3) (*remind* and *warn* are already in the table in different groups) 3 Other reporting verbs in the text are as follows: A announce, urge, recommend, confess, criticise; B inform, encourage, explain, claim, report; C report, add, claim, explain; D notify, predict; E request, advise

3 Ss discuss the questions in pairs. Elicit ideas in open class and why Ss think like that (1 is the only one that does not include the object *she*).

Answers 1 a 2 b

4 Tell Ss that all the sentences are grammatically correct. Elicit what the person might have actually said in each case: eg 1, 2 *I'm not gullible.*

Answers The situation was already in the past: 3, 4, 5 **Passive:** 4, 5

Check it out

Refer Ss to the Check it out section at the back of the book and encourage them to use reporting verbs in their written work to practise the verb patterns.

5 Tell Ss to read through the different choices and see which ones sound wrong. They mark these and then check their ideas.

Answers 1 he wouldn't give / not to give 2 that I tried / trying / that I should try 3 to be / that they should be 4 to be / that she was 5 not being able to / that he couldn't 6 being / having been / that she'd been 7 me that I had to see / me to see

6 Ss match the verbs to the sentences in pairs first. They then do the transformations alone. Point out other changes eg *here* to *there* in sentence 2.

Answers 1 She urged us to start looking for a job. 2 He asked (us) if we were enjoying our holiday there. 3 She invited us to (come to) her party the following week. 4 She wondered why they hadn't phoned. 5 He suggested that I (should) cancel my credit card./He suggested cancelling my credit card. 6 He denied causing/having caused the accident./He denied that he had caused the accident. 7 She regretted not being told/not having been told. 8 He congratulated us on having passed.

7 Put As together and Bs together in small groups to help each other before they join up in pairs (A and B).

Answers A 1 The customer complained that he had seen the waitress's thumb in his soup when she was carrying it. The waitress told him not to worry explaining that the soup wasn't hot. 2 The doctor informed his patient that he was very ill. The patient asked if he could get a second opinion. The doctor told him that he could and that he was very stupid too. B 1 One asked if the other was worried about Mad Cow Disease. The other replied that it didn't worry him (her) because he (she) was a horse. 2 The pupil asked his teacher if the teacher would punish him/her for something he/she hadn't done. The teacher replied that of course he/she wouldn't. The pupil told the teacher that was good, explaining that he/she hadn't done his/her homework.

ADDITIONAL PRACTICE: Photocopiable resources. Resource 27: *Regrets, I've had a few.* Page 196

SPEAKING

> This section introduces ways of preparing listeners for good and bad news when making announcements.

Warm-up Review of reporting verbs. *Go betweens.* Put Ss into groups of three. Each student writes one message for the other two people in the group. Encourage Ss to make them varied, some questions, some advice etc. They should write who the message is to and who it is from. Tell Ss that they have been having a few arguments and they are not speaking to each other. Ss report each others' messages, eg *Anna, David apologised for breaking your CD player.*

1 Ss describe what they can see in the photos (a headline from an article about the economy, an engagement card, a mobile phone bill, a headline from an article about exam passes, a large envelope inside which are some X-ray photos, a pop-up window on a website), then answer the questions.

Answers 1 photo 1 bad news ('new fears'); 2 good news (engagement is a happy time); 3 could be either as the bill could be high or low; 4 seems to be good news although some people may complain about falling standards in the actual exams if pass rates are too high; 5 could be good or bad; 6 it may lead to a prize or spyware/a virus

2 Tell Ss to make notes of the answers as they listen and then play the recording again to allow them to check and complete their answers.

Tapescript `CD 4 Track 1`

One
Officer: *[Southern English accent]* Mr Wakefield?
Man: *[Southern English accent]* Yes?
Officer: May we come in?
Man: Er, yes.
Officer: Mr Wakefield. I regret to inform you that your wife was arrested at Gatwick Airport this afternoon ...
Man: Airport?
Officer: ... and she's been charged with blackmail. If it's OK with you, we'd like to make an initial search of the property.
Man: Blackmail?

Two
Dan: *[slight English Midlands accent]* I'm home!
Mum: *[slight English Midlands accent]* Oh, I was wondering where you'd got to. You'll be lucky if there's any tea left – your brothers have already helped themselves.
Dan: Oh, never mind.
Mum: Anyway, what are you so pleased about? You look like the cat that got the cream!
Dan: Well. What would you say ... if I told you that ... I've been picked for the rugby team?!
Mum: What, is that all?
Dan: What do you mean 'is that all'? I'm chuffed to bits, man!

Three
Debbi: *[neutral English accent]* Dan. Have you seen Ben Fisher's new car? It's such a horrible colour!

Dan: No, I haven't.
Debbi: Well, it's parked outside their house at the moment. I wonder why he changed it when ...
Dan: Debbi. I've got something to tell you.
Debbi: Hmm?
Dan: Listen, you'd better take a seat for a moment.
Debbi: What's happened?
Dan: You know we were planning to go down to London for the weekend?
Debbi: What's happened, Dan?
Dan: Look. I don't want to beat around the bush so I'll come straight out with it.
Debbi: Da-an!
Dan: I'm afraid the trip to London is off. You see the thing is we've got our first rugby match on Saturday and there's no way I can get out of ...
Debbi: You are kidding, right?

Four
Manager: *[London accent]* Ladies and gentlemen – sorry to have kept you waiting for so long. Er, I'm pleased to inform you that the group have actually arrived now so hopefully they'll be on stage in just a few minutes. Thank you for your patience and my apologies once again for the delay.

Answers 1 Policeman and man; formal; they have arrested his wife; bad news **2** Mum and son; personal; the boy has been chosen for the school rugby team; good news **3** Boyfriend/ girlfriend or husband/wife; personal; he can't take her to London as promised; bad news **4** A theatre/concert hall/band manager; formal/ public; the group will be appearing in concert shortly; good news

SPEAK OUT

3 Ss look through the Speak Out box to find the phrase that is used in both preparing for bad and good news. Elicit what it is and show Ss that, although the same words are said, the tone of voice would be very different depending on the type of news being given.

Answers You know/remember (that)

4 Ss read through the six phrases and discuss where they think they should go. Elicit ideas before playing the recording and then go through the answers with Ss. Ss try to say them in an appropriate tone of voice.

Answers 1 B **2** A **3** B **4** B **5** C **6** A

5 Give Ss two minutes to read their situations and think about how to start the conversation. Not all phrases even from the correct section will work, eg A 1 is not serious enough for something like *I hate to be the bearer of bad news.* Suggested phrases to use: A 1 *I've got something to tell you ...* 2 *Please don't take this the wrong way, but ...* 3 Any of the phrases in C would work, eg *You'll never guess what!* B 1 *You know ... That cake was for his/her 40th birthday. I just thought you ought to know that ...* 2 *I'm pleased to inform you that ...* 3 *I've got something to tell you ...*

WRITING

This section introduces ways of writing essay introductions to make them eye-catching and interesting and to inform the reader clearly about what they are about to read.

Warm-up Review of preparing people for good or bad news. *Complete the announcement.* Put Ss in groups of three. Read out some of the phrases from Speak Out on page 101. The Ss complete the announcements (in writing) in whatever way they want. Read out about five or six and then elicit ideas. Make sure that, if the phrase signalled bad news then the Ss completed the announcement with bad news.

1 Set a time limit of three minutes for Ss to discuss the three questions and then elicit ideas in open class.

Possible answers 1 There are lots of newspapers bookmarked which indicates that the person is interested in the news. There are newspapers in three languages bookmarked (Spanish, French, English – UK and USA) so he/she is interested not only in their own country. **3** Comments sections after news stories; people send news items or photos to be included in the online newspaper. Positive: It makes people feel involved, it gives a different viewpoint than normal. Negative: The newspaper can cut costs (and quality) by using readers' stories, journalists are valued by the amount of feedback they get thus encouraging more sensational stories.

2 Look at the question with the whole class. Elicit the key words, i.e. 'essay' – the type of text, '220–260 words' – the length required, 'for and against' – need to include both, 'state your own opinions'.

Answers A 'for and against' essay. The instructions ask for arguments for and against the statement in the question as well as their own opinion.

3 Tell Ss that this is the essay without the introduction. Ss discuss the questions in pairs and then as a class. Point out that this is the usual format for such an essay: introduction; arguments for the essay title; arguments against; conclusion including the writer's opinion.

Answers 1 In the conclusion **2** In addition to this; On the other hand; One particularly positive influence is; Furthermore; Finally **3** eg what has been happening recently to newspapers and online versions

4 After Ss have shared their ideas of the points that could be made in an introduction, read through the checklist with the whole class and see how many of the points they mentioned. Point out that the checklist recommends using two or three of the ideas, not all of them.

5 Ss read the two introductions alone and then discuss their ideas in pairs. Elicit ideas in open class and point out that there is no correct answer to question 2. It is up to the Ss to decide which they prefer as long as they can justify their opinion.

Answers 1 introduction 1 Points 3, 5 and 6 **introduction 2** Points 1, 2, and 4 **2** It may be possible to argue that introduction 1 refers more explicitly to the actual topic of the essay whereas the second introduction focuses too much on the Internet in general, not just its effect on newspapers. Number 1 is also more forceful using words such as *irrelevant*, *risk* and *threat* which makes it more interesting. On the other hand, the fact that 2 introduces the Internet in general first may be seen as positive and a good way to lead on to the effect of the Internet on newspapers.

6 Ss match the phrases to the six approaches. Tell Ss to try to remember one phrase from each category that they can use in an exam if necessary.

Answers a 2 **b** 4 **c** 5 **d** 6 **e** 1 **f** 3

7 Ss look through the essay on page 102 and replace the underlined words with both *so* and *because of* to see which one makes sense. They then complete the table.

Answers Thus – therefore, consequently, as a result **Since** – as **Owing to** – on account of, thanks to, due to

Optional activity: Ss can be given further practice of the two different types of linking words by trying to change the sentences from the essay on page 102 so that, where there is a result linker, they now write it with a cause linker. For example:

Critics of the effect of the Internet on newspapers point out that the Internet has grown in importance and, therefore, sales of newspapers have dropped dramatically and, owing to this, newspapers are no longer able to make money.

In addition to this, newspaper websites are updated several times a day and so many claim that the Internet has led to a decline in the quality of journalism.

Because readers are invited to send their own accounts or photos, newspaper websites can carry information about events as soon as they happen. Furthermore, since readers can share their views with others on message boards, there is a livelier debate than there was …

Finally, newspaper websites have made them more popular and well-known and, as a result, many newspapers have seen a significant increase in their readership …

To my mind, newspapers are aware of the constant presence of their readers online and consequently they feel less remote and elitist.

8 Ss use the same approach as in Exercise 7 if they are not sure which word is correct. Where appropriate, they replace them with *so* or *because of* and see which sounds correct. They can then check the table in Exercise 7 and see which word is needed.

Answers **1** due to **2** consequently **3** Thus **4** as a result **5** owing to **6** On account of **7** Thanks to **8** since **9** Therefore; because of **10** As

9 Once Ss have chosen their topic, set a time limit of ten minutes for Ss to brainstorm arguments for and against the statement and to think of vocabulary they will need. Tell Ss that, when they write their introduction, they can use the example paragraph in Exercise 5 with minimal changes of words when necessary. Go through the two introductions and highlight the words which could possibly be used in the Ss' own essays:
1 *The issue of whether … is a complicated one. Some people claim that … while others believe that … It is my own belief that …*
2 *Most people would agree that … An example of this is … which many … However, there is considerable disagreement about whether …*
Ss could then write an introduction for each of the essays in pairs and discuss their ideas as a class.

Example introductions:

A *The issue of whether public figures have a right to privacy is a complicated one. Some people claim that they are simply normal human beings who have the same rights as everyone else while others believe that, as they use publicity to help their careers, they cannot complain when we demand to know more about their lives. It is my own belief that public figures who keep their lives private should be allowed to remain private whereas those who court publicity for their own gain cannot complain when they are unable to stop the glare of publicity.*

B *The issue of whether or not reality TV is harmless entertainment is a complicated one. Some people claim that the viewers and contestants are willing participants so there is nothing wrong with it while others believe that it is destroying vulnerable people's lives by putting them in a situation they are unable to cope with. It is my own belief that, rather than being harmless entertainment, reality TV promotes selfishness and greed in society.*

C *Most people would agree that the Internet has already had a huge impact on our lives and changed the way we read and write. An example of this is the growth of blogs and newspaper comment sections which many people contribute to and which are littered with spelling and grammatical mistakes. However, there is considerable disagreement about whether these mistakes are a result of the Internet or whether the Internet simply makes it easier for us to notice how widespread such illiteracy is.*

Ss then write their essay alone either in class or for homework.

Beyond belief

Read, listen and talk about society and beliefs.
Practise relative clauses; prefixes and suffixes.
Focus on reacting to surprising news.
Write an opinion article.

EXAM FOCUS

Topic: Society and beliefs

Speaking
Reacting to surprising news: SB p.111, ex.7

Listening
True/False: SB p.105, ex.4
Multiple choice: SB p.111, ex.3

Reading
Gapped text (paragraphs): SB p.108, ex.3
Gapped text (sentences): SB p.113, ex.4

Grammar and vocabulary
Prefixes and suffixes: SB p.105, ex.7, ex.8, ex.9
Wordbuilding: SB p.105, ex.10; p.110, ex.7

Writing
A news article: SB p.113, ex.11

Unit 10 Materials

Success Workbook Unit 10

Photocopiable resources 28, 29, 30

Testing and Evalution Programme tests

VOCABULARY AND LISTENING

This section extends the Ss' knowledge of wordbuilding looking at different types of words as well as prefixes and suffixes.

Special difficulties: There are a large number of words in the lesson which may be overwhelming for Ss at first but, as they look at the exercises, they should find that they are aware of many of the words. It is often possible for Ss to guess words that they think they do not know because they have seen the word before and have subconsciously remembered it.

Culture notes

Martian poetry was a movement in British poetry in the late 1970s and early 1980s. Poets most closely associated with it are Craig Raine and Christopher Reid as well as the novelist Martin Amis. *Martianism* is an anagram of his name. Martian poetry became a popular

topic in the teaching of poetry to schoolchildren. The poem *A Martian Sends a Postcard Home* was published in 1979.

Warm-up Review of cause and result linkers. *Write and rewrite.* Put Ss into groups of four and give each a sentence with the question: *Why?* The Ss have to make a sentence answering the question. They then pass this sentence to a second group who have to rewrite it in two ways: one answering the question *Why?* using a different linking word to the one used by the original group and one changing the sentence to use a result clause. Elicit sentences in open class.

Example sentences:

Lots of people watch reality TV shows. Why?

People are reading less. Why?

Some people don't care about international news. Why?

Some people put personal information on social-networking sites. Why?

Some people break the law. Why?

1 Put Ss into pairs. Tell them to spend a minute describing what they can see in the picture and then another minute discussing the question. Elicit ideas in open class.

2 Explain the idea of the poem: a Martian comes to Earth and sees things which are surprising or confusing. He then writes home about what he has seen and what he thinks it is. Ss discuss their ideas as a class with their reasons, eg the caxton has many wings – the pages of the book; the markings are the covers or illustrations on pages; they perch on the hand – we hold them open to read. The haunted apparatus snores – the dialling tone; if it cries – rings – we pick it up and soothe it with words – speak into it; we tickle it with a finger – dial a number.

Answers caxtons – books **haunted apparatus** – phones

3 Ss discuss the questions in pairs and as a class. Elicit ideas, eg 1 war, greed, homelessness, pollution etc. We are intelligent enough to have new technologies but not intelligent enough to live in peace and cleanliness. 2 Impressive – art, food, freedom etc. Unimpressive – weakness, violence etc. Play the recording and elicit the answers.

For tapescript see page 211.

Answers 1 royal families as entertainment; inequality; strange comparative wages for different jobs; illogical beliefs **2** Impressive: technological progress; more democracies; material progress; sensible at times Unimpressive: technological limitations; crime – dishonesty and corruption; complete insanity at times **3** dishonest, illogical, insane, selfish, sensible, thoughtless, unscrupulous

4 Ss read through the statements to see what they remember from the first time they listened. Ss then listen to the recording again. Elicit the answers and justifications for them: 1 'They've even managed to send people into space!' Q: 'Gosh! That is a surprise.' 2 'They still believe you can't travel faster than the speed of light!' 3 'They won't discover they're not alone in the universe in the foreseeable future. It's quite inconceivable!' 4 'To be honest, some of them are more like a branch of the entertainment industry.' 5 'Are you sure you're not the victim of some kind of misunderstanding?' 6 'If we were to provide them with a proper non-polluting source of energy'.

Answers 1 F **2** T **3** F **4** T **5** T **6** F

5 Before Ss look at the exercise, write the headings on the board. Look at the first, *Government*, and elicit any words Ss know to describe people or types of government, eg *president, communism* etc. Repeat the process with the other four headings. Ss then brainstorm more words in pairs. Elicit ideas and then Ss look at the words in the exercise. Elicit their answers and justifications and the meanings of the words.

Suggested answers 1 dictatorship, kingdom **2** industrialise, redistribution of wealth, inequality **3** inequality, imprisonment **4** pre-emptive attack, intolerance **5** consciousness, irrationality, scientific proof

6 Ss work in pairs and match as many of the words as they can. Ss then join up in groups of four to check their ideas and discuss what each collocation means. Elicit the answers and any definitions and then Ss add them to the correct categories.

Answers 1 e (justice) **2** c (economy) **3** f (coexistence) **4** a (coexistence) **5** j (justice) **6** b (government) **7** i (coexistence) **8** d (government) **9** g (economy) **10** h (coexistence)
Other possible collocations: 2a, 2f, 2h, 3b, 3i, 4b, 4h, 4i, 6a, 8a, 8j, 9a, 9b, 9g, 10a, 10d, 10i

7 When Ss have finished the exercise, they define the example words from the exercises using the word in the box, eg *A co-worker is someone you work **with***. *Coexistence is living **with** each other in peace*. Tell Ss that they must be sure that the words they choose really have a prefix added. *Intervene* is not an example because *tervene* is not a word on its own. Ss may also identify *im-* as a prefix meaning

not but *imprisonment* is not an example of this kind of prefix. Other prefixes meaning *not* also come up in the exercises, i.e. *il(logical)*, *in(sane)*, *ir(rational)*, *(dis)honest*.

Answers 1 with (coexistence) **2** between (international) **3** wrong/bad (misunderstood) **4** many (multinational) **5** after (post-war) **6** before (pre-emptive) **7** again (redistribution) **8** not (unimaginative, unscrupulous)

8 When Ss have found the words, elicit the answers and what they mean. Ask Ss if they can think of any other words which take the same prefixes and for a general meaning for each prefix.

Answers antisocial (against), dishonest (not), extraterrestrial (outside/away from), foresee (in the future), illogical (not), impolite (not), insane (not), irrational (not), monotheistic (one), non-polluting (not)

9 When Ss have found the words, again try to elicit different examples of words which change in the same way, eg *weaken, lengthen*. Also point out that, sometimes, when we add suffixes, there are other spelling changes that need to be made, eg the removal of a final *-e* (*create → creative*).

Answers adjective → verb simplify, industrialise **verb → noun** imprisonment, cooperation, redistribution, behaviour, coexistence, intolerance, growth **adjective → noun** irrationality/inequality, justice, consciousness **noun → noun** monarchy, dictatorship, kingdom, capitalism **noun → adjective** logical, scrupulous, mindless, selfish, economic, scientific, parliamentary **verb → adjective** amusing, creative/sensitive, imaginative, sensible, changeable, tolerant

10 Ss work together to think what kinds of words are needed (noun, adjective etc, negative or positive) and to find them in the unit or try to guess what they should be. Elicit answers in open class.

Answers 1 foreseeable; inconceivable **2** industrialise **3** redistribution **4** unbelievable **5** misunderstanding **6** illogical **7** unimaginative **8** thoughtless; selfish; unscrupulous **9** sensible; dishonesty; corruption; intolerance, insanity

11 Continue the conversation in the example: *Society is all of us. The people. So government is a way of organising people and constitutional monarchy has some people who can tell us what to do and one family who look important but actually can't tell us what to do at all. They are just there to look nice.* Ss choose a word each from Exercise 5 and carry out similar conversations in pairs. Nominate Ss to act out their conversation in front of the class. The other Ss are also Martians and can also ask for extra information if the Martian in the roleplay doesn't.

ADDITIONAL PRACTICE: Photocopiable resources. Resource 28: *Find and use.* Page 197

GRAMMAR

This section extends the Ss' understanding of relative clauses.

Special difficulties: Most of the information should be known to Ss at this level although there may still be some fossilised errors with *what* which have been caused by L1 interference. The Mind the trap! box should clarify this problem.

Culture notes

Panama hats actually originated in Ecuador but were transported to Panama for export. They are also known as Jipijapa after the town in which they were produced.

Theodore Roosevelt (1858–1919), known as Teddy to the public, was the 26th President of the USA. He was an explorer and famous for his energy and cowboy personality. He was the first president to be awarded the Nobel Peace Prize.

Antonio Meucci (1808–1889) was an Italian inventor who many believed invented the telephone. In 2002, the USA House of Representatives passed a bill saying that, if he, Meucci, had been able to pay the $10 to register his invention, Bell could never have been awarded the patent.

Warm-up Review of prefixes and suffixes from the previous lesson and introduction to the topic of the lesson. *Predict the topic.* Write on the board: *believe, educate, combine, natural, dead, estimate, danger, invent.* Ss work in groups of three or four and try to think of as many words as they can from the root words on the board. Elicit ideas and then give the Ss the words from the Grammar section: *unbelievable, educational, combination, naturalist, deadly, overestimate, endanger, invention.* Ss work in their groups to guess the topic of the lesson based on the words given. Elicit ideas and then Ss open their books and look at Exercise 1.

1 Allow Ss three minutes to look at the pictures and discuss the questions. Elicit ideas in open class and ask the Ss if they enjoy these programmes and why or why not.

Answers 1 It's a quiz show with a panel of experts about science and things that we thought were true but are actually not. **2** They learn things, facts are introduced in an interesting, lively fashion.

2 Think Back! Elicit the answers and example sentences which demonstrate the five points, eg 1 *Amy is the woman who presents 'Unbelievable!'* Without the clause we have *Amy is the woman* which is meaningless.

Answers 1 defining **2** non-defining. Because the clause can be removed and still leave an understandable sentence. **3** defining **4** defining **5** non-defining

3 Tell Ss to put a dash (–) as a choice where the pronoun can be left out. Elicit the answers and their choices for the best guests (David and Peggy may be good choices because they are knowledgeable about their specialist subjects but Adam may be more fun).

Answers 1 which/that **2** that/which/ – **3** that/which **4** who **5** that/which/ – **6** whose **7** who/that **8** that/who/ – **9** who **10** which **11** which

4 Again there may be more than one possible answer so elicit all possibilities for the four sentences, i.e. 1 *where/ – /that/which.* Elicit ideas for the endings, then play the recording for Ss to listen to the relative pronouns used in the text and the correct answers.

Tapescript CD 4 Track 3

Amy: *[neutral English accent]* So, the place where Panama hats come from is … Adam?

Adam: *[Manchester accent]* Panama.

Amy: No, sorry, Adam. David?

David: *[neutral English accent]* Ecuador. The reason why they're called Panama hats is that they came to Europe via Panama.

Amy: Yes, it's Unbelievable! But Panama hats actually originated in Ecuador. They were popular with the people building the Panama canal. And while visiting the canal in 1906, US president Theodore Roosevelt put one on, as a result of which the hat was forever linked with Panama. For a bonus point, where do the fibres with which the hats are manufactured come from?

Adam: Ecuador.

Amy: Yes, Adam, but which plant do they come from?

Adam: Oh! I had no idea it was the plant you were talking about. I thought it was the country. Em … the fibres Panama hats are made with come from … the potato.

Amy: No, Adam. The potato has many uses, none of which involve hats. No, the plant from which the fibres for Panama hats are extracted is a palm tree, *Carludovica palmata.*

Adam: Oh, right. Of course.

Amy: Now, the deadliest animal that has ever lived is … Adam?

Adam: Human beings.

Amy: Sorry! Peggy?

Peggy: *[London accent]* The mosquito. In fact, it's hard to overestimate the extent to which mosquitoes endanger our lives. They carry hundreds of diseases.

Amy: That's right. In the history of the world it is estimated that about 90 billion people have died, half of whom were killed by mosquitoes. Unbelievable!

Peggy: Fortunately, the late 19th century was a period in which there were many medical advances and that's when we discovered mosquitoes carry diseases.

Amy: Thank you, Peggy. Now, the man who invented the telephone was … Adam?

Adam: I know what you think I'm going to say …

Amy: Oh yes?

Adam: Yes, you think I'm going to say Alexander Graham Bell, but …

Amy: Well, you are the man I rely on to get the wrong answers.

Adam: ... but I'm not – thank you – I'm not because this is the part where I surprise you and get the right answer.

Amy: Uh huh?

Adam: Yeah, it was an Italian whose name was ... oh ... Antonio something ... Antonio Munchio!

Amy: Not quite. The person to whom you are referring was called Antonio Meucci, and he ...

Adam: That's the guy I was thinking of.

Amy: ... and he invented his 'telettrofono' in 1860. Unfortunately for Meucci, Alexander Graham Bell registered the invention in 1876, and became known as the inventor of the telephone. Meucci died in 1889, by which time Bell had made a fortune from the invention. Unbelievable! Now, the biggest thing a blue whale can swallow is a) a peanut, b) a grapefruit or c) a sailor. David!

David: A sailor!

Amy: No! Peggy?

Peggy: A grapefruit.

Amy: Correct. Hard though it is to believe, the blue whale has quite a narrow throat.

David: Wait a minute! I read a story in which a sailor survived in a whale's stomach for ages!

Amy: Yes, the sailor you read about was James Bartley, who is said to have spent 15 hours inside not a blue whale, but a sperm whale. However, that really is unbelievable. It never happened. There is no reason why a sperm whale couldn't have swallowed him – its throat is wide enough. And conceivably, he could have slid into the whale's stomach, in which case he would have been killed instantly by the extreme acidity of the stomach juices. Now, the people to whom we must give thanks for inventing champagne are ... Adam?

Adam: The French.

Amy: No, it wasn't the French ...

> **Answers** 1 where; Ecuador 2 that; mosquito 3 who; Antonio Meucci 4 –; a grapefruit

Work it out

5 Ss work in pairs to decide which sentences are true and which false. Where they are false, ask Ss to rewrite the sentences so that they are true, eg 2 *It is more informal to put the preposition at the end.*

> **Answers** 1 T 2 F (more informal) 3 T 4 F (*which* for things and *whom* for people) 5 T 6 T

6 Ss work in pairs. Note that in informal spoken English, sentence 4 could also be said as: *I read a story where a sailor ...*

> **Answers** 1 He's the mate I play tennis with. 2 Is this the game you paid $10 for? 3 I've got the book you were talking about. 4 I read a story in which a sailor survived in a whale's stomach. 5 He is the man without whom we could not have completed this project. 6 These are the principles on which our plan to bring peace to all nations is based.

> **Mind the trap!**
>
> Read through the box with the Ss and give them other examples of sentences taking *what*, eg *I know what you did last summer./I know the things that you did last summer.*

Check it out

7 Look at the first two sentences with the whole class and then tell Ss to work alone to complete the exercise.

> **Answers** 1 I know what you think I'm going to say. 2 Wherever it is, I'll find it. 3 Whoever said that can't be serious. 4 Adam's ready to show us what/whatever he knows. 5 You can come back whenever you like. 6 Just say whatever comes into your head. 7 What I like about *Unbelievable!* is you learn a lot. 8 Whichever answer I give you, I'll be wrong.

8 Look through the phrases with the Ss and elicit what they refer to where possible, eg (a) people, (b) a situation, (c) things, (d) possibly a book or film. Ss work in pairs. Elicit the answers and ask Ss to rephrase the sentences, eg 1 *They are called Panama hats because they came ...* 2 *Because Roosevelt put one on, the hat was ...*

> **Answers** 1 g 2 j 3 c 4 i 5 a 6 h 7 d 8 e 9 f 10 b

9 Put Ss into groups of four. Elicit ideas for both the missing word and the missing information and write these on the board. When Ss listen to the recording they can see who was correct both grammatically and with their facts.

> **For tapescript** see page 212.

> **Answers** 1 which (that); fruit fly 2 –; whip 3 who; which; hippopotamus and elephant ivory 4 whose; which; ant 5 –; from; rabbits 6 to; as many different species of animals as possible 7 result; work-related accidents 8 extent; 2% 9 which; 11–14 months

10 Set a time limit for the activity rather than a specific number of questions as it may take some Ss much longer to think of questions than others. Ss ask each other in groups of four, then ask and answer in open class.

ADDITIONAL PRACTICE: Photocopiable resources. Resource 29: *Dr What? Dr Who.* Page 198

READING AND VOCABULARY

This section introduces more collocations, phrasal verbs, and examples of wordbuilding through a reading on myths.

Culture notes

The **J.F. Kennedy** quote was from a speech given at Yale University in June 1962. He was talking about myths about the USA and its economy.

The (Age of) Enlightenment does not represent a single school of thought. The philosophies often did not agree with each other. What they all had in common was a critical questioning of traditional institutions, customs, and morals. There are no clearly agreed beginnings or endings to the period but it started at some point between the middle of the 17th and start of the 18th century. The ending was at some point between the French Revolution of 1789 and the Napoleonic wars of 1804–1815.

Peter Popoff (born 1946) is a German televangelist and faith healer. He now lives in California. During shows in the 1970s he pretended to be able to state names, addresses and other information about people in the audience. His deception was revealed in 1983. He returned to television in 2007. He is now promoting his 'miracle manna bread'.

Arthur Conan Doyle became attracted to spiritualism and occult topics after the death of his son during First World War. While researching the topic of fairies he was given some photographs from a working-class family in Yorkshire. These photographs appeared to show fairies dancing in front of two teenage girls, Elsie and Frances. Many years later the girls admitted that they had faked the photos and the book destroyed Conan Doyle's reputation at the time.

Warm-up Review of relative clauses. *Our group*. Put Ss into groups of four. Tell Ss to find something that is true of all of them, one of them, two of them and three of them, eg *No one speaks German, one person lives in a village, two people have got sisters, three people like heavy rock music and all of us have done our homework*. While they are doing this, write: *none of whom, one of whom, half of whom, three of whom* and *all of whom* on the board. Each group comes out in turn and writes on the board: *We are a group …* They give one of their facts … *have got sisters* and the rest of the class have to guess what the true sentence is, eg *We are a group, half of whom have got sisters*. Award points for correctly formulated sentences and correct answers.

1 Check the word: *myth* (a usually ancient story which may tell you about some aspects of a certain culture but which is not necessarily true). Elicit from the Ss what they think they can see in the pictures and discuss what the class thinks of them all. Accept any opinions from the class as long as they can give a good reason.

Answers 1 the Loch Ness monster 2 Santa Claus 3 Bigfoot/Yeti 4 fairies 5 crystals that can ward off bad energy 6 faith healers 7 Elvis Presley is still alive 8 telepathy

2 Ask Ss where they can find a summary of what an article is about and what the writer's opinions are (usually the introduction and conclusion). Ss read these two paragraphs only and discuss in pairs what they think the correct opinion is. Elicit answers and reasons for them: (a) It says in the conclusion that people will never allow myths to die but not that this is the writer's opinion. (b) Both the introduction and conclusion contradict this: 'despite the Enlightenment (...) despite science (...) millions of people still firmly believe ...'. (c) There are many examples of these useful functions – answers, consolation, make us feel like children, make money.

Answer c

3 Remind Ss of the techniques for doing this. First, look at the overall subject matter before and after each number in the text. Then look at the overall subject matter of the paragraphs to insert. This will help give an idea of where they should go. Having done this, make sure that the text is coherent, i.e. that grammatical and lexical clues in the text and the inserted paragraphs fit logically together, eg pronouns referring back to something written previously, linkers of cause and effect, contradiction and addition making logical sense.
Elicit the answers and the textual clues that Ss used to help them decide: 1 The previous paragraph asks 'Why?' and the paragraph to insert starts 'One explanation'. 2 The paragraph to insert finishes 'And others go to see faith-healers' and the following paragraph talks about a famous faith-healer. 3 The paragraph to insert finishes 'It's human nature' and the next paragraph starts by talking about 'Another human trait'. 4 The link between 'no (...) evidence (...) has ever been found' and the contrasting linker 'However, people don't like the facts to get in the way'. 5 The contrast between 'Nessie is extremely profitable' and 'Not all myths are money-making exercises'. 6 The link is the mention of fairies in both the text 'published a book entitled *The Coming of the Fairies*' and the paragraph to insert 'believing there are fairies at the bottom of your garden.'

Answers 1 B 2 G 3 A 4 F 5 E 6 D

4 Ss find and underline each myth mentioned. Elicit how many there are and what they are. Ss then read the text about them to see what the writer's attitude is in each case. Elicit answers with justifications from the text and then discuss as a class whether he is fair or not.
Crystals and magic stones – 'the power of suggestion', increase your chance of recovery'.
Fairies – 'make life more colourful and interesting', 'What's so bad about that?'

Students' Book ➡ pages 108–110

Elvis – 'self-deception', 'sincere', 'unwillingness to admit the truth'.
Yeti – 'We love telling tall tales'.
Miracle cures – 'hardly surprising that' people place their faith in them.
Evangelist – 'fraud', 'risked people's lives'.
Nessie – 'money-making exercise'.
In general – 'search for simple answers', 'comfortable', 'good fun', 'appeal to the child', 'consolation', 'enticing explanations', 'unhealthy profit for the cynical people'.

Answers He understands why people believe in myths and is sympathetic to all except those that involve deception for financial gain which he disapproves of.

5 Ss find the underlined phrasal verbs in the text and attempt to work out their meaning from the context of the article. Ss then complete the sentences in the exercise. Elicit the answers and ask Ss to rephrase the sentences replacing the phrasal verbs, eg 1 *Aliens are doing/undertaking a study.* 2 *You have no facts to justify your theory.* 3 *I'm not lying/ telling a story.* 4 *My grandfather is a great believer in garlic.* 5 *You can rely on her.* 6 *I believed his hard-luck story.*

Answers 1 carrying out 2 back up 3 making (it) up 4 swears by 5 count on 6 fell for

6 Ss work in pairs to guess the collocations. When they have finished, elicit what the less obvious ones mean (all the collocations with *discover* mean to find out, all with *disseminate* mean to spread, all with *genuine* mean real/true), eg *dispel a myth* – disprove it; *peddle a myth* – try to make people believe it; *irrefutable proof* – impossible to deny; *tangible proof* – visible; *blind faith* – without thinking or questioning; *a leap of faith* – a sudden increase in faith in order to believe something new; *disseminate lies* – to spread them; *a plausible explanation* – believable.

Answers 1 myth 2 proof 3 discover 4 faith 5 disseminate 6 genuine 7 explanation

7 Tell Ss that there may be more than one word possible for each gap and some boxes with words already in could have another word added, eg *believe/disbelieve*. Ss do as much as they can in pairs and then get together in groups of four to share ideas. Make sure that all Ss have a copy of the completed table at the end.

Answers believe/disbelieve; belief/disbelief/believer/ unbeliever; (un)believable **prove**/disprove; proof; proven/provable/disprovable **persist**; persistence; persistent **persuade**; persuasion; persuasive/persuaded/ persuadable **comfort**/discomfort (v); comfort/discomfort (n); (un)comfortable/comforting **tempt**; temptation/ tempter/temptress; tempting/tempted **forgive**; forgiveness; (un)forgiven/(un)forgivable **verify**; verification; verified/verifiable **deceive**; deception/deceit; deceptive **delude**; delusion; delusive/deluded

8 Look at the example and ask what it describes (a myth). Elicit what the relative clause is (everything following the word *which*) and the word from the previous exercises (*belief*). Ss do the same in pairs. Nominate pairs to read one sentence each.

Possible answers 1 It is something which, unbelievably, makes us better without any scientific reason why. 2 It is someone who tries to persuade you that he/she can make you better without medicine. 3 It is a story which is made up. 4 It is something which takes the place of genuine medicine and can sometimes make you feel better because you think you are taking genuine medicine. 5 An object which people believe will protect them from disease or evil spirits if they wear it. 6 It is an unverifiable technique in which one person is able to read another person's mind. 7 It is a trick in which someone persuades others to believe something. 8 It is a crime in which someone deceives others for money. 9 It is a creature which is very small and can carry out magic spells.

9 Ss discuss the cartoon in pairs and then as a class. Ss then work together to complete the text. Play the recording and then elicit the answers in open class.

Tapescript CD 4 Track 6

Dr: *[slight German accent]* So, Mr Claus. How are you feeling today?
Santa: *[RP accent]* I've been having terrible stomach pains, doc.
Dr: Have you been to see a doctor?
Santa: Yes, but he said it was all in my head, so I went to see a faith-healer.
Dr: Really?
Santa: Yes, but she said she'd lost faith in herself and had given up providing miracle cures. She confessed she was nothing but a fraud.
Dr: Oh dear! And how have you been feeling mentally?
Santa: Depressed.
Dr: Why's that?
Santa: Well, yesterday I read an article in a newspaper that accused me of being just another tall tale. It explained that the only thing we do by persistently 'peddling the myth' of Santa Claus is to disseminate lies to innocent little children. Tell me the truth, doc. Am I guilty of deceiving children?
Dr: Do you think you are?
Santa: No, of course not! But the thing is this article gave an extremely plausible explanation of why I can't possibly exist. It said I was just about as believable as fairies at the bottom of the garden! It was very persuasive. By the end I'd stopped believing in myself! Be honest with me, doc. Am I just a delusion?
Dr: If it's any help, Mr Claus, it's perfectly normal to fall into the temptation of self-doubt.
Santa: That's no comfort to me, doc. What I need is irrefutable proof that I exist. Tell me I'm not a hoax.
Dr: I'm afraid I can't give you that proof. You're just going to have to take a leap of faith.
Santa: I don't know if I can do that, doc.
Dr: Well, you'd better try. It's Christmas Eve tomorrow.

10 Ss choose one idea each making sure they do
not choose the same one. Allow two minutes for Ss
to think about their own topic and a further two
minutes to think of arguments against their partner's
topic. Ss then take it in turns to defend their topic.
When they have finished, elicit what the Ss really
think of the ideas mentioned and ask about other
supernatural phenomena that they may have heard
of, eg horoscopes, sixth sense etc.

LISTENING AND SPEAKING

This section introduces ways of reacting to
surprising news.

Special difficulties: Sometimes the expressions
can be used for more than one emotion, eg *I don't
believe it* can show anger, disappointment,
sorrow or delight. Make sure Ss understand that
the tone of voice is as important as the words
spoken and encourage them to really act during
roleplays.

Warm-up Review of vocabulary from the previous lesson.
Telepathy. Tell Ss you are going to try an experiment
on telepathy. You will write a word on the board, eg
honest, and write another word on a piece of paper
made from that root, eg *dishonesty.* The Ss have to
guess what word you have written. Those that are
correct move on to the second word and so on until
you have given them five words or there is only one
student left. Repeat the process with a second set of
five words to see if the same student does well again
and shows signs of telepathy.

Words to use:

1 *prove (proof), forgive (unforgivable), tempt
(temptation), believe (belief), deceive (deception)*

2 *comfort (uncomfortable), religion (religious),
persist (persistence), verify (verification), delude
(delusion)*

1 Ss work together in pairs. Any adjectives that they
do not understand, they look up in a dictionary. They
then discuss the people in the photos. Elicit ideas but
don't give any answers yet as they will find out the
actual facts from the recording.

2 Play the recording once for Ss to do the matching
task and to note down the news each has received
and how they are feeling. Ss may disagree about
some of the adjectives. Allow them to justify their
opinions and tell them that more than one answer
may be correct.

Tapescript CD 4 Track 7

One
Mum: *[Newcastle accent]* Are you sure you want me to
do this, Gwen?
Gwen: *[Newcastle accent]* Yes, Mum!
Mum: You won't be too upset if you've failed some of
them, will you?
Gwen: No, I won't. I know I've failed Maths, anyway.
Mum: You're sure?
Gwen: Yes, go on Mum. Just open it, alright!
Mum: OK ... Right ... Oh dear!
Gwen: What? What is it?
Mum: You've failed them.
Gwen: What? All of them?
Mum: Yes. Every one.
Gwen: No, you're having me on, right?
Mum: No, I'm not.
Gwen: I don't believe it! All of them?
Mum: Yes.
Gwen: What even Art?
Mum: Yes. You must be really disappointed.
Gwen: Disappointed! I'm heartbroken!
Mum: I know.
Gwen: Oh, Mum ... I'm really cut up about this. I feel
like I'm useless.
Mum: It's a terrible shame!
Gwen: What am I gonna do?
Mum: You can do them again in September.
Gwen: I wanted to get a job this summer, but now I'm
gonna have to spend all my time in the library!
Mum: Never mind, love, you'll get over it. The
important thing is you mustn't get too worried ...

Two
Gavin: *[Welsh accent]* Hello.
Sue: *[Welsh accent]* Hi Gavin, it's me.
Gavin: Are you alright?
Sue: Of course, I'm alright. Why wouldn't I be?
Gavin: Well, you said you would call as soon as the
plane landed. That was six hours ago!
Sue: Yeah, I'm sorry, but first of all I couldn't get a
signal ...
Gavin: I didn't know what to do. I was worried sick.
Sue: ... and then my batteries ran out, so I couldn't ...
Gavin: I've been sitting here biting my nails!
Sue: Yeah, well I said I was sorry.
Gavin: Thank goodness you're alright. Was the flight
alright?
Sue: Yeah, it was fine. Listen Gavin ...
Gavin: It's a load off my mind. I'll tell you that for
nothing.
Sue: Gavin! Don't you want to hear the news?
Gavin: I'm dying to hear the news.
Sue: Well, shut up a minute and let me tell you.
Gavin: I'm all ears.
Sue: I got the job.
Gavin: That's brilliant!
Sue: Yeah, I start next month.
Gavin: Oh, I'm really chuffed.
Sue: And guess what? There's a free house with the job!
Gavin? Are you still there?
Gavin: Yeah.
Sue: What's wrong?

Gavin: I'm speechless. I don't know what to say. A house?

Sue: Yeah, with a swimming pool!

Gavin: It's beyond belief! You could knock me down with a feather.

Sue: So, listen. When are you going to come …

Three

Tracy: *[Scottish accent]* OK, Colin, do you want the good news or the bad news?

Colin: *[Scottish accent]* Whatever!

Tracy: No, go on choose, what do you want to hear first?

Colin: OK, Tracy, give me the good news.

Tracy: We've got a gig next Saturday, and you'll never guess where!

Colin: Where?

Tracy: At the Students' Union!

Colin: So what?

Tracy: I thought you'd be pleased. It's the best venue we've ever had!

Colin: It's no big deal! It's only a bunch of spoilt students.

Tracy: I can't believe you! I was really surprised when Baz told me!

Colin: Well, I'm not. It was on the cards, wasn't it? I saw it coming! What's the bad news?

Tracy: Oh! Baz wants us to learn a couple of new songs.

Colin: Oh what a drag! More songs!

Tracy: Yeah.

Colin: Oh, it's a real pain, that is. Which songs does the dictator want us to do?

Tracy: Em … you won't like them …

Colin: Which ones?

Tracy: Em … *Baby one more time* and *What goes around*.

Colin: What? Oh no … We're not playing those songs. No way!

Tracy: Look, they're not that bad, we can rearrange them and …

Suggested answers **1** She has just received bad exam results. She is feeling disbelieving/distraught/ disappointed. **2** He has been waiting for his girlfriend's/wife's phone call. He hears about her new job. He is feeling apprehensive/furious/disbelieving/ relieved/delighted. **3** He hears about a gig and the songs they have to play. He is furious/disappointed/ indifferent/suspicious/indignant.
Matching A 3 **B** 1 **C** 2

3 Ss read through the questions and note any answers they think they remember. Play the recording and elicit what was actually said on the recording which gave them the answers: 1 'I know I've failed Maths, anyway.' 2 'I'm gonna have to spend all my time in the library!' 3 'I couldn't get a signal (…) and then my batteries ran out.' 4 'I'm speechless. I don't know what to say.' 5 'It was on the cards, wasn't it? I saw it coming!' 6 'We're not playing those songs. No way!'

Answers 1 b 2 c 3 b 4 c 5 a 6 b

4 Tell Ss to close their eyes. Say the following with pauses to allow Ss time to think: *You are at home. The phone rings. Pick it up. Who is calling? … They tell you something surprising. What is it? … How do you feel now? … What do you think is going to happen next?* Ss then open their eyes and tell their partner what they thought about. If anyone then wants to share a real anecdote with the class, let them do it after the pairwork.

SPEAK OUT

5 Ss read through the phrases a–k in pairs and guess when people would say them. Then they match them to the emotions in the Speak Out box. Elicit answers and ask Ss to say the phrases in the emotion they are meant to express. Eg *I'm all ears* would be said with excited anticipation. Point out that the emotions disbelief and surprise are very similar and the phrases may be interchangeable.

Answers 1 h 2 j 3 a 4 e 5 k 6 d 7 f 8 c 9 g 10 i 11 b

6 Look at the first one with the class. Elicit that there are a number of ways of reacting to this, eg *Never mind. What a drag. It's no big deal. It was on the cards. You're having me on. You could knock me down with a feather.* These could all be appropriate as it may be no surprise if the person's father and elder brother are also bald. You could say that it does not matter if you are the person's girlfriend and want him to know that you will love him whatever his hair is like. Ss work in pairs to think of different ways of reacting to each piece of news. Elicit feedback by nominating one student to say one of these sentences to a second student. The second student reacts appropriately. Repeat with different Ss for each sentence.

7 Set a time limit of three minutes for Ss to think of their 'news'. Ss practise responding to their own news in pairs, then tell each other in open class and react to each other.

ADDITIONAL PRACTICE: Photocopiable resources. Resource 30: *Act it out.* Page 199

WRITING AND SPEAKING

This section looks at how to write an article for a newspaper or magazine, focusing on the organisation, style, useful vocabulary and other useful features.

Culture notes

Roswell is a city in New Mexico. The Roswell incident happened on 7 June 1947. The first press release on the incident stated that a flying disc had been recovered. This was then changed to say that it had been a weather balloon.

Lee Harvey Oswald, who was arrested for killing Kennedy, was himself murdered before he could be questioned. Witnesses say that bullets were fired from more than one position.

When **Princess Diana** was killed she was with Dodi Fayed. His father has claimed that the Royal Family were behind their deaths as they did not want Diana to marry a Muslim.

The reasons why people believe that the US government faked the **Apollo moon landings** are because, at the time with the problems in Vietnam, the country needed a morale boost.

Conspiracy theories about the **9/11** attacks mainly revolve around the destruction of building 7 which was not hit by the planes and the fact that planes were not sent to intercept hijacked aircraft even after it was known what was happening.

The **Watergate** story was not a conspiracy theory, and the story was uncovered by two journalists from *The Washington Post* who were played by Robert Redford and Dustin Hoffman in *All The President's Men.*

Conspiracy Theory was released in 1997 and starred Mel Gibson and Julia Roberts. Mel Gibson is a taxi driver and Julia Roberts is a lawyer who he once saved from a mugger. Although she thinks at first that he is a harmless eccentric, she finds out that there are sinister people chasing him and they may have even killed her father.

Warm-up Introduce the topic of the lesson. *Anagram race.* Put Ss into groups of four. Give each group two words, chopped up into individual letters. Ss work together to try to find the two words. Keep the two words separate to make the task easier or combine all the letters together to make it very difficult. If Ss are having problems, give them the first letter of each word and, after another thirty seconds, give the second letters and so on until one group find the words.
Words to use:
C O N S P I R A C Y   T H E O R I E S

1 Ss look at the cartoon and the two questions. After they have discussed them in pairs, elicit ideas and ask Ss what they think about conspiracy theories.

Answers 1 It is a theory that what we are told about a major news story is not actually true and that certain people, in government or business, are conspiring to keep the truth secret for some reason. **2** The man is making his own conspiracy theory: what the government tells us is untrue but the conspiracy theories are also made up by the same government so that people won't find out what the real truth is.

2 Tell Ss that, even if they have never heard about these conspiracy theories, they should use their imaginations to try to think what conspiracy theorists say. Play the recording and elicit the answers. Then discuss any other conspiracy theories that they know about as a class.

Tapescript CD 4 Track 8

[neutral English accent] Thanks to the Internet, conspiracy theories reach a wider audience today than ever before. In tonight's programme we're going to look at some of the best-known conspiracy theories and judge whether there is any credible evidence for them. Some people swear that man has never set foot on the moon. They say the 1969 Apollo 11 moon landings were faked and were actually filmed in a TV studio. One of their main arguments is that the US flag seems to be flying in the wind when there is no wind on the moon. However, this is easily explained. The flag had a horizontal pole along its top edge to ensure it would be flying proudly and not just hanging limply on the flagpole.

And speaking of space travel, what about the Roswell aliens? According to the conspiracy theorists – and many screenwriters for film and TV – in July 1947 an alien spacecraft crashed in New Mexico. The US Air Force is said to have examined the aliens' dead bodies before covering up the whole incident. Apparently, most of the technological progress of the last sixty years has come about as a result of copying the advanced technology found in the aliens' spaceship. In fact, the most likely explanation of the 'alien crash' is that a weather balloon blew up at high altitude and fell to earth.

Some cases are so puzzling and the official explanations so unsatisfying, that it seems natural to keep looking for alternative explanations. This is the case with the assassination of President Kennedy. Unhappy with the idea that it was all the work of lone madman, Lee Harvey Oswald, conspiracy theorists have searched high and wide for more believable culprits. In Oliver Stone's film *JFK* the conspiracy goes all the way through the US government from the FBI and the CIA to the Pentagon and the White House. The only problem is that despite decades of searching no irrefutable evidence has been found.

In more recent times the CIA has also been blamed for organising or at least turning a blind eye to the 9/11 attacks on the World Trade Center. The theory goes, they did it so that the US government would have a good excuse to launch a war against terror. The only thing is that such a conspiracy would require so many people to be involved it is unthinkable that in a society so obsessed with news and fame that nobody would have stepped forward to reveal the truth.

Conspiracy theorists love a good story. They feel
unhappy that a life as dramatic and romantic as that of
Princess Diana should end in a sad little car crash due
to a driver drinking too much and driving too fast. So
they invent stories involving the British Royal Family
actually being blood-crazed murderers. Again, just one
problem: no evidence.

However, some conspiracy theories do turn out to be
conspiracy facts. Look at the Watergate case. After
ordering spies to break into the Democratic Party
Headquarters, President Richard Nixon then
desperately tried to cover it up, telling lie after lie until
he was eventually forced to resign from office in the
biggest political scandal of the 20th century. After the
break we'll be looking at these theories in more detail
and I'll be speaking to ...

3 Ss read the article and decide which view the
writer holds and which extracts helped them to
decide. It starts as if the writer holds opinion (b) but
this is just a dramatic device to get the reader
interested. The writer's opinions are shown in the
conclusion: 'be neither dismissed nor accepted lightly'.

Answer c

4 Ss work in pairs. Elicit the answers and the reasons
for them, i.e. 1 'like these' – these examples given in the
previous sentences. 2 The word 'So' links 'unscrupulous
people have conspired' to 'some (...) have been (...)
facts'. 3 'On the contrary' contrasts 'It does not mean
we should take them at face value' and 'they should be
taken with a pinch of salt'. 4 'He' is Mel Gibson's
character. 'One of them' refers to one of the crazy ideas.
5 The second sentence follows the first logically:
'Conspiracy theories should be neither dismissed nor
accepted lightly' – they should 'be analysed objectively'.

Answers 1 h 2 g 3 c 4 d 5 a

5 Ss work in pairs to match the sentences and
reasons. Elicit more details, eg *furthermore* is an
additive linker whereas we need a contrastive one.
The personal anecdote is about how the writer had
enjoyed the film. *Primary objective* and *examine the
validity* are both formal expressions.

Answers 1 b 2 e 3 f

6 When Ss have read the introductions and
conclusions and discussed the questions in pairs,
note that they should avoid phrases such as *I
wonder*, *to me* and *I suppose*.

Answers 1 In the article. It immediately catches the
attention. *I wonder* and *seems to me* make the other
one sound vague. The rhetorical question is also a
useful device for making people read on. **2** In the
article. *I suppose* sounds vague. The passive structure
with *should be* sounds much better. '[I]t's important to
have fun in life' is also irrelevant and the wrong style.

7 Ss work alone to find examples in the text. Elicit
answers in open class: 1 'Should we take conspiracy
theories like this seriously? 2 'Throughout history',
'Nixon spied' etc; 3 'lack serious evidence, are simply
illogical, would require so many conspirators ...'.

Answers 1 b 2 c 3 a

TRAIN YOUR BRAIN

8 Sometimes both choices may seem sensible so the
Ss should refer to the article on page 112 to decide.
Elicit answers with reference to the text, eg 1 the
introduction does not really inform as the writer
does not really believe these theories are true.

Answers 1 b 2 b 3 b 4 a 5 a 6 a, b, c, e

9 Ss underline key words in the question to find out
what and who the article is for (to disagree with a
politician's views for a local newspaper). Ss then
look at the introduction and conclusion in pairs and
find problems with them.

Answers **Introduction** vague (I'm not sure); not very
interesting **Conclusion** vague (probably unfair)

10 Ss decide on the best four or five to put in their
article and also any they definitely would not use and
why. Elicit ideas, eg points 1, 8 and 9 show why
young people do not live in a virtual world. Points 3
and 10 show that, although technology is widely
used, it is not necessarily a bad thing.

11 Ss look at the introduction to the article on page
112 and try to write in a similar style for the question
in Exercise 9. Ss work in pairs or small groups and
then compare ideas as a class.
Example introduction:
*Twenty-four-hour-a day satellite film channels,
mobile phones with Internet connections and games
constantly at our side. A computer in every
bedroom. The possibility of getting lost in a virtual
world certainly does exist but are young people
slaves to this technology or its masters, able to use
it to enhance and improve their real world lives?*
Ss then write their article alone either in class or for
homework.

THINK FORWARD TO EXAMS REVISION 5
UNITS 9–10

VOCABULARY AND GRAMMAR

1 Ss look at the first group of words, one at a time. Try to elicit a definition for each, eg *trivial – unimportant*, undemanding – *not difficult*, in-depth – *in detail*, superficial – *very basic*. Ss then say which is different and why. Ss work in pairs and do the same for the other words. Elicit the answers and the reasons for them.

Answers **1** in-depth (It means *in detail* and implies seriousness whereas the others all mean *simple, basic* or *unimportant*.) **2** tabloid (The other words can all be used to describe 'good' newspapers.) **3** parody (The other words are all crimes. A parody is a humorous copy of music, acting, art etc.) **4** listing (The others are types of TV show. A listing shows you all the shows that are on TV on a particular day.) **5** gullible (All the other words describe being sad or upset. A gullible person is someone who is easily fooled.) **6** far-fetched (The other words mean something is believable and could be true. *Far-fetched* is the opposite.)

2 Ss look at the gaps to decide what kind of word is needed. Look at the first one with the class and show or elicit that what is needed is a noun that is singular or uncountable (to agree with the verb *has*). Therefore, *The readers* cannot be correct. Ss do the same for the other gaps. Elicit the types of words needed: 2 plural noun; 3 adjective; 4 noun, negative connotation; 5 noun; 6 noun, negative connotation; 7 adjective. Then Ss complete the exercise alone.

Answers **1** readership **2** inconsistencies **3** downloadable **4** irresponsibility **5** imprisonment **6** inequality **7** speechless

3 Tell Ss to look at the title and the photo. Ss work in pairs or small groups to predict who or what Piltdown Man might be. Elicit ideas and then Ss read through the text quickly to get a general idea of what the text is about. Then they work in pairs to complete the gaps. When Ss have finished, tell one of them to close their eyes and listen carefully while the other reads through the text. The one with eyes closed tries to hear whether the text sounds right with the words they have used. Elicit answers in open class.

Answers **1** theory/idea/view **2** mystery **3** been **4** coverage **5** next **6** proof/evidence **7** myth **8** until **9** out **10** than **11** joke **12** in **13** up

4 Ss work in pairs to try to think of how to write the second sentence in each case. When they have finished, pairs join up in groups of four to compare their ideas. If possible, give each student in each group a number from 1–4 and then make four new groups consisting of all the number ones, all the twos etc. The Ss again compare answers and try to agree

on one correct answer for each sentence. Elicit these in open class and correct where necessary.

Answers **1** Thanks to her parents (parents' generosity) **2** on account of a drop in **3** Since there is no evidence **4** due to heavy traffic **5** owing to bad light **6** recommended buying travel/recommended that we buy travel **7** threatened to take us **8** claimed that he was a descendant/claimed to be a descendant

5 Tell Ss to read through the text without looking at the choices. They think of words that could possibly fit the gaps, eg 1 *told*, 2 *in which*, 3 *asked*. Ss then look through the choices to see if any of the words they have used are listed. If not, they try to work out the correct answer alone and then compare answers in pairs.

Answers **1** a **2** c **3** b **4** d **5** d **6** c **7** c **8** b **9** c **10** b **11** a

LISTENING SKILLS

1 Ss work in groups of four and look at the four historical characters. Ask Ss if they know anything about any of them. Ss now look through the statements and predict what they might hear. Play the recording twice. Ss compare answers in pairs. Elicit the answers and extracts from the recording which helped the Ss decide on the answers: 1 'there really was a Lady Godiva'; 'There really was a Macbeth'; 2 'Shakespeare probably thought it was wise to exaggerate the good and bad sides of the characters!' 3 'from Japan and Brazil to Russia and Eastern Europe there are examples of folk heroes who robbed the rich to give to the poor'; 4 'added later to add a clear element of a deserved punishment'; 5 'Historical records suggest that the taxes in Coventry were, if anything, rather low and apart from this, Coventry was basically a tiny village at the time'; 'records suggest that Macbeth was actually a generous, religious man with a pretty good reputation'; 6 'the story of King Lear (...) probably started as a Celtic myth'; 7 'added some historical background to make it seem like it really happened'; 8 'historians haven't yet managed to convincingly match one individual to the Robin Hood of the stories'; 9 'the Macbeth we know from the Shakespeare tragedy'; 'King Lear is extremely old, much older than Shakespeare's play.'

> **Tapescript** `CD 4 Track 9`
>
> **Peter:** *[RP accent]* Well, believe it or not, there are plans in the pipeline for yet another TV adaptation of the Robin Hood story. What with several Hollywood films, the Disney cartoon and a musical, it seems that our fascination with the man is as strong as ever. But where did these legends come from and did people like Robin Hood really exist? I'm joined in the studio by Sally Weems, a social historian at Thamesdown University. So, Sally, what do we know about Robin Hood?

124   Students' Book ➡ pages 114–115

Sally: *[RP accent]* Well the first evidence we have of Robin Hood is from narrative songs from the 1400s. But it's clear that the story was already by then several hundred years old. Er, as to whether or not he actually existed – well, the stories do contain a great deal of reference to identifiable places in Yorkshire and Nottinghamshire which does tend to suggest that he really did exist. But one problem is that Robin Hood was a fairly common name in medieval England and, although there are many mentions of Robin Hoods in various historical records, historians haven't yet managed to convincingly match one individual to the Robin Hood of the stories. But another line of thinking, which I think is equally valid, is that Robin Hood was simply invented when the song was written and he was nothing more than a fictional character who caught the popular imagination. It's interesting to note that from Japan and Brazil to Russia and Eastern Europe there are examples of folk heroes who 'robbed the rich to give to the poor'.

Peter: Hmm, so the jury's still out on that one. What about the ladies? There are some fascinating examples of strong women who have passed into legend. I'm thinking of Boadiccea, Lady Godiva, people like that ...

Sally: Ah, yes, Lady Godiva. That's an interesting one.

Peter: Remind us of the story there, Sally.

Sally: Well, according to the legend, Lady Godiva's husband was charging the people of Coventry very high taxes which made life very difficult for them. Lady Godiva urged her husband to reduce the taxes and he eventually agreed but only on condition that she ride through the town on a horse, completely naked.

Peter: Which she did!

Sally: That's right! But only after warning the townspeople to stay inside and keep away from the windows as she went past. And according to the legend, only one man, Peeping Tom, dared to watch her and of course he immediately went blind. But how much of this legend is true? Well, there really was a Lady Godiva whose name pops up several times in various records, including the Domesday Book. And yes, she did live in Coventry, probably at the end of the eleventh century. However, most of the story just doesn't add up. Historical records suggest that the taxes in Coventry were, if anything, rather low and apart from this, Coventry was basically a tiny village at the time when Lady Godiva would have been alive.

Peter: Oh! Mind you, I always found that bit about Tom going blind a bit improbable!

Sally: Quite! Although that part of the story would have been added later to add a clear element of a deserved punishment, which would have suited the public's taste at the time. But actually this sort of thing is very common. Take, for example, Macbeth. There really was a Macbeth, King of Scots, who again lived during the eleventh century. But I doubt whether anyone who knew him at the time would recognise the Macbeth we know from the Shakespeare tragedy. In the latter, Macbeth is a murderer, notorious for his violent temper - perhaps Shakespeare's least likeable tragic hero – whereas records suggest that Macbeth was actually a generous, religious man with a pretty good reputation as Scottish kings go!

Peter: How strange! So what happened to the story along the way?

Sally: Well, the king at the time Shakespeare wrote *Macbeth* was James the First, who was a descendant of one of the 'good guys' in the play. So Shakespeare probably thought it was wise to exaggerate the good and bad sides of the characters!

Peter: Well, as they say, the winners always get to rewrite history! And what about that other tragic king we know from Shakespeare? Was there also a King Lear?

Sally: Er, it's highly unlikely. But the story of King Lear is extremely old, much older than Shakespeare's play. It probably started as a Celtic myth – like the Greeks and Romans, the Celts had a rich mythology based on the lives

of various gods – and then gradually over time, they kept the basic story but invented new characters to go with it and added some historical background to make it seem like it really happened in Britain's distant past.

Peter: So it's not just Hollywood that recycles the same plots.

Sally: No! And let's face it, it's a great story!

Peter: What about that Welsh ...?

Answers 1 B, C 2 C 3 A 4 B 5 B, C 6 D 7 D 8 A 9 C, D

SPEAKING SKILLS

1 Ss choose one of the topics in pairs that both of them are going to present. They have two minutes to brainstorm ideas about what to say in the presentation and then a further five minutes on their own in which they plan the presentation in more detail. Ss then take it in turns to make their presentations to each other in their pairs. Ss then tell each other what they thought and should learn how to improve their own presentations. Nominate one or two Ss to present each topic to the class.

2 Look at the first task (As) with the class and say: *There's a man reading a newspaper and a woman watching TV. You can get the news from newspapers or the TV.* Ask Ss how well you think you would have done in an exam with that answer (not very well) and why (too short). Tell Ss to try to talk for one minute each on their tasks and then two minutes talking together.

Suggested answers A newspaper, mobile phones, TV, radio, computers etc **B** The man could be tired early in the morning or worried about work. He may be on his way home, relaxing after a day's work. The woman may be relaxed or bored. She looks a bit worried so maybe the news is bad or affects her personally.

Students' Book ➡ pages 114–115

Right or wrong?

Read, listen and talk about ethics, the economy, crime and justice.
Practise modal verbs and phrases.
Focus on expressing opinions and agreement.
Write a formal transactional letter making suggestions.

EXAM FOCUS

Topic: Ethics, the economy, crime and justice

Speaking
Opinions and agreement: SB p.121, ex.5, ex.6

Listening
Multiple matching: SB p.117, ex.7, ex.8, p.121, ex.2

Reading
True/False/No information: SB p.117, ex.2
Multiple choice: SB p.120, ex.4

Grammar and vocabulary
Sentence transformations: SB p.123, ex.7, p.125, ex.8
Verbs in brackets: SB p.123, ex.8
Wordbuilding: SB p.120, ex.7

Writing
A transactional letter: SB p.125, ex.9

Unit 11 Materials
....
Success Workbook Unit 11
....
Photocopiable resources 31, 32, 33
....
Testing and Evaluation Programme tests

VOCABULARY AND LISTENING

This section introduces formal and informal expressions on the topic of money and wealth.

Warm-up Introduction to the topic of the lesson. *Guess my job.* Ss work in pairs. Give each student a job title from the unit: Prime Minister, Chief Executive Officer of a top company (CEO), GP (doctor), footballer, head teacher, nurse, police constable, bus driver, store checkout worker, fast-food restaurant worker (from Exercise 1), factory worker, research scientist (from the listening in Exercise 7). Tell Ss that you have thought of a job of your own, eg farmer. They have to find out what it is by asking *Yes/No* questions. Help them with ideas for question, eg *Do you work outside? Is it a difficult job? Do you need special qualifications? Do you have to wear a uniform?* etc. Ss then ask each other questions to try to find each other's jobs.

1 Give Ss two minutes to discuss their ideas in pairs and then they read the text alone. After reading, they discuss again in pairs what they found out from the reading. Ss work together to write a one-sentence summary of the main point of the article. Elicit answers in open class.

Answers It is about how much footballers are paid in comparison to other people.

2 Ss find the extracts from the text which show the answers. Elicit the answers and the Ss' reasons for them: 1 the minister says that the footballer's wages are outrageous and obscene but is comparing them to poor people's earnings, not her own; 2 'that's without counting performance-related bonuses (...) endorsements, modelling deals and other business concerns'; 3 'grass-roots fans are being priced out'; 4 'I earn every penny I make'; 5 'contrasts with his early years' – doesn't say exactly when; 6 five are thought to be too high, five too low.

Answers 1 NI 2 T 3 T 4 F 5 NI 6 F

3 Ss read through the text to get the general meaning of the underlined words and then match them to the words and phrases in the exercise. Elicit the answers. As a follow-up, Ss could use the words to talk about the situation in their country, eg *Name someone, apart from footballers, who earns an immoral/obscene amount of money. What ticket prices are exorbitant?* etc.

Answers 1 outrageous 2 lavish 3 obscene 4 bonuses 5 flaunting his wealth 6 exorbitant 7 run-down housing estate 8 basic salary 9 scraping together every penny

4 Ss work in pairs. Elicit the answers and definitions of the words. Point out that *go bankrupt* is often something that happens to the rich when their investments go wrong but that, if they do go bankrupt, they are no longer rich.

Answers **The rich** inheritance, massive profits, mansion, inflated salaries, rolling in money, heiress, go bankrupt **The poor** on the dole, make ends meet, the needy, scrape by, the poverty line

5 Ss work together in pairs to discuss the cartoons and what they can see. Then they look at the adjectives given and check what they mean and which cartoon they relate to.

Answers A affluent, prosperous, wealthy, filthy rich, loaded, well-off **B** destitute, impoverished, poverty-stricken, badly off, broke, hard up

6 Ss work in pairs, trying to complete the gaps without looking and then checking with the vocabulary from the previous exercises. Point out that in 3 *loaded* is the only extreme adjective for 'rich' so the only one that collocates with *absolutely*. Ss then work alone to complete the story. Nominate Ss to read out their stories in open class.

Answers **1** rich **2** well **3** loaded **4** profits **5** bonuses **6** inheritance **7** rolling **8** mansion **9** estate **10** heiress **11** flaunting **12** lavish **13** exorbitant/obscene/immoral

7 Tell Ss to look through the list of people a–h. Ask them to think of any vocabulary that might be used which would help them recognise who was speaking, eg (a) *used to work, pension, old*. Elicit ideas and then play the recording. Ss note key words which help them to decide who the speakers are.

Tapescript CD 4 Track 10

Kylie: *[neutral English accent]* So health minister Liz Barnet accused football star Teddy Wainwright of earning an 'obscene amount of money'. So let's hear what you've got to say ... The number is 0207 48 48 448 and the question once again: Do the rich get paid too much? And we have our first caller ... It's Frances from Oxford. Hi Frances.

Frances: *[neutral English accent]* Hi Kylie. There's absolutely nothing wrong with Teddy Wainwright earning so much. Football clubs aren't charities, they're business enterprises and if they don't pay the going market rate for top players, then foreign clubs will, and the Premiership will become a second-rate product and then everyone will lose out. It's simply a question of supply and demand, you know, the invisible hand of the market. I'm writing an essay on this at the moment, actually. Market forces dictate how much each player is worth. As long as a club is making money, they'll pay their players what they ask for. If they pay their players too much, they'll have to reduce their wage bill. It's that simple.

Kylie: Thanks, Frances. Our second caller is Geoffrey from Manchester.

Geoffrey: *[Manchester accent]* Thank you, Kylie. I'm old enough to remember when footballers in Britain were on a maximum wage of £20 a week, which was a decent wage for a skilled worker then. But the owners of the clubs were making a fortune and they weren't sharing it out. So in 1960 the players threatened to go on strike and the maximum wage was abolished and very quickly footballers' salaries shot up. So now players get a fair share, and that's the way it should be. In my firm, our employees get the best wages we can offer. After all, if you pay peanuts, you get monkeys, and I don't want monkeys working for me.

Kylie: I'm sure you don't. Thanks, Geoffrey. Now we have Alan from Liverpool.

Alan: *[Liverpool accent]* Nowadays, football clubs are making massive profits thanks to exorbitant ticket prices, overpriced merchandise, corporate sponsorship and multi-million pound TV deals. And it all goes to pay enormous dividends to the owners and the shareholders and inflated salaries to the footballers and their agents.

But who's paying for it all? The fans. I used to go to lots of games with my mates from the factory, but I can't afford it any more, especially now that I'm out of work. I think Wainwright and the other top players are just greedy. You can see it when they play for the national team. They don't try nearly as hard as they do when they're playing for the clubs that pay their salaries.

Kylie: Alright, thank you, Alan. Our next caller is Raj from Leeds.

Raj: *[slight Indian accent]* Hello, Kylie. I think it's ridiculous to pay footballers such astronomical amounts. And the same thing goes for super models, singers, actors and other fat cats! Especially those Chief Executive Officers who delocalise companies causing thousands of job losses just to increase profits, or even worse the managing directors who do their jobs so badly, their companies go bankrupt but they still walk away with a golden handshake worth millions! I'm doing research into cancer and I have to scrape by on a grant of £150 a week. Even if I found a cure and won the Nobel Prize, I still wouldn't earn in my entire career as much as these people earn in a year. It's all wrong.

Kylie: Good point, Raj. And next up is Margaret from Bournemouth.

Margaret: *[neutral English accent]* Well, Kylie, I don't see what all the fuss is about. If you don't approve of the money Wainwright gets, it's simple. Don't buy a replica shirt with his name on it and don't go to football games or watch them on TV. Personally, I'd rather watch paint dry than sit through a football match so I don't contribute a penny to footballers' salaries. Obviously, some people are paid far too much, but rather than just moan about it, I prefer to spend my time doing something about it, you know, raising money for good causes and helping the needy. I work part-time for Oxfam and although I'll be 65 next year, I have no intention of retiring.

Kylie: Thank you, Margaret. And now it's time for ...

Answers **1** h **2** b **3** e **4** c **5** f

8 Play the recording and elicit the answers and justifications: 1 'It's simply a question of supply and demand (...). Market forces dictate how much each player is worth.' 2 'So now players get a fair share, and that's the way it should be.' 3 'But who's paying for it all? The fans.' 4 And the same thing goes for super models, singers, actors and other fat cats!' 5 '... rather than just moan about it, I prefer to spend my time doing something about it.' Ss then discuss who they agree with in pairs and then as a class.

Answers **1** f **2** c **3** b **4** h **5** d

9 Give Ss one minute to read the role and decide what they are going to say. When they are ready, Ss act out the roleplays in pairs. Nominate one or two pairs to act out their roleplay in front of the class.

10 Ss decide alone what they think each person should be paid and why and then get into groups of three or four to compare ideas and discuss their reasons. Elicit ideas in open class.

ADDITIONAL PRACTICE: Photocopiable resources. Resource 31: *If you've got it, flaunt it!* Page 200

READING AND VOCABULARY

> This section extends the Ss' knowledge of crime and punishment related vocabulary.

Culture notes

Minority Report is a 2002 science fiction film based on a Philip K. Dick book. It was directed by Stephen Spielberg and set in Washington DC in the year 2054. Tom Cruise stars in the film as Chief John Anderton who heads the Pre-Emptive Crime department but is then accused of being about to murder someone who he hasn't even met. He has to escape from the surveillance in the city to prove his innocence. At the end of the film, the Pre-Crime section is closed down and all the prisoners imprisoned by it are released and pardoned.

Philip K. Dick (1928–1982) was an American science fiction writer. He sold his first story in 1952 and his first novel in 1955. His stories were often dominated by authoritarian governments and monopolistic companies. *Minority Report* was published in 1956 and is one of nine of his books to have been made into a film.

Warm-up Review of vocabulary from the last lesson.
What's happened to me? One student goes out of the classroom or hides their eyes for a moment while you write a word or phrase on the board. Tell Ss that this is what has happened to the person and they should either give them advice, ask questions or make comments which will give the person a clue as to what has happened but without using the words on the board. Write: *You're on the dole.* When the student who this refers to is ready, help the class with ideas of what to say: eg *Is it hard to scrape by? You should look for a job. Maybe you should move to a bigger city. You should have worked harder when you had a job.* The student at the front guesses what has happened. Allow guesses which are correct but worded differently, eg *I am unemployed.* Ss now get into groups of three or four. One person looks away while the others choose a phrase from the book. They follow the process above until the guesser guesses correctly. When all the Ss have had a turn at guessing, elicit some of the phrases used and whether people guessed them or not.

1 Check the words *hawk* and *dove* and what they symbolise (the hawk is a bird of prey so a hawk believes in heavy punishment and the dove is a symbol of peace so a dove believes in giving people a second chance although may still see the need for punishment if the crime is very serious) and when else they are used (eg politicians' views on war). Ss do the quiz in pairs, checking any vocabulary that they do not know. When they have checked their own results at the back of the book, elicit Ss' views and reasons for them.

Optional activity: Ss look through the quiz and results to find different words related to crime and punishment but not crimes and criminals as these will be looked at in Exercise 5. Tell Ss to list them in different categories, eg
adjectives: *petty (criminal), lenient, reformed, permissive, authoritarian*
related nouns: *breathalyser, proof, evidence, (on) trial, hostage, compassion, retribution, victim, suspended sentence, life imprisonment, death penalty*
related verbs: *admit, accused of, claim, confess to, frame, commit, release, sentence, deter, acquit, let someone off with a warning.*
Ss work in pairs or small groups to make sure they understand all the vocabulary. Then they write definitions for one or two words that they did not know before and test other Ss to see if they know which word is being defined.

2 Give Ss two or three minutes to discuss the two questions and then elicit ideas in open class. Ask Ss whether they mind having their details on a database or not and why.

> **Possible answers 1** Information is gathered when we get: credit cards, mobile phones, passports, ID cards, driving licences, Internet bank accounts, work, go to the doctor, travel etc **2** intercepting messages, infiltrating gangs, observation etc

3 Check *AI* (artificial intelligence) – the intelligence of machines, an intelligence that enables them to make decisions for themselves based on the environment they find themselves in. Set a time limit of two minutes for the reading so that Ss do not look at it in too much detail at this point. Elicit ideas from the Ss and ask what they found out from the reading.

> **Possible answers 1** An article in a magazine or on the Internet. An academic essay. **2** It has an extract from the film and then discusses whether or not the ideas in the film would work and be fair in real life.

4 Tell Ss that one way to approach a multiple choice task is as a true/false/no information task. Look at the four sentences from question 1 and ask the Ss as a class to decide if they are true, false or if there is no information.
1a It does not make the information any more attractive.
1b The first part is the book extract and the second part is analysing what this means about the possibility of really implementing such a scheme.
1c Nothing has really happened.
1d There is no indication that the second part (or first) is more important.
Ss work in pairs and do the same for the other five questions, saying why the choices are either right or wrong. Elicit answers and justifications for them and allow Ss to argue with justifications if there are differences of opinion.

2a Lines 1–2 say she 'had worked miracles' but not worked hard.

2b Line 17 says that sentences were actually much more lenient.

2c Line 10 says that 'People could be tested' but it does not mention schools.

2d Lines 8–9 say that 'Advances in computing and AI now made it possible.'

3a Although no drawbacks are mentioned, the text does not specifically say that there were none. As it is written from Andrews' point of view, this is not an objective look.

3b Lines 2–4 show that crime has decreased not been eliminated.

3c Line 17 says 'sentences were much more lenient'.

3d Contradicted by line 17.

4 There are four reasons given in lines 39–40: reform, public protection, retribution and deterrence. The next three paragraphs look at three of them (reform, protection and deterrence). In lines 55–56 it says that 'Retribution is the one justification of punishment that doesn't fit pre-emptive justice.' Therefore 3 out of 4 do fit which means (b) is correct.

5 In lines 75–76 the writer states: 'there are reasons for doubting such a scheme could ever become a reality.' In lines 81–83 he states: ' there may be good reasons for thinking that human behaviour can never be predicted ...'. The words 'doubting' and 'may' indicate he is not completely sure but that he believes it unlikely.

6a Lines 78–79 'human free will can always step in'.

6b Lines 68–70: 'they may lose the sense that they are in control of their criminality' implies that, at the moment, they are in control.

6c Not mentioned. It talks about the authorities not knowing what we are going to do, not ourselves.

6d Lines 82–83: 'human behaviour can never be predicted with 100 per cent accuracy.'

Answers 1 b 2 d 3 c 4 b 5 c 6 a

5 Tell Ss that, if they find the crime but not the criminal in one of the texts, or vice versa, they should write down the other word as well if they can. Also elicit criminals and crimes from the words given in the box: *smuggler, hijacking, assassination, burglar, to pick someone's pockets, forger, –, –, drug dealing, mugging, fraudster, blackmailer.*

Answers **Crimes:** reckless driving, destroying private property, trespassing, killing in cold blood, assault, vandalism, shoplifting, arson, kidnapping, murder, robbery, street crime, car theft, conspiracy to murder (smuggling, burglary, forgery, fraud, manslaughter, bribery, blackmail) **Criminals:** reckless driver, –, trespasser, killer, –, vandal, shoplifter, arsonist, kidnapper, murderer, robber, street criminal, car thief, – (hijacker, assassin, pickpocket, drug dealer, mugger)

6 It may be worth doing an example with the whole class. Choose a crime yourself and elicit questions from the class. Write the questions on the board and

answers *yes* or *no* as appropriate. Help Ss with ideas if necessary, eg *Is the crime to do with money? Do people get hurt? Is it a big problem in our country?* etc. Ss then play the game in groups of three with each student having a turn as the person who thinks of the crime and answers the questions.

7 Ss work in pairs to try to work out how to rewrite the sentences. Tell Ss to be very careful with the verb patterns needed following some of the verbs that they will be using. Ss should also remember that they cannot change the form of the word given so that sentence 6 cannot be: *I'm going to be released.* Elicit answers in open class and allow Ss to correct each other's mistakes if they make any.

Answers **1** to three-months' imprisonment for **2** have deterred people from **3** accused of stealing **4** was acquitted of committing **5** Locking someone up for **6** They're going to release me/I'm due for release

8 Ss work together in pairs. They should look at all three sentences in a group as one of them may be easier to work out than the others. When they think they have the answer for one of the sentences, they can test the other two with the same word. Eg in 1 Ss could look at sentence (a) for a long time without working out the word needed. However, if they look at sentence (c), they will notice a collocation from this lesson and should be able to complete it without problem. Elicit the answers. Ss should make a note of all the useful collocations and phrases from the exercise, eg *a random sample, pick at random, dead serious, dead right, life insurance, life sentence, the right side of the law, side effects.*

Answers **1** committing **2** random **3** dead **4** life **5** side

9 Ss work alone to note their own thoughts about each of the two questions. Put the Ss into groups of four. They discuss their ideas and try to convince each other of their point of view if there are any differences of opinion. Continue the conversation with the whole class.

Optional activity: Put Ss into groups of about five. In each group, one person is the accused/defendant. He/She hasn't committed a crime but the computer has identified that he/she is going to at some point in the near future. A second student is a lawyer for the defendant. They discuss together how they can argue that the system is flawed. On the other side, there is a prosecution lawyer and a police expert who get together to discuss why pre-emptive justice works and is justified. The fifth person is a judge who can stop people and ask questions or ask people to respond to points made by the other side. This student should think of questions to ask the two sides (eg about the defendant's background, about how the computer system works etc). When Ss are ready, they act out their roleplays in their groups of five.

SPEAKING AND LISTENING

This section introduces ways of offering opinions, asking for opinions, agreeing and disagreeing and asking people to reconsider their opinion.

Special difficulties: Ss can sound unnatural when they first use these phrases. However, as they keep practising, the phrases will become more fluent and their discussions will become more natural.

Warm-up Review of crime vocabulary. *Odd one out.* Read out four crimes, criminals or punishments. Ss work in groups of four to say which is the odd one out and why. There is no right answer. As long as Ss can think of a reason, they can choose that one. When the groups are ready, one group says who their odd one out is and the other groups have to say why.

Example: *burglary, smuggling, murder, reckless driving*

Burglary – it is the only one you can't do in a car.

Smuggling – it is the only one that needs more than one country.

Murder – it is the only one that has to involve death.

Reckless driving – it is the only one that has to involve some kind of transport.

1 Give Ss two minutes to look at the drawings and heading but tell them not to read the text at all yet. Elicit ideas of what the situation may be and then Ss read to check. Check that the New Year's Honours list is where worthy people in all walks of life are honoured by the British government for their efforts. The highest honour is to be knighted which means you can use the title Sir before your name.

Answers A bribe could be good if it consisted of a donation to good causes in return for an award such as a knighthood which doesn't give any power to the recipient.

2 Before Ss look at the opinions in Exercise 2, elicit what Ss think could be reasons for and against giving the man a knighthood. Ss then listen to the recording and discuss their own opinions in pairs and as a class. Elicit the answers and check some of the useful vocabulary from the reading that helped to find the answers: 1 Thomas says 'It's a no brainer', i.e. you don't need a brain to know the answer, it's so simple; 5 Thomas says we should be 'pragmatic' i.e. flexible with our principles; 6 Simone says he is a 'crook'.

Tapescript CD 4 Track 12

Narrator: Three philosophy students, Simone, Thomas and Ludwig are having an informal discussion about the dilemma of the Good Bribe.

Ludwig: *[slight German accent]* So, he knows it's a bribe and a bribe is wrong, but this bribe could do a lot of good to a lot of poor people. It's a real dilemma.

Simone: *[French accent]* It's not easy, is it?

Thomas: *[RP accent]* What do you mean it's not easy, Simone? It's a no brainer.

Simone: Go on then, Thomas, tell us what you think.

Thomas: It's really simple. You've just got to ask yourself what the consequences of his decision would be. If he accepts the bribe, hundreds of thousands of poor people get clean water, right?

Simone: Yes?

Thomas: So the way I see it the only drawback is that a rich man gets a knighthood from the Queen and can ask people to call him 'Sir'. So, it's clear the Prime Minister has to accept the bribe.

Simone: That's one way of looking at it, I suppose, but I really don't think it's as simple as that. He's the Prime Minister for goodness' sake! He's got to follow the rules.

Thomas: What rules?

Simone: The normal procedures of government. He can't put official titles and important honours up for sale! It would set a precedent that anyone could buy anything they want.

Ludwig: That happens already, Simone.

Simone: Well, maybe it does, Ludwig, but it shouldn't. Honours and rewards should go to those who deserve them, not to those who can pay for them!

Thomas: You're so naive, Simone. You're not living in the real world.

Simone: Maybe, but I still think the Prime Minister would be stupid to accept the bribe.

Thomas: Not stupid, pragmatic. He'd only be bending the rules, not breaking them. And as a consequence thousands of lives would be saved. It's all very well to have ethical standards, but it's foolish to be inflexible.

Simone: Yes, but try looking at it from a different angle.

Thomas: What?

Simone: The Prime Minister's got a reputation for being honest, right?

Thomas: Yeah?

Simone: He's trying to run a clean government, to avoid any hint of corruption, but if ...

Thomas: So just to save himself getting his hands dirty, he'd be willing to make thousands of people suffer by making them walk for miles to get clean drinking water. That's not ethical!

Simone: But if he accepts the bribe and gives this crook a knighthood ...

Thomas: He's not a crook, he's just an unscrupulous businessman.

Simone: Yeah, OK, whatever, but if he does that, everyone will say he's just as bad, just as corrupt as all the other politicians and that will lead to apathy in the political system and it'll be bad for the whole country.

Thomas: Hmm, I'm not convinced.

Simone: You're being very quiet, Ludwig.

Thomas: Yeah, that's just what I was thinking. Come on, what's your take on it?

Ludwig: Well, Simone's got a point. Very often one lie leads to another. If the PM can break his moral code for this, where does it end? Maybe he'll lie to the people who voted for him to get their support for a war that they wouldn't support otherwise. Or maybe he'll support an evil dictator somewhere because if not, his country might lose some trade deal or something.

Thomas: Yeah, but ...

Ludwig: But I know what he should do.

Simone/Thomas: What?

Ludwig: He should give the man the knighthood and then afterwards call a press conference and tell the truth, the whole story about the bribe.

Thomas: No way!

Simone: You can't be serious.

Ludwig: I am. Think about it for a second. The PM would come across as trustworthy ...

Answers 1 T 2 S 3 L 4 T 5 T 6 S 7 S 8 L 9 L

SPEAK OUT

3 Ss look at the Speak Out box alone and tick the informal phrases. Go through all the phrases and ask Ss to talk again as a class about the dilemma in the previous exercises, this time using the phrases in the box as they do so.

Answers **Less formal:** 1, 4, 5, 8, 10

4 When Ss have finished, elicit the answers and check which phrases could be used in an exam situation (all of 1–10 are OK but *Come off it!* and *You're dead right!* sound very informal and may not be appropriate in an exam situation). Ask Ss for any other phrases they know which could be used for the different categories. Elicit whether these are formal, informal or neutral, eg Introducing opinions – *In my opinion* (neutral), Asking for opinions – *What do you think?* (informal), Agreement – *That's a good point.* (neutral), Disagreement – *No way!* (informal), *I understand what you're saying but ...* (formal), Asking someone to reconsider their opinion – *I think you should try to consider the situation a little more objectively* (formal).

Answers **Introducing opinions:** For my part ... In all honesty ... **Asking for opinions:** What's your stance on this? **Agreement:** You're dead right! (I) I totally concur with ... (F) **Disagreement:** Come off it! (I) I beg to differ ... (F) **Asking someone to reconsider:** Look at the other side of the coin.

5 Give Ss five minutes to read their dilemma and to write a summary of it in their own words. They also think of their opinions on the issue and the reasons for them. When they are ready, put the Ss into groups of three. Student A starts with their dilemma. All Ss should contribute to the discussion. Try to encourage Ss who agree not to just use an appropriate phrase from Speak Out but also to give extra reasons for their agreement. When Ss have discussed all three dilemmas, talk about them in open class.

6 Ss read through the situations alone and think about what they would do. If they agree with each other, tell them to think of arguments for their actions that they would give to someone who disagreed with them.

ADDITIONAL PRACTICE: Photocopiable resources. Resource 32: *Hmm ... What do you think?* Page 201

GRAMMAR AND READING

This section extends the Ss' ability to make deductions and understand other uses of modal verbs.

Special difficulties: Although Ss should be able to use modals at this level there may be one or two fossilised errors, such as using *can* to make deductions, eg *He can be a doctor.*

Warm-up Review of opinions and agreement. *Pass the statement.* Ss work in groups of three or four. Each group thinks of a topic that they are all interested in, eg computers, and a statement about that topic that people might agree or disagree with, eg *Laptops are better than home computers.* The Ss have one minute in their groups to give their opinions on the topic and agree or disagree with each other. Ss then pass on the statement to a different group. The process is repeated until all the groups have discussed all the statements. Ss then discuss their opinions as a class.

1 When Ss have discussed the quote in pairs, elicit what it means (it is a joke because if he cannot resist temptation, he cannot really resist anything). Ss talk as a class about a time they were tempted to do something that they know they should not have done.

2 Tell Ss to cover all except the first two pictures so they are not tempted to look ahead. Ss discuss ideas in pairs and then as a class. Elicit ideas and predictions.

Answers She needs something to wear to a cool party and sees something belonging to her sister/flatmate. The temptation is to take the clothes without asking.

3 Allow Ss two minutes to read the story and discuss what the missing words could be. Elicit answers and then play the recording for Ss to check their ideas.

Answers present; present; birthday present

Work it out

4 Check that Ss understand the word *deduction* (working out what something means or what the situation is without knowing it for certain). Elicit the three sentences and the differences between them (sentences 1 and 6 are deduction about the present, sentence 3 is a deduction about the past). Ss then look back at the text to find three more examples.

Answers 1, 3, 6 Two other deductions: Liz must have bought it in the sales. She may even have been hoping you'd find it.

5 Before Ss look at the examples, elicit modals which have the same or similar meaning, eg *must/have to* – rules; *might/could* – deductions; *mustn't/can't* – rules. Ss then complete the activity. Elicit answers in open class. Try to elicit the functions that are shown in each sentence or give these if Ss do not know how to say them in English.

Answers 1 No: mustn't – prohibition, don't have to – lack of obligation 2 Yes: obligation 3 Yes: weak prohibition/negative advice 4 Yes: advice/weak obligation 5 No: didn't need to – lack of necessity known in advance; needn't have – lack of necessity subsequently realised 6 Yes: lack of ability 7 No: could – general past ability; managed to – specific past ability 8 No: may well – deduction; may as well – idiom meaning *There is no reason why not*

Mind the trap!

Go through the box with the Ss pointing out that modals can be confusing in that some can be used for one function but not others and that opposites can change: *must* and *mustn't* are opposites for obligation but *must* and *can't* are opposites for possibility/speculation. *Can* cannot be used for speculation.

Check it out

Having looked at the Mind the trap! box with the Ss, tell them they can find more rules for using modals in the Check it out section on page 159.

6 Ss look at the sentences and think of situations in which they may be used. Elicit the functions and the situations demonstrating them and then play the recording.

Tapescript CD 4 Track 14

1a *[both speakers have neutral English accents]*
A: I saved my little sister from a rabid dog.
B: You must be brave.
A: Yes, I am.
1b *[both speakers have neutral English accents]*
A: Now, this might hurt you a little.
B: Ow! Mummy! It hurts!
C: Don't cry! You must be brave.
2a *[both speakers have neutral English accents]*
A: Excuse me, sir. Can I get up?
B: Yes, of course, Sarah. Why?
A: I need a dictionary.
2b
[American accent] Right now, just one more Christmas decoration to put up. Ow! That's so painful! OK, keep calm. Now, I don't think I've broken anything. Ow! But can I get up? No, I can't. Oh no!

3a *[both speakers have neutral English accents]*
A: Oh dear!
B: What's wrong?

A: It's Annette's project.

B: What's the matter with it? It's very good. I had a look at it yesterday.

A: Yes, but it's supposed to be in by tomorrow and I'm worried she won't finish it in time.

3b *[both speakers have neutral English accents]*

A: Hello?

B: Mrs Collins. This is Patti.

A: Yes, Patti. Is something wrong?

B: Well, yes ... I've given Ashley her dinner, but she won't finish it!

A: Oh, don't worry about that, just give her an apple or ...

4a *[both speakers have slight Bristol accents]*

A: Penny! Where's my games console?

B: I don't know. Why do you think I know where it is?

A: Because you borrowed it from me last week?

B: Did I?

A: Stop messing about and tell me where it is.

B: Well, I'm not sure. I mean you might have given it to me, I suppose, but I really can't remember it.

A: Penny!

4b *[both speakers have Liverpool accents]*

A: What's the matter with you?

B: I've just done my History exam. And it was all about French history. I wish you'd given me that book on Napoleon.

A: I did give it to you.

B: Yeah, this morning, when it was too late. You might have given it to me when I asked you for it. It really would have helped me, you know.

A: Sorry.

Answers 1a speculation **1b** obligation **2a** permission **2b** ability **3a** prediction **3b** refusal **4a** possibility **4b** annoyance

7 Ss work in pairs and try to work out the sentences without referring to the Check it out box. When they have finished, Ss should check their answers. Elicit the functions demonstrated in each sentence and the answers: 1 negative advice/weak prohibition; 2 refusal; 3 ability; 4 advice about a past situation; 5 lack of necessity; 6 speculation; 7 annoyance.

Answers 1 are not supposed to be/are not allowed to be **2** won't tell me **3** managed to find **4** shouldn't have said **5** needn't have spent **6** may well have been involved **7** might have warned me (that)

8 Ss read through the text quickly to get an overall understanding of what it is about before they try to complete the gaps. Look at the first gap with the whole class. Elicit ideas about what the function is (speculation) and what the modal could be (*must, might, could, may*). Then point out that, although all these are possible, *must have cost a fortune* is by far the best answer because it is a commonly used phrase. Ss work in pairs to think about the other gaps. Elicit the functions before eliciting answers in each case: 2 lack of necessity; 3 past regret;

4 speculation; 5 inability; 6 past ability; 7 speculation about the past; 8 personal obligation.

Answers 1 must have cost **2** needn't have bothered **3** should have asked **4** must have waited **5** couldn't resist **6** managed to keep/succeeded in keeping **7** wouldn't have understood/might not have understood/may not have understood **8** must remember

9 If Ss enjoy the activity, it would be nice to allow all three Ss to have a turn in each of the three roles so that they actually act out all three conversations. At the end of the activity, nominate groups to come to the front of the class to act out one conversation each. Encourage the Ss to really play the role of the angel and devil to make the activity more enjoyable and memorable.

ADDITIONAL PRACTICE: Photocopiable resources. Resource 33: *This must be yours.* Page 202

WRITING

This section looks at techniques for writing transactional letters looking at appropriate style, organisation and planning.

Culture notes

The **Mosquito ultrasonic deterrent** was first used at a Spar shop in Barry, South Wales. It has a range of 15–20 metres. It works because of a medical phenomenon known as presbycusis or age related hearing loss. This begins in the 20s and it first affects the highest frequencies (18 to 20 kHz). It is therefore possible to generate a high frequency sound that is audible only to teenagers. It has also been used by teenagers in school as a mobile phone ring tone so that no one over the age of twenty-five knows that they are texting each other in class.

Warm-up Review of modals. *Blankety blank.* Ss work in groups of four. Tell one student in each group that they are going to complete a sentence dictated by you so that it is true for them. They should not tell the other people in their group what they have written. The other three Ss then try to guess what the student has written. Repeat with a different sentence and a different student until all four Ss have had a chance to write:

Example sentences:
I am supposed to ... but I don't.
I was very happy last weekend because I didn't need to ...
I really must ...
I have never managed to ...
I am unable to ...

1 Put Ss into groups of three or four to discuss the questions. You could give them a clue by telling the Ss that whatever the Mosquito is, it can only affect teenagers for some reason. Businesses do not want to drive all their customers away. Elicit ideas and then play the recording.

Tapescript CD 4 Track 15

Andrew: *[Scottish accent]* And now, the time has come to talk about Mosquitoes. No, not the insects that suck your blood, but the devices which are being used by private businesses and town councils to combat antisocial behaviour by teenagers. They emit a high-pitched sound which is inaudible to anyone over the age of twenty-five, but which is uncomfortable or even painful for young people. Several thousand of them are thought to be in operation all round the country. Shopkeepers find them useful and the police support them. However, a new campaign, backed by the children's commissioner for England and Wales, is calling for them to be banned. In the studio with me today is one of the representatives of the new campaign, seventeen-year-old Gabriel Knight. Hello, Gabriel.

Gabriel: *[Manchester accent]* Hi.
Andrew: Why do you want the Mosquito banned?
Gabriel: Well, there are basically three reasons. One: they don't ...

Answers **1** A device which emits sound. **2** The sound it emits is at a frequency that only affects people under twenty-five. **3** Shopkeepers **4** The police

2 Make sure the Ss do not look at the letter before they have thought of their answers. Elicit ideas in open class and then Ss read the letter to see which of their ideas were mentioned.

Answers **1** discriminatory, unfair, indiscriminate, affect babies and young children as well as teenagers, possibly harmful to health **2** investment in leisure activities for teenagers

3 Ss work in groups of three or four. Remind Ss of the phrases they have learnt to share opinions and agree and disagree. Set a time limit of two minutes for the discussion and then elicit ideas in open class.

4 Ss work in pairs finding examples in the text to support their answers. Elicit answers and useful phrases from the letter, eg 1 *on behalf of*; *Furthermore*; *Might I suggest*; 3 *on behalf of 'Buzz Off!'*; *aim is to outlaw* ... Ss may have been told that *Dear Sir/Madam* is used with *Yours faithfully* and that we use *Yours sincerely* when using the person's surname (*Dear Mr Smith*). Although this is often the case, the rules are slightly more flexible than that.

Answers **1** Fairly formal although it is active (We believe) rather than passive (It is believed). It is formal because she is writing to a person in authority and wants to make a favourable impression so that her arguments are listened to. **2** Dear Madam; Yours sincerely **3** He says who he represents and why he is writing. **4** He sums up what they want the Mayor to do. **5** Intended effect: to make the Mayor understand the feelings of the young people of the town and their reasons.

5 Explain to Ss that the eight sentences appear in letters to different people. The Ss use both their knowledge of style and register and the context of each to decide who they are being written to. Elicit the answers and why the Ss think that: 1 Topic – senior students; 2 Topic – late-night shifts, very informal; 3 Topic – scene, quite formal; 4 Topic – who do you see (Young people), Register – forcefully disagreeing; 5 Register – very informal; 6 Topic – a measure like this, Register – formal, forceful but polite; 7 Topic – sensational images; 8 Topic – arguments like these, Register – forceful.

Answers **1** d **2** b **3** c **4** a **5** b **6** d **7** c **8** a

6 Ss read the memo alone and then discuss their views on it in pairs. Elicit what the problem is (there has been fighting and vandalism recently). Ask Ss why the principal has taken this decision, i.e. what he thinks it will achieve (banning Ss from loitering outside the school building will prevent them from becoming bored and committing acts of vandalism or fighting). Finally elicit any arguments there might be against it (innocent Ss are also affected, the problem will not go away, it will just move elsewhere). Ss then discuss what they would think if it happened in their school and why.

7 When Ss have underlined the key words, ask questions and tell the Ss that their underlined words should answer the questions. If they do not, then they are not really key. *Who are you representing?* – your classmates; *What do you want?* – to complain about the decision and reverse it, to suggest alternative measures; *Who are you writing to?* – the school head; *How much should you write?* – 180–220 words; *What do you agree with the head about?* – the nature of the problem; *Why do you disagree?* – indiscriminate, unfair ... etc; *What do you suggest?* – focus on troublemakers ... etc. When they have finished, ask Ss how they would organise their letter:

Dear Sir

• introduction – who you are writing on behalf of and why
• the fact that you agree with him about the problem but not his solutions
• reasons why you are against his solution
• your suggestions
• a one-sentence summary of what you want

Yours sincerely (faithfully)

8 Ss work alone, using the letter on page 124 and the principal's memo to help them. When they have finished, Ss check in pairs. Elicit answers in open class. More than one answer may be possible.

> **Suggested answers** **1** on behalf of my classmates
> **2** banned students from using the school grounds
> **3** complete disagreement with this measure **4** an upsurge in fighting and vandalism **5** lack of places to go and things to do **6** of identifying/to identify the culprits would be to install CCTV cameras

TRAIN YOUR BRAIN

9 Read through the Train Your Brain box with the Ss and discuss each point in turn. Point 1 has already been looked at in Exercise 7. Remind Ss why this is so important (to know exactly what to write, who to and how much).

Point 2: Tell Ss that, almost as bad as forgetting a point completely is to remember it late on and add it to the wrong paragraph so that the letter looks disorganised and confusing. The plan should include what each paragraph will be about and all the essential information for them.

Point 3: Look at the memo and elicit from Ss which phrases they should change and which they could keep, eg when disagreeing, if the Ss write *We disagree with this measure because it is indiscriminate and unfair* they are not showing the examiner much range of vocabulary. Therefore they try to rephrase this, eg *We are in complete disagreement with this measure for a number of reasons. Firstly, it is unfair because it affects all students equally whether they are innocent or not.*

Point 4: Exam questions often state that these are not needed so, if Ss read the instructions carefully, they will know this anyway.

Point 5: Re-elicit the phrases that can be used to start or finish a letter. *Dear Sir* – to a man; *Dear Madam* – to a woman; *Dear Sir or Madam* – when you don't know if it is a man or a woman you are writing to; *Yours faithfully; Yours sincerely*

Point 6: Re-elicit the reason for writing to the head and who you represent.

Point 7: Re-elicit what you want from the head (to reconsider his idea and take other measures to stop the problem).

Allow Ss ten minutes to write a plan and think of ways of rewriting the points to include in the letter. Ss then write the letter alone in class or for homework.

Different?

Read, listen and talk about animals and appearance; fashion; conformity and rebellion.
Practise clauses of concession, addition and contrast.
Focus on understatement.
Write a character reference.

EXAM FOCUS

Topic: Describing appearance and personality

Speaking
Roleplay: SB p.133, ex.6

Listening
Sequencing: SB p.132, ex.11

Reading
True/False: SB p.131, ex.5

Grammar and vocabulary
Sentence transformations: SB p.129, ex.9
Cloze: SB p.127, ex.7

Writing
A testimonial: SB p.135, ex.8

Unit 12 Materials

Success Workbook Unit 12

Photocopiable resources 34, 35, 36

Testing and Evaluation Programme tests

VOCABULARY AND SPEAKING

This section introduces new adjectives to describe people and animals as well as some new phrases to describe relationships.

Culture notes

Professor Krause graduated in Biology at the Free University of Berlin, Germany, in 1990. He took an M.Phil. in Applied Biology at Queens' College, Cambridge and a Ph.D. at St. John's College, Cambridge for which he studied the evolution of group-living using fish shoals. He was appointed as a Lecturer at the University of Leeds in 1996 and promoted to Professor of Behavioural Ecology in 2004.

Warm-up Introduction to the topic of the lesson. *What animal?* Put Ss into pairs. Each pair needs a piece of paper which they fold into three columns. In the first column, they write three animals. Next to each animal, in the second column, the Ss write three

adjectives which could describe each of their animals, i.e. nine adjectives altogether. Then they fold their paper so that the first column is hidden. Ss swap papers with a second group. The second group look at the nine adjectives written and try to guess the three animals and write the animals' names in the third column. Ss then join up in groups of four and discuss what they guessed and why and then tell each other the original animals. Elicit the animals and adjectives used to describe them.

1 Elicit anything the Ss know about the animals pictured. Ss then read the facts and guess which each refers to. Again, elicit ideas and then play the recording.

Tapescript ⬛ CD 5 Track 1

[neutral English accent]
1 The male **seahorse** gives birth to the young.
2 A **winteria** or **barrel-eyed fish** can light up its whole body to help it to see.
3 A **thorny devil** or **moloch** has peculiar spikes that change colour depending on its mood.
4 **Sloths** usually only move about 0.5km an hour – but are excellent swimmers.
5 The **armadillo** has four babies at a time and, bizarrely, they are always the same sex.
6 A **kakapo** or **owl parrot** has a distinctive smell, similar to milk and cinnamon.

Answers **1** A **2** B **3** D **4** F **5** E **6** C

2 Play the recording again and ask Ss to note adjectives used, i.e. *peculiar, excellent, distinctive.* Elicit what these mean (strange, very good, easily recognised). Tell Ss they are going to see more adjectives and should try to guess what they mean. Ss then look up words in dictionaries if they are unsure. Elicit answers and discuss what else these words could describe, eg *a distinctive sound; colourful clothes; weird behaviour; freakish hairstyles; typical daily routine.* When Ss describe the animals in the photos, elicit reasons for their choice of adjectives. Tell Ss that different people may use different adjectives to describe the same thing.

Answers **1** unique **2** distinctive **3** peculiar **4/5** grotesque/outlandish **6/7** nondescript/unremarkable

3 Ss work in pairs, using a dictionary to find the differences between two words with similar meanings. Elicit the answers and why the other word is wrong: 1 There is no typical bird appearance. It could be used to describe behaviour – it sings, it eats worms. 2 Da Vinci may have been strange but that is not what the first half of the sentence is suggesting. 3 *Abnormal* is not strong enough to emphasise the strangeness. 4 *Typical* is not a negative word but we need a negative meaning. Also it needs more information – typical French food, typical fast food etc. 5 Typical animal behaviour cannot be described as eccentric as all of that species acts the same way. 6 *Grotesque* has a negative connotation which does not go with *I love*. 7 *Ordinary* does not show that more and more people have them.

Answers 1 nondescript **2** a one-off **3** outlandish **4** unremarkable **5** distinctive **6** quirky **7** commonplace

4 Ss look at the cartoons and describe the situation, and then discuss what they might mean. Elicit the meanings of the phrases and then Ss discuss whether they have ever felt like that.

Answers A the black sheep – different from everyone else, an outsider **B** a fish out of water – not being able to cope with your situation, unprepared

5 Ss read through the sentences and discuss in pairs what they mean. Play the recording and, after they have listened to it, the Ss discuss their ideas and what they heard. Elicit answers and what the phrases mean: 1 to have the same career as them; 2 was similar in attitudes and interests to them; 3 had a different way of thinking to them; 4 he felt as if he were in the right place for him, he felt comfortable; 5 he felt different, unable to fit in; 6 he had similar interests and views; 7 he was different from everyone else; 8 he is now happy/in the perfect place; 9 the Ss joked that he stood out like a sore thumb but he feels as if he is really in his element.

Tapescript `CD 5 Track 2`

[neutral English accent] My parents were both teachers and everyone expected me to follow in their footsteps, just like my brothers and sisters did. But I had realised quite early on in life that I didn't really fit in with my brothers and sisters and I was definitely on a different wavelength to my parents. I suppose I was always the black sheep of the family. When I decided not to go to university but to go to art college instead, they found it hard to hide their disappointment. Unfortunately, I found it hard to get a job when I finished my art course and ended up working in a call centre for an insurance company. Well, right from day one I really felt like a square peg in a round hole. Not only was the job incredibly soulless and boring, I found I had next to nothing in common with my colleagues, even though we were all pretty much the same age. I felt pretty down about life in general. Then, to cut a long story short, I started working as a teaching assistant at the local college, working with students with special needs. Some of them are physically handicapped which

means that many of them are confined to wheelchairs, while others have learning difficulties and need help with basic Maths and English. Well, on my first day I felt I'd made a terrible mistake. The other teaching assistants were a lot older than me and were all married with kids so I really felt like the odd one out. But after a few days I began to feel at home. I feel I'm really in my element working with the students – they've got such a positive attitude to life which rubs off on all the staff. The kids can be cheeky too – last week we went on a day trip and they teased me because I was the only person not in a wheelchair and they said I stuck out like a sore thumb! And of course the big irony is that I ended up working in education after all!

Answers 1 T **2** F **3** T **4** F **5** T **6** F **7** T **8** T **9** F

6 Look at the first sentence and elicit all the possible phrases that could be used in this case with justifications: *I feel like a fish out of water (because I can't cope). I don't fit in. I'm on a different wavelength to everyone else (because I'm a feminist in a class full of chauvinists). I feel right at home. I (don't) have a lot in common. I'm the odd one out. I'm in my element. I stick out like a sore thumb.* Ss then choose the best phrase for them for all situations and justify them with reasons. Ss should try to use a different phrase each time. Elicit answers and reasons in open class.

Possible answers 1 I'm the odd one out. **2** I feel like a fish out of water. **3** I stick out like a sore thumb. **4** I feel like a square peg in a round hole. **5** I feel right at home. **6** I have a lot in common with the other people here. **7** I feel like the black sheep of the family.

7 Ss read the text quickly to find out what it is about. Elicit answers (the similarities between people in crowds and the way sheep act together). Ss then complete the gaps alone and check in pairs. After checking their answers, Ss discuss the questions in pairs. Elicit the answers and their opinions. If Ss have used *report* for gap 4, show that this cannot be correct because the verb *show* is not in the third person singular form.

Answers 1 like **2** seem **3** which **4** results/findings **5** a **6** without **7** What **8** despite **9** another **10** us **11** even **12** more **13** prefer/tend **14** because/when

8 Ss look at the two statements alone and decide their opinions and reasons for them. When they are ready, tell Ss that question 1 is about individual feelings so the Ss should not disagree with each other or try to change each other's minds. Question 2 uses a general *you* so in this case Ss can agree and disagree and try to come to an agreement. Elicit ideas in open class.

ADDITIONAL PRACTICE: Photocopiable resources. Resource 34: *Who is it?* Page 203

GRAMMAR AND READING

This section extends the Ss' knowledge of clauses of concession, addition and contrast.

Special difficulties: Ss should be aware of most, if not all, of these clauses but may still make errors in sentence structure when using them. Allow Ss to attempt to complete exercises without much input beforehand so that they can see that they have made mistakes and realise that they have learnt something during the lesson.

Culture notes

Vans were originally called Van Doren Rubber Company. They were founded in 1966 in California. Today, Vans produce clothes for the bmx, skateboarding, snowboarding, urban and punk markets. Two songs have been written about Vans shoes. The punk The Suicide Machines wrote *The Vans Song* and the rap group The Pack released *Vans*.

DKNY stands for Donna Karan New York and is a range of clothing made by fashion designer Donna Karan. The label was founded in 1984 and there are now seventeen stores around the world. Donna's real name is Donna Ivy Faske and she was born in 1948.

Dolce and Gabbana is an Italian fashion house started by the Italian designers Domenico Dolce and Stefano Gabbana. It is based in Milan where Gabbano was born in 1962. Dolce is from Palermo. They have a more casual range called D&G as well as D&G Junior for children.

Warm-up Review of vocabulary from the last lesson.
Famous people. Ss work in groups of three. Each group writes the name of a famous person on a piece of paper. Then they write one adjective or phrase from the last lesson, in a sentence, to describe them, eg David Beckham: *He sticks out like a sore thumb in the LA Galaxy team.* Ss then pass their paper to a new group who have to write a new sentence about the person using a different phrase or word, eg *He's quite an unremarkable footballer.* Repeat the process until each group have written a sentence about all the other groups' people. Ss then get their own person back and read through the comments deciding which they agree with and which they disagree with. Elicit sentences and opinions, with reasons, in open class.

1 Ss look through the photos in pairs and describe each with an adjective from the previous lesson, eg *He's distinctive.* Then they discuss the two questions. Elicit ideas in pairs and reasons. There is no right answer as long as Ss can justify their opinions.

2 Ss can ask and answer the questions in pairs to make the quiz more fun. When Ss have found their answers, ask the Ss if they are interested in fashion to see if the quiz results are correct.

3 Ss look at the statements in pairs first to see if they agree or disagree. Elicit ideas in open class and then Ss read the blog to see what the writer thinks. Elicit the answer and extracts from the text that demonstrate that it is the correct one: she talks about the extravagance of buying designer brands but this is only one aspect of fashion. She also talks about clothes being a compulsory form of self-expression and that even people like her friend, who say they do not follow fashion, actually have their own fashion.

Answer 3

Work it out

4 Tell Ss that, as soon as they have found the sentence, they should put their hands up. Stop the others and elicit the sentence: 'Although he only earns a pittance' – line 2. Now elicit the form in the three sentences.

Answers **1** In spite of the fact that/Despite the fact that/Even though + pronoun + verb **2** In spite of/Despite + *-ing* form **3** In spite of/Despite + noun

Optional activity: Give Ss further practice of the form. Elicit the name of a famous person who the Ss think does not deserve their fame. Elicit why and write the reason on the board, eg a singer who cannot sing. Write a sentence on the board about the person: *Although … can't sing, he/she is rich and famous.*
Ss then rewrite the sentence using the forms in Exercise 4. Elicit sentences to check that Ss can manipulate the form correctly.
In spite of the fact that … can't sing, he/she is rich and famous.
In spite of not being able to sing … is rich and famous.
In spite of his/her poor singing, … is rich and famous.

5 Ss may find it difficult to understand the subtle differences between the two choices. Elicit ideas and tell the Ss that, in this sentence, *we* refers to everybody. If the word *if* was replaced by *though*, it would change the meaning so that *we* only refers to a group of people all of whom have not much money. In this case, (a) would be correct.

Answer b

6 Ss discuss the two sentences in pairs. Elicit the answers and, again, look in detail at the two sentences. In (a), the contrasting situations are that some people spend a lot of money on clothes and others do not.

Answers **1** b **2** a

Optional activity: Again, give Ss a little more practice of the form. Use the example from the last optional activity, i.e. *… can't sing. … is rich.*
Ask Ss which of the two sentences in Exercise 6 would be appropriate for linking the two facts about the singer – (b) *Whilst I understand that … is rich and famous, I'm still convinced that he/she can't sing.*
Ss can also think of a way of contrasting this situation with another, eg *… is a poor singer whereas … is very good. Some good singers earn a pittance whilst … is rich and famous.*

7 Ss find the sentence (lines 13–15): 'Besides having to pay a small fortune for unremarkable, mass-produced clothes, why would anyone want to look like a walking advert.' Then they look at the form and answer the question.

> **Answers** **1** As well as/Apart from + *-ing* **2** As well as/Apart from + noun

Check it out

Refer Ss to the Check it out section on page 159 and tell Ss to try to do exercises without looking at it, using it only to check their ideas.

8 Check: *slovenly* (untidy/messy in appearance or habits). Ss try to do the exercise in pairs without looking at the text or previous exercises. They then check before you elicit answers in open class. Discuss some of the answers with the Ss, eg ask about sentence 4: *Can you complete the sentence with the other phrase? (In spite of the fact that he doesn't have much money.)* 5 *If the sentence started 'Even if I ironed it' it would be a second conditional so what would have to happen to the second half? (it would still look).*

> **Answers** **1** While **2** Despite **3** even if **4** Despite **5** Even though **6** apart from **7** while **8** although

9 Ss work alone and compare answers in pairs. Tell the Ss that, if they disagree with each other, they should check on the page and the Check it out section to see if they can find out who is correct.

> **Answers** **1** well as being lightweight **2** having retired/being retired/being a pensioner **3** they had long been out of **4** though they are expensive **5** the fact that I have just **6** I'm not particularly interested/not being particular interested **7** some people have style, other

10 Ss look at the four statements alone and decide their own opinions as well as trying to think of one sentence about each which uses a clause from the lesson. Ss then get together in groups of four. Each student starts the conversation about one of the statements with the others agree or disagree as they feel. Elicit ideas in open class.

ADDITIONAL PRACTICE: Photocopiable resources. Resource 35: *But …* Page 204

Students' Book ➡ pages 128–129

READING AND LISTENING

This section introduces more vocabulary to describe people's appearance and personality through a reading of a short story.

Culture notes

Herman Melville (1819–1891) was an American writer. *Moby Dick* was considered a failure at the time of publication and Melville was largely unknown at the time of his death. It was only in the twentieth century that his works were reappraised. In this story, the office owner finally moves premises to escape Bartleby and, when Bartleby 'prefers not to' move out of the building he is jailed and soon dies as he 'prefers not to eat'. The book is considered to be a forerunner of absurdist literature. The photo is from the 2001 film, *Bartleby*, starring Crispin Glover as Bartleby.

Warm-up Review of linking clauses from the previous lesson. *Agree or disagree.* Ss work in groups of three. Write a sentence on the board, eg *English is interesting*. Ask Ss to agree or disagree in their groups. If they agree, they must use a clause of addition to give a second positive thing about English, eg *Besides being interesting, English is easy.* For those who disagree, they find a fact that contrasts with this either about English (*Whilst English is useful, it isn't very interesting.*) or a contrast with a different language or school subject (*English is uninteresting whereas Maths is fascinating.*). Each group in turn writes a statement of their own about any topic they like. Each group reads out their sentence and the other groups have one minute to write a follow-up sentence as in the examples above. When Ss have all read out their sentences, Ss can discuss their statements as a class if necessary.

1 Elicit what an office or clerical job entails. Elicit duties and list them on the board, eg typing, filing, sorting paperwork, answering the phone, writing reports etc. Ss then answer the two questions in pairs and as a class. Try to encourage Ss to use the clauses from the previous lesson in their answers, eg *Whilst it's quite an easy job, it must be really boring. Besides being badly paid, it's also very repetitive.*

2 Ss read through the vocabulary items in pairs, working together to say what the words mean. Then they look up any words that neither of them know and finally use the words to describe the man in the photo.

Possible answers 1 forlorn expression, frail, lean face, stooping shoulders, wan complexion 2 Ss can choose any words as long as they can justify them. The most likely adjectives to use because of his facial expression, clothes and hairstyle: gloomy, reserved, sedate, dependable

3 When Ss have read through the fact box, elicit a one sentence summary of the plot (a man takes on Bartleby as a third worker to help in his office). Ss then discuss their predictions about what effect he will have. Do not tell Ss anything else about the story at this point.

4 Tell the Ss that, if they finish reading before others, they should underline extracts in the text which support their answers. Elicit all the adjectives (or adjectives that could be made from adverbs or nouns in the text), i.e. *pale, neat, respectable, forlorn, sedate manner, silent, mechanical, willful, passive, calm, honest, lean face*. Then elicit the answers and justifications from the text.

Answers Appearance forlorn expression, lean face, wan complexion **Personality** uncooperative, dependable, diligent, gloomy, unpredictable, rebellious, reserved, sedate **Narrator's feelings** He starts by thinking he was a normal, unremarkable, quiet, hard-working man. This feeling changed to being surprised and confused by Bartleby's refusal to carry out certain activities but also an inability to be angry with him.

5 Ss find the extracts in which the answers are given and decide what the correct answers are and why. Elicit the answers and justifications for them: 1 'would have a positive influence'; 2 'I would have been delighted (...) but ...'; 3 'in a mild, firm voice'; 4 'With any other man I would have flown into a rage'; 5 'testimony for an important case I was working on'; 6 'kick him out'; 'a bit mad'; 7 'his incessant industry and great calmness made him a valuable acquisition'.

Answers 1 T 2 F 3 F 4 T 5 T 6 T 7 F

6 Ss look at the highlighted words in the text in pairs and read the sentences in which they occur. Ss try to work out what they mean and what other words or phrases they could be replaced with. Ss then look at the exercise together.

Answers 1 stating 2 led me to 3 dismiss 4 reason with 5 regarding 6 premises 7 inadvertently 8 imperative 9 desired 10 incessant

7 Give Ss two minutes to discuss their predictions in pairs. Elicit ideas before Ss read Part 2 and, after they have finished, ask what the answer was.

Answer He was living there.

8 Ss read through the text alone and underline or mark sections of the text which help to answer each question. Ss compare their ideas in pairs. Elicit answers in open class and justifications: 1 blanket, soap and a ragged towel, crumbs in a newspaper. *Ragged* implies old and the fact that the crumbs are in a newspaper means that he doesn't have any plates. 2 It isn't explained explicitly. Perhaps the thought of him living in an office, not able to clean himself properly. 3 The word *superstitions* implies that he thinks it may bring him bad luck. 4 The last sentence says that Bartleby 'was slowly but surely driving us all insane'.

Answers 1 He is poor, homeless. 2 Pity changes to repulsion. 3 He feels he shouldn't as it might bring him bad luck. 4 Bartleby's strange behaviour was affecting everybody in the office (both the narrator and Nippers involuntarily use *prefer*).

9 Ss work in pairs and check their ideas by replacing the words in the text with the words given to see if the text still makes sense.

Answers 1 to recall 2 austere reserve 3 decline 4 wary about 5 repulsion 6 resolved 7 get into a habit 8 demented

10 Give Ss two minutes to discuss the questions. Ss then join up in groups of four to tell each other their ideas. Play the recording and elicit as much detail about the story as possible without allowing Ss to look at Exercise 11 at this point.

Tapescript CD 5 Track 5

Story Narrator: [East Coast US accent] The next day I noticed that Bartleby did nothing but stand and stare out of the window. Upon asking him why he did not write, he said that he had decided not to do any more writing.

'Why? What next?' I exclaimed. 'And what is the reason?'

'Do you not see the reason for yourself?' he indifferently replied.

I peered at him, and saw that his eyes looked dull and glazed. Instantly it occurred to me that the long hours spent copying by his dim window might have damaged his vision.

I was touched. I hinted that it would be better if he refrained from writing for a while; and urged him to embrace that opportunity of taking some exercise outside. This, however, he did not do. Instead Bartleby would stand next to his desk, staring out the window for hours at a time. Whether his eyes improved or not, I could not say. Some days later he finally informed me that he had permanently given up copying. However, he remained, as ever, a fixture in my office, staring out his window.

After wrestling with my conscience, I told Bartleby that in six days' time he must unconditionally leave the office. I warned him to take steps, in the meantime, to obtain alternative accommodation. I offered to assist him in this endeavour and assured him he would be provided for financially.

When I arrived at my office after the six days had expired, I realised, to my horror, that Bartleby was still there. I advanced slowly towards his desk and said, 'The time has come; I am sorry for you; here is money; but you must go.'

'I would prefer not,' he replied, with his back still towards me.

Ignoring him, I tranquilly turned and added – 'After you

have removed your things from these offices, Bartleby, you will lock the door and leave your key underneath the mat, so that I may have it in the morning. I shall not see you again so goodbye to you. If I can be of any service to you, do not fail to advise me by letter. Goodbye, Bartleby, and the best of luck.'

As I walked home I felt pleased with the masterly way in which I had rid myself of Bartleby. The beauty seemed to consist in its perfect quietness. The more I thought over it, the more I was charmed with it. Nevertheless, the next morning, upon awakening, I had my doubts. I reached my office earlier than usual. I stood listening for a moment but all was still and the door was locked. He must be gone! I was almost sorry for my brilliant success. As I was fumbling under the door mat for the key, I accidentally knocked against the door with my knee.

'Not yet; I am busy.' a voice called.

Bartleby! Not gone!

'Bartleby,' I said, entering the office, 'I am seriously displeased. Will you, or will you not, quit me?'

'I would prefer not to quit you,' he replied.

'What earthly right have you to stay here? Do you pay any rent? Is this property yours?'

He answered nothing.

'Are your eyes recovered? Could you copy a small paper for me this morning?'

He silently retreated to his desk. The others arrived for work and the day passed as usual with Bartleby motionless at his desk.

Some days passed and I began to think that my troubles with Bartleby were some strange act of fate – that it was my humble role in life to provide Bartleby with an office to live in. Yes, Bartleby, stay; I shall persecute you no more; you are as harmless and noiseless as any of these old chairs. But my feelings changed when, to my discomfort, my clients and other lawyers began commenting unkindly about my strange clerk who spent all his time staring out the window. I then knew that something unusual must be done. Since he will not quit me, I must quit him!

Which is exactly what I did. I quickly found suitable premises and a few days later men with carts came to remove the books and furniture to my new office near City Hall. Finally, I entered my old offices for the last time to say farewell to Bartleby. He stood with his back to me, staring out the window.

'Goodbye, Bartleby; I am going – goodbye.'

And then, slipping some money into his hand, I hurried out of the room, relieved to be escaping the man who for so long I had been unable to rid myself of.

Answers 1 No, he doesn't. 2 The owner leaves the premises instead.

11 Ss work in pairs to try to put the story in the correct order from what they remember. Play the recording again and elicit the answers.

Answers 1–7–2–4–6–5–3

Optional activity: Before Ss look at the final questions, they work in groups of four to try to write a summary of the entire story so far in up to fifty words. When the Ss have written their summaries, each group in turn reads theirs out while the other groups try to spot vital information that they think the group has left out. The winners are the group(s) whose summary includes all the important facts or which other Ss find fewest faults with. You act as the judge to decide if criticisms are valid or not to stop Ss making irrelevant ones.

12 Ss work in groups of three or four. Set a time limit of three minutes and then open up the conversation to the whole class. As a follow-up, it may be nice to give the ending of the story to the Ss from the Culture notes.

SPEAKING AND VOCABULARY

This section introduces ways of using understatement to be more diplomatic when discussing views and opinions.

Warm-up Introduction to the topic of the lesson. *Bad news.* Ss work alone. Everyone has to make up a small problem they could have had. Tell Ss they can choose from the list:

A present they didn't like
A holiday they have been on which wasn't very good
A lie someone has told them
A time when they were angry with someone
A time when they felt ill.

Ss then get into groups of three or four. Each student gives clues about their situation without saying what it was. The idea is to disguise the actual problem for as long as possible: *Oh, it was terrible.* (A present?) *It was in Greece.* (A holiday?) *I ate some bad meat and was ill.* (Felt ill?) *And while I was in bed, my sister took my MP3 player. I was really angry.* Ss tell each other their problems in their groups and the others guess what the problem was.

1 Ss work in pairs. They describe what has happened in the cartoon and what they think the speakers are thinking. Then they compare this to the actual caption. Elicit the difference between the two (the words spoken are probably not as strong as what they are thinking).

Answers They are very upset. Everything has been destroyed by a burglar or earthquake. They would probably be thinking: *Oh no! What a mess!* or similar.

2 Ss look through the reasons. Ask if they have ever been in any of these situations. Elicit anecdotes if possible and then play the recording. Elicit the answers and the situations in the recordings: 1 Two work mates are discussing a new man. One likes him, the other thinks he is too quiet. 2 A man and a woman discussing a book. She says she's not keen on it but, when she finds out that he wrote it, she becomes more enthusiastic. 3 The pilot of a plane is telling passengers that they have to make an

emergency landing because two of their engines have failed. 4 Two MPs are arguing over unemployment figures in a parliamentary debate.

Tapescript CD 5 Track 6

One
Lisa: *[Northern English accent]* Hey Sian, have you seen that new guy who's started work in the IT department?
Sian: *[Northern English accent]* What, the guy with the little beard?
Lisa: Yes, that's him. I think he's gorgeous!
Sian: Yes, he helped me set up my printer yesterday afternoon.
Lisa: And what do you think of him? I think I'm rapidly falling in love with him!
Sian: Well, he's got a nice smile, I suppose. And that hairstyle of his is, well, original. But conversation obviously isn't his strong point. I could hardly get a word out of him!
Lisa: Awww! He's new here – he's just a bit shy, that's all!

Two
Man: *[neutral English accent]* Excuse me. I couldn't help but notice that you're reading *The Reluctant Harlequin*. Can I ask what you think of the book?
Woman: *[neutral English accent]* The book? What do I think of it? Well it's a bit long, to be honest. And some of it isn't exactly easy to follow either! Why do you want to know?
Man: Well, I, er, wrote it, you see.
Woman: Oh, really? Well in that case can I just say that it's a marvellous book. I couldn't fault it. The whole of the first chapter had me laughing out loud and I just love the description of ...

Three
Captain: *[RP accent]* Good morning, Ladies and Gentlemen. My name is Captain Geoffrey Bates, and I'd like to welcome you onboard this Sabrina Airlines flight to Helsinki. I'm afraid we're running a bit late this morning – there was rather a delay at Heathrow due to strong winds – but we'll hopefully make up for lost time. As for the weather conditions in Helsinki – well, the temperature is about 1 degree Celsius at the moment with a strong northerly wind, so not especially warm this morning. At present we're flying over northern Denmark and then we'll make our way across southern ...
This is your captain again. Er ... just to let you know that we have a slight problem and we're about to attempt an emergency landing at Copenhagen airport. This is due to the loss of power in two of our engines. Can I just apologise in advance for the inconvenience ... the landing may be rather bumpy.

Four
MP: *[RP accent]* Would the Minister please tell the house why he has repeatedly given Parliament misleading information about the number of unemployed people in this country?
Minister: *[RP accent]* Well, I'm afraid the Right Honourable Member for North Stilton is somewhat mistaken in his assertions. Let me repeat once again, the number of people in Britain who are between jobs has remained steady at 800,000.

Answers 1 b 2 a 3 c 4 d

SPEAK OUT

3 Go through the Speak Out box with the Ss. If they did the warmer activity, they could use an appropriate phrase from the box to talk about their problem, eg *I was rather annoyed with my sister as I was feeling a little under the weather and wanted to listen to music while they were enjoying themselves on the beach!* After Ss have listened to the recording again, elicit the answers and who used the phrases and what about: 1, 2 – speaker 1 about the boy in the office (his haircut and his conversational ability); 3, 4 – speaker 2 about the book; 5, 6, 7 – speaker 3, the pilot (the delay to the flight, the temperature in Helsinki, the emergency landing which may be bumpy); 8, 9, 10 – speaker 4, the MPs (information about unemployment, about the unemployment figures, the number of unemployed people in Britain).

Answers 1 g 2 d 3 i 4 e 5 j 6 f 7 c 8 a 9 b 10 h

Mind the trap!

Elicit other example sentences from Ss making sure that the adjectives are always negative, eg *It's a bit cold today. It's a bit of a cold day today.*

4 Ss work in pairs to discuss how many of the adjectives they know. If they cannot complete the table, they look up the remaining words in the dictionary. When all Ss have completed the table, look at the examples given and tell Ss to imagine they were talking about an unattractively skinny person in their class. They would not refer to the person as *skinny* as this would be rude so they could say that the person is *a bit underweight* or *not exactly well-built*. Ss then do the same with the other words. Encourage Ss to use different modifiers to each adjective.

Answers unintelligent – slow ≠ bright
lazy – indolent ≠ conscientious
odd – peculiar ≠ typical
disgusting – unappetising ≠ delicious
rude – blunt ≠ well-mannered

2 They're a bit slow. They're not exactly very bright.
3 He's rather indolent. He's not terribly conscientious.
4 This example is rather peculiar. This example isn't entirely typical. **5** The food was somewhat unappetising. The food wasn't exactly delicious.
6 She can be rather blunt. She's not particularly well-mannered.

5 Give Ss three minutes to read through the situation and find as many phrases as possible that they could use to talk to the parents. Ss could then act out a roleplay between the teacher and parent if necessary.

Possible answers Uncooperative – He can be rather a nuisance at times. Acts strangely – He doesn't act particularly normally. Aggressive – He is rather unfriendly towards the other students. Hard to teach – He's quite a challenging student to teach. Lacks motivation – He's not terribly motivated.

6 Tell Ss to look at Situation One to start with. As think about the questions they will ask. Bs think about how to complain about the problems they are having in an understated way. When the Ss are ready, A starts by ringing up and asking questions. When B responds, A should use their imagination to ask follow-up questions and B should give more details, not just follow the instructions without making it sound natural. When they have finished, Ss read the second situation and Bs start the new roleplay.

ADDITIONAL PRACTICE: Photocopiable resources. Resource 36: *Soften the blow.* Page 205

WRITING

This section looks at how to write a character reference or testimonial for someone.

Special difficulties: This is possibly the most difficult writing task for Ss to find realistic as it will probably be many years before they are asked to write one in real life. However, they should be able to understand the importance of being able to write one if it should appear in an exam.

Culture notes

GCSEs (General Certificate of Secondary Education) is a qualification usually taken by students in Britain (not Scotland) at the age of sixteen. There are eight pass grades from A* to G. Many jobs require at least a C grade and this is also the standard expected if students want to continue studying a subject to A-level. In most subjects a final mark is given for a combination of coursework and final exam grade.

Rochdale is a town in Greater Manchester, about 15km north of the city of Manchester. It was a centre for the wool trade and textile mills during the Industrial Revolution. It was also the birthplace of the cooperative movement.

Warm-up Review of understatement and lead-in to the topic of the lesson. *Write about me.* Tell Ss to write down three positive things about themselves and one negative, eg *hard-working, out-going, honest, often late.* Ss swap papers with a partner. Tell the Ss that they are going to write about their partner using the information given. To do this they should use linkers to link the positive aspects and contrast with the negative. They should also use understatement to make the negative aspect sound less serious and use their imagination to add details.
Example: *Besides being honest and hard-working, ... is an out-going person who loves meeting new people. On the other hand, he doesn't always arrive for lessons at the same time as his classmates.*
Ss read their descriptions to their partners to see if the partner thinks it sounds positive enough. Elicit some descriptions in open class.

1 Give Ss one minute to carry out the task. Tell Ss that they should try to spend half the time describing the two photos and the other half pointing out the major differences and what they think might have happened. Elicit ideas in open class.

Suggested answers Her appearance has changed from casual to smart. She is smiling (happy-go-lucky) in the first and serious in the second. She looks as if she has got a good career for which she must dress smartly.

2 Ss read through the questions. Tell Ss to underline words or phrases that help them to find the answers, then to discuss what they read and think in pairs. Elicit ideas and justifications in open class.

Answers 1 Positive – hard-working, mature, not allowed ill-health to interfere with her work, commitment, elegant and insightful written work, cheerful, calm, considerate, delightful sense of humour, popular. She is quiet and probably shy in large groups but the teacher excuses these things. **2** A quiet, hard-working student. **3** Yes – give future employers or universities a clear idea of what someone is like. No – teachers may not be objective, you may not show aptitude for work in the classroom.

3 Again, Ss work alone, finding words and phrases which show her character and her behaviour at work. Then they discuss their ideas with their partner and as a whole class. Elicit all the positive and negative attributes mentioned in the text: *dependable, highly motivated, comfortable working as part of a team, ability to work independently, calm under pressure, punctuality not a strong point, hasn't missed a day through illness, increasingly confident, professional, excellent rapport with customers, insightful written reports, considerate, mature, rather earnest, lacks a sense of humour, well liked, highly regarded.* When Ss discuss the third question, ask them to think of jobs she would be good at (eg working in a bank where customers want a serious, professional person to talk to) and what she might not be good at (eg a teacher – you cannot arrive for lessons late).

Answers 1 She has become more confident and is able to communicate well with clients. **2** She is sometimes late for work, she has lost her sense of humour. **3** Probably encouraging depending on the job.

4 Ss look through the words in the exercises in pairs to see how many they understand. Ss then look through the texts and do as much of the matching task as they can. Finally, the Ss use dictionaries to check their answers and complete any of the matching that they could not do.

Answers 1 excels at **2** in all she undertakes **3** every success in **4** diffidence **5** hard-working **6** considerate **7** with ... alike **8** insightful **9** earnest **10** dependable **11** I have no hesitation in recommending **12** comes across as **13** favourable **14** well liked **15** highly regarded **16** asset

5 Ss look at the phrases and try to think of verbs that could collocate with them, eg 1 *get/achieve;* 2 *has shown/proved;* 3 *make/create;* 4 *show/ demonstrate/have;* 5 *create/have;* 6 *do/produce.* Ss then look through the texts to see which verbs have been used there. Tell Ss that the wording may not be exactly the same in the texts but they should be able to recognise which section of text relates to each phrase in the exercise. Elicit the section of texts where the collocation can be found: 1 text A, paragraph 1, lines 1–2: 'achieved a very fine set of results'; 'gaining seven grade As'; 2 text B, paragraph 2, lines 1–2: 'She has proved herself to be a dependable and highly motivated member of staff.'; 3 text B, paragraph 2, line 1: 'Catherine has made a very favourable impression'; 4 text B, paragraph 2, lines 2–3: 'she has also demonstrated an ability to work independently'; 5 text B, paragraph 2, line 6: 'and has established an excellent rapport with ...'; 6 text B, paragraph 2, lines 6–7: 'Catherine has produced some insightful written reports.'

Answers **1** achieve/gain **2** prove **3** make **4** demonstrate **5** establish **6** produce

TRAIN YOUR BRAIN

6 Read through the Train Your Brain box with the Ss. Elicit that both the texts only have four paragraphs, therefore some of the points in the Train Your Brain box will be in the same paragraph as each other. Elicit answers and ask Ss to justify their answers by referring to text A and B, eg 'mention any notable personal qualities' – text A – *cheerful, calm and considerate;* text B – *considerate and mature.*

Answers **paragraph 1** briefly summarise the person's career; mention how long you have known the person **paragraph 2** mention the person's strengths; use strong verbs; mention any weaknesses in an understated way **paragraph 3** mention any notable personal qualities **paragraph 4** state that you recommend them for the job; express the hope that the person's future career will be a success

7 Ss look through the six adjectives to see which they understand. Ask Ss to attempt to do the matching even if they are not sure of all the adjectives, eg *fussy/pedantic.* Elicit the answers and then the meaning of the adjectives if necessary (a fussy person is someone for whom nothing is good enough; a pedantic person always has to correct you even for the tiniest of errors).

Answers **1** e **2** d **3** c **4** f **5** a **6** b

Optional extra: As a fun follow-up, Ss look through the two texts about Catherine and find all the negative things about her. Knowing that the writers are using understatement, the Ss work in pairs or small groups to discuss what she might be really like, i.e. they exaggerate her negative traits. Eg *She's really shy. She can't think quickly. She hates large groups of people. She goes for days without speaking. She's always late. She never smiles.* Elicit ideas in open class and make sure Ss do not contradict any information in the texts, eg if they say that she is miserable and has no friends this contradicts the information that she is well liked.

8 If the Ss did the warmer activity, they will already have some adjectives for their partner and will have rewritten the negative trait using understatement. Tell Ss to make a plan for their writing, listing all the adjectives and facts they will need. Ss can either do this alone so that the testimonial is a surprise to their partner when finished or they can discuss their ideas in pairs and ask their partner eg what they are good at. Ss then write the testimonial alone either in class or for homework.

Optional follow-up: It would be a good idea to use the testimonials as the basis for deciding what jobs different Ss might be best for. Ss should cover the name of the person they are writing about so that no one else knows who the person is. Collect in all the testimonials and put the Ss into pairs. Each pair is then given two testimonials at random, making sure they haven't got one that they wrote. They read through the two testimonials and discuss together what they think the people would be good and bad at and whether they would offer them a job. They can also discuss what the people's real weaknesses are. Ss then guess who the testimonial is for and see if they are correct.

THINK FORWARD TO EXAMS REVISION 6
UNITS 11–12

As this is the final review section in the book, it may be a good idea to use this as a form of exam practice, especially the tasks which are likely to be included in their end-of-year or end-of-school exams.

VOCABULARY AND GRAMMAR

1 Tell Ss to look at the words in the box. Ask Ss what kind of word each is, i.e. *badly* – adverb; *confined* – adjective; *fashion* – noun; *label* – noun; *name* – noun; *petty* – adjective; *poverty* – noun; *rich* – adjective; *thinning* – adjective; *under* – preposition; *wage* – noun; *follow* – verb. Ss then work in pairs to think of phrases or collocations that they may appear in, eg *badly paid, badly behaved, confined space, confined to your room.* Elicit ideas and then Ss look at the other halves of the collocations in the exercise and match them together. Elicit the answers and what they mean: 1 very rich; 2 poor; 3 the lowest wage allowed by law; 4 earning less than is considered to be enough to live comfortably; 5 unable to leave the wheelchair; 6 ill; 7 very fashionable; 8 do what everyone else is doing; 9 clothes made by a specific fashion company; 10 someone who breaks the law in small crimes; 11 the name of a company which makes a particular product; 12 starting to go bald. Ss make sentences using the phrases which relate to their own country or people they know, eg *My uncle is filthy rich. He owns his own business and lives in a mansion.*

Answers 1 rich 2 badly 3 wage 4 poverty 5 confined 6 under 7 fashion 8 follow 9 label 10 petty 11 name 12 thinning

2 Ss work alone. When they have finished, they compare answers and reasons for their choices. If there are any differences in opinions, they should look up the words in a dictionary and find out who was correct. Elicit the answers and the meanings of the words in open class.

Answers 1 dilapidated (It means old and run-down. The others are the opposite.) 2 prosperous (It means rich. The others mean poor.) 3 quirky (It means strange or different. The others mean normal.) 4 outlandish (All the words can be used to describe something different than the norm but *outlandish* may have negative connotations.) 5 assault (It involves violence. The others are ways of illegally obtaining money without violence. Ss may possibly choose *corruption* as it is more of a process of criminal action rather than one immediate crime.) 6 hostage (It is a victim of crime whereas the others are criminals.)

3 Ss work on the exercise without any initial help. When they have finished, allow them to compare answers in pairs and then elicit answers in open class. Elicit what Ss must remember in such exercises (keeping the tense of the second sentence the same as the first) and what is often tested (eg passive and active; phrasal verbs; inversions; conditionals; different modals).

Answers 1 You didn't need/have to do all that washing-up. 2 We had better contact the police. 3 I succeeded in closing the gate just in time. 4 You might have phoned to say you were delayed. 5 They were unable to help me trace her. 6 They may turn up later this evening. 7 You should have been at last night's party. 8 It's unlikely/doubtful that he saw/has seen us. 9 I might as well stay (in tonight).

4 Ss work alone and complete the activity. When they have finished, put the Ss into pairs or small groups. Each student first tells their partner(s) how they approached the activity. Ask Ss if anyone first read through the text to get a general understanding of what it was about. Ask if anyone looked at the gaps without looking at the choices to try to guess what the missing words could be. Ss then compare answers in their groups and finally as a whole class.

Answers 1 b 2 d 3 c 4 c 5 d 6 a 7 a 8 d 9 c 10 b

5 Ss quickly read through the task to see what it is testing (linking expressions). Tell Ss that, sometimes, no changes will have to be made to the rest of the sentence whereas at other times, quite substantial changes will have to be made. Ss work alone, then compare in pairs.

Answers 1 Despite the fact that the food was atrocious, we all had a good time. 2 Apart from working night-shifts, she's also studying for a degree. 3 He's coming with us, even if he doesn't want to. 4 Despite having given up full-time work, Tom still works as a volunteer. 5 Although he is (often/usually/always) late / Although he is (not/not often/not usually/never) punctual, he's actually very committed.

READING SKILLS

1 One approach for this exercise is to simply allow Ss to answer the questions alone in a set time limit as if they were in an exam. However, an alternative approach would be to ask Ss to read the text alone and underline any key words, phrases or ideas in it. Then they write a summary of the article in a maximum of fifty words which should include all the main points and arguments in it. Ss compare summaries as a class and decide whether other Ss' summaries have included all the main points or not. Ss then answer the questions, noting extracts in the text which give them the correct answer. Elicit the answers and the justifications for them in open class. Tell Ss that, in an exam, they usually have plenty of time to carry out reading tasks and it is worth reading the texts quickly before starting to get an overall understanding of what they are about and having a better idea of where to find information in the text which will help to answer each question. Justifications: 1 'the devil is generally associated with the left hand and the word *sinister* comes from the Latin for left, *sinistra*'; 2 'left-handed people are more common among the highly innovative'; 3 'Tools like the screwdriver work well for both.' (this doesn't mean it was designed to be so – it is just lucky); 4 'This ought to make left-handed people less productive (...). However, that's clearly not always the case'; 5 'college graduates overall earned an average of 30 percent more than high-school graduates', 'left-handed males with a college education earned 10 to 15 percent more than their right-handed counterparts.' 6 'in Britain and Ireland (...) 5 percent lower pay for left-handed females compared to right-handed females.' 'In a US study (...) no systematic difference between the pay of left-handed and right-handed females.' 7 'those who are left-handed on average came up with nearly 30 percent more uses (...) only holds true for left-handed males'; 8 (a) is disproved as left-handed people actually often earn more than right-handed; (b) is stated at the end as a conclusion but that is not the main idea of the text; (d) is wrong as the study is not showing new hope but new evidence about an existing situation; (c) sums up the article as a whole which is looking at evidence to see whether left-handed people are at a disadvantage or not.

Answers 1 T 2 T 3 F 4 T 5 T 6 F 7 T 8 c

SPEAKING SKILLS

1 As this is the last Think Forward to Exams section, allow Ss to choose a topic as if they were in an exam. Ss have a set time limit to plan their presentation, eg five minutes. Nominate one or two Ss to present each topic to the class and then discuss with the whole class what information could be included in each one and a logical way of presenting the information.
For example:

1 A short, interesting introduction which will hold the listeners' interest.

Throughout history, there have been many punishments for crime, some of which have been very gruesome. However, people have always committed crimes so it would seem as if these have been unable to prevent people from reoffending.

Follow up with reasons why people commit crimes, eg need, human nature, revenge, temptation.

Follow up with a look at different countries with different punishments. Eg USA – capital punishment, 'three strikes and you're out' (in some states, if you are caught three times, regardless of the severity of the offences, you can be jailed for life) but still high crime rates. Scandinavia – liberal punishment regime and low crime rates.

Follow up with your conclusions.
We can't change human nature.
The ability of the police to catch criminals is more important than the punishment they will get if caught.

2 Introduction: What does it mean? Again, an interesting start.
The quote seems to be saying that the most difficult thing in life is to be independent in thought and action from everyone else. The world, governments, teachers, family and friends want us to conform to their view of what is right and acceptable and to fight against this can mean losing friends, being laughed at or even losing your job.

Arguments for the opposite view to that which you hold, eg if you agree that it's the most difficult thing then argue against it.

Arguments for the view you hold with examples of people you know or who are famous.

Conclusion. Restate what the presentation was about and again give your view.

CULTURESHOCK1

Lead-in to the topic of the lesson. *Gapped sentence.* Use some of the idioms that have appeared in the book as the basis for a game. Put the Ss into two groups and write on the board a gapped sentence for each, eg:

____ ____ ____ ____ ____ ____ ____
____ ____ ____ ____ ____ ____ ____
____

1 I fell head over heels in love with the girl who sat next to me in History. / 2 I laughed my head off at a joke that my friend told me this morning in History.

Each group guesses words that might be in their sentence. Elicit three guesses, eg words such as *the*, *a*, *in*, *of* etc, and then give Ss the first two letters of each word in their sentence. Elicit two more ideas and then give them two more letters. Keep going until one group has guessed their entire phrase. Ask what both sentences include and try to elicit the word *idiom* and what an idiom is. Elicit definitions but do not tell the Ss the real definition yet as they will find this in Exercise 3.

1 Ss look at the seven cartoons and captions in pairs and discuss what they show. Then they try to match the idioms to the correct caption. Elicit ideas and tell Ss the correct answers without saying what their meanings are at this stage.

> **Answers** A 4 B 2 C 6 D 3 E 5 F 1 G 7

2 Ss should now be able to do the matching easily. Elicit the answers in open class. Check the difference between *very expensive* (although it may be worth that much money) and *overpriced* (not worth the money being charged).

> **Answers** 1 g 2 a 3 b 4 d 5 f 6 c 7 e

3 Tell Ss to read the first sentence of the text to find the real definition of an idiom and see how close it is to their own ideas from the lead-in activity. Ss then complete Exercise 3 alone.

> **Answers** 1 lose face (to lose some respect or standing in society) 2 by and large (usually, often) 3 the salt of the earth (a good, honest, trustworthy person) 4 in a pickle (in a difficult situation)

4 Ss read the article first and underline any information they find on the origins of the different idioms. Elicit ideas, eg 1 seems English – actually from the USA – 1815; 2 1696 – brick up windows to avoid tax – story not true – dates from 1916 – in a book 1949; 3 football managers – popular since 1970s – originates 16th century nursery rhyme; 4 words changed 14th century – *numbles* = heart, liver, kidneys – then *umbles* – popular with humble people; 5 boat race to find king – cut off hand to win – not true – poaching animals or killing – 1819 book

Ivanhoe. Tell Ss that, if they underlined the correct words and phrases, they should be able to complete the exercise without looking at the text. If not, they should check again. Elicit the answers.

> **Answers** 1 Eat humble pie 2 Over the moon 3 Keep a stiff upper lip 4 Daylight robbery; Caught red handed

5 Set a time limit of two minutes for Ss to read through all the sentences and discuss their ideas in pairs. Elicit ideas as a class and then play the recording. Ss compare what they heard in pairs.

Tapescript `CD 5 Track 7`

Meredith: *[neutral English accent]* OK, so the next idiom is 'cost an arm and a leg'. This definitely doesn't come from eating the arms and legs of bears, which is the origin my six-year-old son suggested. No. A much more credible explanation is that in the 17th century when rich people loved to have their portraits painted, it was cheaper to have only your head and shoulders done, slightly more expensive to have the arms too, and the most expensive paintings were the ones with everything including arms and legs, so that's why people started using the expression, 'it costs an arm and a leg'. I wish it were true, but in fact, it appears to have a much grimmer origin. It was first coined in the USA after the Second World War, when many ex-combatants returned home missing arms and legs, and people started using it to describe anything that was unreasonably expensive. I love the idiom the French use for this, by the way. They say 'ça coute les yeux de la tête' which means 'it costs the eyes from your head'. Lovely! Right, the next one is 'to bury the hatchet'. Obviously there's a connection with fighting, with war, and in fact, it originated with the Native American Indians. At the end of a war, the chiefs of the warring tribes would smoke the peace pipe and ceremoniously bury their hatchets to signal the end of the conflict and the return of peace. The story that the Comanches had a kind of spiritual object, a hatchet made of gold that they called 'Tatzinupe' that they would bury at the end of a war is a fictional variation on this theme, and the idea that the phrase originated with a certain US general called Wilbur Hatchet who was obsessed with war and massacring Native American Indians and that the wars ended when he was killed and buried is in fact entirely without foundation.
Now, you don't need to keep any of this 'under your hat'. I'm telling you no secrets. The phrase 'keep it under your hat' has nothing to do with Al Capone, casinos, and …

> **Answers** 1 b 2 a

6 Give Ss one minute to look back, alone, over all the idioms and to choose one. Then they discuss their choices in groups of three or four. Nominate Ss to tell the class their ideas.

7 Prepare answers to the questions in advance so that, if Ss cannot think of equivalent idioms, you can help them. It would also be good to find out the true origins of some of the idioms so that, once Ss have invented their own origins, you can tell them what the true origins are.

CULTURESHOCK 2

Lead-in to the topic of the lesson. *Foreign TV.* Ss work in groups of four. Ask them to list as many TV channels as they can from countries other than their own. Set a time limit of two minutes and then elicit the channels to see who had the most. If anyone mentioned a BBC channel (eg BBC World or BBC Prime) ask if they know what BBC stands for. Elicit ideas and then Ss look on the Culture Shock page in their books. Ss then look at the glossary in small groups, sharing any knowledge they have about what the different words mean. Elicit definitions in open class and define any words that none of the Ss knows.

1 Ss work in groups of three. Set a time limit of two minutes for the Ss to answer the questions and then elicit ideas in open class.

Answers **1** Top left: wildlife documentary; top right: comedy (*Little Britain*); centre: children's show (*Teletubbies*); bottom left: quiz show (*The Weakest Link*); bottom right: costume drama **2** radio, website, magazines (eg *The Radio Times*, a *TV and Radio listings magazine* and other magazines based on BBC programmes; books; DVDs)

2 Ss look through the points, find examples alone and compare in groups of three. Elicit answers and ask Ss what they found most surprising.

Possible answers **1** too objective in times of war or crisis; dumbing down the quality in recent years **2** it was set up to sell radios; radio wasn't allowed to broadcast news until 7p.m. to help newspapers; it was the world's first regular TV service; *The Archers* has been going since 1950 **3** 22 million watched the coronation in 1953; *Teletubbies* is shown in 75 countries **4** A presenter at the end of Second World War introduced the TV service by saying: *As I was saying before we were so rudely interrupted …* **5** 1922 – set up; 1936 – first regular TV service **6** There is no advertising; it is independent of government interference; its aims are to inform, educate and entertain **7** 1936 – TV service starts; 1953 – huge surge in viewers after the coronation; 2007 – children's channel started

3 Ss read through the opinions before they listen to the recording and predict what each person might say. Elicit ideas, then Ss listen to the recording.

Tapescript `CD 5 Track 8`

Speaker 1: *[Ulster accent]* I don't have much time to watch TV to be honest. I'm far too busy with my job and the children. But I do try to watch the local news once a day just to keep in touch with what's going on. I appreciate nature documentaries and current affairs programmes and the occasional film, although to be honest I think I spend more time listening to music and reading.

Speaker 2: *[slight Spanish accent]* I'm not much of a reader and I never really got into computer games so I spend most of my leisure time in front of the TV screen watching all the programmes I enjoy. I always try to make sure I have the remote control because I love zapping to see what's on and to avoid having to watch all those terrible commercials.

Speaker 3: *[Scottish accent]* I watch TV a lot, too much probably. Well, if I have to pay the licence fee, I may as well get my money's worth, eh? I watch all sorts of stuff but what I really like are the programmes which are made in or set in the area where I live, you know, which tell me something about my own community. I don't get out much so that helps me find out what's going on.

Speaker 4: *[London accent]* Every Saturday I get a magazine which shows all the radio and TV programmes of the coming week and I sit down with a pen and circle all the programmes I'm interested in. I am quite a well-organised sort of person and it annoys me if I forget to watch my regulars. My children say I only watch dull programmes because I don't like reality TV and game shows.

Speaker 5: *[Newcastle accent]* Unfortunately, I have to travel a lot in my job, but before I leave I set up my digital TV to record all the programmes I'm going to miss. It's so much easier than the days of video recorders! I love all the programmes that have been around for ages, you know *The Archers* on the radio and *EastEnders* on the TV. I'm really hooked on soaps. They're a great way to escape from the pressures of work.

Answers **1** c **2** e **3** b **4** d **5** a

4 Ss tick the statements which best relate to themselves and other people in their family, then tell each other in more detail why they have ticked those statements. Nominate Ss to share ideas in open class.

5 Again Ss look through the statements and try to predict how the opinions may be rephrased. Elicit ideas, eg (a) *Too many reality TV shows. Trying to compete with cheap satellite shows.* Play the recording and elicit the answers and key words and phrases which helped Ss decide.

For tapescript see page 212.

Answers **1** f **2** e **3** d **4** a **5** b

6 Put Ss into groups of three or four. One student reads the first question to their group and each student in turn has to make a comment. The reader of the question then has to sum up what was said and give their opinions. The other Ss can then keep the discussion going if there is still disagreement. Repeat with a different student reading out the second question. When the Ss have discussed each of the questions, elicit ideas in open class.

Lead-in to the topic of the lesson. *British towns.* Ss work in groups of three. Ask them to list as many British towns or cities as they can. Elicit a few obvious ones to start with (London, Edinburgh) and then set a time limit of two minutes. Elicit ideas and ask Ss what they know about any of the places, eg Ss may know about Manchester or Liverpool because of the football teams or Stratford because of Shakespeare. Ss then look at the glossary in their groups of three to see how many of the words they know. Elicit all the definitions in open class and explain any words that none of the Ss know.

1 Check: *AD* (Anno Domini, after Christ) and *BC* (Before Christ). Tell Ss to look through the factfile and write down when each language was first used in Britain. They will have to use Maths for Latin and Gaelic (Anglo-Saxon 5th century AD, Latin 0AD, Celtic 600BC, Old Norse 9th century AD, Gaelic 500AD). Elicit all and write them in chronological order on the board.

Answer Celtic

Optional activity: If Ss did the lead-in activity, they can look at the towns and cities they listed and see how many of them have a suffix or prefix from the lists and so find out what language the name comes from.

2 Ss look at the photos and the meanings of the town names. Elicit ideas about what we can learn, eg that Birmingham was once a village and the people who lived there were called the Birmas; Derby was a village and lots of deer lived there, etc. Play the recording and Ss make notes about what is said. Ss compare ideas in pairs. Elicit answers in open class.

Tapescript CD 5 Track 10

Simon: *[London accent]* You're listening to *History Hour* here on Radio Thamesdown with me, Simon Frith. Well, this morning we're talking about place names and I'm delighted to be joined in the studio by Karen Moulding, who's written several books on British place names. Welcome to the programme Karen.
Karen: *[English West Country accent]* Thanks, Simon.
Simon: Well we're both sitting here in the studio with a lovely view of Swindon below us so perhaps I can start by asking what Swindon means.
Karen: Oh, that's quite an easy one. It's from Anglo-Saxon – *Swin* from the Anglo-Saxon for pig and *don* meaning hill or slope.
Simon: Hmmm – Pig Hill. I'm sure the estate agents were pleased when they came up with that name!
Karen: Well, Simon, it's one of the reasons why I find place names so fascinating. They're so immediately evocative. You can just picture how Swindon must have once looked, without the housing estates, factories and shopping centres. Just some pigs peacefully wandering around a hill. But really place names are history in a nutshell. They not only tell us what a place once looked like and what sort of function the place had but also they tell us a lot about different immigrant groups who lived in Britain, the languages they spoke and how these people later moved around the country.

Simon: Mmm, it all sounds very intriguing. Well, we're going to take a short break now but we'll continue our discussion after the latest traffic news.

Answers What a place once looked like; what sort of function the place had; about different immigrant groups who lived in Britain, the languages they spoke and how these people later moved around the country.

3 Ss read through the questions and predict the answers in pairs using the factfile, prefixes and suffixes to help them (eg 2 river mouth, headland/hill) or guessing the answers (eg 3 maybe Scotland as Gaelic is a Celtic language). Play the recording and elicit the answers.

For tapescript see page 212.

Answers 1 3,000 years and more **2** rivers, hills and mountains **3** the west – Wales, Cornwall and Scotland **4** Anglo-Saxon **5** North America and Australia

4 Some of the towns on the map might be places the Ss named in the lead-in but they will not have seen them on a map so this activity will still be interesting. Ss write the origins of each name on the map so they can easily see where each group predominated. Tell Ss they only need to look in one box for each place, eg *Aber-* is in the prefix box so Ss do not then have to check for *-deen* in suffixes.

Answers 1 Celtic **2** Celtic **3** Anglo-Saxon **4** Anglo-Saxon **5** Anglo-Saxon **6** Celtic **7** Anglo-Saxon **8** Old Norse **9** Anglo-Saxon **10** Gaelic **11** Anglo-Saxon **12** Celtic **13** Anglo-Saxon **14** Old Norse **15** Gaelic **16** Gaelic **17** Celtic **18** Latin **19** Celtic **20** Celtic **21** Old Norse **22** Gaelic **23** Anglo-Saxon **24** Anglo-Saxon

5 It may be a good idea for the teacher to look into the questions before the lesson and find examples of town names that have been exported (eg Paris, Texas; Warsaw, Ohio; Cordoba, Argentina), examples of other languages influencing town names in the Ss' country and some interesting names of towns in the Ss' country. Ss discuss the questions in groups of three or four for four minutes and then as a class.

CULTURESHOCK 4

Lead-in to the topic of the lesson. *We are what we eat.* Ss work in groups of four. Elicit ten countries which Ss know a lot about. For each country, Ss write down one stereotype about the people, the food or the culture of the country, eg France – the men wear blue and white striped shirts and berets; Germany – everyone eats sausages and drinks litre glasses of beer etc. When the Ss have finished, elicit stereotypes from different groups and the other Ss try to guess the country. If the stereotype is widespread, it should be easy for Ss to guess the country easily. If they cannot guess, then the stereotype probably is not widely believed. When they have finished, tell Ss they are going to look at some common stereotype views of Britain. Ss open their books and look at the glossary in their groups. Elicit definitions for each word and give definitions of any words unknown by any Ss.

1 If Ss have done the lead-in they will have answered some of these questions but this will still give them an opportunity to look at the pictures they didn't talk about in the lead-in and discuss what these show and whether these are things which people in their country associate with England. If there are any the Ss are not sure about or want to know more about, tell them they will be reading about them in the next exercise.

Answers 1 a hot-water bottle **b** double-decker buses **c** full English breakfast **d** five o'clock cup of tea **e** milkmen **f** non-decimal measurements (inches and feet) **g** bowler hats **h** smog **i** English accent

2 Although Ss could match the descriptions to the photos by skimming the texts quickly, they should be given time to read the texts carefully and get as much as possible from them. Elicit the answers to the matching and ask Ss what else they found out about each item and whether there was any surprising information for them, eg 1 hot-water bottles originated in Croatia; 2 fried eggs became popular in the First World War; 3 smog is caused by a combination of wet weather and pollution; 4 milk floats ran on electricity; 5 there are no doors on the buses; 6 the hat has an iron top; 7 only 2 percent of people use Received Pronunciation; 8 five o'clock tea was introduced deliberately by one person; 9 the measurement 'foot' was based on the size of a foot.

Answers 1 a **2** c **3** h **4** e **5** b **6** g **7** i **8** d **9** f

3 Ss read the captions in pairs and discuss what the words mean using the information in the book to help them. Elicit ideas and go through what they all mean with the class.

Answers Disappearing – becoming less common. **Axed** – got rid of. **A rare treat** – something special that you don't have very often. **Enduring myth** – something untrue or no longer true that is still believed. **Under threat** – in danger of disappearing or being axed. **Doomed** – almost certainly going to disappear or be axed. **Out of fashion** – no longer popular. **Good riddance** – something that we are not sad to see go. **Evolving** – changing over time.

4 Ss read through the items and the factors and try to predict which match with which. Elicit ideas and reasons for them, eg *full breakfast – health conscious. It's all fried food and very unhealthy. People now try to keep slim and fit so don't want to eat sausages, bacon and fried eggs.* Ss then listen to the recording and make notes about what is said. They compare ideas in pairs and then as a class. Elicit the answers and what was said on the recording about each item.

> **For tapescript** see page 213.

Answers 1 c **2** b, d **3** c **4** b **5** a **6** a

5 Ss work in pairs and try to write advantages and disadvantages for each one, eg *milk floats – milk is delivered but more expensive than buying in the supermarket; routemaster buses – tourist attraction but dangerous; hot water bottles – easy to use but boiling water can leak out and burn you.* Elicit as many ideas as possible and then Ss look on page 149. Elicit the answers and see if the Ss had thought of these reasons or not.

6 Put Ss into groups of three or four and set a time limit of ten minutes for them to discuss the three questions. Have some ideas prepared in advance to give the Ss an idea of what is needed. When they have discussed the ideas in their groups, elicit ideas in open class.

Photocopiable resources

Contents

Resource	Language point	When to use	Time (minutes)
UNIT 1			
1 Body talk	Body part idioms	After Vocabulary and Speaking, page 7	20–30
2 Past, Present and Future	All tenses	After Grammar and Listening, page 10	20–30
3 I've always wanted to meet you …	Managing conversations	After Speaking and Listening, page 12	5–20
UNIT 2			
4 Letter of complaint	Strong and base adjectives and modifying adverbs	After Vocabulary and Speaking, page 16	20
5 I see what you mean, but …	Talking about preferences	After Listening and Speaking, page 18	15–20
6 Dramatic opinions	Cleft sentences	After Grammar, page 23	20–30
UNIT 3			
7 Explaining the graphs	Collocations	After Vocabulary and Listening, page 28	25
8 They match but are they right?	The passives	After Grammar, page 32	20
9 Argue your point	Making predictions	After Speaking, page 34	up to 30
UNIT 4			
10 Banned words	Education vocabulary	After Reading and Vocabulary, page 40	20
11 The exam	Inversion	After Grammar and Speaking, page 42	20–30
12 Complete the job application	Writing job applications	After Writing, page 47	30
UNIT 5			
13 The proof of the pudding …	Food idioms	After Vocabulary and Speaking, page 50	20
14 On condition …	Conditionals	After Listening and Grammar, page 54	20–30
15 Solve it together	Problem solving	After Speaking, page 56	10–20
UNIT 6			
16 Noise bingo	Collocations	After Vocabulary and Grammar, page 60	15
17 Ask your friends	Verb patterns	After Grammar and Speaking, page 65	20
18 Just our opinions	Talking about differences and similarities	After Speaking and Listening, page 66	up to 30

Resource	Language point	When to use	Time (minutes)
UNIT 7			
19 Stop stress	Illness vocabulary	After Reading and Vocabulary, page 74	15
20 Rumours and lies	Impersonal reporting structures	After Grammar, page 77	20
21 A talk with Tom	Being assertive	After Listening and Speaking, page 78	30
UNIT 8			
22 Travellers' forum	Collocations	After Vocabulary and Speaking, page 83	20–30
23 What's the story?	Participle clauses	After Grammar and Listening, page 84	20–30
24 What are they saying?	Clichés	After Speaking, page 86	20
UNIT 9			
25 Sort them out	Newspaper vocabulary	After Reading and Speaking, page 94	25
26 Differing opinions	Vocabulary to describe TV programmes	After Speaking and Vocabulary, page 97	15
27 Regrets, I've had a few	Verb patterns	After Grammar, page 100	30
UNIT 10			
28 Find and use	Word formation	After Vocabulary and Listening, page 104	20–30
29 Dr What? Dr Who	Relative clauses	After Grammar, page 106	25
30 Act it out	Reacting to surprising news	After Listening and Speaking, page 111	10–30
UNIT 11			
31 If you've got it, flaunt it!	Formal and informal adjectives	After Vocabulary and Listening, page 117	30
32 Hmm … What do you think?	Stating opinions, agreeing and disagreeing	After Speaking and Listening, page 121	5–40
33 This must be yours	Modals	After Grammar and Reading, page 123	20
UNIT 12			
34 Who is it?	Describing people	After Vocabulary and Speaking, page 126	15–20
35 But …	Contrastive linkers	After Grammar and Reading, page 128	15–20
36 Soften the blow	Giving bad news	After Speaking and Vocabulary, page 133	up to 20

Photocopiable resources
Instructions

1 Body talk

Aim: To revise body part idioms.
Interaction: Groups of 3 or 4
Exercise type: Matching activity
Time: 20–30 minutes
Language: *have a mind of your own, under her thumb, hold your tongue*, etc
Materials: One copy of the resource, cut up, per group.
Instructions: (1) Divide the Ss into groups of 3 or 4. (2) Give each group the parts of the body sheet. (3) Ask each group to brainstorm as many idioms as they can using these parts of the body. Elicit ideas in open class. (4) Hand out the text cards so that each student has 3–4 cards. (5) The first student reads out one of their texts, emphasising the underlined words. The other Ss have to make an idiom which means the same as the emphasised words, using one of the body parts. (6) The person who read out the text tells them if they are right or wrong. If wrong, the reader tells the other students the correct answer and keeps the text card. If right, the person who made the idiom takes the card. (7) Repeat until all the cards have been read out. (8) Go through all the idioms with the whole class.

Answers On the cards

2 Past, Present and Future

Aim: To practise all tenses including the Future Perfect and the Future Continuous.
Interaction: Individual, then groups of 4 or 5, then pairs
Exercise type: Information gap
Time: 20–30 minutes
Language: *How long has John been working at this company? He's been working there since 1996.*
Materials: One copy of resource A or B, cut up, per student.
Instructions: (1) Hand out gapped text A or B to each student. Ss read the text and complete the gaps using the verbs in brackets. (2) Ss check and compare their ideas in groups, As working together and Bs working in different groups. The teacher checks that each group has the correct answers. (3) In the same groups, Ss think of what questions they will need to ask to find out the missing information. (4) Put the Ss in pairs so that one A and one B are working together. Give each student the information that their partner is going to be asking about. Make sure Ss do not show their partner the information. (5) Ss ask and answer questions to find out the missing information. (6) Elicit the questions and answers in open class, nominating Ss to ask and answer each one.

Answers A **1** has worked/been working; 1996 **2** has had **3** was; administrative assistant **4** personnel manager **5** will have been working/worked **6** will be driving; London **7** will be meeting/will meet; company directors **8** 9p.m. (to) 3a.m.; will be flying **9** will have been

Questions to ask: **1** How long has John worked/been working at this company? **2** – **3** What was his first job? **4** What does he do now/is his job now? **5** How long will he have been working/worked in this job by next April? **6** Where will John be driving between 7a.m. and 9a.m. next Monday? **7** Who will he be meeting in the afternoon? **8** When will he be flying to New York? **9** –

B **1** have been; 2001 **2** will have been; *Answer dependent on what year it is* **3** spent; Barbados **4** have celebrated **5** will celebrate/are going to celebrate/will be celebrating; Paris **6** 4p.m. (and) 7p.m; will be travelling **7** have reserved **8** will be eating; 9p.m.; 11p.m. **9** will be dancing

Questions to ask: **1** How long have Mary and Richard been married? **2** How many years will they have been married for next May? **3** Where did they spend their honeymoon? **4** – **5** Where are they going to celebrate their anniversary next year? **6** When will they be travelling to Paris? **7** – **8** When will they be eating? **9** –

3 I've always wanted to meet you ...

Aim: To practise managing conversations.
Interaction: Pairs
Exercise type: Mingling; speaking
Time: 5 minutes per conversation; four conversations possible
Language: *Excuse me, do you mind if I ...? Have you heard the news about ...?*
Materials: One set of cards, cut up, for each pair.
Instructions: (1) Put Ss into pairs and give them the role cards in three piles: start cards, change cards and finish cards. (2) Student A takes one of the start cards and starts the conversation as instructed. The two Ss continue the conversation for one minute. (3) After one minute, student B takes a change card and acts as instructed. Again, the two Ss carry on talking for one minute. (4) Student A now takes a finish card and brings the conversation to a close as instructed. (5) The two Ss can swap roles (and partners if necessary) and repeat the process with different role cards.

UNIT 2

4 Letter of complaint

Aim: To practise strong and base adjectives and modifying adverbs.
Interaction: Pairs
Exercise type: Gap-fill reading; discussion
Time: 20 minutes
Language: *absolutely furious, utterly impossible* etc
Materials: One set of the resource, cut up, for each pair.
Instructions: (1) Put Ss in pairs and give each the cut up adjectives and adverbs. Ss work together to sort the adjectives into base and extreme adjectives and the adverbs into three groups: those which can go with extreme adjectives only, those that can go with base adjectives only and those that can be used with both. (2) Hand out the gapped text to each pair. Ss work together to decide where to put the adverbs and adjectives from stage (1). Tell Ss that there are lots of possible choices for most of the gaps. (3) When they have finished, go through the text, eliciting any information you can about the words needed and then eliciting the actual words Ss used. Give feedback on whether the Ss' choices are possible or not.

Answers for Stage 1
Base adjectives: excited, disappointing, crowded, surprised, poor, upset
Extreme adjectives: impossible, furious, magnificent, exhausted
Adverbs that collocate with base adjectives only: extremely, terribly, slightly, pretty
Adverbs that collocate with extreme adjectives only: utterly, absolutely, simply, totally
Adverbs that can be used with both base and extreme adjectives: very, really

Suggested answers for Stage 2 (**Note:** Other combinations will also be possible.)
1 very/really/extremely/terribly/pretty excited
2 very/really/extremely/terribly/pretty/slightly disappointing
3 absolutely/utterly/simply/totally/really/pretty impossible
4 very/really/extremely/terribly/pretty crowded
5 very/really/extremely/terribly/pretty/slightly surprised
very/really/extremely/terribly/pretty upset
absolutely/utterly/simply/totally/really/pretty furious
6 very/really/extremely/terribly/pretty/slightly surprised
very/really/extremely/terribly/pretty upset
absolutely/utterly/simply/totally/really/pretty furious
7 absolutely/utterly/simply/totally/really/pretty magnificent
8 very/really/extremely/terribly/pretty/slightly poor/disappointing
9 absolutely/utterly/simply/totally/really/pretty exhausted
10 very/really/extremely/terribly/pretty/slightly surprised
very/really/extremely/terribly/pretty upset
absolutely/utterly/simply/totally/really/pretty furious

5 I see what you mean, but …

Aim: To practise talking about preferences.
Interaction: Groups of 3
Exercise type: Discussion; roleplay
Time: 15–20 minutes
Language: *I'm a big fan of …, I know what you mean but …* etc
Materials: One copy of the resource, cut up, per group. Copies of paintings if possible for the art gallery roleplay.
Instructions: (1) Put the Ss into groups of 3 and give the Ss a role card: A, B or C for the art gallery. Ss read their role to make sure they know what they should say. If the number of Ss in the class is not divisible by three, one or two groups can be made up of four Ss with two Ss working together on one of the roles. (2) If there are copies of paintings, Ss should look at them as if they are in a gallery. If not, they should still stand up and pretend to be looking at something. (3) Student A starts by praising the pictures, then B contradicts them. (4) A and B should try to get quite emotional about their views and then C should join in as a peacemaker. Set a time limit of three minutes for each roleplay and stop all the groups even if they are still talking so that all the groups are working at the same pace. (5) Hand out the next role cards. Make sure Ss have a different role (A–B, B–C, C–A). (6) Repeat the process as before and repeat again for the restaurant role if required.

6 Dramatic opinions

Aim: To practise cleft sentences.
Interaction: Individual, then groups of 3
Exercise type: Sentence completion; discussion
Time: 10 minutes for the sentence completion, 10–20 minutes for the follow-up discussion
Language: *What struck me first was …, It's the guitar introduction that I like best.* etc.
Materials: Two cards per student.
Instructions: (1) Give Ss two cards each and ask them to complete the cleft sentences. (2) Ss then get together in groups of 3 with other Ss who had the same card as them. They compare their sentences and ask the teacher for help if there are any doubts. They then discuss the follow-up task together, using cleft sentences as before. (3) Elicit sentences about teachers that the Ss know from the groups that were looking at this topic and encourage other Ss to join in the discussion, making their own cleft sentences. (4) Repeat the process with all six topics.

155

UNIT 3

7 Explaining the graphs

Aim: To revise collocations.
Interaction: Individual; then pairs
Exercise type: Information exchange
Time: 10 minutes for the speaking activity, 15 minutes for writing and comparing
Language: *steady increase, sharp fall, dramatic decline* etc
Materials: One complete (fast food sales or music downloads) graph and one blank graph per student. One bullying in school graph per pair.
Instructions: (1) Put Ss into pairs. Give each student one of the graphs. Ss work alone to think of how to describe the trends shown. They should not show their graph to their partner. (2) When they are ready, give the Ss a blank graph each. One student starts by describing their graph. The other student tries to draw the information on their blank graph. (3) Repeat the process for the other student's graph. (4) Ss compare their graphs to see how well they drew the information and any mistakes made. (5) The pairs now look at the bullying in school graph and write a description of the trends. (6) Elicit descriptions in open class and correct where necessary.

Possible answer for fast food sales graph Between 2000 and 2001, there was a dramatic decline in bullying. There was no change between 2001 and 2002 and then a very slight decrease by 2003. There was a steady increase in bullying for the two years between 2003 and 2005 and then a significant rise between 2005 and 2006. The following year saw a small fall in bullying and, after another year with no change in the amount of bullying, there was a sudden drop between 2008 and 2009.

8 They match but are they right?

Aim: To practise the passives.
Interaction: Groups of 3, whole class, individual, then pairs
Exercise type: Matching
Time: 20 minutes
Language: *Global warming will have been stopped by 2050.* etc
Materials: One copy of the resource, cut up, per group.
Instructions: (1) Hand out the beginnings of the sentences. Ss work in groups to discuss how they might finish, using passive structures. (2) Hand out the endings. Ss work together to match the beginnings to the endings. (3) When they have finished, Ss discuss which they agree with and which they disagree with, giving justifications for their opinions. (4) Ss discuss their ideas as a class. (5) Ss now work alone to rewrite the sentences to make them true for them, eg 1 *Global warming will never be stopped.* Then they compare ideas in pairs or small groups.

9 Argue your point

Aim: To practise making predictions.
Interaction: Groups of 3 or 4
Exercise type: Discussion
Time: Up to 30 minutes
Language: *It's bound to happen. I doubt if ...* etc
Materials: One copy of the resource, cut up, per group.
Instructions: (1) Hand out the certainty expression cards to each group. Ss work together to put them in order from the most likely to the least likely. Remind Ss that some expressions mean the same, eg *bound to/certain/inevitable*. (2) Check Ss' answers and hand out the discussion topics in a pile, face down on the desk. (3) The group turn over the first sentence to discuss. The Ss discuss the topic and have to try to use all the certainty expressions, turning them over as they do so. (4) When all the expressions have been turned over, the Ss turn them back and pick the next discussion topic card. (5) Ss repeat the process for each discussion point. (6) Follow up by asking each group what topic they found most interesting and what their opinions are on that topic.

Answers for Stage 1 (from the most likely) Bound to, Certain, Inevitable, In all probability, Likely to, The chances are, Conceivably, Not much chance, Doubt if, Very faint chance, Highly improbable, Extremely doubtful, Not a hope of, There's no way, Sure not to, Inconceivable

UNIT 4

10 Banned words

Aim: To revise education vocabulary.
Interaction: Five groups
Exercise type: Reading multiple matching
Time: 20 minutes
Language: *a grant, an undergraduate, morning assembly, rag week* etc
Materials: One paragraph from the reading for each student.
Instructions: (1) Put the Ss into five groups. Give each student in each group one paragraph from the reading, eg all the Ss from group A get paragraph 1. (2) Ss read their paragraph alone and then discuss it as a group, making sure they all understand it. (3) Ss place their paragraphs face down on the desk and cannot look at them during the next stage. (4) Read the questions to the class. After each question, ask which group has the answer and why. Eg read question 1: Group A have the answer and say that their person got 2,000 pounds a year while they were a student which is a grant. Write the key vocabulary (*grant*) on the board. (5) If no one thinks they have the answer to a question, or if two groups think they have the answer, give the correct answer and why it is correct. (6) As a follow up, re-elicit the meanings of all the key vocabulary written on the board.

Questions for teacher to read out (with answers) Who ...

1 got a grant? (A)
2 has got two undergraduates in their family? (D)
3 likes rag week? (E)
4 doesn't like parents' evenings? (C)
5 wrote a dissertation? (A)
6 used to go to parents' evenings? (D)
7 is a lecturer? (E)
8 goes to morning assembly? (B)
9 gets lots of assignments to do? (C)
10 had to resit exams? (C)
11 didn't like the halls of residence when he/she first saw them? (D)
12 has got a form tutor? (B)
13 likes the lecture theatres? (E)
14 has seminars and tutorials with students? (E)

11 The exam

Aim: To practise inversion.
Interaction: Pairs
Exercise type: Sentence completion
Time: 20–30 minutes
Language: *On no account can you ..., Never before have I ...* etc
Materials: One copy of the resource, cut up, for each pair.
Instructions: (1) Hand out the twelve beginnings, cut up, to each pair. Ss work together to put the vocabulary in the correct order. Tell Ss they must use inversions, so eg *I have never been so (nervous)* is wrong. It should be *Never before have I been so (nervous)*. Elicit the answers so that Ss can correct their work if necessary. (2) Ss work together to predict how the sentences could end. Elicit ideas. (3) Hand out the endings, cut up. Ss match them to the beginnings. (4) Tell Ss that the sentences make up a story about an exam with four of them in each part, separated by three introductory sentences. There is also an ending sentence. (5) Give Ss the three introductory sentences which separate the sections of the story and the ending. Ss now try to put the whole thing in the correct order to make a story. (6) Nominate Ss to read out one sentence each in order to see if the order they have is correct.

Answers 1 On no account can anyone talk **2** Not until everyone has finished can **3** Not only do you have to answer part A **4** Under no circumstances will I **5** Scarcely had we started the exam **6** No sooner had the lights come back on **7** Seldom have I seen so **8** Never before have I written so **9** Little did I know that **10** Only three months later did **11** Never have I been so **12** Not only had I passed all subjects

12 Complete the job application

Aim: To practise writing job applications.
Interaction: Individual, then groups of 4
Exercise type: Writing; brainstorming
Time: 30 minutes
Language: *I am writing in connection with ..., In addition to this ...* etc
Materials: One copy of the resource per student.
Instructions: (1) Give Ss a copy of the job advert and gapped letter. (2) Ss work alone to complete the application with suitable words. Those numbered 1–15 are fixed expressions, others freer ideas. Ss should sign the letters with a false name so that other Ss do not know who wrote them. (3) Ss join together in groups of 4. They swap letters with a second group. Each student now reads one of the letters from the other group and decides the good and bad things about it. They also check whether the fixed expressions were completed correctly. (4) Ss tell the other members of their group about the application they read and the group choose the best candidate. (5) Ss now tell the group they swapped letters with who they chose and why. (6) Elicit the correct answers to the fixed expressions in the letter. As a follow-up, ask the Ss to sum up the most important qualities and skills a perfect applicant for this job should have.

Answers 1 in **2** connection **3** appeared **4** of **5** working **6** well-suited **7** number **8** of **9** addition **10** would **11** to **12** attend **13** at **14** your **15** enclosed

157

13 The proof of the pudding …

Aim: To revise food idioms.
Interaction: Groups of 3 or 4
Exercise type: Matching
Time: 20 minutes
Language: *a hot potato, a pie in the sky, a tough nut, the salt of the earth* etc
Materials: One copy of the resource, cut up, per group.
Instructions: (1) Hand out the picture cards to each group. The Ss look at them and try to think together about what idiom they represent and what the meaning of that idiom is. Check the idioms with the class but not their meanings. (2) Now place the sentence cards face down on the desk. One student picks up the first card and reads the sentence. The other students try to find the picture card that matches the sentence. (3) Whoever chooses a picture makes a sentence and the reader tells them if they are right or wrong. The sentences do not have to be exactly as written on the card as long as the Ss use the correct idiom and are grammatically correct. If wrong, the other Ss continue trying to guess. If they are correct, the student takes the sentence card and reads out the next one. (4) The winner is the student with the most cards at the end of the activity. (5) Go through all the idioms to check their meaning at the end of the activity.

Answers 1 K 2 B 3 N 4 C 5 E 6 H 7 J 8 A 9 G 10 O 11 F 12 M 13 D 14 I 15 L

14 On condition …

Aim: To practise conditionals.
Interaction: Pairs; then groups of 4
Exercise type: Matching; putting verbs in brackets into the correct form
Time: 20–30 minutes
Language: *Had I had …, Should I finish …* etc
Materials: One copy of the resource, A or B, per pair. Response cards should be cut up but not the question cards.
Instructions: (1) Put Ss into pairs and give A their question card and B their response card. Tell them that A is a customer asking B, a salesman/woman about a new diet they are trying to sell. (2) A reads out their questions and B must respond using the appropriate response. (3) When they have finished, hand out Bs question cards and As response cards. Give them roles again – B is a husband or wife just returned home from work. A is their partner who has been at home all day but is now going out. (4) B asks the questions and A responds appropriately. (5) Put the Ss into groups of 4 by joining two pairs together. Give the two A students their transformation cards and give the two B students theirs. They work together to complete the transformations so that they

have a similar meaning to the original sentences. (6) Nominate pairs to act out the roleplays using the transformed sentences and make sure they are correct. If there are any errors elicit or give the correct forms.

Answers A 1 Had I had time, I would have cooked something. **2** Should I come home early, I might. **3** Providing you have done the washing up by the time I get home, I will think about … **4** You won't get a cake for a month if the dishes aren't clean/unless the dishes are clean **5** I would have made one had someone done the shopping. **6** If I had had the car, I would/could have done the shopping.

B 1 Were you to go on this new diet, you would feel like a new person. **2** Had you started one month ago, you would have lost ten kilos by now. **3** Not unless you eat the wrong food or have/eat snacks while no one is looking. **4** You won't lose weight unless you try/buy our diet. **5** Should you not lose 5kg in the first month, we will give you your money back. **6** If I'd known that you weren't interested, I wouldn't have wasted thirty minutes talking to you!

15 Solve it together

Aim: To practise problem solving.
Interaction: Pairs
Exercise type: Discussion
Time: 10 minutes for each task
Language: *Personally, I quite like the idea of …, I think we all feel that …* etc
Materials: One copy of the resource, cut up, per pair.
Instructions: (1) Put Ss into pairs. Give the Ss the expression cards. Ss work together to put the expressions in categories, i.e. Expressing your point of view; Asking for opinions; Agreeing; Proposing an alternative; Summarising. (2) Check that Ss have grouped the words correctly. (3) Hand out task A to each pair. As they discuss the problem, they turn over the expression cards which they use. They should continue the discussion until all the cards have been turned over. (4) Hand out task B to the Ss. Ss repeat the process but, this time they divide the expression cards between them. When one student uses an expression, they pass the card to their partner and the aim is for the Ss to have a fairly even number of cards at the end of the activity to show that they have both taken an equal part in the discussion. (5) Ask Ss what decisions were reached in both discussions.

Answers for Stage 1 Expressing your point of view The way I look at it …, Personally, I quite like the idea of …, I think we can discount the idea of …, Thinking about it, perhaps …, The more I think about it, the more I'm convinced …
Asking for opinions What do you reckon? Any thoughts?
Agreeing You've got a point there. We could do worse.

Proposing an alternative Let's not forget that …, We have to take the fact that … into consideration. Perhaps we should go for …, We could just play safe and …

Summarising So that's settled. I think we both feel that …, I'm afraid we'll have to agree to disagree about …

UNIT 6

16 Noise bingo

Aim: To revise collocations.
Interaction: Individual OR pairs (up to 16 cards can be used at one time)
Exercise type: Bingo game
Time: 15 minutes
Language: *clock ticking, lorry rumbling* etc
Materials: One card per individual/pair.
Instructions: (**1**) Hand out a bingo card to each student or pair. (**2**) Explain that you are going to read out some sentences with one word (a verb) missing. If the Ss think the word is on their card, they should cross it out. The winner is the first student to cross out all their words and shout *Bingo!* (**3**) Read out the sentences in the correct order. (**4**) When one person/pair has won, elicit which words the others were waiting for. (**5**) Read the sentences again, this time eliciting the correct missing word for each one. (**6**) The game can be played again if required with Ss getting a different bingo card and with the teacher reading the sentences in a different order.

Sentences to be read out in this order:

1 My heart _____ fast when I read the letter . (*beat*)
2 The church bells _____ every hour. (*chime*)
3 I was just holding the gun and it went _____. (*bang*)
4 The chandeliers _____ when the wind blows gently. (*tinkle*)
5 I hate the _____ of chalk on the blackboard. (*screech*)
6 Don't _____ the door. Shut it quietly. (*slam*)
[*All groups should have one by now.*]
7 I love it when you _____ quietly in my ear. (*whisper*)
8 I can't concentrate because of the _____ _____ _____ of your mouse. (*click, click, click*)
9 I know it's winter when I hear the _____ of footsteps in the snow. (*crunch*)
10 The only noise on the train to work is the _____ of newspapers. (*rustle*)
11 There was a sudden _____ as the motorbike sped past me. (*roar*)
12 The baby sounds happy. Does he always _____ away to himself like that? (*babble*)
13 I could hear the _____ of his computer when I went to the bathroom at 3a.m. (*hum*)

14 Oh wow. I love the sound of sauces as they _____ away on the cooker. (*bubble*)
15 I couldn't sleep because the clock had a loud _____. (*tick*)
[*There should be a winner now.*]
16 When I opened the bedroom window, the _____ of lorries going past stopped me from going to sleep. (*rumble*)
17 There was a sudden _____ from my mum when she saw a mouse in the kitchen. (*shriek*)
18 The tray of glasses fell to the floor with a terrible _____. (*crash*)
19 I sat nervously in the waiting room listening to the _____ of the dentist's drill in the room next door. (*whine*)

17 Ask your friends

Aim: To revise verb patterns.
Interaction: Whole class, then groups of 4
Exercise type: Mingling
Time: 20 minutes
Language: *I enjoy …ing, I'm thinking of …ing.*
Materials: One *Tell me about something* card per student.
Instructions: (**1**) Give each student one card. If there are more than 16 Ss in the class, either make double copies of some of the question cards or allow Ss to work in pairs. Tell them they are going to ask as many people as possible their questions in five minutes and should note the names of the people they ask and the answers given. (**2**) When they have finished, Ss sit down in groups of 4 and tell each other what they found out, using full sentences. (**3**) The groups of 4 now try to remember the questions asked by the Ss not in their group of 4, eg *Cathy asked what we hate doing.* (**4**) Ask Ss how many questions they remembered in stage (3). The group who remembered the least start by telling the class what they remember. Ss may use a variety of ways of reporting the questions and different students may prefer different forms, eg *Cathy asked about things we hate doing. Jack asked 'What can't you imagine being without' and wanted to know what our parents are trying to discourage us from doing.* Allow direct and indirect question forms in the second person or the first person plural but correct if Ss mix different forms in their answers.

18 Just our opinions

Aim: To practise talking about differences and similarities.
Interaction: Pairs, then groups of 4
Exercise type: Discussion
Time: Up to 30 minutes (5 minutes per topic and 5 minutes per topic for extra ideas)
Language: *Brad Pitt is not quite as cool as George Clooney.* etc
Materials: One copy of the resource per pair. Notebooks or extra paper to write on.
Instructions: (**1**) Give Ss the pictures in pairs.
(**2**) Ss use the expressions on the cards to make sentences that they think are true. (**3**) Ss get together

with a second pair to tell them their sentences.
(4) Ss now work together as a group of 4 to discuss the three topics and expand on them using new expressions and introducing new actors, countries or aspects of school life (subjects etc) to compare.
(5) Elicit sentences in open class and allow Ss to agree or disagree with each other.

UNIT 7

19 Stop stress

Aim: To revise illness vocabulary.
Interaction: Pairs
Exercise type: Word completion
Time: 15 minutes
Language: *headache, insomnia, acne* etc
Materials: One copy of the resource per pair.
Instructions: (1) Ask Ss in pairs to think of good advice to combat stress. **(2)** Elicit ideas. **(3)** Hand out the resource to each pair and tell Ss that, by completing the words, they are going to find a way of combating stress. **(4)** Tell Ss that the first pair to finish should shout *Finished!* as soon as they have all the words and the message. It is not enough to guess the message without finding the words. When one pair has finished, elicit all the words and the message.

Answers Message: Don't worry, be happy

1 headaches 2 stomachache 3 acne 4 heartburn
5 mood swings 6 anorexia 7 fever 8 mouth ulcer
9 allergy 10 backache 11 eczema 12 chest
13 insomnia 14 pneumonia 15 oversleeping
16 hay fever

20 Rumours and lies

Aim: To practise impersonal reporting structures.
Interaction: Pairs, then groups of 4
Exercise type: Matching; giving opinions
Time: 20 minutes
Language: *It has been said …, It was believed …*
Materials: One copy of the resource per pair.
Instructions: (1) Hand out the pictures to each pair. Ss quickly discuss anything at all they know about the eight people and things in the pictures, eg *The Pyramids are in Egypt.* **(2)** Hand out the sentences and verbs to use. Tell Ss to write one sentence about each picture without naming the person or thing in the picture and using a different verb from the box each time, eg *It is rumoured that they were built by aliens.* They should try not to write the sentences in the same order as the pictures as there will be a matching task later. **(3)** Ss swap sentences with a second pair and match the sentences to the correct pictures. **(4)** Ss get together as a group of 4 and discuss what they think about the sentences written – are they facts, opinions or rumours. If they are not facts, do the Ss believe them? **(5)** Elicit sentences about each picture in open class and make sure the sentences are written correctly.
Note: Area 51 is the nickname for an American Air

Base in Nevada, in the west of the USA. It is a very secretive place as it is used for testing new weapons and planes and, because of this secrecy, it has become the subject of conspiracy theories about the finding and storage of alien spacecraft as well as their occupants who have been recovered both dead and alive. Many films have used the idea of Area 51 holding aliens, eg *Independence Day* and *Tomb Raider 3.*

21 A talk with Tom

Aim: To revise being assertive.
Interaction: Pairs
Exercise type: Dialogue completion; ordering
Time: 30 minutes
Language: *I was wondering when we could …,*
I couldn't help but notice that …
Materials: One copy of the resource per pair. Tom's responses should be cut up. Recording.
Instructions: (1) Hand out the gapped resource to each pair. **(2)** Ss complete the ten missing words from the boss's side of the conversation. **(3)** Ss listen to the first part of the recording to check their answers. **(4)** Give the pairs ten minutes to read through the boss's side of the conversation and complete what Tom might be saying. **(5)** When they have finished, the pairs act out their conversation. **(6)** Now hand out Tom's responses, cut up. Ss work in pairs to try to put them in the correct order. **(7)** Ss listen to check their order and to complete Tom's responses. **(8)** Elicit answers from the class or nominate a pair to act out the full conversation.

Tapescript `CD 5 Track 13`

Manager: *[RP accent]* Ah, Tom. I couldn't help but [1] ***notice*** that you were late again this morning.
Tom: *[neutral English accent]* Oh, yes. I'm sorry. I had a few problems (a) ***at home***.
Manager: I was [2] ***wondering*** when we could have a little chat.
Tom: Well, er … maybe this (b) ***afternoon***.
Manager: Now is a good time for me.
Tom: I really should (c) ***start my work*** now.
Manager: It won't take long. I really do [3] ***think*** we need to talk. Sit down. Now, I [4] ***realise*** that you're having a hard time at home.
Tom: Yes, my son's having a lot of problems with (d) ***his exams***.
Manager: And I know you're trying your [5] ***best*** to do extra work in the evenings.
Tom: Oh yes, last night I managed to …
Manager: And I know your family is very important [6] ***to*** you. I really [7] ***appreciate*** that you want your daughter to do well in her exams but you can't ignore your work here.
Tom: Er … son. No, I would never do that. I always (e) ***try my hardest***.
Manager: I [8] ***hope*** you understand that some of the other people here are getting upset.
Tom: Really? I had (f) ***no idea***. Who is upset? What are they upset about?
Manager: I don't want to mention any names at this time. And this might not be a good moment to [9] ***mention*** this but your report was due yesterday.
Tom: Oh no! I completed it last night but I left it (g) ***in the kitchen***. I can ask my wife to bring it, if you want.
Manager: No, no. That's alright. I've got Jackie's report. It's very good. I don't think I need yours now. Back to you. Don't you [10] ***agree*** that it'd be better if you took your two weeks holiday now and then came back feeling much better and ready to work in July?

> **Tom:** But I've booked a holiday to (h) ***France*** in July.
> **Manager:** It's much nicer now. Fewer tourists. I'm sure you can change the dates. Good, so that's settled. When are you planning to start your holiday? Now or will you be staying for lunch? It's steak and kidney pie today. My favourite …

Answers In the tapescript

UNIT 8

22 Travellers' forum

Aim: To revise collocations.
Interaction: Whole class, then pairs
Exercise type: Open cloze; class discussion
Time: 20–30 minutes
Language: *come across, rip off, off-peek fares* etc
Materials: One copy of the resource per pair.
Instructions: (**1**) Talk to Ss about travellers advice forums on the Internet. Ask Ss what sort of things people want to know when they travel. (**2**) Elicit ideas and ask Ss what the most important information about their country would be for a traveller, eg safety, food and drink etc. (**3**) Hand out the resource. Ss work in pairs to complete it. (**4**) Elicit ideas and discuss whether the advice would be the same for the Ss' own country.

Answers **1** come **2** cost **3** save **4** made **5** off
6 keep **7** off **8** in **9** value **10** around **11** put
12 discounts **13** tax **14** charge

23 What's the story?

Aim: To revise participle clauses.
Interaction: Pairs, then groups of 4
Exercise type: Matching; rewriting
Time: 20–30 minutes
Language: *Reports written …, On returning …* etc
Materials: One copy of the resource, A or B, per pair.
Instructions: (**1**) Put Ss into pairs, each pair being either A or B. (**2**) Hand out paragraph A to pair A and the alternative sentences B to pair B. Allow one minute for Ss to read through their handouts. (**3**) The two students in A read, out loud, half of their text each and, as they do so, Bs tick the correct sentences that give the same story, choosing either 1a or 1b, 2a or 2b etc. (**4**) Hand out Bs text and As alternative sentences. Repeat processes (2) and (3). (**5**) Elicit the correct answers, asking Ss only for the first two or three words of the correct answers so they do not give away too much of the next stage. (**6**) As a follow-up, the pairs tell each other the first words of their alternative sentences. The pairs then try to rewrite their text using participle clauses. When they have finished, they check how well they did as groups of 4.

Answers **Alternative sentences A (text B):** **1** b
2 a **3** a **4** a **5** b **6** a
Alternative sentences B (text A): **1** a **2** b **3** b
4 a **5** a **6** b

24 What are they saying?

Aim: To revise clichés.
Interaction: Pairs, then groups of 3
Exercise type: Matching; discussion
Time: 20 minutes
Language: *That's easier said than done. I'm going round in circles.* etc
Materials: One copy of the resource, cut up, per pair/group.
Instructions: (**1**) Hand out the cartoons to each group. Tell Ss that they should look at the pictures and work together to decide what the people may be saying. (**2**) Elicit ideas in open class. (**3**) Hand out the actual words being said. (**4**) Ss work together to match them to the pictures. (**5**) Elicit answers and what the clichés mean.

Answers **1** G **2** D **3** H **4** B **5** A **6** E **7** C **8** F

UNIT 9

25 Sort them out

Aim: To revise newspaper vocabulary.
Interaction: Pairs, then groups of 4
Exercise type: Problem solving; giving and justifying opinions
Time: 25 minutes
Language: *gutter press, in-depth news* etc
Materials: One copy of the resource per pair.
Instructions: (**1**) Hand out the resource and tell Ss to look at the list of words at the bottom of the page. Ss work together to match them to quality newspapers and tabloids. (**2**) Elicit the answers and check the meanings of all words. (**3**) Ss work together to match the headlines on the resource to the correct newspaper. As they do this, they should try to use as many of the words as possible. (**4**) Elicit the answers and reasons for them. (**5**) Tell half the class they have to think of reasons why people prefer tabloid papers. The other half think of reasons why people prefer broadsheets. (**6**) Ss join up in pairs: a tabloid pair with a broadsheet pair. Ss discuss their ideas. (**7**) Elicit ideas and then discuss which newspapers the Ss prefer and read, if any.

Answers **The Daily Tabloid** 1, 5, 6, 7, 8, 9, 10, 13, 14
The Quality Broadsheet 2, 3, 4, 11, 12, 15

Tabloid dramatic, colloquial, sensational, celebrity gossip, undemanding, populist, human interest stories, gutter press, paparazzi, light-hearted, tongue-in-cheek **Broadsheet** sophisticated, neutral, restrained, quality press, opinion-forming, extensive coverage of foreign news, in-depth news analysis, serious

26 Differing opinions

Aim: To revise vocabulary to describe TV programmes.
Interaction: Individual, then pairs
Exercise type: Listening True/False/No information
Time: 15 minutes
Language: *canned laughter, clichéd characters* etc
Materials: One copy of the resource per student. Recording.
Instructions: (**1**) Tell Ss to write down one TV programme they like and one they hate. (**2**) Hand out the resource. Play the recording for Ss to complete the task alone. (**3**) Ss compare answers in pairs, then listen again to check. (**4**) Ss then get into pairs and discuss the two programmes they wrote down in (1) to see if they agree or disagree. (**5**) Elicit ideas in open class.

Tapescript   CD 5 Track 14

Dan: *[London accent]* What's on TV tonight?
Kathy: *[slight Bristol accent]* There's a great comedy on, *My Dad*.
Dan: Why do you like that? I think it's awful.
Kathy: I like the dialogues. They're really witty and well written.
Dan: Unnatural more like. People just don't talk like that in real life. And I hate that canned laughter.
Kathy: It's not canned. There are people there watching it while they make it. I love the characters too. The dad is so nice. I'd really like him to be my dad.
Dan: Yes, OK. He's quite funny and makes you feel sorry for him when things go wrong. But why does he have to say: 'It wasn't my fault!' at the end of each episode?
Kathy: The viewers like it. Everyone can copy him – it's funny: 'It wasn't my fault!'
Dan: It's not funny. I hate it when people at school say that: 'It wasn't my fault'. The main problem though is that you know exactly what's going to happen after about five minutes.
Kathy: You're probably right. Like the time he went to work on a Saturday. It was really obvious that it wasn't a working day but he's such a good actor it doesn't matter. It's still hilarious.
Dan: He's the only good actor. The others are so wooden they look like puppets on strings. The mum is appalling.
Kathy: Oh, I like her. She used to be in *Market Square*, the soap opera.
Dan: Oh no! You didn't watch that, did you?
Kathy: Yes, every week. I loved it.
Dan: It had the most annoying theme tune ever and the characters were all from the *How to Make a Soap Opera* book. You need one evil manager, one unhappily married woman who drinks too much, one misunderstood teenager, one middle-aged woman, working in a bar or a shop who solves everyone's problems, one …
Kathy: Alright, alright. I understand. It's funny though. You seem to know a lot about these programmes you don't like!
Dan: Well, I might have seen them once or twice!

Answers 1 F 2 T 3 NI 4 T 5 T 6 T 7 F 8 NI 9 NI 10 T 11 T 12 F

27 Regrets, I've had a few

Aim: To revise verb patterns.
Interaction: Pairs
Exercise type: Story writing
Time: 30 minutes
Language: *He denied being ..., He was accused of ..., He regretted that ...* etc
Materials: One copy of the resource for each pair.
Instructions: (**1**) Hand out the cartoon story to the Ss in pairs. (**2**) Ss work together to decide what the story might be about. (**3**) Hand out the writing task. Tell Ss that they have to use all the verbs given to write the story. (**4**) When the Ss have finished their stories, either nominate Ss to read them out or display them so that all the Ss can read each other's stories. (**5**) Correct the verb forms used where necessary.

UNIT 10

28 Find and use

Aim: To practise word formation.
Interaction: Groups of 4
Exercise type: Guessing game
Time: 20–30 minutes
Language: *dishonesty, simplify, creative* etc
Materials: One word formation sheet and 15 words (cut up) per student; dictionaries.
Instructions: (**1**) Put Ss into groups of 4. Hand out a word formation sheet to each student. Tell Ss that, for each root word that they have, there are five word cards on which there are related words to add in the different categories. Tell Ss that sometimes there is more than one word for one category, eg there may be two nouns, and sometimes there may be a word in the same category as their root word. As each student has five words to collect for each of their root words, some related words may not be included. Ss try to think about related words for their root words but do not write anything yet. (**2**) Hand out fifteen words for each student in the group. Ss see if any of the words are theirs. (**3**) Ss then get into pairs with one other person in the group. They tell the other student their root words (the ones written on their word formation sheet) and the second student looks to see if they have any related words. They tell each other how many words they have for each root, eg A tells B that one root is *create* and B tells A that they have two words from that root. (**4**) Ss try to guess the words that the other student may have. If they say the word, their partner gives them it. If not, the partner keeps the words. Ss can guess as many times as they like until they cannot think of any other possible words. (**5**) The Ss then change pairings and repeat the process so that they talk to all three other Ss in their group. (**6**) Ss see who has found the most words and now swap those words not guessed in stages (3) – (5). (**7**) Ss complete their word formation sheet with the words in the

correct places. Ss can use dictionaries to help them if necessary. If Ss are using dictionaries, they could also find more related words for each of their root words. (8) Ss choose three of their words and write a sentence which includes that word. They then tell the other Ss in their group their root word and read out the sentence, saying *BLANK* instead of the word chosen. The other Ss have to guess what the word is.

Answers create creative (adj), uncreative (adj), creativity (n), creation (n), creatively (adv)
logic logical (adj), illogical (adj), logician (n), logically (adv), illogically (adv)
imagine imaginative (adj), unimaginative (adj), imagination (n), imaginatively (adv), unimaginatively (adv)
believe believable (adj), unbelievable (adj), belief (n), disbelief (n), believably (adv)
understand misunderstand (v), misunderstood (adj), understanding (adj/n), misunderstanding (n), understandably (adv)
equal equalise (v), unequal (adj), equality (n), inequality (n), unequally (adv)
science scientific (adj), unscientific (adj), scientist (n), scientifically (adv), unscientifically (adv)
politics politicise (v), political (adj), apolitical (adj), politician (n), politically (adv)
lead mislead (v), misleading (adj), leader (n), leadership (n), misleadingly (adv)
elect re-elect (v), unelectable (adj), elector (n), election (n), electorate (n)
tolerant tolerate (v), intolerant (adj), tolerance (n), intolerance (n), intolerantly (adv)
honest honesty (n), dishonest (adj), dishonesty (n), dishonestly (adv), honestly (adv)

29 Dr What? Dr Who

Aim: To revise relative clauses.
Interaction: Whole class discussion, then pairs
Exercise type: Reading text insertion; discussion
Time: 25 minutes
Language: *wherever, whoever, all of whom* etc
Materials: One set of materials per pair.
Instructions: (1) Before handing out the material, talk about TV programmes that appeal to both adults and children. Elicit ideas and ask Ss why they are popular. (2) Tell Ss they are going to read about a very popular British TV programme which has been on TV since 1963. (3) Hand out the gapped text and tell the Ss to read it, trying not to worry about the gaps. (4) When Ss have read it, put the Ss into two groups. Tell Ss to turn over the text so they cannot see it. Write words from the text on the board and Ss have to say what they are, eg Gallifrey – a planet, Dr Who – a Timelord, dalek – a robot, The Master – Dr Who's enemy, Tardis – Dr Who's spaceship, 1963 – the first year it appeared on TV, ten – the number of actors who have played Dr Who, Saturday – the day of the week it is on TV. (5) Hand out the phrases to insert. Ss complete the task in pairs. (6) Elicit the

answers. (7) As a follow-up, put the Ss in pairs. Each pair has to try to use three of the inserted phrases in sentences about a TV programme that they know. Elicit some of the sentences in open class.

Answers 1 D 2 G 3 A 4 N 5 J 6 E 7 M 8 K 9 B 10 H 11 F 12 L 13 C 14 I

30 Act it out

Aim: To practise reacting to surprising news.
Interaction: Pairs
Exercise type: Roleplay
Time: 5 minutes for the initial reaction and checking; 5 minutes for each roleplay
Language: *I've been worried sick. I don't believe it! That's brilliant!* etc
Materials: One role card per pair. A set of expression and emotion cards, cut up, per pair.
Instructions: (1) Remind Ss of the different ways of reacting to surprising news. Tell Ss that, sometimes, more than one way may be possible, eg they may show surprise or anger to the same piece of news. (2) Hand out the expression cards and emotion cards to each pair. Ss work together to match the expressions to the correct emotions. Elicit the answers. (3) Hand out a role card to each pair. Allow them one minute to think about what they are going to say. Tell Ss they should use the expressions from stage (2) as appropriate but also try to add their own information to make the conversation more interesting. Ss have to keep talking for three minutes using their imaginations as to how they will develop. (4) Ss then act out the conversation together. Stop the conversations after three minutes. (5) Nominate one pair to act out their roleplay. (6) Ss swap role cards with another pair and repeat the process as many times as required.

Answers for Stage 2 Apprehension – I've been worried sick! **Relief** – Thank goodness! **Interest** – I'm dying to hear ... **Delight** – That's brilliant! **Surprise** – I'm speechless. **Indifference** – So what? **No surprise** – I saw it coming. **Disappointment** – It's a real pain. **Disbelief** – I don't believe it! **Sorrow** – I'm heartbroken. **Sympathy** – It's a terrible shame.

UNIT 11

31 If you've got it, flaunt it!

Aim: To practise formal and informal adjectives.
Interaction: Pairs
Exercise type: Discussion; writing
Time: 30 minutes
Language: *affluent, filthy rich, scrape by* etc
Materials: One set of pictures per pair. One task, A or B, per pair.
Instructions: (1) Hand out the picture story to the Ss. They work together to discuss what they think the

story is all about. (**2**) Elicit ideas in open class and make sure there is one version of the story which is accepted by the whole class. (**3**) Give out a task to each pair. (**4**) Ss write their article in an appropriate style. Elicit that the informal article should not only have the more informal vocabulary but it should be written in a more dramatic, sensational style whereas the formal article should be neutral and restrained. Refer Ss to the two stories on pages 94 and 95 in SB if necessary. (**5**) As a follow-up, Ss could swap articles with another pair who act as editors, checking that the style is consistent throughout or all the articles could be displayed for the Ss to read and decide which is the best formal and informal article.

32 Hmm ... What do you think?

Aim: To practise stating opinions, agreeing and disagreeing.
Interaction: Groups of 3
Exercise type: Discussion
Time: 3–5 minutes per topic
Language: *The way I see it …, I'm afraid I can't go along with that.* etc
Materials: One copy of the resource, cut up, per group.
Instructions: (**1**) Put Ss into groups and hand out the expressions card and topic cards. Place the topic cards face down in a pile on the desk. (**2**) One student from each group picks up the first topic card and reads it out. They nominate one other student to begin the discussion, using one of the phrases on the expressions card. Each student in the group takes turns to give their opinion and their reasons for it, again using a phrase from the expressions card. Each student has to add something new to the discussion – they cannot just say that they agree with what has already been said. (**3**) The student who read out the topic acts as the group leader. They can keep the conversation going by asking further questions, ask one student to let the other one speak and stop any arguments or L1 use. At the end, the leader decides which opinion they agree with most and why. (**4**) Continue for as many topics as are required with a different student reading out the topic card and acting as leader each time. (**5**) Elicit opinions in open class on all topics.

33 This must be yours

Aim: To revise modals.
Interaction: Groups of 5
Exercise type: Matching
Time: 20 minutes
Language: *He might have been …, He may as well …, He should have …* etc
Materials: One set of materials, cut up, per group.
Instructions: (**1**) Put Ss into groups of 5 and give each student a number 1–5. Give each student their picture and the four sentences with their number on. Tell Ss not to show these to the other Ss. If the number of Ss is not divisible by five, put some Ss into groups of 4, taking out one picture and the sentences that refer to it. (**2**) Student 1 describes their picture in as much detail as possible. As they listen, the other students

decide which of their sentences relates to the picture being described. They do not say anything but write number 1 on that sentence. (**3**) Students 2–5 repeat the process. At the end of the activity, Ss should have decided which pictures all their sentences relate to. (**4**) Students now pass each other their sentences and read those given to them to make sure they make sense. If there are any problems, Ss should ask the teacher for help. Otherwise it can be assumed that Ss have done this correctly. (**5**) Ss now write one more sentence about their picture using a different modal to the four used on the sentences they have been given. (**6**) Elicit the new sentences in open class and correct where necessary.

Answers Picture 1 2 He might have been to a party. 3 He should go to the hairdresser's. 4 He won't need to buy a Halloween costume. 5 They must think he looks very strange.

Picture 2 1 He should have gone to bed five hours ago. 3 He could be studying for an exam. 4 He may as well stay up all night now. 5 He doesn't have to go to school tomorrow.

Picture 3 1 He'll be able to go to loads of parties. 2 He must have done well in his exams. 4 He'll have to learn how to cook and do his washing. 5 He succeeded in getting on a course.

Picture 4 1 He'd better leave it alone. 2 He should phone the police. 3 It might have been used in a crime. 5 He must be playing football.

Picture 5 1 He should have done more training. 2 He won't even win one game. 3 He may as well give up now. 4 He'd better take up a new sport.

UNIT 12

34 Who is it?

Aim: To practise describing people.
Interaction: Groups of 3
Exercise type: Speaking; matching
Time: 15–20 minutes
Language: *eccentric, one of a kind, colourful* etc
Materials: Three individual picture cards for each person. One whole resource per group.
Instructions: (**1**) Elicit ways of describing people's appearance which do not specifically mention things like hair colour, the actual clothes being worn etc. Write the words Ss come up with on the board under three headings: negative (eg *strange, ugly*), positive (*beautiful, interesting*), neutral/either (*normal, distinctive*) and add any from page 126 in the Students' Book that Ss do not mention. (**2**) Put the Ss into groups and give each person three picture cards. Tell them not to show anyone else in their group their card. Also hand out a group picture containing all the people in the exercise to each group. (**3**) Each student in turn has to describe one of their people using the adjectives on page 126 in the SB or other general adjectives referring to appearance, eg *pretty,*

friendly etc. Ss cannot use normal descriptions, i.e. describing hair, type of clothes etc. (**4**) During each description, the other Ss note down the adjectives used and guess who was being talked about, writing the number of that person on a piece of paper. If the other Ss think the description is too vague, eg *He's strange. He's stupid*, they can ask for more details, eg *Does he look aggressive? Do you think he's friendly or not?* (**5**) At the end of the activity, when Ss have described all three of their people, the Ss compare their guesses. If there are any disagreements, the Ss justify their descriptions or guesses by referring to the adjectives used. (**6**) When they have finished, elicit adjectives for each picture in open class.

35 But …

Aim: To practise contrastive linkers.
Interaction: Pairs
Exercise type: Matching; sentence transformation
Time: 15–20 minutes
Language: *Although …*, *In spite of …* etc
Materials: One copy of the resource, cut up, per pair.
Instructions: (**1**) Put Ss into pairs. Hand out the sentence halves to each student so that they both have eight halves. Ss see if they have any matching halves and then work together to match the rest.
(**2**) Ss read the sentences and discuss whether they agree with them or if they are true for them.
(**3**) Elicit opinions in open class. (**4**) When Ss have finished the discussion, hand out the sentence transformation task. The Ss work together in pairs to rewrite the sentences using the linking word given in brackets. When Ss have finished, elicit the answers and correct where necessary. (**5**) As a follow-up, if Ss need further practice, Ss could rewrite sentence 1 in as many different ways as possible.

Answers **1** Although Goths look quite frightening, they are often very shy, peaceful people. **2** In spite of stopping people from wearing old clothes, nightclubs can't stop them from fighting. **3** Whereas schools always had a uniform when my parents were young, now quite a lot of schools don't.
4 Despite complaining about the price of designer label clothes, people still love wearing them.
5 While I like watching fashion programmes on TV, I would never wear any of the clothes they show.
6 Even though heavy metal music is great, the fashion is awful. **7** Whilst I don't have to look smart at the weekend, I often wear a jacket and a tie when I meet my friends. **8** Although wearing fur is cruel, some people think coats made from dead animals are very elegant.

36 Soften the blow

Aim: To practise giving bad news.
Interaction: Pairs
Exercise type: Roleplay
Time: 2 minutes per roleplay
Language: *I'm a little annoyed, I have a few misgivings.* etc
Materials: One role card, A and B, per pair (maximum of thirty students altogether). One vocabulary card per pair.
Instructions: (**1**) Put the Ss in pairs and give them a vocabulary card to look at. Ss discuss how they could use each phrase in a sentence. Elicit examples.
(**2**) Give each pair role cards A1 and B1, one role for each student. Ss read the situation and decide which phrases from the vocabulary card they could use. Ss have thirty seconds to think about what they are going to say and then act out their conversation.
(**3**) Nominate one pair to act out their conversation in front of the class. (**4**) Now hand out role cards A2 and B2. Ss repeat the process with a new role. Repeat with other role cards as many times as required.

Resource 1   Body talk

Don't listen to Mike. He isn't always right. You should be more confident and <u>think for yourself.</u>

(have a mind of your own)

Jack's wife makes all the decisions. She doesn't let him go out and he has to wear clothes she likes. He's really <u>controlled by her</u>.

(under her thumb)

It doesn't matter what they say, you must <u>keep quiet</u>.

(hold your tongue)

Everyone's angry with Terry. We've all been <u>ignoring him</u>.

(giving him the cold shoulder)

I know you're sad. I know you've been through a terrible time but you're British and you have to <u>stay unemotional</u>.

(keep a stiff upper lip)

We were on a yacht when the storm hit us but we all <u>stayed calm</u> and got back safely.

(kept cool heads)

Mark told me a really funny joke during the lesson. The teacher was looking at me so I had to <u>stop myself from laughing</u>.

(keep a straight face)

Jackie told me that we were going to have an exam today but it wasn't true. She was just <u>joking</u>.

(pulling my leg)

I offered Susie some of my old clothes but she <u>didn't want</u> them.

(turned her nose up at)

I met a girl at a party and started talking to her about our terrible local hospital. I really <u>said the wrong thing</u>. Her mum works there!

(put my foot in it)

James is always telling lies and making fun of us. He's <u>really annoying</u>.

(a pain in the neck)

I was miserable for days and didn't tell anyone. Then my mum sat down with me and I <u>told her everything that was wrong</u>.

(got it off my chest)

MIND	THUMB	TONGUE
SHOULDER	LIP	HEAD
FACE	LEG	NOSE
FOOT	NECK	CHEST

166

PHOTOCOPIABLE

A   **Put the verbs in the correct form.**

John [1]_____ (work) at his company since _____. He [2]_____ (have) lots of jobs since he joined the company. His first job [3]_____ (be) an _____. Now he is a [4]_____. Next April he [5]_____ (work) in this job for three years.

Next Monday is going to be a very busy day. Between 7a.m. and 9a.m., John [6]_____ (drive) to _____. He [7]_____ (meet) with _____ for most of the afternoon. Then, from [8]_____ to _____, he _____ (fly) to New York. By the time he gets to bed on Monday night, he [9]_____ (be) awake for about 24 hours.

A   **Read this information. Your partner will be asking you questions about it.**

Married: 2001. Honeymoon – two weeks in Barbados. Great!
Anniversary – different country every year.
Next year (May 15th) Paris.

Anniversary plans:
May 15th – leave for Paris 4p.m.
Arrive 7p.m.
Get to hotel 8p.m.
Table at a restaurant on the Champs Elysees booked 9–11p.m.
Disco 11p.m.–4a.m.!

B   **Put the verbs in the correct form.**

Mary and Richard [1]_____ (be) married since _____. On May 15th next year, they [2]_____ (be) married for _____ years. They [3]_____ (spend) their honeymoon in _____ and, since then, they [4]_____ (celebrate) their anniversary in a different country each year.

Next year they [5]_____ (celebrate) their anniversary in _____. Between [6]_____ and _____, they _____ (travel) to Paris. They will go to their hotel and then to a restaurant. They [7]_____ (reserve) a table at a restaurant on the Champs Elysees and they [8]_____ (eat) there from _____ until about _____. After that, they're going to go dancing. They won't be going to bed until morning. They [9]_____ (dance) until the disco closes at 4a.m.

B   **Read this information. Your partner will be asking you questions about it.**

Started at this company: February 10th, 1996.
Lots of jobs. First: administrative assistant – 1996–1997.
Now: personnel manager.
Next April: three years as personnel manager.

Plans for Monday:
Get up 5a.m.
Drive to London 7–9a.m.
Meet company directors.
Fly to New York 9p.m.–3a.m.

I've always wanted to meet you …

START

You're at a party. You don't know the person next to you. Start a conversation by saying …

Excuse me, do you mind if I …

The two of you should continue talking for one minute.

CHANGE

You've now been talking for one minute and want to change the subject. When an opportunity arises, say …

What do you think about …?

The two of you should continue talking for one more minute.

FINISH

It's time to finish the conversation. When an opportunity arises, look at your watch and express surprise about the time. Tell the other person that it was nice to meet them and say goodbye.

Don't finish the conversation too suddenly!

START

You are introduced to someone you've always wanted to meet. Start a conversation by saying …

Pleased to meet you. I've heard so much about you …

The two of you should continue talking for one minute.

CHANGE

You've now been talking for one minute and want to change the subject. When an opportunity arises, say …

**That's enough about …
Tell me something about …**

The two of you should continue talking for one more minute.

FINISH

It's time to finish the conversation. When an opportunity arises, apologise for having to leave and ask the other person for their phone number. Promise to call sometime.

Don't finish the conversation too suddenly!

START

You see someone at a club. You are sure you recognise him/her. Start a conversation by saying …

Have we met somewhere before?

The two of you should continue talking for one minute.

CHANGE

You've now been talking for one minute and want to change the subject. When an opportunity arises, say …

**I love your …
Where did you get it/them?**

The two of you should continue talking for one more minute.

FINISH

It's time to finish the conversation. When an opportunity arises, tell the other person you don't want to keep them any longer as they are probably busy.

Don't finish the conversation too suddenly!

START

You are on holiday. You hear someone saying that they are from your home town. Start a conversation by saying …

Sorry, but I couldn't help overhearing that you …

The two of you should continue talking for one minute.

CHANGE

You've now been talking for one minute and want to change the subject. When an opportunity arises, say …

Have you heard the news about …?

The two of you should continue talking for one more minute.

FINISH

It's time to finish the conversation. When an opportunity arises, tell the other person that it was lovely to meet them. Suggest meeting again.

Don't finish the conversation too suddenly!

PHOTOCOPIABLE

really	excited	extremely	disappointing	utterly
impossible	terribly	crowded	absolutely	furious
slightly	surprised	simply	magnificent	very
poor	totally	exhausted	pretty	upset

Dear Sir,

I'm writing about the exhibition at the art gallery which I have just returned from. I was
[1]_____ about going to see it. However, the day was [2]_____.
It was [3]_____ to get close to the painting as the gallery was
[4]_____. There were hundreds of schoolchildren there, running and
shouting. One of them knocked into me and laughed. I was [5]_____ but
there was no sign of a teacher anywhere. I was also [6]_____ that no one in
the gallery tried to stop them.

I must say that the paintings themselves were [7]_____ but the organisation
was [8]_____. I had to walk along corridors and up and down stairs to
see them all. Why couldn't they all be put in one room? By the time I had finished,
I was [9]_____. I was also [10]_____ to find that there were no
guide books left when I arrived. Why didn't you realise that there would be such a big
demand?

I hope this letter may help to improve exhibitions at your gallery in the future.

Yours,

Mrs L. Philips

A

You are at an art gallery. You love the paintings.
Give your opinion about them and explain why.

- **Use some of these words:**
  superb
  marvellous
  wonderful
  brilliant
  big fan of
  soft spot for

B

You are at an art gallery. You don't like the paintings.
Give your opinion about them and explain why.

- **Use some of these words:**
  mediocre
  second rate
  not a patch on
  leaves me cold
  nothing to write home about
  atrocious

C

You are at an art gallery with two friends. They are disagreeing quite loudly. You don't know much about art but you want everyone to get on. Try to agree with both of them.

- **Use some of these words:**
  not bad
  I know what you mean
  I understand where you're coming from
  acquired taste

B

You went to see a film with your friends. You loved it.
Give your opinion about it and explain why.

- **Use some of these words:**
  superb
  marvellous
  wonderful
  brilliant
  big fan of
  soft spot for

C

You went to see a film with your friends. You didn't like it.
Give your opinion about it and explain why.

- **Use some of these words:**
  mediocre
  second rate
  not a patch on
  leaves me cold
  nothing to write home about
  atrocious

A

You went to see a film with your friends. You don't know much about films and you thought it was OK. You want everyone to get on. Try to agree with both of your friends.

- **Use some of these words:**
  not bad
  I know what you mean
  I understand where you're coming from
  acquired taste

C

You are at a restaurant with your friends. You love it – the food, the service, everything.
Give your opinion about it and explain why.

- **Use some of these words:**
  superb
  marvellous
  wonderful
  brilliant
  big fan of
  soft spot for

A

You are at a restaurant with your friends. You are really disappointed by it – the food, the service, everything.
Give your opinion about it and explain why.

- **Use some of these words:**
  mediocre
  second rate
  not a patch on
  leaves me cold
  nothing to write home about
  atrocious

B

You are at a restaurant with your friends. It's OK, nothing special but you want everyone to get on. Try to agree with both of your friends.

- **Use some of these words:**
  not bad
  I know what you mean
  I understand where you're coming from
  acquired taste

A SPECIAL TEACHER

- struck first by his friendly smile
- knowledge – very impressive
- best thing – the way he explains things

What _____
_____ smile.
It _____
_____ impressive.
It _____
_____ thing.

*Now think of a teacher you really know
and make sentences about him/her.*

A MODERN BUILDING

- impressive size
- architect has used lots of different styles
- the thing I like most – the restaurant on the roof

What _____
_____ size.
What _____
_____ styles.
It _____
_____ most.

*Now think of a building you really know
and make sentences about it.*

A SONG

- I like the guitar introduction best
- most people know him for his lyrics
- surprising that this is an instrumental

It _____
_____ best.
What _____
_____ lyrics.
What _____
_____ instrumental.

*Now think of a song you really know
and make sentences about it.*

THE WORST PLACE YOU'VE EVER BEEN

- worst thing – the noise
- the smell of old chips depressed me
- shocked by how expensive it was

It _____
_____ thing.
What _____
_____ chips.
What _____
_____ was.

*Now think of a place you really know
and make sentences about it.*

A TERRIBLE FILM

- ending was really strange
- annoying choice of actors
- I disliked the message it gave about life most

What _____
_____ ending.
It _____
_____
annoying.
What _____
_____ life.

*Now think of a film you really know
and make sentences about it.*

A SPORT

- boring – nothing happens for long periods of time
- shocked by how popular it was in England
- most people remember the white clothes they wear to play it

What _____
_____ time.
What _____
_____ England.
It _____
_____ remember.

*Now think of a sport you really know
and make sentences about it.*

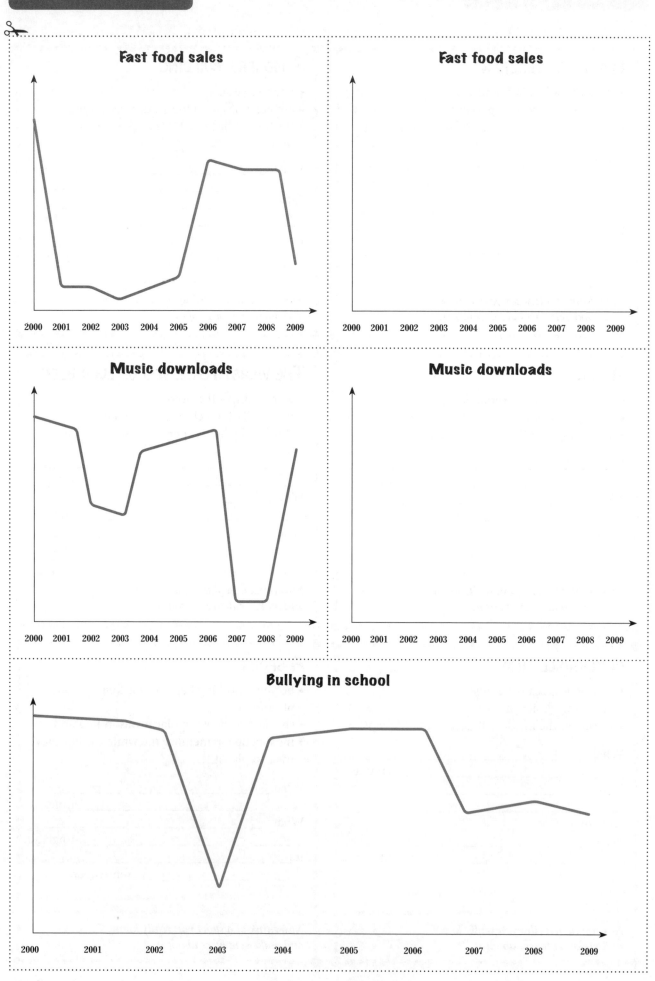

Global warming will have	been stopped by 2050.
CD players won't	be made after the year 2010.
The problem of crime will	never be solved.
In recent years, the problem of bullying in our school has	been reduced.
Nothing can	be done about poverty.
The centre of our town will	be rebuilt in the near future.
Our class will	be forgotten by this school soon after we leave.
I will	be recognised all over the world by the time I'm 25.
Our fashion, music and hairstyles will	be laughed at by students in year 1 when they are our age.
We have	been treated badly whilst in this school.

CERTAINTY EXPRESSION CARDS

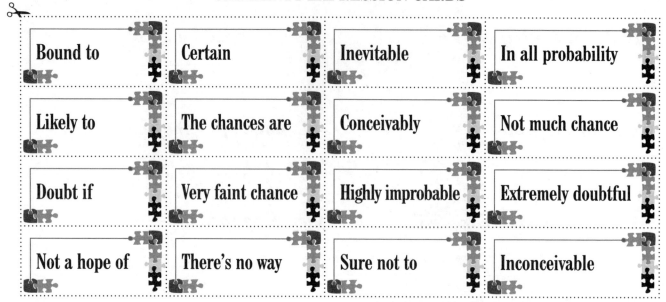

Bound to	Certain	Inevitable	In all probability
Likely to	The chances are	Conceivably	Not much chance
Doubt if	Very faint chance	Highly improbable	Extremely doubtful
Not a hope of	There's no way	Sure not to	Inconceivable

DISCUSSION CARDS

UFOs will land on Earth.

Women will run 100m faster than men.

The world will end before the year 2100.

Global warming will stop.

The world will live in peace.

We will all be happy in life.

There will be a huge earthquake in the world this year.

Tourists will travel in space in the next two years.

Our school will be on the TV news this term.

Roads will be less crowded next year.

174

PHOTOCOPIABLE

A I wasn't rich at university but at least I did get some money from the government. I think it was about 2,000 pounds a year which paid for my room at the university and a few evenings a week out with my friends. I enjoyed being a student but it was hard work, especially the 20,000 words I had to write in my final year.

B Our school is very big. There are about 2,000 students altogether so we can't all meet at once. We get into school at nine o'clock and on four days a week we sit with the teacher who looks after our class. Once a week we go to the school hall from 9–9.30a.m. to listen to the headmaster telling us what has happened and what's going to happen. We used to sing as well but we don't now.

C I'm still at school. I don't like it much and I have to admit I don't work very hard. My mum always goes to meetings with the teachers. They're terrible. The teachers always say that I 'could do better' and my mum always comes home angry. Last year I had to take three exams twice because I failed them the first time and we always get homework tasks from our teachers which take up most of my free time.

D My husband and I left school when we were sixteen so it's quite a surprise to find that we've got two children at university. They were always very clever. I remember that whenever I went to meet their teachers they were always very positive. I remember when we took our eldest to university for the first time. He had a room in a big block near the lecture halls. It looked very sad but he enjoyed it and made lots of friends. Now he's in his final year and our daughter is just starting her first.

E I work at a university. I have to teach the students about English Literature. I have a busy life. First, I teach big groups of about fifty. Luckily the rooms are bright and modern. Then I teach smaller groups, about five to ten students and finally I have one-to-one sessions. I love the students. They're so enthusiastic about everything. The best time of year is when they are taking part in crazy events to raise money for charity.

We arrived early for the exam and sat at our desks. The teacher read out the exam rules ...

Rule number 1 as always: no / anyone / can / talk / account / on _____	... during the exam
Secondly, has / not / can / everyone / until / finished _____	... you leave the exam.
Don't forget: do / answer / only / have / not / to / part A / you _____	... but you also have to answer three questions from part B.
That's everything. Now you can start. I / no / circumstances / under / will _____	... help you from now on.

The exam started ...

had / the / we / exam / scarcely / started _____	... when the lights went out.
on / no / the / lights / back / come / sooner / had _____	... than my friend's mobile rang.
have / I I / seldom / so / seen _____	... many people trying to keep a straight face.
After that, there were no more problems. so / before / written / I I / have / never _____	... much in one exam.

My worries weren't over when the exam finished ...

little / I I / that / know / did _____	... the results would take so long to arrive.
only / did / later / months / three _____	... the postman bring them.
been / have / never / so / I _____	... nervous about opening an envelope.
I was worrying unnecessarily. I / all / passed / not / subjects / only / had _____	... but I had got As in Maths and English.

University, here I come!

176

PHOTOCOPIABLE

SOUTH COAST FESTIVAL COMPANY

requires young people for summer work.
We need flexible, enthusiastic but responsible young people to help organise
and run music festivals during the summer holidays.

DUTIES INCLUDE:

- Cooking and cleaning for musicians
- Ticket selling
- Security and first aid duties
- Putting up and taking down the stage
- Driving cars and small vans
- Helping to advertise the festivals locally

Please send a covering letter and photograph clearly stating why you think you would be a good person to employ and which of the listed duties you could and couldn't carry out.

Dear Sir/Madam,

I am writing [1]_____ [2]_____ with your job advert for summer workers to help organise music festivals which [3]_____ in the latest edition of *Student News*. I am very interested in the possibility [4]_____ [5]_____ for your organisation.

I am _____ and I have just _____. In September, I am due to _____. In the meantime, I would like to _____.

I believe I am [6]_____-_____ for this position for a [7]_____ [8]_____ reasons. I have _____.
I can _____.
I have also got _____ _____.

In [9]_____ to this, I believe I am _____ and _____.
I am always _____ and I _____.
I have had _____ for the last six months and I can _____. I am a(n) _____ _____.

I [10]_____ be very pleased [11]_____ [12]_____ an interview [13]_____ [14]_____ convenience. Please find [15]_____ a recent photograph as requested.

Yours faithfully,

1 This is a controversial issue. *It's a hot potato.*	2 Your idea is not practical. *It's a pie in the sky.*	3 It's difficult to understand her behaviour. *She's a tough nut to crack.*
4 He's a very normal, nice, genuine person. *He's the salt of the earth.*	5 They're almost identical. *They're like two peas in a pod.*	6 My way of dealing with people is to reward the good and punish the bad. *I use the carrot and stick approach.*
7 I don't feel sorry for Roger. He caused his own problems and now he can take the consequences. *He can stew in his own juice.*	8 Don't do that! It'll be terrible! *It's a recipe for disaster.*	9 I know you're wrong and when I prove it, I'll make you admit it. *I'll make you eat your words.*
10 You can't have everything. You've got to choose sometimes. *You can't have your cake and eat it.*	11 I'm sorry but I can't believe you. You're not telling the truth. *I can't swallow your lies.*	12 If we do that, we'll just swap one difficult situation for another that is probably worse. *We'll be out of the frying pan and into the fire.*
13 You should always have an alternative, backup plan. Just in case something goes wrong. *You shouldn't put all your eggs in one basket.*	14 The news from the war was horrible to watch. *It was stomach turning.*	15 My friend had some really exciting news to tell me about my classmates. *My friend had some really juicy gossip to tell me about my classmates.*

K
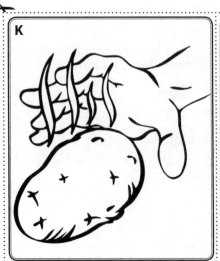

B

N
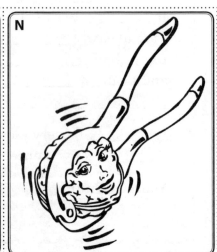

© Pearson Education Limited 2009

PHOTOCOPIABLE

C

E

H

J

A

G

O

F

M

D

I

L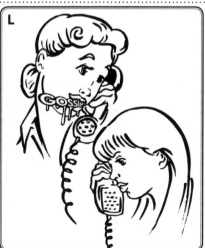

A QUESTION CARD	B QUESTION CARD
Why should I go on your new diet?	Where's my dinner?
How much weight will I lose in a month?	Will you cook something later?
Can it fail?	What about a cake?
I could use a different, cheaper diet.	Is that a promise?
It's very expensive. What if I don't lose weight?	Why didn't you make a cake yesterday?
No, it's OK. I don't really want to lose weight anyway.	You could have gone shopping.

A RESPONSE CARD	B RESPONSE CARD
I didn't have time to cook any.	It would make you feel like a new person.
I don't know. I might, providing I get home early.	Well, imagine you had started one month ago, I think by now you would be about ten kilos lighter.
That depends on whether you do the washing up while I'm out. If it's all done, I'll think about making one.	Not if you eat what we tell you to with no extra little snacks while no one is looking!
Yes, it is but if the dishes are still dirty you won't get one for a month.	Only our diet really works if you want to lose weight.
Because no one did any shopping last weekend!	We'll give you your money back.
You had the car, remember!	Why didn't you tell me that before! I've wasted thirty minutes talking to you instead of selling my diet to someone else.

A TRANSFORMATION CARD	B TRANSFORMATION CARD
1 _____ I _____ time, I _____ _____ cooked something.	1 _____ you to _____ on this new diet, you _____ _____ like a new person.
2 I don't know. Should I _____ home early, I _____ .	2 _____ you _____ one month ago, you _____ _____ lost ten kilos by now.
3 Providing you _____ _____ the washing up by the time I get home, I _____ _____ about making a cake.	3 Not _____ you eat the wrong food or _____ snacks while no one is looking.
4 You _____ _____ a cake for a month _____ the dishes _____ clean.	4 You won't _____ weight _____ you _____ our diet.
5 I _____ _____ _____ one _____ someone done the shopping.	5 Should you _____ lose five kilos in the first month, we _____ _____ you your money back.
6 If I _____ _____ the car, I _____ _____ _____ the shopping.	6 If I'd _____ that you _____ interested, I _____ _____ wasted thirty minutes talking to you!

   PHOTOCOPIABLE

A

a new uniform

parents invited to watch lessons

more CCTV cameras

student coffee bar

more choice of school dinners

a school newsletter

> You are on a student council. You have been asked to think of five things which would improve the school without costing too much money. Try to agree on the best five ideas.

students sorted into 'houses'

more after-school activities

re-painting the building

guest speakers from local businesses

more choice of subjects

B

Get the waiters and waitresses to hand out brochures dressed as items of food.

Advertise more in the local paper.

Invite a TV chef in for a meal.

Start a website.

> You own a restaurant which isn't doing very well. The food is excellent and it isn't very expensive. Try to agree on the best five ideas to make your business a success.

Lower the prices.

Change the chef.

Make a giant pizza and give pieces away in the street.

Re-decorate the restaurant.

Have a giant TV screen showing sports/ music videos.

Give free meals to journalists.

Have a kids play room.

Change the name of the restaurant.

EXPRESSION CARDS

The way I look at it ...	Personally, I quite like the idea of ...	I think we can discount the idea of ...	Thinking about it, perhaps ...
The more I think about it, the more I'm convinced ...	What do you reckon?	Any thoughts?	You've got a point there.
We could do worse.	Let's not forget that ...	We have to take the fact that ... into consideration.	Perhaps we should go for ...
We could just play safe and ...	So that's settled.	I think we both feel that ...	I'm afraid we'll have to agree to disagree about ...

© Pearson Education Limited 2009   **181**

Card 1

Bang		Click	
	Tick		Shriek
Rumble		Crunch	

Card 2

	Bang		Click
Tick		Shriek	
	Tinkle		Rustle

Card 3

Bang	Click		
		Shriek	Roar
Hum	Beat		

Card 4

		Bang	Click
Tick	Slam		
		Whine	Chime

Card 5

	Shriek	Rumble	
Rustle			Babble
	Whisper	Screech	

Card 6

Rumble			Tinkle
	Roar	Whine	
Bubble			Chime

Card 7

Crunch		Rustle	
	Hum		Slam
Whine		Babble	

Card 8

	Crunch		Rustle
Hum		Crash	
	Chime		Screech

This card wins if words are read out in the order given.

	Click	Tick	
Screech			Whisper
	Babble	Slam	

Tinkle	Rustle		
		Hum	Crash
Bubble	Whisper		

		Beat	Slam
Crash	Bubble		
		Babble	Whisper

	Whine	Tick	
Rumble			Crunch
		Tinkle	Roar

Roar		Hum	
	Beat		Slam
Crash		Whine	

Bubble			Chime
	Babble	Whisper	
Bang			Shriek

Rumble	Tinkle		
		Roar	Beat
Slam	Bubble		

	Crunch	Rustle	
Hum			Crash
		Whine	Chime

Tell me about something ...

1 you enjoy doing.

2 you have tried to do but failed.

Tell me about something ...

1 you can't imagine being without.

2 your parents are trying to discourage you from doing.

Tell me about something ...

1 you've got a chance of becoming.

2 you hate doing.

Tell me about something ...

1 you're too old to do.

2 you want to keep doing.

Tell me about something ...

1 you remember doing when you were young.

2 your parents encouraged you to do.

Tell me about something ...

1 you can't stand doing.

2 you're too young to do.

Tell me about something ...

1 you'd love to have.

2 that made you feel very happy.

Tell me about something ...

1 you have no intention of doing.

2 that's guaranteed to make you feel good.

Tell me about something ...

1 you mean to do this week.

2 you worry about doing.

Tell me about something ...

1 you've got the opportunity of doing.

2 it took you ages to choose.

Tell me about something ...

1 you are excited about doing.

2 you forgot to do.

Tell me about something ...

1 you'll never forget doing.

2 you wouldn't mind doing.

Tell me about something ...

1 you're thinking of doing.

2 you'd be a fool to turn down.

Tell me about something ...

1 you're looking forward to doing this year.

2 you haven't got the strength to do today.

Tell me about something ...

1 you don't feel like doing today.

2 you're scared of doing.

Tell me about something ...

1 you're not very good at doing.

2 you're planning to do before the end of the year.

PHOTOCOPIABLE

not quite as cool ✳ **a much better actor** ✳ **by far the best looking** ✳ **quite similar to** ✳
just the same as ✳ **not nearly as good as**

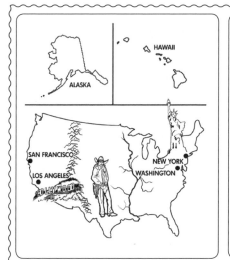
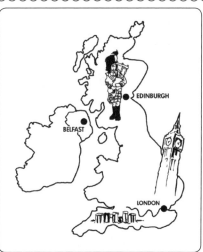

fairly similar to ✳ **a lot more expensive than** ✳ **slightly less interesting than** ✳
by far the most romantic ✳ **totally different from** ✳ **quite similar to**

not quite as difficult ✳ **much more interesting** ✳ **a bit less stressful** ✳ **just the same as** ✳
by far the most enjoyable ✳ **marginally less free**

HOW TO STOP STRESS:

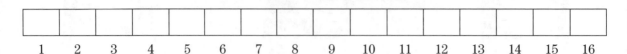

1	2	3	4	5	6	7	8	9	10	11	12	13	14	15	16

1 I get these terrible _ e _ □ a _ h _ _ when I've been watching TV or sitting out in the hot sun without a hat. I have to take an aspirin and lie down in a dark room.

2 I'm not surprised that you've got a _ t □ _ _ c _ _ c _ _. All those ice creams and crisps you eat.

3 Sweets and fatty food are bad for your skin and they may lead to _ c □ _ when you reach 14 or 15 years old.

4 I ate too quickly and now I've got _ e _ r □ _ u _ _. Well, I hope it's that and not a heart attack!

5 Jenny has terrible _ o _ _ _ □ _ n _ s. One minute she's happy and the next she's really depressed.

6 I think Cathy's got _ n □ _ _ x _ _. She never eats and she's really skinny.

7 Good grief! 40.5°. You've got a _ e _ e □. Get to bed at once.

8 Ow! This _ o _ t _ _ l _ e □ is really painful. Every time I eat something it hurts.

9 I've got an a _ _ e _ g □. Every time I go near an animal I sneeze.

10 I was carrying heavy boxes at work and now I've got □ a _ k _ c _ _. I can't stand up straight.

11 Look at my hands. They're really red and sore. Do you think it's □ _ z _ m _?

12 Breathe in. Breathe out. Hmm, yes, you've got some kind of _ □ _ s _ infection.

13 I suffer from _ n _ o _ n _ □. Sometimes I don't fall asleep until 5 or 6 in the morning.

14 This is very serious. You've got □ n _ u _ _ n _ _. Your left lung is infected. You'll have to take antibiotics.

15 I'm not lazy. I just have a problem with _ v _ _ s _ _ e □ _ n _ in the mornings!

16 Summer's nearly here. I guess my _ a □ _ e _ e _ will start soon and I'll be sneezing all day.

PHOTOCOPIABLE

believe	feel	think	expect	say
report		claim	rumour	

1 It is _____

2 It was _____

3 It has been _____

4 It_____

5 _____ is/are _____

6 _____ was/were _____

7 _____ has/have been _____

8 _____

PHOTOCOPIABLE

Manager: Ah, Tom. I couldn't help but [1]_____ that you were late again this morning.

Tom: _____

Manager: I was [2]_____ when we could have a little chat.

Tom: _____

Manager: Now is a good time for me.

Tom: _____

Manager: It won't take long. I really do [3]_____ we need to talk. Sit down. Now, I [4]_____ that you're having a hard time at home.

Tom: _____

Manager: And I know you're trying your [5]_____ to do extra work in the evenings.

Tom: _____

Manager: And I know your family is very important [6]_____ you. I really [7]_____ that you want your daughter to do well in her exams but you can't ignore your work here.

Tom: _____

Manager: I [8]_____ you understand that some of the other people here are getting upset.

Tom: _____

Manager: I don't want to mention any names at this time. And this might not be a good moment to [9]_____ this but your report was due yesterday.

Tom: _____

Manager: No, no. That's alright. I've got Jackie's report. It's very good. I don't think I need yours now. Back to you. Don't you [10]_____ that it'd be better if you took your two weeks holiday now and then came back feeling much better and ready to work in July?

Tom: _____

Manager: It's much nicer now. Fewer tourists. I'm sure you can change the dates. Good, so that's settled. When are you planning to start your holiday? Now or will you be staying for lunch? It's steak and kidney pie today. My favourite …

- ✂

Tom: Oh, yes. I'm sorry. I had a few problems (a) _____.

Tom: Well, er … maybe this (b) _____.

Tom: I really should (c) _____ now.

Tom: Yes, my son's having a lot of problems with (d) _____.

Tom: Oh yes, last night I managed to …

Tom: Er … son. No, I would never do that. I always (e) _____.

Tom: Really? I had (f) _____. Who is upset? What are they upset about?

Tom: Oh no! I completed it last night but I left it (g) _____. I can ask my wife to bring it, if you want.

Tom: But I've booked a holiday to (h) _____ in July.

Jack	Has anyone ever [1]_____ across any really good travel guides about travelling in Poland? Any help appreciated. Or if you've got any advice …
Neil	Don't worry about guide books. They [2]_____ an arm and a leg. You can [3]_____ a fortune by using the Internet. Unless you're [4]_____ of money, of course. ☺
Jack	No way. Just like to have something to read in cafés.
Patricia	Don't take taxis parked outside train stations. They'll rip you [5]_____. If you haven't got many bags, walk away from the station and [6]_____ your eyes peeled for a taxi rank. Take a taxi with a phone number on it.
Jack	Cheers. What about trains? Are there cheap [7]_____-peak fares?
Sue	Not sure about that but, if you book [8]_____ advance, you can get great Intercity fares. They're really good [9]_____ for money. Go to www.intercity.pl
Jack	Great.
Ben	You should try emailing language schools – IH, Bell or whatever. They're full of young travellers. Someone will probably be happy to show you [10]_____ and may even [11]_____ you up in their flat for a night or two. Take your student ID card too. It may entitle you to [12]_____ at some clubs or when travelling.
Jack	Wow! That's a great idea. Final question. Are there any hidden extras on bills I need to look out for?
Rachel	No, don't worry. All the prices in shops include sales [13]_____ and there's never a service [14]_____ in restaurants. And the waiters don't chase you into the street if your tip is less than 10% which happened to me in New York once!
	add a comment

PHOTOCOPIABLE

A Captain Cook left school in 1741 and, five years later, moved to a fishing village where he first fell in love with the sea. When he got his first job on a boat he started studying algebra, geometry, navigation and astronomy, all of which were to help him later in his career. He was promoted very quickly and soon became a Master's Mate and then, later, a Master. As he was in the navy, he was sent to Canada during the seven years' war. While there he spent his time drawing up maps of the Canadian coastline. The maps that he drew up were extremely accurate and used by General Wolfe in his attack on Quebec. When Cook returned to England, he was hired to travel to the Pacific Ocean to record the movement of Venus across the Sun.

B After passing Cape Horn, Captain Cook sailed across the Pacific to Tahiti. Later he arrived at New Zealand and he mapped the entire coastline. He then moved on to Australia and was the first to map the east coast of that continent too. When Cook returned to England, he published his journals which made him a hero amongst the scientific community. He was promoted to Commander and again sent to find the mythical land of Terra Australis. Reports he wrote during this second voyage made it clear that Terra Australis didn't exist. Cook was always concerned about the men under his command and, on his voyage around the world between 1768 and 1771, not one man died of the disease scurvy, a disease which was usually deadly for sailors who couldn't get fresh fruit to eat.

A

1a Before passing Cape Horn, Captain Cook sailed across the Pacific to Tahiti.	1b Having passed Cape Horn, Captain Cook sailed across the Pacific to Tahiti.
2a Arriving at New Zealand, he mapped the entire coastline.	2b Having mapped the entire coastline of New Zealand on a previous journey, Cook arrived there.
3a Returning to England, he published his journals which made him a hero amongst the scientific community.	3b Having published his journals, he returned to England a hero amongst the scientific community.
4a Promoted to Commander, Cook was again sent to find the mythical land of Terra Australis.	4b Having again been sent to find the mythical land of Terra Australis, Cook was promoted to Commander.
5a Having returned to England, Cook wrote reports making it clear that Terra Australis didn't exist.	5b Reports written during this second voyage made it clear that Terra Australis didn't exist.
6a Always concerned about the men under his command, Cook ensured that, on his voyage around the world, not one man died of the disease scurvy.	6b Sailing around the world, Cook became concerned about the disease scurvy but none of his crewmen died of the disease during that voyage.

B

1a Having left school five years previously, Captain Cook moved to a fishing village in 1746 where he first fell in love with the sea.	1b On leaving school in 1741, Captain Cook moved to a fishing village where he first fell in love with the sea.
2a Having studied algebra, geometry, navigation and astronomy, all of which were to help him later in his career, Cook got his first job on a boat.	2b On getting his first job on a boat, he started studying algebra, geometry, navigation and astronomy, all of which were to help him later in his career.
3a On being promoted to Master's Mate, he quickly moved up to the position of Master.	3b Promoted quickly, he soon became a Master's Mate and then, later, a Master.
4a Being in the navy, he was sent to Canada during the seven years' war.	4b Having been in the navy, he was sent to Canada during the seven years' war.
5a The maps drawn up by Cook were extremely accurate and used by General Wolfe in his attack on Quebec.	5b Drawing maps, Cook was used by General Wolfe in his attack on Quebec.
6a While returning to England, Cook was hired to travel to the Pacific Ocean to record the movement of Venus across the Sun.	6b On returning to England, Cook was hired to travel to the Pacific Ocean to record the movement of Venus across the Sun.

© Pearson Education Limited 2009   **191**

PHOTOCOPIABLE

Use the vocabulary to decide which things should go in which newspaper.

1 **Useless! England lose again**

2 **Hurricane approaches Cuban coast**

3 ECONOMIC PROBLEMS CONTINUE

4 The EU and your rights. Four page special inside

5 **Leave our pound alone!**

6 Film stars on holiday – exclusive photos inside

7 **BIG BROTHER PAGE 39**

8 Football stars in nightclub fight

9 Twins meet for the first time in 56 years!

10 **WE NAME ENGLAND'S TEN WORST EVER PLAYERS!**

11 FRENCH PRESIDENT VISITS MOSCOW

12 **Editor's comment: The government should have acted more quickly over currency problems**

13 **Editor's comment: Global warming? You're kidding!**

14 ALL YOUR TV TIMES ON PAGE 38

15 Reviews pages 30–34. Art, opera, theatre, film and music

---

dramatic, colloquial, sophisticated, neutral, restrained, sensational, quality press, opinion-forming, celebrity gossip, undemanding, extensive coverage of foreign news, populist, human interest stories, gutter press, in-depth news analysis, paparazzi, light-hearted, tongue-in-cheek, serious

     PHOTOCOPIABLE

Decide whether the sentences are true (T), false (F) or there is no information (NI).

1 They both like *My Dad*.

2 When you watch the programme you can hear people laughing.

3 Kathy's dad is nice.

4 They both agree that the father's character is sympathetic.

5 The programme has a catch phrase.

6 The storylines in *My Dad* are predictable.

7 Dan thinks that all the actors in *My Dad* are bad.

8 One of the actors in the comedy played a mother in a soap opera.

9 Dan's got a book about soap operas.

10 Dan doesn't like the theme to the soap opera.

11 The characters in the soap opera were clichéd.

12 Dan never watches programmes he doesn't like.

1   Jimmy was in court. (accuse; deny; claim)

_____

_____

_____

2   Finally, ... (admit; beg; promise)

_____

_____

_____

3   The judge sat and thought. (decide; warn; thank)

_____

_____

_____

4   When the judge got outside, he had a surprise. (regret; wonder; ask)

_____

_____

_____

5   There was the car and there was Jimmy. (congratulate; apologise; order)

_____

_____

_____

PHOTOCOPIABLE

VERB	ADJECTIVE	NOUN	ADVERB
create			
_____		logic	
imagine			

VERB	ADJECTIVE	NOUN	ADVERB
believe			
understand			
	equal		

VERB	ADJECTIVE	NOUN	ADVERB
_____		science	
		politics	
lead			

VERB	ADJECTIVE	NOUN	ADVERB
elect			_____
	tolerant		
_____	honest		

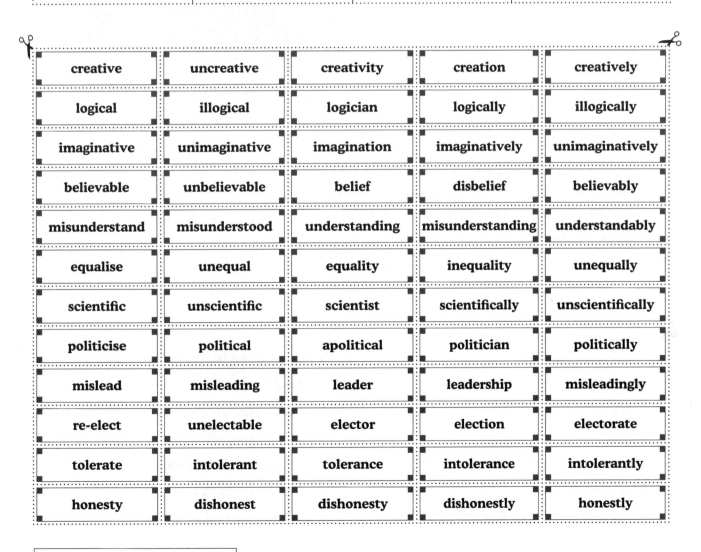

creative	uncreative	creativity	creation	creatively
logical	illogical	logician	logically	illogically
imaginative	unimaginative	imagination	imaginatively	unimaginatively
believable	unbelievable	belief	disbelief	believably
misunderstand	misunderstood	understanding	misunderstanding	understandably
equalise	unequal	equality	inequality	unequally
scientific	unscientific	scientist	scientifically	unscientifically
politicise	political	apolitical	politician	politically
mislead	misleading	leader	leadership	misleadingly
re-elect	unelectable	elector	election	electorate
tolerate	intolerant	tolerance	intolerance	intolerantly
honesty	dishonest	dishonesty	dishonestly	honestly

Dr Who? That's right.

I'm currently reliving my childhood with my son. [1]_____ is because of *Dr Who*. *Dr Who* has been on TV since 1963. Of course, it's a bit different now. The budget is bigger and the special effects are better but it's the same plot.

Dr Who is a Timelord from the planet Gallifrey. The evil daleks, a kind of robot, fought the Timelords, [2]_____ except the doctor and his enemy, The Master. Dr Who can travel [3]_____ in the universe and can go backward or forward [4]_____ he wishes. He travels in a Tardis [5]_____ on the outside. [6]_____, they take one look at it and can't believe that it's a space ship. [7]_____ is that Timelord technology can make things bigger on the inside than on the outside.

Dr Who has been on TV now for nearly fifty years, [8]_____ there have been ten different actors [9]_____ have played the same person. Doesn't this make it strange? Not at all. You see, the doctor cannot die. [10]_____, he regenerates and comes back with a new face and personality so, [11]_____ to play the part can act it however they like.

Why is it so popular? Millions of people watched it every Saturday [12]_____. And the new series cleverly appeals to both a new generation of children and their parents, [13]_____ are happy to have a chance to bond with their children and share an interest. And they may both find themselves hiding behind the sofa during [14]_____ the monsters appear!

A wherever he likes

B all of whom

C many of whom

D One of the reasons why

E Whenever he shows it to people

F whoever is chosen

G none of whom survived

H Whenever he is killed

I the parts where

J which looks like a small, blue box

K a period in which

L when they were children

M What they don't know

N to whatever period in time

PHOTOCOPIABLE

You are a parent and teenage child. The child should have come home at 10p.m. It is now 3a.m. and he/she has just walked in the door.

PARENT: SHOW APPREHENSION AND RELIEF.
CHILD: SHOW INDIFFERENCE.
PARENT: REACT TO THE CHILD'S INDIFFERENCE WITH ANGER.
CHILD: REALISE YOU HAVE DONE WRONG AND APOLOGISE.

You are a parent and teenage child. The child is on holiday in Mexico. The parent has just heard a news item about a large earthquake there.

CHILD: RING HOME TO SAY ALL IS OK.
PARENT: SHOW RELIEF.
CHILD: SHOW DISAPPOINTMENT ABOUT HOW IT HAS AFFECTED YOUR HOLIDAY PLANS.
PARENT: SHOW SYMPATHY.

You are two friends, one of whom had a date yesterday. You now meet on the way to school.

STUDENT 1: ASK YOUR FRIEND HOW THE DATE WAS.
STUDENT 2: GIVE SOME INTERESTING DETAILS.
STUDENT 1: SHOW SURPRISE.
STUDENT 2: REACT BY SHOWING NO SURPRISE.

You are two friends. You bought tickets to a concert weeks ago and were very excited. The concert was due to be held tonight but one of you has just found out that it has been cancelled.

STUDENT 1: RING YOUR FRIEND AND TELL HIM/HER THE BAD NEWS.
STUDENT 2: SHOW NO SURPRISE AND GIVE A REASON WHY.
STUDENT 1: SHOW DISAPPOINTMENT.
STUDENT 2: SHOW SYMPATHY.

You are two friends. You arrive at school together and find a note pinned to the front door saying that school has been cancelled for the day. There is no explanation and no one else is around.

STUDENT 1: SHOW DISBELIEF.
STUDENT 2: SHOW DELIGHT.
STUDENT 1: SHOW MORE DISBELIEF AND DISAPPOINTMENT.
STUDENT 2: SHOW DISBELIEF AT YOUR FRIEND'S ATTITUDE.

You are two friends. One of you is a great fan of a soap opera on TV. The other hates soaps. The soap has recently had a dramatic story line.

STUDENT 1: TELL YOUR FRIEND THE DETAILS OF THE SOAP OPERA PLOT.
STUDENT 2: SHOW INDIFFERENCE AND CHANGE THE SUBJECT.
STUDENT 1: SHOW INDIFFERENCE IN THE NEW TOPIC AND TALK ABOUT THE SOAP OPERA.
STUDENT 2: SHOW DISBELIEF THAT YOUR FRIEND IS STILL TALKING ABOUT THE SOAP.

EXPRESSION CARDS

I've been worried sick!	Thank goodness!	I'm dying to hear ...
That's brilliant!	I'm speechless.	So what?
I saw it coming.	It's a real pain.	I don't believe it!
I'm heartbroken.	It's a terrible shame.	

EMOTION CARDS

Apprehension	Relief	Interest
Delight	Surprise	Indifference
No surprise	Disappointment	Disbelief
Sorrow	Sympathy	

PHOTOCOPIABLE   © Pearson Education Limited 2009   **199**

A You are writing an INFORMAL article about the events in the pictures above. Think of the vocabulary an informal article would use and use APPROPRIATE words from the list below:

affluent, badly off, broke, destitute, exorbitant, filthy rich, flaunt wealth, go bankrupt, hard-up, impoverished, inflated salaries, inheritance, lavish lifestyle, loaded, make ends meet, mansion, massive profits, (the) needy, on the dole, obscene amounts, outrageous wages, (the) poverty line, poverty stricken, prosperous, run-down housing, scrape by, scraping together every penny, wealthy, well-off

B You are writing a FORMAL article about the events in the pictures above. Think of the vocabulary a formal article would use and use APPROPRIATE words from the list below:

affluent, badly off, broke, destitute, exorbitant, filthy rich, flaunt wealth, go bankrupt, hard-up, impoverished, inflated salaries, inheritance, lavish lifestyle, loaded, make ends meet, mansion, massive profits, (the) needy, on the dole, obscene amounts, outrageous wages, (the) poverty line, poverty stricken, prosperous, run-down housing, scrape by, scraping together every penny, wealthy, well-off

PHOTOCOPIABLE

Your favourite football team is going to be taken over by a billionaire. He has promised to spend lots of money on your club but he has a reputation of being a ruthless businessman and is possibly linked to organised crime.

Your government is going to deal with another country to sell them weapons. This will mean lots of jobs and money for the people of your town but the weapons may be used by the other government to kill innocent civilians.

The police can question people for two days. After that, they have to charge them or let them go. They say that it is difficult to find all the information in two days. They want to be able to hold people for as long as they like.

Energy companies in your country have recently made billions of pounds in profits while some people are unable to afford heating. Your flatmates at university have found a way to get free gas and electricity and want you to agree to allow them to do it.

You are organising a party next week. You've got some music but not very much. A friend tells you how to get free music from the Internet although it is illegal. You only want the music for the party – you don't want to keep the songs forever but you're not sure if you should.

You are a politician and there's an election coming up. At the moment the opposition are more popular than you but only because they've been lying about you. A colleague suggests spreading lies about your opponent's personal life. His idea could win you the election but it might cost the other person his marriage.

You are in a band. At the moment you aren't very successful but your manager tells you that he can bribe people to get your record in the charts. Then you'll be on the radio and TV and could become stars. If anyone finds out, though, it could destroy you.

You are a teacher. You have given a test and the worst student in the class has come first. You're sure he must have cheated but you didn't see anything in the exam. If you give him such a good mark the headmaster will want to know how it happened and it might encourage other students to cheat next time.

EXPRESSIONS CARD

Asking for opinions: What's your point of view? What's your take on it? What do you think? What's your opinion?

Introducing opinions: The way I see it …, As far as I'm concerned …, In my opinion …

Agreeing and disagreeing: That's just what I was thinking. You've made a very valid point there. I'm afraid I can't go along with that. That's one way of looking at it I suppose, but …

Asking someone to reconsider their opinion: There's something else you should take into consideration. Try looking at it from a different angle.

© Pearson Education Limited 2009

1 He should have gone to bed five hours ago.	1 He'll be able to go to loads of parties.
1 He'd better leave it alone.	1 He should have done more training.
2 He might have been to a party.	2 He must have done well in his exams.
2 He should phone the police.	2 He won't even win one game.
3 He should go to the hairdresser's.	3 He could be studying for an exam.
3 It might have been used in a crime.	3 He may as well give up now.
4 He won't need to buy a Halloween costume.	4 He may as well stay up all night now.
4 He'll have to learn how to cook and do his washing.	4 He'd better take up a new sport.
5 They must think he looks very strange.	5 He doesn't have to go to school tomorrow.
5 He succeeded in getting on a course.	5 He must be playing football.

PHOTOCOPIABLE

1

2

3

4

5

6

7

8

9

© Pearson Education Limited 2009

1 Goths look quite frightening but ...	... they are often very shy, peaceful people.
2 Some nightclubs stop people from wearing old clothes but ...	... they can't stop them from fighting.
3 Schools always had a uniform when my parents were young but ...	... now quite a lot of schools don't.
4 People always complain about the price of designer label clothes but ...	... they still love wearing them.
5 I like watching fashion programmes on TV but ...	... I would never wear any of the clothes they show.
6 Heavy metal music is great but ...	... the fashion is awful.
7 I don't have to look smart at the weekend but ...	... I often wear a jacket and a tie when I meet my friends.
8 Wearing fur is cruel but ...	... some people think coats made from dead animals are very elegant.

1 (Although) _____

2 (In spite of) _____

3 (Whereas) _____

4 (Despite) _____

5 (While) _____

6 (Even though) _____

7 (Whilst) _____

8 (Although) _____

© Pearson Education Limited 2009

PHOTOCOPIABLE

VOCABULARY CARD

Modifiers: a little / a bit / rather / somewhat + adjective
to have rather / a slight + noun

Phrases with *not*: not exactly / entirely / especially / terribly / particularly + adjective

Euphemisms: eg unmotivated (lazy), nuisance (problem), under the weather (ill), well-off (rich), incident (accident), challenging (hard), ill-advised (stupid)

A1 Your friend has just had a trendy new haircut. He spent all his pocket money on it.

You meet him in the street and he looks very strange.

A2 You've been waiting for your new boy/girlfriend for an hour. You're cold and hungry and very annoyed.

A3 Your friend persuaded you to go to a film saying that it was really good. It was really bad.

A4 There is a new person at work. You are responsible for training them. They don't listen to you and aren't very good. Your boss has just asked you to come into his/her office for a chat.

A5 Your friend is in a band. You have just seen their first concert. It was awful. Most people in the crowd seemed to think the same as you.

A6 You asked your friend to book a cheap holiday for the two of you. You love camping and hope that he/she has found a nice quiet campsite somewhere.

A7 A friend who moved away from your school several years ago phoned you last night unexpectedly.

You meet a school friend the next day and tell them about the phone call.

A8 Your friends have been discussing a camping holiday in the mountains. You're not sure it's a good idea. A lot of people have had accidents in the mountains.

A9 You are parents. Your child has been caught playing in an old building which has lots of broken glass and loose bricks in it. You want to make it clear that it was stupid.

B1 You have just had a trendy new haircut. You spent all your pocket money on it.

You love it. You're going to be the coolest boy/girl in town.

Ask your friend what he/she thinks of it.

B2 You've had a terrible day. You're really angry with everyone. It's nice to meet your boy/girlfriend though.

Smile and say 'Hi. How are you?'

B3 You have taken your friend to see a great film. It's the second time you've been this week but it was so good you wanted your friend to see it and you spent your last £5 on a ticket. As you come out of the cinema, ask your friend what he/she thought.

B4 You are the boss at work. A new employee has just complained about their training. The person responsible is impatient and rude. You need to find out what's going on. Ask the trainer how the new person is getting on.

B5 You are in a band. You have just played your first concert. It was brilliant. The crowd were shouting for more. You are sure you are now going to be big stars.

Ask your friend what he/she thought.

B6 You have just booked a holiday for you and your friend. You are really excited and pleased with yourself because you found a 5* hotel at a bargain rate. Your friend usually has cheap, camping holidays so you're sure he/she will be pleased.

B7 Your friend had a phone call from someone who used to be at your school. You were very pleased when the person left and have no interest at all in hearing about them.

B8 You are planning on going camping in the mountains. It will be a great time. You are really excited and want to know what your friend thinks of the idea.

B9 You are a child. You were caught playing in an old empty house. Everyone plays there, it's full of interesting things and there's nowhere else for children of your age to play.

Extra tapescripts

Tapescript `CD 1 Track 6`

Exercise 6 page 21 (SB page 10)

Tina: OK, the call lines are closed, so if you haven't voted for the couples, it's too late this week. You've missed the chance of a romantic holiday in Venice, but there's always next week's show ... Now, let's hear what the girls have to say for themselves, and we're going to start with Maggie ...

Maggie: *[English West Country accent]* Superficially we're so different. I really need to lose a few kilos, and he's built like an athlete. He's a bit younger than me too. We may not look alike but we have similar personalities. He's sensible, reliable and really mature for his age. We're both crazy about computers and games. We met in the library. I was trying to write an essay when he sat down next to me, and although he was really nervous, he asked me out. Apparently, he'd been thinking of asking me out for a while, but he was too shy. He's so sweet.

Tina: Aw! Lovely, isn't it? I think it's pretty clear who Maggie's in love with. But now let's listen to Natalia ...

Natalia: *[Scottish accent]* He's really temperamental and he gets depressed sometimes, you know because he wants to be an artist, but it isn't easy. I can usually cheer him up when he's down though. He's in a good mood now 'cause he's sold a painting. It's great 'cause he really needs the money. He's working in an art gallery this summer, but the money's rubbish. It's strange how you just click with someone, isn't it? We met at a friend's house and when he talked to me, I knew immediately he was the one. The special one.

Tina: You must have worked out who Natalia's crazy for, but let's just make everything crystal clear, shall we? It's Yasmina's turn ...

Yasmina: *[RP accent]* He's not at all the kind of guy I thought I would fall for. The first time I saw him I thought he was a bit big-headed. I didn't fancy him at all. However, just a few minutes after he started talking to me, I was laughing my head off. I'd never met such a funny person. We've been together for over a year. It's true love, I know it. I thought he was having a laugh when he asked me to marry him. I mean, he's always pulling my leg about something or other, so how could I know he wasn't joking then?

Tina: ... and now it's time to meet our couples and to check if you guessed right on *Love Stories* ... Welcome, Maggie and James ... Natalia and Tommy ... and Yasmina and Simon ... And the winner of our prize of a romantic holiday in Venice is ... Wendy Smith from Brighton ... And we have her on the line now ... Hello, Wendy ...

Tapescript `CD 1 Track 20`

Exercise 2 page 38 (SB page 28)

Jarvis: *[Northern English accent]* It's 8a.m. and you're listening to *Good Morning* with Rita Collins and me, Jarvis Scott. The news headlines today ...

Rita: *[London accent]* House prices tumble, air fares soar and there's been a huge rise in the number of deaths on the road ... Nothing but good news, eh, Jarvis?

Jarvis: Unfortunately not, Rita ... New figures show there's been a dramatic collapse in the housing market as a result of the disastrous slump in the world economy. The Prime Minister is planning to make an announcement on the crisis later today, but the leader of the opposition claims that the government has lost control of the situation. However, it isn't bad news for everyone. Later in the programme, we'll be talking to some first-time home buyers who are delighted with the sudden reduction in prices.

Rita: Airline shares plummeted on the London stock exchange this morning reaching record lows and causing scenes of tremendous tension, even panic. It's all because of last week's announcement of a new 35% tax on airline fuel. Most airlines have already said they will raise prices

by up to 30% to make up for the tax. Travel agents around the country have raised their concerns for the future of their industry. Ecological groups, on the other hand, have welcomed the news. Every cloud has a silver lining for somebody, eh Jarvis?

Jarvis: Yes, Rita ... The number of deaths on our roads has surged dramatically in the last year. Accidents involving drivers under the age of thirty have registered a significant increase of more than 20% over last year's figures. The government is considering introducing speed control devices on all private vehicles in an attempt to cut down the number of accidents.

Rita: But there is some good news too ... A nationwide study carried out by scientists from Cambridge University has revealed that there has been a gradual decrease in the use of cars in city centres right across the country. Apparently, there's been a steady decline of almost 12% in the amount of city centre driving over the last five years. Congestion charges, the tremendous surge in the price of petrol and a gradual increase in environmental awareness are given as the reasons for the change.

Jarvis: And there's some good news for women too. The equality gap is shrinking. There's been a spectacular growth in the number of women in top jobs in government and major private companies according to the government's latest report into gender equality. There's still some way to go, but you're catching up with us!

Rita: It's about time! And finally if you enjoy playing computer games, you'll love this. Due to increased competition in the computer games market and a sharp fall in sales since Christmas, prices have been slashed. Games are now on average 50% cheaper than they were last month ... I'm not sure that's good news for teachers and parents, though.

Jarvis: No, I think perhaps a few parents ...

Tapescript `CD 1 Track 26`

Exercise 2 page 46 (SB page 36)

Speaker 1: *[Australian accent]* I had a good job in a private hospital in Melbourne, but I split up with my girlfriend and decided I needed a change. I'd always wanted to see the world, but not as a tourist. I'd feel guilty about flying around the world just for fun. So I joined *Médecins Sans Frontières*, you know *Doctors Without Borders*, and I've never regretted it. It's not easy, but I really feel I'm doing something to make the world a better place. At the moment I'm working in the Democratic Republic of Congo where there's been an outbreak of the Ebola virus. It's deadly and extremely contagious. If you catch it, there's a strong likelihood you won't survive, so we have to be very careful not to get infected. For the moment there's no cure, no vaccine. In all probability a cure will be found one day, but I shouldn't think it'll happen any time soon ... unless the virus spreads to richer countries. I feel strange when I'm in Australia or Europe and there are so many shoppers buying things they don't need when organisations like ours are so short of money. It's not right.

Speaker 2: *[English West Country accent]* There's me, my sister Tracy, and my cousin Jason. We're called Changes and we play pop rock. We're pretty good – I'm not saying we're sure to be famous one day, but we've got a chance. Unfortunately, it's not easy to find a place to practise. Mum and Dad work at home so we can't rehearse there. And even when they go away, we can't play too loud because it bothers the neighbours – one of them even complained to the police! We live in a small town and there's absolutely nowhere for groups to perform. There's nothing for young people to do here. That's why we started the group, to have something to do. Anyway, we decided there was no point just sitting about complaining, so we started up a pressure group and we talked to church groups and local businesses, sent letters to politicians, designed a poster and printed a leaflet, organised a demonstration, got people to sign a petition ... And last week they announced a new community centre's going to be built with a stage and a rehearsal room and there might well be a recording studio too! If you want something, just do it!

Speaker 3: *[English Midlands accent]* My doctor told me I had to lose weight and recommended taking up a sport. My daughter suggested tennis, but I've never had much coordination, you know. My brother offered to take me sailing, but I get seasick on boats. My wife wanted me to take up dancing. No chance! And then, I thought of cycling. I work for an engineering company and the office is about five miles away so I thought if I cycled to work, it would kill two birds with one stone. I could lose weight, and I wouldn't have to sit in traffic jams. But the first time I cycled to work, I realised there was a problem. It was really dangerous. There were no bike lanes. So I joined a cycle group that works to persuade people to use bikes instead of cars. Thanks to our work the council is going to build twenty miles of bike lanes including one that goes right past my office! It's not surprising that more people are commuting by bike nowadays. It's cheaper, quicker, cleaner, and good for your health. I've lost ten kilos and I feel much fitter. Get on your bike! It's the future.

Tapescript CD 2 Track 2

Exercise 5 page 49 (SB page 39)

Martha: OK, time for some of your calls. First on the line is Martin, from Bristol. What's your comment, Martin?

Martin: *[English West Country accent]* I think the first time I realised I was an adult was when I received a birthday card from my local Member of Parliament on my eighteenth birthday. Inside there was a printed message: it said 'Many happy returns' and 'I hope I can count on your vote in the forthcoming elections'. It really brought home to me the fact that I was now part of the 'adult world'. I threw the card straight in the bin!

Martha: Thanks for that, Martin. Next up is Kerry, from Rochdale. Welcome to *Have Your Say*, Kerry.

Kerry: *[Northern English accent]* Well, perhaps in common with the last caller, I also realised I was an adult when I received an official government letter. It was just before my fourteenth birthday. I remember I received a plastic card with my National Insurance number on it. I was the first person in my class to get one and I remember feeling terribly grown-up. I carried it around with me everywhere in my purse for several months. I was tickled pink! Nevertheless, I also remember thinking that I was now on their database until the end of my life. Which is a really creepy thought!

Martha: Thanks for your story, Kerry. Next we have, I think, Mr Hayes from High Wycombe. Are you there, Mr Hayes?

Mr Hayes: *[RP accent]* Hello? Oh, yes well I just wanted to say that I totally agree with your expert's comment about young people not having a role and the problems that creates. Until, regrettably, National Service was abolished in, er, in ... I'm racking my brains to remember the date, now!

Ted: 1963.

Mr Hayes: Yes, until 1963 young people had very clear, useful functions in society. After two years in the army, every chap came out again a mature, responsible adult. If you ask me, it's high time the government brought back some kind of military service, preferably as part ...

Martha: Yes, National Service is rather a can of worms, isn't it? Perhaps we can talk about it another time. But thanks for your comment, Mr Hayes.

Ted: Although, of course, he's made a good point. In many countries, young people still have to do National Service in the army and this is a very good example of a rites of passage.

Martha: Next we have Agnes from Ealing in London. Agnes, you're on air.

Agnes: *[RP accent]* Well, in my day, girls officially became an adult after they 'came out' at their Debutante's Ball.

Martha: Could you perhaps explain what that is to our listeners, Agnes?

Agnes: Yes, of course. A debutante was a lady from an aristocratic family. When she was nineteen, she was introduced to high society at a splendid ball, during which she would be introduced to the Queen. It meant that she was now an adult, she was now free to meet young men from families of a similar social standing and eventually get married. It was a marvellous tradition – I remember being over the moon meeting the Queen. It's such a great shame that it was abolished soon afterwards.

Martha: Thank you for that. We've just got time for one more caller – Nathan from Friern Barnet.

Nathan: *[neutral London accent]* Hello. The point I'd like to make is that there are actually many communities in Britain who have kept their rituals connected with becoming an adult. People who are practising Muslims, Christians or Jews still undergo ceremonies that mark the beginning of adulthood. I have to say I'm surprised and disappointed that your expert hasn't brought this subject up. In my own culture, the Bar Mitzvah ceremony, which takes place just after your thirteenth birthday, gives a very clear message that you have become a morally responsible adult. It's given me a clear purpose in my life ever since. Your expert's comments about the 'emptiness of teenage years' just don't hold up, as far as I'm concerned.

Ted: Well, I was in two minds about whether to extend our discussion to include religion. But of course you make a very valid point.

Martha: Well, I'm afraid we're just coming up to the news now so we'll have to call it a day. Thank you to Ted for joining us and everyone who's rung in this morning.

Tapescript CD 2 Track 12

Exercise 2 page 66 (SB page 56)

Ailsa: *[Scottish accent]* Well, listen guys – I've been thinking about what to do when the exchange students are over from Greece and it struck me that it would be a really nice idea if we laid on a big meal for them on their first evening. You know, it'd be a way of breaking the ice and also of welcoming them to Scotland. And their plane gets in early in the evening so they'll probably be starving anyway.

Steve: *[Scottish accent]* Good idea.

Fraser: *[Scottish accent]* That makes a lot of sense. What sort of meal did you have in mind, Ailsa?

Ailsa: Well, I'm not exactly sure, but the way I look at it I think we've got four options. We could either take them somewhere posh and over-the-top in the city centre. You know, somewhere like *The Ubiquitous Tip*, that does really brilliant food. Or we could take them to one of the cheap student places near the university. Especially one that does authentic Scottish home-cooking. Or we could just play safe and go for a pizza or a burger.

Steve: Or?

Ailsa: Or, failing that, as a last resort, we could actually cook something ourselves. What do you reckon?

Fraser: Well, if you ask me, I think we can discount the idea of the big, posh restaurant straightaway. I mean, even if we get some money from the exchange committee, it's still way out of our price range.

Ailsa: You're probably right. And besides, sometimes those exclusive restaurants can be a bit snooty and unwelcoming. Hardly the place to let your hair down on your first evening. Any thoughts, Steve?

Steve: No, I think you're both right. Personally I quite like the idea of cooking something ourselves. I mean, there are fourteen of us so if we all lent a hand we could come up with something quite special. For example, I can make great *potted heid*, which we could have as a starter, and then if someone else did some ...

Ailsa: *Potted heid*? What on earth's that?

Steve: Surely you know what *potted heid* is, Ailsa! It's an absolute classic of Scottish cuisine. You just boil up a sheep's head and then after a few hours you scrape the meat off it and use the jelly that's left in the pot to make wee …

Ailsa: Sorry but that sounds absolutely disgusting.

Fraser: Well, exactly. Let's not forget that not everyone is going to find our traditional cooking very appetising. We want the Greek students to have a good time, not sit picking at their food, worrying if they're offending us.

Ailsa: And also we have to take the fact that some of them might be vegetarian into consideration.

Fraser: Very true!

Ailsa: And just thinking about it, perhaps in that case we shouldn't go for the traditional Scottish restaurant either. It just might not be to everybody's taste. I'm sure the more adventurous students will get a chance to try some more, er, interesting dishes at some point during their stay. I mean, they are going to be in Glasgow for over two weeks.

Fraser: Yes, you've got a point there. Well then, what does that leave us with?

Ailsa: The bland, safe option. Pizza.

Steve: Seems a real shame. You could eat pizza in any city in the world.

Fraser: Yeah, but to be honest, the more I think about it, the more I'm convinced it's the best option. OK, so it's safe and predictable – but we know in advance what we're going to get. And everyone's bound to find something they can eat. And it's going to be within everyone's price range.

Ailsa: Yes, we could do worse, I suppose. I mean places like *Pizza Fresh* are quite fun and unpretentious and the service is pretty reliable. It means we can all just relax and enjoy ourselves.

Fraser: Yeah. So that's settled, then – we've decided on the pizza restaurant.

Ailsa/Fraser: Yes./Yes, I think so.

Tapescript CD 2 Track 17

Exercise 11 page 71 (SB page 61)

The following sounds can be heard: Floor creaking; something crashing to the floor; a muffled scream; clock ticking; the beating of Kirsty's heart; music – a bit horror-movieish; high-heeled footsteps clicking as Kirsty walks tentatively towards the door. She stops at the door and slowly turns the door handle. We can hear the ticking of the clock and the beating of Kirsty's heart. A clock chimes, a sharp intake of breath from Kirsty. A balloon bangs from the room next door, it sounds like a gun shot. A woman shrieks once from the room next door, it is cut off as if someone has put a hand over her mouth. Kirsty opens the door and tries to click the light on – she tries several times and mutters worriedly 'There's no light!' She walks into the next room, glass crunches as she walks across the broken glass. Suddenly the door slams. Kirsty shrieks. As someone clicks another light on, another person knocks over a chair which crashes to the floor. Kirsty's friends roar out 'Surprise!' and 'Happy Birthday!' Fade out to a babble of happy voices and Kirsty sounding shocked and surprised, but relieved too.

Tapescript CD 2 Track 23

Exercise 3 page 76 (SB page 66)

Megan: *[East Coast US accent]* OK, right guys, the next one is for the SoundSnake. You're teenagers, friends, and you meet in a shopping centre. Kelly, you're bright and enthusiastic, OK?

Kelly: *[Yorkshire accent]* Yes, OK.

Megan: And Fred, you're Jay, Mr Cool. And you feel even cooler than usual 'cause you're wearing your new SoundSnake, right?

Fred: *[upper-class London accent]* Yeah.

Megan: OK, ready when you are.

Kelly: Hi Jay, that's a really cool necklace.

Megan: OK, sorry, Kelly, but you need to sound slightly less … em laid-back than you were there, not so relaxed. Could you do that?

Kelly: Less laid-back?

Megan: Yeah, not quite so mellow. OK, from the top … Ready.

Kelly: Hi Jay, that's a really cool necklace.

Megan: Stop! Sorry, Kelly, but that was just the same as the first time.

Kelly: Just the same?

Megan: Well, it wasn't absolutely identical to the first time, but it was quite similar to it, wasn't it? You still sound too laid-back. You need to be a lot more enthusiastic. Can you try again? From the beginning.

Kelly: Hi Jay, that's a really cool necklace.

Fred: Necklace? What necklace?

Megan: Cut! Kelly, that was much better than before. Eh, Fred, that was good, but it was a little bit too aggressive, not quite as cool as I'd like it to be. I want a warm, velvety, confident sort of voice. Less shrill than you were there. Try making it a bit deeper.

Fred: Like this?

Megan: That's perfect. OK from the beginning of your line. Go.

Fred: Necklace? What necklace?

Kelly: The one around your neck.

Fred: That's not a necklace. It's my new SoundSnake.

Kelly: SoundSnake?

Fred: Yeah, it's a music and video player.

Kelly: Like my iPod?

Fred: No, it's totally different from your iPod.

Kelly: Really?

Fred: Yeah, traditional MP4 players aren't nearly as good as the SoundSnake. The sound quality is amazing.

Kelly: Can I try it? Oh, wow! That's incredible!

Fred: Yeah! It's by far the best music player on the market.

Megan: Great! That's brilliant. Oh, and by the way do you say 'different *from*' here?

Fred: Yes.

Megan: Oh, right, we say 'different *than*' in the US. Never mind … Now, the next one is …

Tapescript CD 3 Track 2

Exercise 1 page 77 (SB page 67)

Richard: *[English West Country accent]* … I'm absolutely delighted to be here, so thank you for inviting me onto the show.

Cynthia: *[English West Country accent]* What gave you the idea for the book, Richard?

Richard: Well, I've always been fascinated by recording devices, and I started thinking about how people today take it all for granted.

Cynthia: You mean the technology?

Richard: Yes, you know, it's so easy nowadays to record your own voice and what's happening around you, and to listen to commercial recordings. There are so many formats …

Cynthia: Like CDs and DVDs?

Richard: And iPods and MP3 players, even mobile phones and digital cameras can record sound and play music. And then there are Internet downloads too. I mean, nowadays – perhaps because of the prevalence of music piracy – some groups are only marketing their albums through the Internet. We're living in the digital age, but people don't know much about where it's come from, and so I thought it would be a good moment to try to explain it all.

Cynthia: It hasn't always been so easy to record voices and music, has it?

Richard: Oh, no, not at all. It started in the late 1850s when inventors recorded sound waves and other noises for the first time. At that time the inventor of the telephone, Alexander Graham Bell, made a recording device using a human ear and a piece of skull from a corpse!

Cynthia: Ugh … So those inventors only recorded sound waves, not voices?

Richard: That's right, and their devices didn't work very well either. In fact, it wasn't until 1877 that Thomas Edison, the great American inventor, made the first successful recording of a human voice on his 'phonograph'.

Cynthia: What did he record?

Richard: A nursery rhyme.

Cynthia: A nursery rhyme?

Richard: Yes, 'Mary had a little lamb'. It would have sounded something like this ... 'Mary had a little lamb, its fleece was white as snow. And everywhere that Mary went that lamb was sure to go.'

Cynthia: Fascinating.

Richard: Unfortunately, the original recording was lost years ago so that's a copy, but along with the book we are giving away a CD that includes many other historical recordings.

Cynthia: Edison's phonographs didn't use discs, did they?

Richard: That's right, they used cylinders, instead of discs, to capture the sound, but the disadvantage with them was that the recordings couldn't be mass-produced.

Cynthia: So, commercially speaking the technology was useless.

Richard: Yes, but then along came Edison's great rival Emile Berliner. In 1888 he demonstrated his 'gramophone' which used flat discs, and they had a much better sound quality than Edison's cylinders. By 1895 he had also developed a way of making several discs from a master copy.

Cynthia: Mass-producing them?

Richard: That's right, and so the modern recording industry was born. By 1914 over one third of all British households owned a gramophone!

Cynthia: Makes you wonder what happened to all of them, doesn't it?

Richard: They're worth a fortune now ... What happened next was that in the 1920s record players with electric motors and electronic amplifiers were developed.

Cynthia: So you didn't need to turn the handle to keep the music playing anymore.

Richard: Hmm, and the electronic amplifiers gave a much clearer, louder sound. Until the 1940s most records were 78s.

Cynthia: 78 rpm.

Richard: Yes, 78 revolutions per minute. That means they turned 78 times in one minute. But in 1948 the first 12-inch 33s and 7-inch 45s were released. The 33s were called LPs – long playing records and the 45s were called singles because they only had one song on each side.

Cynthia: Isn't it odd they were called singles if they had two songs?

Richard: Hmm.

Cynthia: What about tapes and cassettes?

Richard: Well, the first magnetic tape recorder – the magnetophone, was made in Germany in the 1930s. In 1963 Philips produced the first compact cassettes and in 1979 Sony produced its famous Walkman and a new age of personal music listening had begun.

Cynthia: And the Walkman led to the discman and now we're in the digital age.

Richard: Yes, that's right, the age of the iPod, which was first marketed by Apple in 2001, and it's not going to stop there. New technologies are constantly being developed and the changes are likely to be astronomical ...

Tapescript CD 3 Track 8

Exercise 3 page 83 (SB page 73)

Alex: Hi Megan! Had a good day?

Megan: [Neutral English accent] Yeah, fine. Hey, what's wrong? You look really cheesed off! Don't tell me – you've had another row with Mr Barnes. What was it this time?

Alex: Well, I'd just got back from lunch and he just started to rant and rave at me, accusing me of leaving the shop unattended!

Megan: And had you?

Alex: Of course not. I was having half-an-hour lunch break, just like I do any other day.

Megan: So did you stick up for yourself?

Alex: Well, yes. I tried. But he just jumped down my throat and said I had an attitude problem and then threatened to sack me on the spot. Again!

Megan: He's such a bully. It's just because you're a threat to him. He knows you could probably do his job better than he does. You should make an official complaint.

Alex: It's not that simple. I need to keep my head down and finish the six months for my work experience. But I'm at the end of my tether – he really gets my back up.

Megan: But I take it that you didn't actually lose your job?

Alex: No. Funnily enough, Gareth stuck up for me and explained that it was actually his fault that there was no one around. And Barnes just sort of calmed down eventually.

Megan: Gareth?

Alex: One of the guys I work with. We were actually at school together.

Megan: I don't think I've heard you mention Gareth before.

Alex: Well, I suppose I was too ashamed. You see, we all used to pick on him at school. The usual stuff. We'd call him names and hide his things. We used to wind him up and enjoy watching him lose his temper. And we'd make a point of never sitting next to him in any of the lessons.

Megan: Why?

Alex: Well, no reason really. He was a smart kid and basically pretty harmless. But you know how it is when you're fourteen – it makes you feel stronger when you can exclude someone, I suppose.

Megan: You've never mentioned anything like this before! And, what, did you bully him too?

Alex: Yes. Actually, probably worse than anyone else.

Megan: Alex!

Alex: Of course, I feel really bad about it now. I couldn't believe it on my first day at the store when I realised he was working there.

Megan: Did you apologise to him?

Alex: Well, I've tried to be friendly to him. And after he stuck up for me today I thanked him and he just said 'No problems, mate. I'm sure you'd have done the same for me.'

Megan: Well that was pretty big of him!

Alex: Yes, it was. And there was something about the way he said it. 'I'm sure you'd have done the same for me'. He was so cool about it. I think he was trying to clear the air and tell me that he'd got over it, and that he'd forgiven me.

Tapescript CD 3 Track 13

Exercise 8 page 89 (SB page 79)

Susan: You need to learn to be more assertive. In other words, your priority is to make sure that people understand what you want from them, but you don't hurt their feelings. So when you're dealing with someone you're having problems with, you should start by giving them some positive recognition or at least try to show that you understand or empathise with their situation.

Justine: So, for example, I should start by saying that I really appreciate that she washed up my glass!

Susan: Exactly! Or, alternatively, show that you understand that she is annoyed about it. 'You've got every right to be annoyed about having to wash up our things.' Another example – it annoys you that Chrissy would rather write you an email than say something to your face, even when she's in the flat at the time. So you could start by saying, 'I realise you're the kind of person who prefers to deal with problems in writing.'

Justine: Uh-huh.

Susan: And now the important bit. You then state clearly what your own feelings are but without apologising or making up excuses. 'I really do think you overreacted a little.' Or 'Don't you agree it would be better if we all sat down and discussed this together?'

Justine: OK.

Susan: If you're still worried that the person is going to be aggressive a good way of 'softening' your message is to use phrases like 'I was wondering whether' or 'I was really hoping'.
Justine: Yes, I can see that it sounds less threatening. Well, thank you, Susan, that makes a lot of sense.

Tapescript CD 3 Track 18

Exercise 3 page 94 (SB page 84)

Narrator [N]: In a quiet village in Lincolnshire, John Harrison, an uneducated carpenter with a gift for making clocks, was convinced he could solve the problem of longitude.

John Harrison [JH]: *[Northern English accent]* Clocks can't keep true time at sea because of the rocking of the ship and the changes in temperature, humidity and pressure. But I believe that I can make a clock that will keep time on board ship.

N: After explaining his ideas to the Astronomer Royal in London, Harrison was given money to build his first clock, H1. By 1736 it was ready for a trial at sea. Harrison himself accompanied it on a voyage to Lisbon and back. On returning to England, Harrison saved the ship from a possible shipwreck by calculating its longitude more accurately than the navigator could. He reported to the Board of Longitude ...

JH: My clock works and it works well ... But it lost 5 to 10 seconds a day, which is not good enough. Given more money, I could make a better clock.

N: The scientists on the Board of Longitude were mainly astronomers, men of theory who thought the problem of longitude could only be solved by careful study of the moon and the stars. Many of them disapproved of Harrison and did not understand his machines. However, they did agree to give him additional funds to build another clock. Many years passed as Harrison worked on his second clock, H2. But having discovered a flaw in its design, he abandoned it without even testing it at sea. By 1755 his third clock, H3, was almost ready.

JH: Oh, dear ...

William Harrison [WH]: *[Northern English accent]* Father, what's wrong?

JH: The clock is too big, William. We need something smaller, more practicable.

WH: But father ...

JH: Imagine, William. A watch, not a clock, a watch. Small enough to fit into a man's hand. That would be a practicable solution, would it not?

N: Four years later, in 1759, H4 was ready. Measuring only five inches wide, it is the most famous timepiece ever made. Harrison's son, William, tested it by sailing to Jamaica and back. The results were astounding. It had lost less than a minute since leaving London ten weeks before. Delighted, the Harrisons returned to the Board of Longitude. But to their surprise, the astronomers were not convinced. They ordered another trial to the West Indies in 1764. This time H4 produced even better results. In those days the best clocks usually lost about a minute in a day, but during the six-week voyage to the West Indies and back H4 lost under thirty seconds. In January 1765, feeling sure they had won the prize, John and William Harrison went to the meeting of the Board of Longitude. However, they were to receive an unpleasant surprise. The new Astronomer Royal was Nevil Maskelyne, a young scientist convinced that his own method of calculating longitude through observations of the moon should win the prize.

Nevil Maskelyne [NM]: *[English West Country accent]* Mr Harrison, this Board finds that your watch kept correct time during the recent trial to Barbados. However, we cannot award you the prize money.

WH: What? But ...

NM: The terms of the longitude prize are very clear. The solution must be useful and practicable. Your machine appears to be useful, but is it practicable?

JH: Of course, it's practicable.

NM: To prove it you must take your watch apart and explain how it works. You must make two exact replicas for us to test. And you must give us all your sea clocks so we can examine them in detail.

JH: Gentlemen, it is thirty years since I first appeared in front of this board and in all that time I have never spoken to one man who had the slightest understanding of my clocks. We have won the prize and I demand my money.

NM: It is not for you, sir, to demand anything from us. Our resolution is final.

N: Harrison's clocks were 150 years ahead of their time. They solved the problem of longitude saving thousands of sailors' lives and allowing the British Navy to rule the seas. Eventually the Board of Longitude paid him £10,000, half the prize money, but at the age of 71, having dedicated his whole life to making his sea clocks, John Harrison felt as if he had been cheated. Desperate for justice, his son, William, wrote to the King. George III was a keen amateur scientist and on hearing the story, he felt Harrison had been cruelly treated. Finally, in 1773, thanks to the insistence of the King, John Harrison received the full £20,000.

Tapescript CD 3 Track 22

Exercise 2 page 106 (SB page 96)

Speaker 1: *[Scottish accent]* Erm, I usually buy *The Daily Record* every day or very occasionally one of its rivals if the cover looks more interesting. I suppose I ought to feel ashamed of myself for buying it when I'm a university student, although to be fair a lot of other students I know buy it as well. The thing is, I sometimes feel I'm suffering from information overload and *The Daily Record* is a great antidote to that. I don't actually believe half the stories and most of the articles seem pretty light-hearted or 'tongue-in-cheek' anyway. Nobody I know takes what they read in them very seriously – it's just undemanding entertainment really, celebrity gossip and ridiculous news. And the sports coverage is probably better than in a lot of the more serious papers and being a bit of an avid sports fan, I appreciate that.

Speaker 2: *[Northern English accent]* Even when I was much younger I seemed to have an insatiable appetite for news. My folks always had several papers delivered every morning and I used to spend hours poring over them. If anything, it's got worse since then! I'm now a total news junkie – I can never get enough news. My start page when I open up my Internet browser is *The Independent's* site and I have bookmarked loads of other online newspaper sites and news magazines from all over the world. I like *The Independent* because I suppose it's a real opinion-forming newspaper and I've grown to prefer reading it online to its print version because it's all so interactive now – you've got a chance to air your own views as well.

Speaker 3: *[slight English Midlands accent]* I pay pretty scant attention to the news these days so I'm pretty clueless about current affairs. I just can't be bothered with all that doom and gloom. I used to occasionally sit and gawp at Sky News for ten minutes or so but I always found I didn't take much of it in. If there's one paper I tend to read thoroughly it's the *Evesham Admag*. You won't have heard of it because it's just a local newspaper everyone gets through their letterbox once a week. It's full of stories about roads being dug-up, couples celebrating their diamond wedding anniversaries and changes to various bus routes, that kind of thing. If I'm honest, I find the local trivia much more absorbing than any of the latest political scandals.

Speaker 4: *[neutral English accent]* I'm so rushed off my feet these days I'm finding it hard to keep up with the news, which I regret a lot. I used to get *The Guardian* but it ended up unread in the bin every evening. But I do make a point of buying one of the glossy weeklies, such as *The Economist*, which I'll read from cover to cover. These days it's rather right-wing for my tastes but the articles are so well-written that it's still a pleasure to read.

Speaker 5: *[RP accent]* I like to stay informed about international news and that's why I gave up on TV news a long time ago. I was appalled at how superficial the coverage of foreign news was – one or two news stories at most. That's why I switched to the radio instead – BBC Radio 4 and the World Service are both really excellent for news. Actually these days I get most of my news as podcasts from the World Service website – my computer automatically downloads the programmes as MP3 files every morning so I can listen to them on my iPod on the bus.

Tapescript CD 3 Track 23

Exercise 4 page 107 (SB page 97)

Sophie: *[slight English West Country accent]* So what do you think of our new Sociology lecturer, then?

Tim: *[neutral English accent]* Yeah, he seems like a nice enough bloke!

Sophie: I really like him. I tell you who he reminds me of ... Tom Carter. The way he brushes his fingers through his hair when he's talking. But his personality is quite similar too, I think.

Tim: Er, who exactly is Tom Carter?

Sophie: Oh, you know! From *Selly Oak*. He used to go out with that irritating Canadian girl.

Tim: Hang on a minute – you're comparing one of our lecturers with a character from a soap. That's just ridiculous. He's not a real person, you know! How can you say they've got the same personality?

Sophie: Oh, come on, Tim – don't take things so seriously.

Tim: Well, I do take it seriously actually. What horrifies me the most is that people seem to be more interested in what's happening in a soap opera than what's going on in their own families. I mean, when was the last time you spoke to your sister, Sophie?

Sophie: Well that's not exactly fair ... Anyway, you've always got your head in a book. How is reading a novel any different from watching a soap opera?

Tim: When you're reading a classic novel, you're in touch with some of the greatest minds that ever lived.

Sophie: Ooooh!

Tim: Whereas a soap opera is ... is just banal rubbish.

Sophie: You can be such a snob sometimes, Tim. Reading a book and watching a good soap gives you exactly the same sort of enjoyment. You start sympathising with the characters, you become immersed in their situation and because of that they become interesting and real. Anyway, do you mind if I switch on the TV for a bit? It's the semi-final of *Celebrity Circus* and I want to see who's going to win it.

Tim: I suppose so!

TV Announcer: So which three of our lucky celebrity contestants will go through to next week's finals of *Circus Celebrities*? Just call the number at the bottom of your screen to vote for the star of your choice. Our phone lines are open until ten o'clock and calls cost no more than ...

Sophie: Hey, why have you turned the sound down? I was watching that!

Tim: I'm sorry but I find this kind of programme really depressing. Respected politicians and sports stars acting like complete idiots!

Sophie: What's got into you this evening? It's just a bit of harmless fun. It's quite nice to see what famous people are really like!

Tim: But don't you see how damaging it is, Sophie? Nobody's allowed to be serious any more! I mean, if a politician wants to be popular nowadays then the best thing they can do is appear on a celebrity talent show.

Sophie: OK, OK, I get the message, Tim. So, let's watch something that you actually approve of. Perhaps the news? It'll be on now.

Tim: OK, suits me!

Newsreader: Channel Six have announced plans to launch the UK's first completely interactive TV news bulletins.

They are said to be investing £2 million pounds in the scheme, which – they claim – will allow members of the public to vote for only those news stories they are interested in hearing. Here's our media correspondent, Nigel Crowe.

Tapescript CD 4 Track 2

Exercise 3 page 114 (SB page 104)

Q: *[RP accent]* Hello. Q here.

Z: *[RP accent]* Hello Q. It's Z here reporting from planet Earth.

Q: Lovely to hear from you old chap, how are you getting on?

Z: Well, I must say it's a lot more interesting than I'd thought it was going to be.

Q: Oh yes?

Z: Yes, Earth civilisation has really come on by leaps and bounds since I was here last. Especially in the fields of science and technology. They've even managed to send people into space!

Q: Gosh! That is a surprise. Do you think they'll be able to ...

Z: Oh, no, no, no. They still believe you can't travel faster than the speed of light!

Q: No!

Z: Yes, seriously. They won't discover they're not alone in the universe in the foreseeable future. It's quite inconceivable!

Q: That's a relief.

Z: There have been some changes in government too.

Q: In what way?

Z: Well, there used to be lots and lots of feudalistic societies, dictatorships, absolute monarchies and so on. There are still quite a few totalitarian regimes here and there, but now most countries have adopted a democratic system with parliamentary elections.

Q: Oh! So there are no more kings and queens?

Z: Oh no, there are.

Q: Oh good. I do like royal families.

Z: But they tend to be constitutional monarchies now, you know, they don't actually have any real political power. To be honest, some of them are more like a branch of the entertainment industry.

Q: And what about the economy?

Z: What can I say? Could do better. Most countries have a mixed economy, you know, capitalism with some state intervention. And there are some enormous multinational corporations which have a lot of power. I must say they have made incredible material progress since they began to industrialise a few centuries ago. However, they're not so good at the redistribution of wealth. I mean, some of the things they do are quite unbelievable!

Q: What do you mean?

Z: Well, they pay some people a fortune for doing things they enjoy, like singing a song or kicking a ball around or ...

Q: Sorry, they pay people money for singing?

Z: Yes! Vast amounts of money! On the other hand, some people who work incredibly hard at extremely unpleasant jobs don't earn enough to survive!

Q: Oh, I say! Are you sure you're not the victim of some kind of misunderstanding?

Z: No! For supposedly intelligent beings, humans have some completely illogical beliefs.

Q: For example?

Z: Well, they believe in all sorts of things that don't really exist. You certainly can't accuse them of being unimaginative! And don't let me get started on crime and violence!

Q: Crime?

Z: Yes, they're riddled with criminal instincts. They can be so thoughtless and selfish and unscrupulous! Their civilisation is plagued by dishonesty, corruption and intolerance. Frankly, it's almost beyond belief!

211

Q: Oh dear!

Z: It's curious because they can be quite sensible but they seem to suffer from periods of complete insanity!

Q: Well, it all sounds most interesting; a tad depressing, but interesting nonetheless.

Z: Yes, it is. You know, I was wondering if we shouldn't help them out a little with their environmental problems. If we were to provide them with a proper non-polluting source of energy, then maybe they wouldn't want to be so …

Tapescript CD 4 Track 4

Exercise 9 page 117 (SB page 107)

1 The first animal which was sent into space was a fruit fly, not a dog.

2 The first invention the sound barrier was broken by was the whip, not the aeroplane.

3 George Washington, who was not the first president of the USA, had false teeth which were made of hippopotamus and elephant ivory, not wood.

4 An animal whose brain is about 6% of its body weight and which lives in a complex society is the ant, not the human being.

5 The enemies Napoleon ran away from in great embarrassment in 1807 were rabbits, not the British – he was attacked by hungry rabbits during a hunt and had to flee in his carriage.

6 The purpose of the 'Glutton Club', to which biologist Charles Darwin would go once a week, was to eat as many different species of animals as possible, not vast amounts of normal food.

7 The cause of death as a result of which more than two million people die every year is work-related accidents, not war – only 650,000 are killed in wars.

8 The extent to which the Earth is made up of water in percentage terms is about 2%, not more than 50%. Although about 70% of the surface of the earth is covered in water, only about 2% of its mass is water.

9 The period in which most children learn to walk is from 11 to 14 months, not 6 to 9 months.

Tapescript CD 5 Track 9

Exercise 5 page 149 (SB page 141)

Speaker 1: Don't get me wrong. I like the BBC, especially BBC 2. I probably watch it more than all the other channels put together. I think, by and large, the BBC has managed to maintain their traditions, they haven't dumbed down the content of their programmes as much as the commercial channels have, and I certainly don't miss the advertising interrupting the films. But what bugs me is the TV licence. I mean I know it allows the BBC to resist commercial pressures and to remain objective, but I just don't think it's fair especially in the days of satellite and cable TV. Some people hardly ever watch BBC programmes but they have to pay anyway, and it's not cheap, is it?

Speaker 2: It's so different from what I'm used to. Generally, the programmes are better and of course there are no interruptions. When I'm back in Spain, I only ever watch films on cable TV or on DVDs. I mean, you just can't watch a film on the normal channels. They're cut to pieces with commercial breaks, a 90-minute film can take almost three hours to watch because of all the ads! But here there are no cuts at all. And I love the radio too. They don't break into programmes to try to sell you a car or a foreign holiday! I'd happily pay a licence fee to have something like the BBC in Spain.

Speaker 3: It's going downhill, so it is. It used to be a lot better. I wouldn't bother paying the licence fee any more if it wasn't for the fact I'd be fined if I didn't. You know what really annoys me more than anything, though? They only ever talk about London on the news. They don't seem to realise we exist up here! And those weather maps! Have you seen them? It's unbelievable the way, they're tilted

---

down so that the Isle of Wight seems huge and the North of Scotland is a tiny narrow piece of land disappearing into the North Pole. The sooner we have access to more home-grown programming, the better.

Speaker 4: The news and current affairs programmes are very good. They've managed to maintain their independence and high standards. Frankly, it's worth the licence fee just for that and the documentaries too. I must say, though, I wish they'd kept the traditional BBC accent. I can't always understand the regional accents some presenters have. And of course the radio, especially Radio 4, is first rate. But other than that I confess I've been a bit disappointed with the way the BBC seems to be following its competitors towards more commercial programmes such as *Big Brother* on Channel 4. I mean, they seem to be made for people with a mental age of five!

Speaker 5: I'm proud of it. I've travelled to a lot of places in the world and wherever I've been, people always say they envy us for having the BBC. When I'm away, I keep in touch with what's going on with the BBC website. It lets me see what's been happening at home in Newcastle and other parts of the country. But the thing I really love about the Beeb, is that thanks to the licence fee, it's free from competition and commercial pressures and all the dumbing down that usually brings. So, they'll keep a programme like *The Archers* or *Gardener's Question Time* running year after year even if they're not fashionable any more.

Tapescript CD 5 Track 11

Exercise 3 page 150 (SB page 143)

Simon: OK, Karen, you mentioned that the name Swindon came from Anglo-Saxon, which, correct me if I'm wrong, could mean that it's well over a thousand years old. Which is pretty old! Are there many other place names that go back this far?

Karen: Er, yes. In fact, there are quite a few place names in Britain that have been in existence for 3,000 years or more.

Simon: That's incredible!

Karen: The earliest place names are actually Celtic. You have to remember that at one point Celtic-speaking people lived across much of modern-day England, Scotland and Wales and many names of rivers, such as the Thames, are from Celtic as well as many of the names of hills and mountains. This isn't just true of Britain – there are many names of rivers and mountains across Europe that are probably from Celtic words. Before the Romans arrived, most place names in Britain would have been Celtic at one point. Then, over the centuries as the Roman presence grew stronger, these Celtic-speaking people moved west to present-day Wales, Cornwall and Scotland. Meanwhile, in the south and east the Celtic names they had given to their villages and settlements were slowly replaced. With a few exceptions – Dover, for example, which is from the Celtic for *water* – is a Celtic place name that has survived.

Simon: OK. You mentioned the Romans. Did they give us many place names?

Karen: Um, there are many towns throughout England whose names end in *-ster*, such as Leicester or Gloucester, and these are all are from the Latin *castra*, which meant they had an army camp. But apart from that, the Romans had surprisingly little influence on place names. But when the Romans began to leave Britain, they were quickly replaced by the Anglo-Saxons from Germany and Holland and they had a huge impact on place names across Britain. In fact, the vast majority of place names in England and quite a few in Wales and Scotland are from Anglo-Saxon. And let's not forget the Vikings either. They controlled much of north-eastern Britain for over 200 years and they gave us many names of islands and coastal features as well as the names of towns such as Derby and Rugby.

Simon: In other words there are very few place names in Britain that are less than a thousand years old.

Karen: Yes, that's right.

Simon: Hmm, I'm beginning to see what you meant when you said these names show thousands of years of history in a nutshell.

Karen: Yes, and of course it doesn't stop there. When British people later emigrated to North America and Australia they took their old place names with them. I wonder if the people of Birmingham, Alabama realise that their town is named after a tiny Anglo-Saxon village, for example.

Simon: Or I wonder next time people watch a derby horse race or a game of rugby whether they realise they're named after Viking towns.

Karen: Exactly!

Simon: OK. Well, I think it's time to take some of your calls now. If you have a question for Karen give us a ring on 01945 56 ...

Tapescript `CD 5 Track 12`

Exercise 4 page 151 (SB page 145)

One

Woman: *[London (Cockney) accent]* A quarter of a pound of radishes, please.

Man: *[London (Cockney) accent]* Certainly. That's 44 pence. Anything else, my dear?

Woman: Er, how much are the spring onions?

Man: They're on special offer – just £6.80 a kilo!

Woman: That doesn't mean anything to me! How much is that *in English*?

Man: Let's see – that's £3.10 a pound, love. I have to write all my prices in kilos and grammes now, you see – otherwise I'm breaking the law. It's EU regulations, isn't it?

Woman: Well I think it's a terrible shame. I mean, we've had these ...

Two

Pat: *[London accent]* Here's your breakfast, Eduardo.

Eduardo: *[slight Spanish accent]* Mmm – smashing! I could get used to having these English breakfasts every morning.

Pat: Well, to be honest, we don't usually have a full breakfast in the mornings now.

Eduardo: No?

Pat: Well, you know. We don't usually have time. We just have them occasionally as a treat at the weekends or when we've got guests. It's not very healthy if you have all that fried food too often either.

Tony: *[London accent]* A heart attack on a plate!

Eduardo: Well, I love it!

Paul: *[London accent]* So how are you enjoying England then, Eduardo?

Eduardo: Well, I have to say I'm a bit disappointed!

Paul: Oh, really? In what way?

Eduardo: Well, it's nothing like how I expected. I was really looking forward to seeing a real London fog with my own eyes. And so far there's been nothing!

Paul: Nah! That's a thing of the past mate.

Tony: Well, when I was a lad, we sometimes had terrible smogs in London. There was a particularly bad one in ... oh, it must have been 1952. Lasted for weeks, it did. And lots of people were ill or even died. But then the government introduced strict regulations about burning coal in towns and cities and since then it's been a lot better.

Pat: So any other 'disappointments', Eduardo?

Eduardo: Well, before I came here, I thought that the British stopped what they were doing at five o'clock so they could have their 'five o'clock tea'!

Pat: Everyone's too busy to have afternoon tea nowadays.

Paul: At five o'clock most people are still working or travelling home!

Tony: Yes, I think it was only a tradition amongst upper-class ladies, really.

Eduardo: Oh, and I also expected everyone to wear those hard, black hats like on *Monty Python*!

Paul: Bowler hats! I don't think I've ever seen anyone wearing a bowler hat. Except for the odd pop star. Pete Doherty ...

Tony: Well, when I was a lad you would still see businessmen in the City wearing bowler hats. But they disappeared almost overnight in the 1960s. I suppose it was a social change – people saw them as a symbol of the establishment and they didn't want to be associated with it. A lot of things changed in the sixties ...

Three

Announcer: *[Yorkshire accent]* In fifteen minutes, a roundup of the latest national and international news from the BBC. But first, here's Simon Scanlon with *Language Matters*.

Simon: *[Manchester accent / 'mimics' RP for a time]* Hello and welcome to the last in the present series of *Language Matters*. Well, it may have come to your attention that the BBC, that last bastion of Received Pronunciation, is employing increasingly greater numbers of speakers with regional accents. Does this mean an end to impeccable BBC English pronunciation? Does it mean that the standard of spoken English is in decline? Should we be concerned? Or should we just get used to it? To discuss the apparent decline of Received Pronunciation, I'm now joined in the studio by Professor John Burrell ... So John, in a nutshell, what's happening to RP?

John: *[neutral English accent]* Well, first of all I should point out that RP has always been evolving. If you compare speakers of RP before the last war with speakers today, you'll notice a marked difference. Even the queen herself has slowly changed her accent over the past fifty years. But I think the main change is how people regard this accent. When I was younger, many young people, even from working-class backgrounds, adopted Received Pronunciation to show they were well educated. Then I think beginning in the 1960s, and certainly since the 1980s, the opposite has been happening. Well-educated young people, or people from wealthy backgrounds are more likely to disguise this fact by speaking in a neutral or regional accent. Look at Tony Blair – he had an expensive private education where he obviously picked up RP. But quite often he slips into a neutral or classless accent.

Simon: To show he's one of us. That he has the common touch?

John: That's right.

Workbook answer key

Unit 1 Pleased to meet you
Reading and Vocabulary
1
c
2
1b 2c 3a 4d 5c
3
2 taken aback 3 brought to its knees 4 moved on
5 wrote up 6 raised eyebrows 7 hold down
4
2 reproductive 3 statistical 4 attractive 5 loyalty
6 boring
5
1 mate 2 rank
6
2 write up 3 rank 4 move on 5 brought to (its)
knees 6 mates

Grammar – Tense revision
Present and past tenses
1
2d 3c 4a 5c 6d 7b 8b 9a 10a 11b 12d
2
2 changes 3 recognise 4 knows 5 collected
6 were watching 7 asked 8 observed 9 lit 10 are
wondering 11 hasn't used

Tenses with the perfect aspect
3
2e 3a 4f 5d 6g 7b
4
2 has published 3 have criticised 4 have read 5 'll
have read 6 've tried 7 have brought 8 have grown
9 have been publishing 10 will have been publishing

Future Continuous and Future Perfect
(simple and continuous)
5
2 won't be living 3 be dancing 4 have been 5 have
been learning 6 have finished 7 have seen 8 have
been running 9 have been going out
6
2 'll have gone 3 'll have got 4 'll have 5 'll be
sunbathing 6 'll be working 7 will (you) have
visited 8 'll have been travelling 9 Will (you) be
staying 10 won't have had 11 'll be leaving
12 won't have finished

Speaking
1
2 Excuse me, a 3 mustn't, sure, c 4 really must
(be) going, c 5 Pleased (to) meet you, a 6 reason
(I) want, b 7 How about, c 8 What (do you)
think, b 9 Whereabouts, b
2
2 Have you heard 3 I wish I could stay 4 Sorry to
bother you, but 5 If you ask me 6 I'd better be
going 7 I couldn't help overhearing 8 Whereabouts
9 that's enough about me

Writing
2
(Students' own answers)

Vocabulary activator
1
2 cheerful 3 exasperating 4 careless
5 irresponsible 6 maturity 7 cocky 8 insensitive
9 charisma 10 assertive 11 strong-willed
12 insecure 13 confidence 14 stubborn
15 sensitive 16 emotional 17 indecisive
18 self-conscious
2
2 staggered 3 glancing 4 stuttered 5 glared 6 flashing
7 glimpse 8 Creeping 9 chattered
3
2 gave Tim the cold shoulder 3 pulling my leg
4 keeps a cool head 5 hold your tongue 6 putting
her foot in it 7 keep a stiff upper lip 8 is under his
girlfriend's thumb
4
2a 3b 4a 5a 6c 7c 8b

Extend your vocabulary
1
2b 3d 4g 5a 6e 7c
2
2 digs her heels in 3 toe the line 4 grit my teeth
5 turn a blind eye 6 drag my feet

Unit 2 Is it art?
Listening and Vocabulary
1
1b 2c 3a
2
1F 2NI 3NI 4T 5T 6T 7F 8NI 9F
3
2f 3b 4a 5g 6c 7h 8e
4
2 trademark 3 iconic 4 regard 5 busts

Speaking
1
2h 3e/b 4g 5a 6b/e 7d 8c
2
2 absolutely/utterly/pretty 3 to judge 4 bit second
5 far the 6 suppose 7 patch on
3
I understand where you are coming from. a I've
got a real soft spot for nineteenth-century
landscapes. e It's not bad. d It's nothing out of the
ordinary. b It's nothing to write home about. b It's
pretty interesting. a It's simply marvellous. e
Perhaps it's an acquired taste? d I'm a big fan of
abstract paintings. e It's absolutely dire. c Who
am I to judge? d It's a bit second rate. b It's by far
the worst one. c It's not bad, I suppose. b It's not a
patch on … c

Grammar
Cleft sentences for emphasis
1
2b 3f 4c 5d 6a
2
2 you can see in Monet's *The Parliament, Sunset*, is
Britain's parliament building. 3 the woman is doing
in Edward Hopper's *Automat* is sitting next to the
table. 4 is *The Parliament, Sunset* which/that is an
Impressionist painting. 5 was Renaissance art
which/that started in the fourteenth century.
3
2 was fog 3 is Juno who/that 4 she did was 5 was
the taxi driver who 6 he did was 7 was the taxi
ride which/that
4
2 do 3 did 4 in the slightest 5 No matter
5
2 The boys had no interest in the slightest in
visiting the sculpture park. 3 Let's hope that our
guest does want to see the exhibition. 4 It's a
terrible thought but Van Gogh did cut off his own
ear. 5 No matter what people say, I'm determined
to be an installation artist.

Writing
2
1 Every weekday morning … squeeze into 2 … the
flattest area of the country./This location is the first
and last place many of our city's visitors see.
3 There are long-forgotten ancient wrecks …
faithful owners. 4 For me … town in miniature.
3
(Students' own answers)

Vocabulary activator
1
2 admire 3 delighted 4 disturbing 5 enchanting
6 enrich 7 evocative 8 provocative
2
2 delighted 3 provoke 4 accomplishment
5 disturbing 6 evoke 7 admiration
3
2 flaw(s) 3 humbling 4 mediocre 5 atrocious
6 inventive 7 sickening

4
2 sculpture, oil painting 3 art installation, vivid
(colours) 4 performance art, blurred 5 still-life,
Surrealist
5
2 anticipated 3 place 4 expectations 5 pandered
6 poses 7 Needless 8 lucrative

Extend your vocabulary
1
2a 3f 4c 5g 6i 7j 8b 9e 10d 11h
2
2 nauseating 3 bewildering 4 pitiable 5 abysmal
6 contemptuous 7 fuzzy 8 bewildering 9 brilliant
10 contentious

Unit 3 Our changing world
Reading and Vocabulary
1
Text A 4 Text B 2 Text C 1
2
2 bombard 3 cinematographer 4 demanding
5 hybrid 6 incentives 7 intrusive 8 subdued
9 scope 10 visibility
3
2 incentives 3 scope 4 visibility 5 bombarded
4
1a 2d 3a 4b 5a 6c

Grammar
The Passive
1
2 Leaflets were handed out near the research
laboratory. 3 Subsidised bicycles are being offered
to employees. 4 Carbon emissions should have
been reduced years ago. 5 Our dependence on
fossil fuels will be reduced by nuclear energy.
6 Unnecessary flights have been cut down on.
7 Broken glass had been scattered in the road.
8 The rainforests have been decimated (by tree
fellers). 9 The same questions are raised at every
meeting. 10 Most of our energy is got from fossil
fuels. 11 Is hunger ever going to be eradicated?
12 Solutions to the economic crisis were being
discussed at the meeting.
2
2 are built/are being built 3 campaign 4 grow
5 was collected 6 have been handed out 7 were
caused 8 is sleepwalking
3
2 have been sent to overseas hospitals by the
medial charities *or* have been sent by the medical
charities to overseas hospitals / have been sent
emergency supplies by the medical charities 3 are
lent by the library to the reading groups *or* are lent
to the reading groups by the library 4 are being
given clothes / are being given to the flood victims
5 had been promised to the cholera epidemic relief
fund / had been promised a large donation
4
2 The government had been sent thousands of
letters by objectors. Thousands of letters had been
sent to the government by objectors. 3 The
visitors had been given an interesting talk about
solar power. An interesting talk about solar power
had been given to the visitors. 4 ✗ 5 The
contribution from the nuclear industry was refused
by the green charity. 6 Free power is offered to
anyone with a solar panel. Anyone with a solar
panel is offered free power. 7 The issue of
reducing carbon footprints is being discussed by
the committee.
5
2 were denied 3 were prevented/were being
prevented 4 protest 5 to find 6 joined 7 shared
8 was founded 9 are sent 10 to give 11 has grown
12 are employed 13 are employed 14 was awarded

Speaking
1
2 likelihood, e/f 3 faint, b 4 slight possibility, b
5 bound, a 6 probability, f 7 doubtful, b

214

8 improbable, b 9 inconceivable, a 10 inevitable, g 11 way, a 12 hope, a

2

1 There's no way I will ever wear them again. 2 You may well wear them again. 3 I shouldn't think so. 4 Fashion always goes in cycles so our grandchildren are bound to wear goth clothes. 5 That means our children will in all probability wear new romantics stuff from the 1980s. 6 Yes, I suppose there's a good/strong chance that will happen.

Writing

1

1e 2b 3b 4c 5d

2

1c 2b

3

(Students' own answers)

4

(Students' own answers)

Vocabulary activator

1

2 rises 3 raised 4 raised 5 raise 6 rise/rising

2

2a 3c 4e 5f 6d

3

carbon

4

2 a significant rise in the average age in Europe 3 has decreased gradually; has grown dramatically 4 a sudden reduction in oil supplies last year (which led to) a sharp increase in prices 5 fell steadily last year 6 have surged dramatically in recent days 7 the world's major currencies is predicted to collapse drastically 8 slumped considerably in the UK in 2008

5

2 emissions 3 fossil 4 energy 5 renewable 6 conventional 7 cooperation 8 catastrophic 9 aviation 10 gases

Extend your vocabulary

2

1 are knocking down 2 are (the police) setting up; broke out 3 knocked down; set (you) up 4 set up; has broken out 5 set up; knock (someone) down

Unit 4 Coming of age

Listening and Vocabulary

1

b

2

1b 2h 3g 4f 5a

3

1b 2g 3e 4c 5f

4

2h 3c 4a 5e 6f 7d 8g

5

2 have money to burn 3 asking for trouble 4 say it to her face 5 have friends in high places 6 crossed my mind

Speaking

1

2 I rarely wear smart clothes. 3 I only realised I was underdressed when I arrived./I didn't realise I was underdressed until I arrived. 4 The other people's clothes were so smart that 5 I seldom see you in a suit. 6 I looked so handsome in it.

2

2 it's important 3 must (you) take 4 will beer or wine be served to 5 can (you) serve 6 should (staff) chat up 7 do

Grammar
Inversion

1

2 Little did they know it was the last time they would see each other. 3 Never are such exotic animals seen in Britain. 4 Rarely do we see a person like Nelson Mandela. 5 Rarely do students hand in their work on time. 6 Seldom had I seen so many people in one place. 7 Only when Tim

saw Anna with someone else did he realise how much he loved her. 8 Scarcely had Bob taken his coat off when Sally said they were going out.

2

2 had the exam started when the fire bell rang 3 did I think of the perfect answer 4 did we know that we had a test that morning 5 do people travel to unmapped parts of the world 6 will I make that mistake again 7 had I sat down when my phone rang

3

2 No sooner 3 Not often 4 Not since 5 No longer 6 Not until

4

2a 3c 4a 5f 6c 7c 8b

5

1 Most of our people have never had it so good. 2 A woman's work is never done. 3 Troubles never come alone. 4 I will never be hungry again.

Writing

1

Sports coach at Camp USA

2

1 I am writing in response to 2 I am in my final year at; I am due to start 3 I believe that I am a strong candidate for the position described in your advertisement. 4 Apart from this 5 I would be free to attend an interview

3

For example, on a recent trip, some of us went to a party and missed the coach home so I had to make alternative travel arrangements.

4

(Students' own answers)

Vocabulary activator

1

2b 3c 4b 5b 6a 7b

2

2 a can of worms 3 learn the ropes 4 in two minds 5 brought home to me 6 felt out of place 7 call it a day 8 over the moon

3

1 grant 2 creep 3 snaps

4

2 hall of residence 3 fresher 4 lecture theatre 5 Tutorials/Seminars 6 seminars/tutorials 7 assignments 8 dissertation

5

2 particular care 3 real boon

6

2 exclaimed 3 dread 4 stammer

Extend your vocabulary

1

1b 2a 3c 4d 5e 6f

2

2 everything under the sun 3 Reach for the stars 4 make hay while the sun shines 5 once in a blue moon

Unit 5 Live to eat?

Reading and Vocabulary

1

Para 1 b Para 2 c Para 3 e Para 4 a Para 5 f

2

1T 2F 3NI 4F 5F 6F 7T 8T 9NI 10T

3

c

4

2 adverb, g 3 noun, d 4 noun, f 5 noun, a 6 adjective, b 7 adjective, c

5

2 joint 3 wholesome 4 maxim 5 crackers 6 plausibly 7 amiable

Grammar
Conditionals

1

2 won't make 3 wouldn't be 4 'd/would become 5 'd/had known 6 'd/had roasted 7 would (you) take 8 cook 9 'd/would order 10 hadn't trained

2

2a you should need some advice, you could ask the

waiter for help 2b you need some advice, you could ask the waiter for help 3a the service were to be bad, I wouldn't leave a tip 3b the service to be bad, I wouldn't leave a tip 4a you should leave without paying your bill, we will contact the police 4b you leave without paying your bill, we will contact the police 5a you should be disappointed by your meal, please tell the manager 5b you be disappointed by your meal, please tell the manager 6a you were to take a vegetarian to a burger bar, he/she wouldn't be very happy 6b you to take a vegetarian to a burger bar, he/she wouldn't be very happy

3

2a the customers hadn't complained, the bill wouldn't have been reduced 2b the customers not complained, the bill wouldn't have been reduced 3a he had learnt to cook, he could have invited the girl he fancied to dinner 3b he learnt to cook, he could have invited the girl he fancied to dinner 4a the health inspectors hadn't seen rats in the café's kitchen, it wouldn't have been closed down 4b the health inspectors not seen rats in the café's kitchen, it wouldn't have been closed down 5a I had agreed to wash up, I would have remembered 5b I agreed to wash up, I would have remembered

4

2 wouldn't speak, hadn't spent 3 hadn't taken, would be able to get 4 hadn't stayed up, wouldn't be 5 hadn't cancelled, wouldn't be 6 would know, had grown up

5

2 were, 'd/would go / would have gone 3 to get, 'd/would give 4 would prefer, could be arranged 5 eat, 'm/am 6 don't fancy, would/can make 7 known, 'd/would have stayed

Speaking

1

2 more (I) think, a 3 play safe, d 4 last resort, d 5 agree (to) disagree, e 6 point, c 7 reckon, b

2

2 Perhaps we shouldn't 3 let's not forget that 4 Thinking about it 5 into consideration 6 as a last resort 7 could do worse 8 I think we can discount the idea of 9 the more I'm convinced 10 So that's settled

Writing

2

1 a on the other hand, however, yet b secondly c last but not least d for example 2 a an interesting and varied diet is enjoyed by most people, ... use of animal feed and fertilisers must be included, the latter has to be given supplementary processed food b Such has been ..., never before have northern Europeans been able ... c Furthermore, were we to return to eating only local produce, our diets would be dependent on ...

3

(Students' own answers)

Vocabulary activator

1

2 allergic 3 beneficial 4 detrimental 5 extravagance 6 feasible 7 insignificant 8 mountainous 9 nutritious/nutritional 10 predictable 11 spontaneity 12 tempting

2

2 temptation 3 allergic 4 benefit 5 acrimonious 6 detrimental 7 feasibility 8 prediction

3

2 nutritious 3 takeaways/packaged foods 4 time-consuming 5 price range 6 chop 7 overcook 8 stir 9 roast 10 staple 11 herbs 12 sow 13 rinsing 14 baked

4

2 like a horse 3 like two peas in a pod 4 the salt of the earth 5 a hot potato 6 a square meal

5

2b 3a 4b 5a 6b 7c

Extend your vocabulary

1

2b 3c 4e 5d

2

2 To put it in a nutshell 3 's/has salted away 4 cooked up

215

Unit 6 Sounds around us

Listening and Vocabulary

1

1T 2F 3F 4F 5T

2

1a 2d 3d 4b 5b 6c 7b

3

twittering, lapping, hum

4

2d 3f 4h 5b 6a 7g 8e

5

2 Search me 3 does the trick 4 the matter in hand
5 swear by 6 lost me

Speaking

1

2 by far 3 fairly similar 4 just (the) same
5 marginally less 6 much better 7 nearly as
8 totally different from

2

1B quite similar to 2A not nearly as good as
2B by far the best 3A totally different from
3B a bit more 'real'

Grammar
Infinitives and gerunds

1

2c 3a 4b 5b 6a

2

2 humming 3 to learn 4 to drown out 5 getting up
6 have

3

2 going 3 passing 4 ticking 5 playing 6 to visit
7 being 8 to get

4

2 to tidy, tidying 3 to get, getting 4 to study,
studying 5 attending, to attend

5

2 go 3 introducing 4 looking 5 playing 6 to save
7 to get 8 reviving 9 produce 10 hearing 11 to put
12 trying 13 hearing 14 to move 15 employ

Writing

1

2a 3e 4d 5c

2

(Students' own answers)

Vocabulary activator

1

2 screech 3 babbling 4 whine, drill 5 crunch,
gravel 6 creaking 7 click 8 crack, gunfire
9 rumble, thunder 10 tinkling 11 crackling
12 rustle

2

2 honk his horn 3 take it for granted 4 put up with
5 fill the pause 6 find some peace and quiet

3

B melodic C shrill D tuneful

4

2 composers 3 conductor 4 chords 5 classic
6 lyrics 7 drowned out 8 cranked up the volume
9 solo 10 show off 11 paying homage 12 catchy
13 anthem 14 humming

Extend your vocabulary

1

2 took to 3 set in 4 comes up 5 come forward,
taking over 6 come for 7 set up

Unit 7 Calm down!

Reading and Vocabulary

1

2g 3e 4b 5f 6c 7d 8a

2

2 jump to conclusions 3 put up with 4 duty of care
5 stand your ground 6 upped the ante

3

1B 2C 3D 4A

4

1B 2B 3D 4A 5C 6D 7A 8B 9C 10D

Grammar
Impersonal reporting structures

1

2 It has been discovered by researchers that more
than 50 percent of busy workers don't take their
lunch break. 3 It is claimed that walking in a park,
the countryside or by the sea is soothing. 4 It is
known that high levels of noise are damaging to our
health. 5 It is estimated that half of all office workers
don't sit at their computers correctly. 6 It is reported
that keeping a pet relaxes people. 7 It used to be
believed that smoking was good for you. 8 It is
thought that teenagers learn more if their lessons
start later in the day. 9 It has been demonstrated that
listening to soothing music can improve academic
performance.

2

2 was proved in the 1950s to cause cancer 3 are
thought to be doing unpaid overtime 4 was
believed to be beautiful 5 is reported to be
increasing 6 are rumoured to be inaccurate 7 are
understood to create feelings of well-being

3

2 is known 3 has been calculated 4 are thought
5 is argued/has been argued 6 was proposed

4

2 it has been suspected that 3 have been rumoured
to 4 has been demonstrated to 5 is estimated to
6 it was assumed that 7 it is proposed that 8 is
intended to

5

Sample answer
Subject: Half-day dance course
It is well known that dancing is a great stress
buster. Combining music with exercise is thought
to allow people to relax in a social environment. It
is believed that dancing is healthy, involves learning
a skill and increases confidence. It is claimed that
students who attended last year did better in their
exams. Early booking is recommended as there are
limited places on the next course which takes place
on Wednesday 5th March. It is guaranteed that
those attending won't be disappointed.

Speaking

1

2 I was wondering whether you could give me a
lift. 3 I (just) thought it might be better for
everyone if I (just) left. 4 You've got every right to
be annoyed. 5 I hope you'll understand that I don't
have time to help you. 6 Will you be helping
tomorrow?

2

2 I was wondering 3 have (my) best interests 4 do
think 5 trying your best 6 the kind of person
7 couldn't help but 8 hope (you) understand
9 really appreciate 10 you agree it'd be better
11 very important to you 12 wondering 13 really
(do) think 14 right (to be) angry

Writing

1

a

2

a We all know about; Below are some dos and
don'ts to help you get a good night's sleep
b Basically; dos and don'ts; wound up; fretting
c (not a problem for many teenagers!); (but not too
late!); it's not the place for sending text messages,
updating Facebook or watching DVDs! d It is said
that e Not until I developed ...

3

(Students' own answers)

Vocabulary activator

1

2 admonish 3 aggressive 4 detrimental
5 dismayed 6 dispute, dispute 7 nourishment
8 resentful 9 stimulate 10 submissive 11 threaten

2

ad·monishment, ad·monish, ad·monishing
a·ggression, a·ggressive ·detriment, de·ter,
detri·mental dis·may, dis·mayed dis·pute,
dis·puted ·nourishment, ·nourish, ·nourishing
re·sentment, re·sent, re·sentful stimu·lation,
·stimulate, ·stimulating sub·mission, sub·mit,
sub·missive ·threaten, ·threatening

3

2 stimulating 3 detrimental 4 dismay 5 threatened
6 resentful 7 nourishing

4

2 dominant 3 humiliated 4 sarcastic 5 lethargic
6 tactless

5

2 calming 3 assault 4 despair 5 misery
6 patronising

6

2 hay fever 3 acne 4 heartburn 5 mood swings
6 mouth ulcer

7

1

2 bear a grudge 3 jumped down my throat 4 keep
my head down 5 makes my blood boil/gets my
back up

2

1 pick on 2 rub along with 3 be on red alert 4 beat
around the bush 5 at (the) end of your tether

Extend your vocabulary

1

2 bad/foul 3 general 4 in a festive/in a party

Unit 8 Getting around

Listening and Vocabulary

1

1b 2c

2

1 accident 2 was too hard up 3 third
4 investigative journalism 5 money-saving tips
6 campsite newsletter 7 break 8 on a tight budget
9 the best job in the world 10 travel light

3

1–2 2–3 3–8 4–6 5–4 6–1 7–5 8–7

4

1h 3d 4c 5e 6f 7g 8b

5

2 up-market 3 a tight budget 4 off the beaten track
5 keep, quiet 6 well-worn

Speaking

1

2e 3a 4j 5i 6c 7b 8f 9d 10g

2

2 jumped at the chance, at the crack of dawn 3 too
good to be true 4 going round in circles 5 on top
of the world 6 It just goes to show

Grammar
Participle clauses

1

2 Not having been paid 3 Not having paid
4 Having been paid 5 Paying extra 6 by paying
7 Having paid

2

2 Waiting for her train 3 Not knowing when his
girlfriend's flight was landing 4 By keeping an eye
on discountholidays.com 5 Having agreed to go
camping with a friend 6 Having been told the price
of the tickets 7 Having heard about the outbreak
of cholera

3

2 Staying with the Clementi family in Piramide, she
is close to the centre of the city. 3 Having been
introduced by a mutual acquaintance, Anna and
the Clementis are now good friends. 4 Having seen
the price of hotels in the city, she is very glad that
she has friends she can stay with. 5 Arriving at the
airport, she rings the son, Alberto Clementi.
6 Working near the airport, he can easily drive over
and pick her up. 7 Having been both quite shy
when they first met, they now always have lots to
talk about.

4

2 ✓ 3 Having visited Buckingham Palace, we
drove on by coach to the Tower of London.
4 While travelling on the bus, I lost my camera.
5 ✓

5

2 Drawn 3 using 4 Showing 5 having used
6 Recognising 7 seeing 8 changing 9 Having had

Writing

1

I know that I avoid eating there! It would be great if could be open for lunch too, wouldn't it?

2

Possible answers

1 a The main purpose of this report is to b In summary, the survey results are: c it was concluded that 2 The guests who were invited to complete the survey; Following discussions with the canteen staff; a second survey needs to be undertaken 3 guests want better value for money and for the canteen to be open for longer hours 4 bullet points under 'Results'; numbered items under 'Recommendations'

3

(*Students' own answers*)

Vocabulary activator

1

2a 3c 4d 5a 6b 7c 8d 9a 10c

2

2 affordable prices 3 off-peak 4 package holidays 5 port (of) departure 6 on board 7 low-cost

3

2 A fool and his money are soon parted. 3 It never rains, but it pours. 4 easier said than done 5 You can't judge a book by its cover. 6 at the end of the day/it just goes to show

4

2 showing visitors around 3 messed up 4 Check out 5 put up 6 come across

5

2 flight 3 suck 4 venue 5 leaks 6 urbane

Extend your vocabulary

1

2f 3b 4a 5d 6c 7l 8g 9h 10k 11i 12j

2

2 get (her) money's worth 3 ten a penny 4 the penny drops 5 money for old rope 6 spend a penny

Unit 9 Media truths

Reading and Vocabulary

1

2 downtrodden 3 circulation war 4 lawsuit 5 docudrama 6 biopic 7 mythology 8 germ of an idea 9 debut 10 co-write/co-produce 11 release 12 crush

2

2 co-wrote 3 crushed 4 debut 5 released 6 biopic

3

1a 2d 3b 4c

4

1E 2C 3D 4A

Grammar
Reported speech

1

2 Gandhi admitted that he believed in equality for everyone, except reporters and photographers.
3 Art Buchwald argued that television had a real problem because there was no page two and that consequently every big story got the same time and came across to the viewer as a really big, scary one.
4 William Randolph Hearst boasted that you could crush a man with journalism.
5 Oscar Wilde claimed that the public had an insatiable curiosity to know everything, except what was worth knowing.
6 William Sherman swore that if he had had his choice, he would have killed every reporter in the world, but he was sure we would have been getting reports from hell before breakfast.

2

2 'Rock journalists are people who can't write, interviewing people who can't speak, for people who can't read.' 3 'Journalism is the first rough draft of history.' 4 'Newspapers seem to be unable to distinguish between a bicycle accident and the collapse of civilisation.' 5 'If you saw a man drowning and you could either save him or photograph the event, what sort of camera would

you use?' 6 'I am more frightened of three newspapers than a hundred thousand bayonets.'

3

2 recommended 3 ordered 4 insisted 5 Informing 6 claims 7 told 8 insisting 9 blamed 10 encouraged

4

2 suggested that Zack should buy a newspaper on his way home 3 wondered whether the journalist would be found guilty of libel 4 doubted whether/that publishing a correction would stop the media frenzy 5 threatened to ground me if my marks didn't improve 6 reported that he/she had seen the international footballer Ryan Lucas in Star Dust night club 7 ordered the newspaper to publish a full apology 8 informed him that the party was illegal 9 denied that her website conned people into giving money to a non-existent charity

5

2 explained that Britain was currently 3 argued that the plan was necessary 4 accused the government of behaving 5 objected to losing 6 asked if she must/had to pay 7 wondered what to do

6 *Possible answer*

… how long he had been singing. Callum replied that he really couldn't remember and that everyone in his family sang, so he'd never known a time when he didn't sing. The journalist asked him where he had grown up. Callum explained that his parents were from Belfast but that he had grown up in Liverpool. The journalist asked when he had realised that his voice was better than average. Callum told him that he didn't think his voice was naturally better than a lot of other singers, but added that he had worked very hard to develop an image and stage presence. The journalist asked whether his parents supported him in his ambitions. Callum replied that his parents had always said that he should follow his dream. The journalist asked him if he thought lots of teenage girls voted for him because he was young and good-looking. Callum said he was sure that was true and that one newspaper had said he'd got more votes from grandmothers over sixty. The journalist asked what his plans were now that his career had taken off. Callum told him that he was going to spend some time with his family as he hadn't seen much of them during the previous few months. He also said that he would be in a recording studio for most of the next month and that after that he might be going on tour. The journalist wished him luck with everything.

Speaking

1

2 ought (to) know 3 delighted 4 regret 5 wrong 6 guess 7 believe

2

2BN 3GN 4BN 5BN 6GN 7GN

3

2 It is with regret that I must tell you that our retired head teacher has died at the age of eighty. 3 You know that photo you showed me? I sent it to a newspaper competition and it's won first prize! 4 I'm delighted to be able to reveal that the club has been awarded £3,000 of government money to spend on new equipment. 5 Do you want the good news or the bad news first? The concert's been cancelled, but we've got a full refund and free seats at the next concert! 6 You'll never guess what! I've got my dream job!

Writing

1

d

2

1 The question that must be asked is whether … 2 Many people think that … 3 Many critics of the 24-hour news cycle argue that … 4 My own belief is that … 5 Due to, Therefore, Owing to the 6 In conclusion, the 24-hour news cycle brings the benefit of constantly updated stories as they unfold. However, the quantity of news needed to fill the programmes may have harmed the quality of the reporting.

3

Consequently, Therefore, On the other hand, However

4

(*Students' own answers*)

Vocabulary activator

1

2 neutral 3 superficial 4 trivial 5 sensational/posh 6 colloquial 7 once-in-a-lifetime 8 countless 9 clichéd 10 ingenious 11 colossal

2

2 posh 3 beforehand 4 gatecrash 5 rowdy 6 mayhem 7 trash

3

2c 3a 4a 5b 6c 7a

4

2 inconsistencies 3 moralistic 4 countless 5 insatiable 6 impersonated 7 circulation 8 restrained 9 mystery 10 illiterate

5

2 tongue-in-cheek 3 forgery 4 practical jokes 5 fabrication 6 spoof on 7 scam

6

1 a taken in b take in c taking in 2 a took off b took off c take off

Extend your vocabulary

1

2 gossip column 3 journal 4 journalese 5 press/media baron 6 media hype

2

1 press corps 2 media hype 3 Journal 4 journalese 5 press/media baron 6 gossip column

Unit 10 Beyond belief

Listening and Vocabulary

1

2g 3f 4h 5b 6a 7c 8e

2

2 obsessive 3 manipulative 4 judgemental 5 fanatical

3

2 manipulate 3 mixed up in/drawn into 4 gospel 5 undue 6 stroppy

4

d

5

1d 2a 3c 4c 5b 6b

Speaking

1

2h 3f 4g 5b 6i 7a 8d 9j 10k 11c

2

2 coming, g 3 speechless, d 4 dying, f 5 cut up, i 6 chuffed, b 7 worried sick, a 8 real pain, c 9 shame, k 10 big deal, e 11 load off my mind, h

3

Suggested answers:

1 I was speechless/You could have knocked me down with a feather 2 I'm dying to see it 3 I'm really cut up about it/It's a real pain, Never mind/It's no big deal 4 Thank goodness/That's a load off my mind

Grammar

1

3b 4a 5a 6b 7a 8b 9b 10a 11b 12a

2

2 She's my co-worker with whom I have lunch/who I have lunch with.
3 The dictator's house, which is in the centre of town, is surrounded by security guards.
4 Some of the victims who were offered emergency relief said they didn't need it.
5 Aspirin, which I take for minor aches and pains, is a simple cure for many things.
6 That's the building where a political party has its offices.

3

2 'The man to whom I spoke had a knife.'
3 'This is the desk where/at which Tolstoy wrote novels.'
4 'Who do I say "thank you" to?'
5 'The girl (who) I chatted to seemed really friendly.'
6 'This is the room where I eat my meals.'
7 'Which platform does our train leave from?'
8 'The article in which the journalist argued for the redistribution of wealth caused a lot of controversy. '

217

4

2 whatever 3 wherever 4 Whenever 5 whoever
6 whichever

5

2 which 3 who 4 which 5 whose 6 who 7 that
8 who 9 whose 10 whom 11 whose 13 who

Writing

2

a *Linking words:* but, and, also
b *Possible answers:* the word 'physic' means
'science of healing'; the garden was founded in the
seventeenth century by apothecaries (chemists) to
grow medicinal plants; the bark of willow trees has
been used for thousands of years to relieve pain
c For: three quarters of modern prescription
medicines are derived from the active ingredients
in the plants used in traditional cures; the bark of
willow trees has been used for thousands of years
to relieve pain and it is the basis for the humble
but widely used aspirin; many treatments which
we regard as alternative, for example,
acupuncture, are long-established
Against: Maybe you were never ill in the first place
and you just wanted a bit of attention;
conventional doctors will point to the lack of
scientific proof for many of the so-called natural
cures; there are well-publicised cases of
unscrupulous people peddling miracle cures to
desperately ill people who will try anything when
conventional medicine has failed to help them

3

(Students' own answers)

Vocabulary activator

1

2 treasured 3 constitutional 4 dictatorship
5 parliamentary 6 numerology 7 astrology

2

2 constitution 3 astrologist 4 treasured
5 dictatorial 6 parliamentarian

3

2 economic 3 redistribution 4 unscrupulous
5 strengthened 6 intervene 7 perpetuate

4

irrefutable supernatural unproven unscrupulous

5

2 indifferent 3 doubt 4 self-doubt
5 interchangeable 6 changeable

6

2 crystals 3 tarot cards

7

2c 3a 4c 5c 6c

Extend your vocabulary

2

2a 3b 4d

3

2 transatlantic 3 extracurricular 4 monogamy
5 monologue 6 polytheistic

Unit 11 Right or wrong?

Reading and Vocabulary

1

1T 2F 3T 4F

2

2d 3c 4b 5g 6e 7f 8k 9h 10j 11i

3

Text A 1b 2a   Text B 1a 2c   Text C 1b 2a

Grammar
Modals and related verbs

1

2c 3a 4d 5a 6e

2

2b 3a 4a 5b 6a

3

2 wouldn't 3 cannot 4 won't

4

2 may have won 3 might/could have stolen 4 May
(he) have hired 5 may have borrowed 6 must have
borrowed 7 might not know 8 does 9 might/could
have got

5

2 could be at work today 3 managed to solve the
problem 4 needn't have bought the tickets in
advance 5 can't have forgotten my birthday
6 should apply for the CEO's job 7 managed to
swim ashore 8 should help me clear up after the
party 9 have to take my birth certificate to the
passport office 10 wouldn't tell my sister what she
was getting for her birthday

6

1

2 must deliver 3 not been able to collect 4 can start
5 must prove 6 are unable to do 7 could avoid

2

1 may ask 2 might also be asked 3 can see 4 can't
see 5 not have to attend 6 have to give 7 should
arrive

Speaking

1

2i 3g 4h 5a 6c 7d 8e 9b

2

1 2a 3b 4c

2 1e 2c 3b 4d 5a

Writing

2

1 to express our concerns about 2 we do not
believe that 3 Further 4 As you are aware 5 We
would suggest that you consider alternative 6 we
would ask you to

3

(Students' own answers)

Vocabulary activator

1

2 destitute 3 dilapidated 4 impoverished 5 heiress
6 prosperous 7 retribution 8 inheritance
9 bankrupt 10 outrageous 11 random

2

2 couldn't scrape by 3 is out of bounds 4 trespass
on 5 wasn't committed in cold blood 6 was
acquitted of

3

2 arson, arsonist 3 hijacking, hijacker
4 assassination, assassin

4

2c 3a 4a 5b 6d 7c 8a

Extend your vocabulary

1

2d 3c 4f 5e 6b 7g

2

2 get away with murder 3 daylight robbery
4 a slap on the wrist 5 was/got caught red-handed
6 throw the book 7 poetic justice

Unit 12 Different?

Listening and Vocabulary

1

1h 2b 3f 4e 5a

2

1 to be well turned out 2 well-tailored 3 to be out
of step 4 haute couture 5 a core belief 6 a soap-
dodger 7 to preen 8 to customise 9 to comb
10 vintage clothing 11 designer outlet 12 quirky
13 a makeover 14 a fashionista

3

b3 c10 d12 e13 f5 g2 h14 i6 j8 k9 l4 m7 n11

4

2 customising 3 makeover 4 be well turned out
5 vintage clothing 6 quirky 7 comb

Speaking

1

2g 3b 4d 5c 6h 7a

2

Possible answers: 1 She's rather energetic.
2 He is a bit boring. He is not particularly
interesting. 3 It's a little breezy. It's not exactly
sunbathing weather. 4 I'm somewhat disappointed.
I'm not exactly overjoyed.

Grammar
Clauses of concession, contrast and addition

1

2 ✓ 3 Although I don't like the fabric, I like the
design. 4 Although Mr and Mrs Stevens are rich,
they dress rather shabbily. / Mr and Mrs Stevens
are very rich, but/yet they dress rather shabbily.
5 ✓ 6 ✓

2

2 In spite of buying her clothes from charity shops,
she always looks well turned out. 3 In spite of the
fact that Ann-Marie works in a designer shop, she
buys her clothes in chain stores. 4 Even though it
was a wedding, Leon wore jeans and a sweatshirt.
5 Despite appearing nondescript from the outside,
the shop has some fantastic clothes. 6 Even
though the shoes were extremely uncomfortable,
Hannah wore them to the party.

3

2b 3a 4a 5b

4

Possible answers: 2e Whilst most visitors to the
zoo behave sensibly, there are a few who are a bit
irresponsible. 3f The children didn't enjoy the
reptile house whereas they liked the petting zoo
with rabbits and hamsters. 4d Whereas in the past
most circuses had performing animals, many of
them don't nowadays. 5a While the idea of a pet
armadillo is interesting, I wouldn't want one in my
house. 6c While a visit to a zoo can be very
interesting, there is nothing better than seeing
animals in the wild.

5

2d 3d 4b 5b 6b

6

2 Despite 3 although/even though 4 though/
whereas 5 As well as 6 though 7 besides

Writing

1

a paragraph 4 b paragraph 3 c paragraph 1
d paragraph 2 e paragraph 3

2

1 Even though he has had to overcome the
difficulties of ...; Despite this achievement;
Although Marco's diffidence; In spite of his busy
schedule; Besides working as 2 Marco's
contribution to this year's art exhibition has been
outstanding with his series of drawings being
highly commended by the judges; Marco has
accompanied the group on various gallery visits
and found this to be a rewarding experience.
3 work of a consistently high standard; Marco's
contribution to this year's art exhibition has been
outstanding; highly commended by the judges; a
diligent, talented and dedicated artist 4 overcome;
commended; helped 5 Although Marco's diffidence
may initially make him seem a little unfriendly,
once he feels at ease in a group, he is a lively and
interesting companion.

3

(Students' own answers)

Vocabulary activator

1

2 on a different wavelength 3 stuck out like a sore
thumb 4 a fish out of water 5 takes a pride in her
appearance 6 in his element 7 a square peg in a
round hole

2

2 unremarkable 3 one-off, eccentric 4 distinctive,
thought-provoking 5 commonplace 6 abnormal,
odd 7 rarest, strangest

3

2 diligent 3 perceptive 4 imperative 5 confined
6 celebrated 7 freckles 8 abnormal 9 austere,
forlorn

4

2b 3c 4b 5a 6a 7c 8c 9c

Extend your vocabulary

1

2f 3i 4c 5j 6b 7g 8d 9a 10e

2

2 dressed up 4 let (them) out

Workbook tapescript

Unit 1 Pleased to meet you

Track 1.2. Reading and Vocabulary

Speaker: A recent survey in the US has raised eyebrows in the world of evolutionary psychology. Previous research had concluded that people prefer life partners with strong reproductive potential and qualities that they think will be good for raising children. However, the more recent study suggests that this is not necessarily the case and that people are attracted to mates with similar personality types as themselves, as it is more likely they will be able to hold down a stable relationship.

Theories of animal behaviour suggest that animals look for attractive physical qualities, such as brightly coloured feathers or shiny coats, because such things can be a sign of reproductive health. In the animal kingdom, a potential mate's 'wealth' – for example, a large, well-built nest and ample food – advertises its ability to provide for the next generation. There has always been an assumption that our behaviour isn't very different, but the more recent publication suggests that humans have a more sophisticated system of mate selection, which includes looking for positive personality traits.

The study began when university students taking a course called *Introduction to Behaviour* each administered questionnaires to ten other people (see sample questions below). The survey, which was voluntary and anonymous, resulted in data from 979 people – most of whom were students aged between eighteen and twenty-four. Hoping to learn what attracts people to each other, the students asked their male and female survey subjects to rank the importance they placed on ten attributes in a long-term partner and to rate themselves on the same qualities.

The students wrote up their reports, got their grades and moved on. However, their tutors were left with an intriguing, if unsorted, mountain of information. When the academics finally got round to doing a proper statistical analysis of the results, the conclusion 'jumped out at us,' they reported. In simple terms, the conclusion was that humans are attracted to people like themselves; reproductive potential is less important.

The scientists were taken aback by the characteristics that people rated as most important. 'Surprisingly, physical attractiveness is not all that important – except to people who rate themselves as physically attractive: the Brad Pitts and Angelina Jolies of the world,' says one of the professors.

'What politicians like to call "family values" characteristics, for example qualities like responsibility, loyalty and trustworthiness, are what people say they're looking for in a long-term relationship. And most people say they perceive those same characteristics in themselves.' However, the research also found particularly strong evidence that women who thought they were physically attractive tended to go for men who were wealthy or of high status. Equally, men who thought they were successful wanted to pair up with good-looking women.

The scientists' analysis concluded that like-minded people are more likely to have a good marriage than dissimilar individuals. A relationship expert commented that she thought the results were common sense. 'The results aren't earth-shattering. Any relationship can quickly be brought to its knees if you don't see eye to eye on important issues and share similar moral values,' she said. 'The safest choice would probably be a mirror image of yourself, but it would be a bit boring. After all, variety is the spice of life.'

Track 1.3. Writing

Speaker: When Della reached home her happiness gave way to good sense. She got out her curling irons and repaired the damage made by love. Within forty minutes her head was covered with tiny curls that made her look wonderfully like a schoolboy. She gazed at her reflection in the mirror and said to herself, 'I hope Jim likes it and understands a dollar and eighty-seven cents wasn't enough to buy him a present.'

At 7 o'clock she heard Jim's footsteps coming up the stairs to their flat. The door opened and Jim stepped in and closed it. Jim stopped inside the door with his eyes fixed upon Della. She could not read his expression. It was not anger, nor surprise, nor disapproval, nor horror, nor any of the emotions that she had been prepared for. He simply stared at her.

'Jim,' she cried, 'don't look at me that way. I sold my hair because I couldn't have lived through Christmas without giving you a present. It'll grow out again. Say "Merry Christmas!" Jim, and let's be happy.'

'You've cut off your hair,' mumbled Jim as if in a dream. 'Your hair has gone.'

'I sold it!' cried Della. 'Don't be angry. I did it for you.'

Coming out of his trance, Jim took Della in his arms and held her tenderly. Then he took a package from his pocket and threw it on the table.

'Don't be mistaken, Della,' he said. 'Nothing could make me love you less. But if you'll unwrap that package you may see why I was shocked.'

Her white fingers tore impatiently at the paper and she gave a cry of joy, which quickly turned to sobs. In the paper lay two beautiful silver hair combs that Della had worshipped in a shop window. They were expensive combs, and she had longed to own them. And now, they were hers, but her hair was gone.

But she hugged them, and at length she was able to look up with glistening eyes and a smile and say: 'My hair grows so fast, Jim!'

Della leapt up. Jim hadn't seen his beautiful present yet. She held the chain in her hand. The precious metal seemed to flash with a reflection of her bright and ardent spirit.

'Isn't it a beautiful, Jim? Give me your watch. I want to see how it looks on it.'

Smiling wistfully, Jim fell back on the couch and put his hands behind his head and said, 'Dell, let's put our Christmas presents away and keep them a while. They're too nice to use just at present. I sold the watch to get the money to buy your combs.'

Unit 2 Is it art?

Track 1.4. Listening and Vocabulary

Speaker: For today's lecture I've brought together some images which I think are absolutely fascinating and are, coincidentally, all monochrome or black and white. You'll see immediately that what links them is Pablo Picasso, who dwarfs all other twentieth-century artists. One of the most remarkably inventive artists to have ever lived, his work and style evolved over his extremely long working life.

I'll briefly introduce each image before talking about them in relation to each other. The one we have here is *Guernica*. This iconic work, which shows the bombing of the Spanish city of Guernica during the Spanish Civil War, was painted in 1937. Abstract in style, the massive painting shows an utterly appalling scene of destruction, which always makes me think of the horror and terror of war. It's a deeply disturbing image.

There are two portraits of Picasso here. Both are by world-famous artists in their own right and show the regard other artists have for Picasso as simply one of the twentieth-century's finest artists. *Picasso and the Loaves* is a photograph by French photographer Robert Doisneau. It is a witty, affectionate image of the artist wearing his trademark striped shirt. Although the subject of the portrait is looking impassively away from the photographer, it is nonetheless an expressive and evocative portrait of a great man as he moves towards old age. The position of the bread to look like large hands is amusing, but possibly also a way of showing the photographer's admiration for the skill of his subject's hands.

This portrait *The Student: Homage to Picasso* is an etching. On the left is a self-portrait of the artist, British-born David Hockney, looking at a bust – the head and shoulders of Picasso. The title *The Student: Homage to Picasso* tells us why Hockney painted the picture: although he was in his thirties at the time he did the work, he sees himself as a learner in the company of a great master. He is showing his respect for the older artist. The bust of Picasso is disproportionate in size – rather like the Doisneau bread hands – larger than life. The artist on the left is smaller; he is humbled in his hero's presence.

Unit 3 Our changing world

Track 1.5. Reading and Vocabulary

Text A

Speaker: Automated transport

Humans did not evolve to drive vehicles safely, at high speed, in conditions of high congestion and poor visibility on motorways or in busy city streets, so it is not surprising that when they do, a lot of accidents happen.

Today nearly all the intelligence involved in controlling a vehicle is in the human behind the wheel, but this will change rapidly in the future. Today we are used to anti-lock braking systems (ABS) to help us operate our cars more safely in a crisis, and in the future we are likely to be handing over a lot more control. Car manufacturers are already researching advanced forms of vehicle control and driver assistance that will radically change how we drive.

Even when humans are experienced drivers, they have very little opportunity to learn how to control a vehicle under demanding crash conditions, so they do not get the benefit of the learning that is available to artificial systems. As artificial control systems develop, they will have the advantage over humans because they can learn through millions of hours of simulated driving. It can only be a matter of time before we start to prefer automated control to the human variety in a growing number of situations.

Looking further into the future, are we heading towards the time when human driving will become a form of extreme sport to be allowed only within controlled areas? At the very least, we will surely insist on drastically reducing the scope of human control in many conditions.

Text B

Speaker: A convincing journey into the future

Steven Spielberg's *Minority Report* is a superior sci-fi film based on a Philip K. Dick short story. *Minority Report* is set in 2054 and the number of murders has plummeted because psychic 'pre-cogs' warn of murders before they happen. In charge of the pre-cog unit is Detective John Anderton (Tom Cruise), who believes in the system of preventative action. Until, that is, the pre-cogs foresee him as a murderer and he goes on the run.

Minority Report presents a future that is scary but convincing. The toy-like cars shoot up the sides of buildings and soar through the air, people are bombarded by personalised advertising and, as predicted in Orwell's *Nineteen Eighty-Four*, there is constant, intrusive surveillance.

The bleakness of the film is enhanced by the atmospheric work of Janusz Kaminski, Steven Spielberg's favourite cinematographer. Kaminski creates a subdued landscape with muted blues and greys. The film is thrilling and, in many ways, disturbing: its depiction of a harsh world is depressingly believable.

Text C

Speaker: Halting the gridlock

The problem

There's **too much traffic** on Britain's roads. This is causing: climate change; congestion; noise and air pollution.

The solutions

People must learn to be less dependent on their cars and to adopt green habits such as walking, cycling and using public transport; buy hybrid cars which use part-petrol and part-electric-driven engines and emit less carbon dioxide.

Car manufacturers must invest more in new technology; speed up the development of cars which are more efficient and less polluting.

Governments must introduce tax incentives to **encourage** (1) manufacturers to develop greener cars and (2) people to buy them; encourage the public to leave their cars at home by investing in public transport and cycle lanes.

Unit 4 Coming of age

Track 1.6. Listening and Vocabulary

Speaker 1: Well, I'm eighteen next week and I'm having like a massive party. It's at the Hatfield Hotel and all my friends are going to be there – I've invited 50 people. It's going to be fantastic: there's a disco and a Thai buffet. Dad's said I can spend £200 on a new outfit, but that's nowhere near enough. I want some Jimmy Choos and they cost a bit more than that. Anyway, I can twist Dad around my little finger so – hey – I'll get them. Of course Mum and Dad are paying for the party so they're insisting on coming. Yawn ... And they've invited all my cousins and aunts and uncles and grandparents.

Speaker 2: It's my granddaughter's 18th birthday party next week. It's being held in some fancy hotel. Between you and me, I think it's ridiculous to spend a lot of money on a party for an eighteen year old. In my day, you were lucky if you had a family party at home for your 21st. It wouldn't have crossed my parents' minds to pay for a party in a hotel. They didn't have money to burn.

There's going to be a disco so I won't be able to hear myself think. However, my son and daughter-in-law will be disappointed if I don't go so I'll show my face for half an hour and get home in time to watch the football highlights.

Speaker 3: We've got an eighteenth birthday party booked in for next Saturday evening. It's for the daughter of the gentleman who owns the big sports shop in town. I'm keen that it goes well – it'll be good publicity for the hotel if everything goes off smoothly. I'm sure he has friends in high places. I haven't actually met him yet, his wife has been dealing with the day-to-day arrangements, but he's footing the bill. Some other hoteliers try to avoid bookings for eighteenths – they say it's just asking for trouble, but I think that if the parents can afford it, it's good for business.

Speaker 4: Who'd have thought it? Our Cassandra 18 years old! It only seems like yesterday that we brought her home from the hospital. She's our only daughter so I suppose she's always been a bit of a daddy's girl. I know you're not supposed to have favourites but ... Anyway, it's a nice opportunity to have a party and get all the family together. She's invited quite a lot of her friends from the pony club. Can't say I like them very much, but you can't choose your kid's friends, can you?

Speaker 5: I've been working at the Hatfield Hotel for two months. I started off in the kitchens but now I'm a waiter. It's very hard work because the hours are long, but the tips are quite good and I get free food and accommodation. My English colleagues call the owner Sybil Fawlty – I think it's the name of the character in a TV comedy but I'm not sure. Anyway, they never say it to her face!

I've enjoyed my time here and I've learnt a lot about being away from home, working with different nationalities and a bit about how not to run a hotel! I'm going home at the end of next month to start a course in hotel management.

Self-assessment Test 2

Track 1.7. Listening

Speaker 1: Just before I started university, for my eighteenth birthday, my parents gave me a palmtop. I'd never seen one before and I was a bit disappointed at the time, but now I find it an indispensable part of university life. While all my friends are scribbling notes which they have to type up at the end of the day, I write on the palmtop and, when I connect it to the computer, it automatically transfers the notes. It's quite old now and doesn't have many functions. One of my colleagues can get the Internet on his. Although he looks busy during lectures, he's usually writing emails or playing games.

Speaker 2: It's probably quite an obvious thing but my laptop is the first thing I'd save in a fire. It's everything in one – an entertainment centre, the Internet, a phone and, of course, a workplace. There have been quite a few thefts from the halls of residence recently, so I always carry it around with me. I was worried sick when I found out it had gone missing from the bar but it turned out that it was just my friends trying to frighten me.

Speaker 3: The thing I would really miss is my iPod, but I don't actually use it much when I'm at university as there's always someone to talk to. I live in the south of England and I go to university in Scotland. Trains are so expensive that I always travel to and from university by bus. It takes 12 hours and I get carsick if I try to read. The films on the bus are awful and my laptop battery only lasts about two hours. A bus journey with nothing to do would be too dull, but I don't like talking to strangers so I sit with my eyes closed listening to music.

Speaker 4: My most important possession is a piece of software. It's called Electronic Student Recipes. I had a real cookbook last year but, in a shared flat, things go missing all the time. After I'd lost two, I decided to get an electronic version for the laptop. I have always listened to the radio on the laptop in the kitchen anyway. There are 200 easy and cheap recipes, but you can also add your own and save them, so my mum helped me to write down all her (and my) favourites. The only problem is that, now, it always seems to be my turn to cook.

Speaker 5: Well, it sounds unoriginal but my mobile phone is my most precious object. It's more than a phone. I mean, it doesn't have many functions – just phone and camera – but it also holds special memories for me. I bought it when I was at summer school in France. All the instructions are in French so it reminds me of the country every time I use it. Also, I know that there's one exactly like it in La Rochelle because I bought one for my boyfriend who lived there at the same time that I bought this one. It was his birthday and that was the first present I bought him.

Unit 5 Live to eat?

Track 1.8. Reading and Vocabulary

Speaker: When I was a small boy at school, a lecturer used to come once a term and deliver excellent lectures on famous battles of the past, such as Blenheim, Austerlitz, etc. He was fond of quoting Napoleon's maxim 'An army marches on its stomach', and at the end of his lecture he would suddenly turn to us and demand, 'What's the most important thing in the world?' We were expected to shout 'Food!' and if we did not do so, he was disappointed.

Obviously he was right in a way. (...) I think it could be plausibly argued that changes of diet are more important than changes of dynasty or even of religion. The Great War, for instance, could never have happened if tinned food had not been invented. And the history of the past four hundred years in England would have been immensely different if it had not been for the introduction of root-crops and various other vegetables at the end of the Middle Ages, and a little later the introduction of non-alcoholic drinks (tea, coffee, cocoa). (...) Yet it is curious how seldom the all-importance of food is recognized. You see statues everywhere to politicians, poets, bishops, but none to cooks or bacon-curers or market-gardeners. The Emperor Charles V is said to have erected a statue to the inventor of bloaters, but that is the only case I can think of at the moment.

So perhaps the really important thing about the unemployed, the really basic thing if you look to the future, is the diet they are living on. As I said earlier, the average unemployed family lives on an income of round about thirty shillings a week, of which at least a quarter goes in rent. It is worth considering in some detail how the remaining money is spent. (...) The miner's family spend only tenpence a week on green vegetables and tenpence half-penny on milk (remember that one of them is a child less than three years old), and nothing on fruit; but they spend one and nine on sugar (about eight pounds of sugar, that is) and a shilling on tea. The half-crown spent on meat might represent a small joint and the materials for a stew; probably as often as not it would represent four or five tins of bully beef. The basis of their diet, therefore, is white bread and margarine, corned beef, sugared tea, and potatoes – an appalling diet. Would it not be better if they spent more money on wholesome things like oranges and wholemeal bread or if they even (...) saved on fuel and ate their carrots raw? Yes, it would, but the point is that no ordinary human being is ever going to do such a thing. The ordinary human being would sooner starve than live on brown bread and raw carrots. And the peculiar evil is this, that the less money you have, the less inclined you feel to spend it on wholesome food. A millionaire may enjoy breakfasting off orange juice and crackers; an unemployed man doesn't. Here the tendency of which I spoke at the end of the last chapter comes into play. When you are unemployed, which is to say when you are underfed, harassed, bored and miserable, you don't want to eat dull wholesome food. You want something a little bit 'tasty'. There is always some cheaply pleasant thing to tempt you. (...) It is unfortunate that the English working class – the English nation generally, for that matter – are exceptionally ignorant about and wasteful of food. I have pointed out elsewhere how civilized is a French navvy's idea of a meal compared with an Englishman's, and I cannot believe that you would ever see such wastage in a French house as you habitually see in English ones. Of course, in the very poorest homes, where everybody is unemployed, you don't see much actual waste, but those who can afford to waste food often do so. I could give startling instances of this. Even the Northern habit of baking one's own bread is slightly wasteful in itself, because an overworked woman cannot bake more than once or, at most, twice a week and it is impossible to tell beforehand how much bread will be wasted, so that a certain amount generally has to be thrown away. The usual thing is to bake six large loaves and twelve small ones at a time. All this is part of the old, generous English attitude to life, and it is an amiable quality, but a disastrous one at the present moment.

Unit 6 Sounds around us

Track 1.9. Listening and Vocabulary

Greg Dale: That was Green Day. Hello to you if you've just tuned in. My guests today are Denise Hope and Ranesh Singh. Denise Hope is an audiologist and Ranesh Singh is a specialist in acoustics. Welcome to you both. We invited them in because last week's discussion on noise pollution prompted so many calls and messages on our website that we've decided to get a couple of specialists in to answer some of your questions. Perhaps you could start by briefly explaining your jobs. Ranesh?

Ranesh Singh: Hi, yes, basically, I'm a scientist and I study the physics of sound. It's really an interdisciplinary subject because it spreads across all sorts of areas – music, architecture, industry ... every area of human activity.

Greg Dale: And what about you, Denise? What is an audiologist?

Denise Hope: Well, in my day job, I work with people with hearing problems. From that, I have developed a general interest in all aspects of sound and the impact it has on us.

Greg Dale: Good. Well, we're going to open up the topic today and try to answer some of our listeners' more general questions. I'll just read out this question from Eleanor who lives in Ware. She asks: 'What is white noise?' Denise, can you get us started on that one?

Denise Hope: Well, white noise is the sound equivalent of white light.

Greg Dale: Er ... yes?

Denise Hope: In the same way as white light contains all the colours we can see, white noise contains all the *frequencies* that the human ear can hear – it's about 20,000 tones playing at the same time. And because it contains all the sounds we can hear, it effectively blocks out other noises.

Greg Dale: How does that work?

Denise Hope: OK, imagine you are listening to one person speaking ... you can understand them perfectly well, can't you? Now imagine you are in a pizza restaurant with ten friends – it's more difficult to hear everyone, but you can still focus on a few people. But if there were a thousand people in the restaurant, it would be a wall of noise and your brain wouldn't be able to 'hear' one voice, just a constant babble. That's the effect of white noise. People buy white noise CDs and machines or even download it from the Internet so they can mask other sounds.

Greg Dale: But aren't they annoyed by the new noise?

Denise Hope: No, not at all. I suppose it would be more accurately called sound, not noise, which suggests something intrusive and irritating. For example, people who live by busy roads use it to block out the rumble of traffic; some companies use it to aid concentration in busy offices; and many people say that it helps them to relax.

Greg Dale: That's extraordinary. Let's hear some ... Strange ...

Denise Hope: I know. I have several patients who swear by it to help them sleep. But I also have patients who say that anything that blocks out background noise and stops their minds working has the same effect.

Ranesh Singh: Can I just chip in?

Greg Dale: Of course. Please do.

Ranesh Singh: OK, if I can't get to sleep, I listen to number stations and they always do the trick. They have the same effect on me as white noise.

Greg Dale: You've lost me there.

Ranesh Singh: I'm not surprised. When I first heard about number stations, I thought they were a joke, but then I did a bit of research on the web and now I'm obsessed with them. They are a bit off the topic but, briefly, they are short-wave radio broadcasts – normally in a woman's voice – that simply list random numbers constantly. The voices are artificially generated and there is a constant stream of numbers, words or letters. And even Morse code sometimes.

Greg Dale: Sorry to interrupt, but who broadcasts these things?

Ranesh Singh: Search me. I wish I knew the answer, but I don't. What I do know is that number stations first appeared during the Cold War. The assumption is that instructions are being sent to spies, but no government will admit to using them. Since the end of the Cold War, there has been a slight increase in the number of broadcasts so they can't be solely linked to the east–west tensions of post-war Europe.

Greg Dale: Well, no doubt there are plenty of anoraks out there who we'll be hearing from about them. But going back to the matter in hand: we've had an email from Don, who wants to know if it's possible to achieve complete silence. Is it?

Denise Hope: Mmmm, that's difficult because we can nearly always hear something. Even in the countryside you can still hear the twittering of birds, the lapping of waves, the faint hum of traffic in the distance, and so on. Experiments have been done with sensory deprivation which means stimuli are deliberately removed from our senses. Simple things can be done like covering your eyes with a blindfold or covering your ears with earmuffs. A more extreme form is to try to remove all five senses by isolating people from all stimulation. For short periods, some people find this relaxing but longer periods generally lead to terrible problems including anxiety, hallucinations, irrational thoughts and antisocial behaviour. Clearly our brains do need a level of stimulation to stop us from going mad.

Greg Dale: So, Don, I think the answer is 'yes', but you may be driven mad so it might not be such a good idea. Ah! I've just been handed an email from a listener called Jason about number stations. It's quite brief, but he has attached a sound clip that we'll be able to listen to in a couple of moments. Jason writes 'I'm a radio ham and I've been listening to number stations for years. They pop up, broadcast for a while then disappear from the airwaves.' That doesn't add much but we do have the sound clip ...

RP voice: one, seventeen, ninety-six, ten (...) thirty-two, four, one hundred, sixty (...) one thousand, three thousand, forty-four, one (...) seventy-nine, eight, ninety-nine, four hundred and one ...

Ranesh Singh: Extraordinary, isn't it? I love the idea of these things being constantly broadcast.

Greg Dale: Well, before we take any more calls and emails, let's have some more music. We'll be back after this track from the Kings Of Leon and the news.

Track 1.10. Listening and Vocabulary

Denise Hope: ... even in the countryside you can still hear the twittering of birds, the lapping of waves, the faint hum of traffic in the distance, and so on.

Track 1.11. Vocabulary Activator

1 [door bell chiming]
2 [screech of tyres]
3 [babbling baby]
4 [whine of a dentist's drill]
5 [crunch of footsteps on gravel]
6 [a creaking door]
7 [click of a light switch]
8 [crack of gunfire]
9 [rumble of thunder]
10 [tinkling chandelier]
11 [a crackling fire]
12 [someone walking through leaves]

Unit 7 Calm down!

Track 1.12. Reading and Vocabulary

A

Speaker 1: Assertiveness training is about helping people to know that there are situations where they have the right to defend themselves from bullying attempts made by others. Once people realise that it is OK, and even proper, for them to stick up for themselves and to allow themselves to feel angry when someone takes advantage of them, they find that defending themselves is not so hard. (...) There is a certain inertia to how people relate to one another in relationships. A dominant partner is used to getting his or her way, and a submissive, passive partner is used to giving the dominant partner his or her way. This pattern feels normal to both partners and any change will leave both partners feeling unsettled. Expect to feel weird when you decide to become assertive and change the pattern, and also expect that your partner will feel weird too and will generally be motivated to act so as to reassert the old, comfortable pattern. Because the normal amount of domination is no longer working, most dominant partners will 'up the ante' and try coming on stronger so as to try to overpower you into submission. Don't fall for this. If you can stand your ground for a while, both of you will get used to the new pattern of you being assertive.

B

Speaker 2: Employers have a duty of care to their employees and this includes dealing with bullying at work. There are measures you can take if you're being bullied.

Get advice

Speak to someone about how you might deal with the problem informally. This might be: an employee representative like a trade union official; someone in the firm's human resources department; your manager or supervisor.

Some employers have specially trained staff to help with bullying and harassment problems; they're sometimes called 'harassment advisers'. If the bullying is affecting your health, visit your GP.

Talk to the bully

The bullying may not be deliberate. If you can, talk to the person in question who may not realise how their behaviour has been affecting you. Work out what to say beforehand. Describe what's been happening and why you object to it. Stay calm and be polite. If you don't want to talk to them yourself, ask someone else to do so for you.

Keep a written record or diary

Write down details of every incident and keep copies of any relevant documents.

Make a formal complaint

This is the next step if you can't solve the problem informally. To do this you must follow your employer's formal grievance procedure, or if one doesn't exist, you can use the statutory grievance procedure.

C

Speaker 3: By law, all schools are obliged to keep an up-to-date anti-bullying policy available to teachers, parents and children. The policy specifies what the school expects from all pupils, how bullying will be dealt with, and the action the school will take.

Most parents are initially contacted by telephone and asked to come into school for a meeting, possibly with the bullied child, and his or her parents. The first step to take is to sit down with your child and find out not just their side of the story, but also how they are feeling, and what else might be wrong. One expert points out that it is essential to take a deep breath and talk to them calmly. 'If you start ranting and raving, you end up being a bully yourself, thereby condoning the behaviour you are trying to stop,' he says. 'Don't jump to conclusions and bear in mind that bullying can mask something more serious. You have to find out what has happened, as well as deciding whether or not they have been fairly accused.'

D

Speaker 4: Have you landed yourself with a friend who drains your self-esteem, confidence, social life or bank account? Relationships come and go, but we're ingrained with the idea that friends are forever. For the most part, mates are a lifeline: you laugh, cry, obsess, analyse and party with them. But a toxic friendship – or a 'frenemy' as featured in *Sex and The City* – has the opposite effect and a night out with a toxic friend can leave you demoralised, resentful and angry.

As Florence Isaacs, author of *Toxic Friends/True Friends: How Your Friendships Can Make Or Break Your Health, Happiness, Family, and Career*, says, 'A toxic friendship (it's the relationship that's toxic) is *regularly* – that's the key word, none of us is perfect – unsupportive, unsatisfying, draining, stifling and/or unequal. You can both be caring people, but the dynamic doesn't do either of you any good. 'Toxic friendships are bad because they're stressful at best, and may be abusive. They also make you feel bad about yourself and take effort, time and emotional energy that could be spent on positive friendships that bring you support and pleasure. We're all so busy these days, why waste precious energy on a negative experience?' Self-obsessed, cruel, boring and needy; these friends are seriously polluting. You wouldn't put up with being humiliated, betrayed or stood up frequently by your partner, so why do we tolerate such bad behaviour from a friend?

Unit 8 Getting around

Track 1.13. Listening and Vocabulary

Hannah: I first got into travel writing by accident during the school holidays about eight years ago. I was really bored and to keep me quiet my mum suggested that I enter a competition in a national newspaper. The competition invited entries under the ironic title of 'What I Did In My Holidays'. And, again ironically, I hadn't actually done anything

during my holidays because I was too hard up to go anywhere. Anyway, I wrote an article about filling your time when all your friends are off doing exciting things. And although I didn't win the first prize, I did win third which wasn't bad for my first try. The experience gave me a taste for writing, seeing my name in print. And winning prizes. What did I win? It was £50 and a camera. It doesn't sound much but I was on top of the world and could see a glittering future in journalism! I still have the camera, although I no longer use it – like everyone else, I've moved on to digital. Looking at it reminds me of how my career started by accident and that you should take every opportunity that comes your way as you never know where it might lead.

Anyway, I went off to university the year after I won the prize and presented myself to the campus newspaper – I had ambitions to be a big name in investigative journalism! Strangely enough, they didn't seem to be very interested in letting me cover any big stories, but they said I could submit any features I wrote. I used to do two or three a term – some of my classics included 'How to get by at a rock festival on less than £10 a day', 'Free things to do in airports when your cheap flight is cancelled' and 'Travelling on a shoe string'. You may have noticed that there was a common theme of money-saving tips – a subject close to the hearts of most students.

When I graduated, I got a job at a campsite in Spain for the summer. While I was there, I was asked to edit the English part of the campsite newsletter – it didn't match my dream of being a big-shot journalist, but it was a tiny step in the right direction. While I was working there, I got my break into travel writing: a friend of my parents, on hearing I was working in Spain, asked me to update the budget section on their travel website. I jumped at the chance. I left my job at the campsite and set off round Spain with my rucksack and a laptop. I had to travel to the places listed on the site and check that the information like opening times, prices, quality of accommodation and so on was still true. I was on a tight budget so I stayed in youth hostels and spent a lot of time finding ways to save money – you know, buying off-peak tickets, saving a fortune by not eating in restaurants, and so on. Nowadays, I'm a full-time writer for the website and their guidebooks. My speciality is still Spain and because my Spanish is fluent, I cover some Latin American countries. A lot of my friends think I have the best job in the world, but it's not as exciting as it sounds. Not many travel writers have the opportunity to go off the beaten track – most of us are on a well-worn path. I still spend most of my time gathering and double-checking facts to make sure that all the information is accurate. Luckily, I no longer work on budget travel so I get to stay in decent hotels and to try out more up-market restaurants and cafés. One thing I have never learnt to do is to travel light. Many other writers manage with a small carry-on bag, but I always have loads of luggage – and at least once a year one of my bags goes missing.

Self-assessment Test 4

Track 1.14. Listening

Travel Agent (TA): Good afternoon, sir. Can I help you?
Customer (C): Yes, I'm looking for a nice weekend break for my wife and me. We were married seventeen years ago in June.
TA: Congratulations! What sort of place were you looking for? Venice is very romantic.
C: No, I think we'd prefer somewhere a little less crowded and not as hot as Venice. We were thinking of Copenhagen. Are there any weekend package deals there?
TA: Yes. There's a deal we run with Budget Airlines. They fly there on Friday evenings at 7.30 from Luton.
C: To Copenhagen?
TA: Yes, well, you know what budget airlines are like. They fly to a nearby city. This flight goes to Malmo.
C: Malmo? But that's in Sweden.
TA: Yes, but now the Oresund Bridge has been completed, they are practically one city. People from both cities commute to the other each day. The bridge is only 7.8 km long and there's both road and rail travel over it. It's well worth seeing.
C: Is that the one which is a bridge for half the distance and then goes into a tunnel?
TA: That's right. The bridge stretches from Sweden to an island called Peberholm. From there to Denmark, the road goes under the water. It's called, er, the Drogden Tunnel.
C: Fascinating. Well, that sounds great. What about hotels in Copenhagen?
TA: Well, we have holidays to suit every pocket from budget one-star hotels to a luxury five-star option.
C: Well, I don't think that would be in our price range, but we'd like something nice. Maybe a four-star. But the most important thing is the location. We'd like to be close to the centre, but somewhere quiet and safe and good for eating out in the evenings and walking.
TA: I suggest Nyhavn, the New Harbour. It's very picturesque and home to many cafés and restaurants. The locals love eating out, and not only in the summer. The restaurants keep their tables out except

in the coldest parts of the year and there are blankets on the back of every seat to keep you warm as you eat. I wouldn't imagine that would be necessary in June!

C: I hope not! It sounds an interesting area.

TA: It certainly is. The oldest building in the area is number 9 Nyhavn, which dates from 1681, and Nyhavn 18 was the home of Hans Christian Andersen for several years.

C: Oh, lovely. My wife is a great fan of his stories. Now, about hotels in the area ...

Unit 9 Media truths

Track 1.15. Reading and Vocabulary

Speaker: The greatest film ever made?

Many people believe that *Citizen Kane* is the greatest film ever made (at least that's what film magazine polls report year after year). Actor Orson Welles starred in, directed, co-produced and co-wrote the film when he was only 24 years old. Although he was already renowned in the worlds of theatre and radio, *Citizen Kane* was an extraordinary film debut for the young Orson Welles.

For those readers who haven't seen *Citizen Kane*, it is, in short, the story of a powerful American newspaper owner who dies alone in a gloomy, antique-stuffed mansion with the word 'Rosebud' on his lips. But is it a true story?

It is easy to think that *Citizen Kane* is entirely true. The story is narrated by an investigative reporter, and the use of (entirely fake) newsreels, interviews and flashbacks adds to the illusion that you are watching a documentary about a real person, not a fictional drama. At the time, such techniques were revolutionary, but they have become standard for the makers of biopics and drama-documentaries.

Not only was the style of filming radical, but the left-wing message of *Citizen Kane* was also controversial. Further, on the release of the film in 1941, there were lawsuits and an attempt to have the film destroyed. There is still debate as to whether this film depicts real people and real events, or is a story that uses the gutter press as a metaphor for human weakness.

Whether you think the *Kane* storyline is fact or fiction depends on how similar you think it is to the life of the real press baron William Randolph Hearst. Hearst, the only child of a San Francisco multi-millionaire, built a US newspaper empire in the late 19th and early 20th centuries. Hearst's career began in 1887 when his father gave him a San Francisco newspaper. Shameless publicity stunts and a ruthless circulation war built the sales and profits of the paper. Hearst went on to buy a New York paper and to lure staff away from competing newspapers.

Hearst evidently thought that *Citizen Kane* was too close to his own life. He banned advertisements for the film from his newspapers and offered to buy the negative from the film studio so he could destroy it. However, Welles himself, perhaps realising that Hearst had enormous power, insisted that *Kane* was fictional drama rather than history. 'Hearst was born rich,' the director wrote in 1975. 'He was the spoilt son of an adoring mother. That is the decisive fact about him. Charles Foster Kane was born poor.'

Welles had to admit, however, that some Hearst mythology was too good not to include it in the film. For example, when a Hearst newspaper sent an artist to do drawings of a war in Cuba, and the artist complained that there wasn't really enough action to keep him busy, Hearst is said to have replied, 'You make the pictures, I'll make the war.' This sentence appears as a line of dialogue in the film.

In addition to this quotation, there are other points of comparison. Hearst built a bizarre Californian palace called *San Simeon* which he filled with art and antiques. He held lavish parties there, and it was at one of these bashes that the co-writer of *Kane*, Herman J. Mankiewicz, had the germ of the idea for the film. In the film, Kane builds an extraordinary fantasy castle, *Xanadu*; the similarities are too obvious to ignore.

The evolution of the fictional Kane from a hero of the downtrodden to corrupt media mogul was *not* a journey Hearst made, however. Hearst was never a liberal at any stage of his career. Asked later in life why he had not got involved in the film industry, Hearst replied, 'Because you can more easily crush a man by journalism.'

Unit 10 Beyond belief

Track 1.16. Listening and Vocabulary

Thomas: Has Sam settled in at university yet? He was having some problems making friends at first, wasn't he?

Lily: Well, he has made some friends and he seems a lot happier, but Mum and Dad are still worried about him.

Thomas: Parents never stop, do they? I don't suppose they've got any reason to be concerned, have they?

Lily: I'm not sure ... It's going to sound crazy, but they think he's getting drawn into a cult.

Thomas: What do you mean 'a cult'? Has he joined a weird religion?

It's not like that lot in Texas or the ones in California who thought they would be rescued by a space ship, is it?

Lily: No, I don't think it's anything as extreme as that – at least I hope it isn't. But that's the problem, we don't really know what he's got mixed up in because he's become very secretive.

Thomas: Well, perhaps he just wants a bit more privacy now he's left home. It doesn't mean he's joined a cult – he might just be doing things he doesn't want to tell your parents about.

Lily: No, I don't think that's the case. I must admit that at first I wasn't that bothered. I just thought he was going through a phase and that Mum and Dad were overreacting. But now I'm beginning to wonder. It's like he's suffering from monomania.

Thomas: Monomania? What do you mean?

Lily: You know, one thing that he thinks and talks about all the time. Sam met some bloke called Hal, and at first we all thought that was great because he'd made a friend. But then all his phone calls were 'Hal says this and Hal says that'. Then the next thing we knew, he'd left his halls of residence to go and move into a shared house where this guy Hal and some other people live – half of whom don't seem to have jobs or do anything.

Thomas: What's wrong with that?

Lily: Obviously there's nothing wrong with sharing a house, but there's something obsessive about it – and this Hal seems to have undue influence over him. Y'know, anything Hal says is gospel. Sam used to be pretty easy-going about everything, but last time he was home he kept talking about global conspiracies and how we were all blind to what was really happening in the world.

Thomas: That doesn't sound like Sam.

Lily: I know. I tried to speak to him about it, but he just said something about this group knowing about 'secret government plots' and that everyone else was too gullible to see what was being done to them. Then he just clammed up.

Thomas: That does sound a bit extreme for someone like Sam. But it sounds to me that it's more likely he's got mixed up in a political group – it doesn't sound like a cult to me. Can't you ring him and ask him about it? You've always been very close.

Lily: Exactly! In the past we always talked about stuff, but he has become very secretive and he accused me of being judgemental and not understanding the real issues that we're facing. I'm with you on this – I think it's more likely to be political than religious. But the way he's behaving, it might as well be a religious sect!

Thomas: I suppose you do hear about these things – you know, someone being influenced by a charismatic leader who is manipulative and unscrupulous. But even so, it's hard to imagine someone as sensible as Sam getting drawn into anything like radical politics.

Lily: If you'd asked me two months ago, I'd have said the same. But it really is like he's been brainwashed. One thing I haven't been able to tell Mum and Dad yet is that I got phone call from Sam this morning asking me for money. I think they're both at home this evening so I'll tell them over dinner. The thing is, I know he had quite a lot of savings from his gap year and Mum and Dad send him a generous cheque every month, so I don't understand why he needs more money.

Thomas: Did you ask him?

Lily: I tried to, but he just got stroppy and put the phone down. I sent him a text asking why he needed the dosh but he just ignored the question. Anyway, the latest thing is that he has said he won't come home for the Christmas holidays. Something about it being a capitalist plot!

Thomas: It does all sound a bit odd, but I don't think it adds up to irrefutable evidence that he's joined an extremist group. There could be another explanation. You don't think he could have got into drugs, do you?

Lily: No, absolutely not. If anything he's got fanatical about health – he does loads of exercise and eats a really faddy diet.

Thomas: Oh well, he needs to lose a few kilos, so it's not all bad.

Unit 11 Right or wrong?

Track 1.17. Reading and Vocabulary

A

Speaker: Sunday saw the return of Seb Green to his home town after his ten-month, 9,300 kilometre walk around the coast of Britain. Seb embarked on the journey with his dog, Flash, to raise £20,000 for the rescue services, who had saved him from the sea when he was just 15 years old.

Seb and a friend had got themselves into difficulties at sea when they stole a boat from a local marina. By his own admission, it was a prank that went horribly wrong and could have ended in tragedy. When he and his friend got into difficulties, they were unable to get back to the shore, but luckily a passerby heard their cries for help and was able to raise the alarm. The two pranksters were rescued by police and coastguard helicopters and the local lifeboat crew. The cost of his rescue was £20,000 and Seb swore that he would make amends by paying the money back.

Having successfully completed his coastal walk, Seb feels that he has

223

literally and metaphorically paid his debt to society. He can put his youthful indiscretion behind him and get on with his plans for the future, which include completing his studies before applying to the armed forces.

A local person commented: 'They should never have taken the boat, but he has done everything he can to put things right. It's the first time he's got himself into trouble and everyone deserves a second chance, don't they? I did some daft things when I was younger and I'm not sure I'd have walked that far to raise the money. You've got to be impressed, haven't you?'

B

Speaker: A teenager who had his offer of a place at Imperial College London medical school withdrawn because of a conviction for burglary has now won a place to study medicine at Manchester University. The straight-A student from Little Horton, a rundown area of Bradford, was rejected by the London college when he revealed that he had a spent conviction for burglary. The college's reason for withdrawing the conditional offer was that they had to uphold the public's trust in doctors. However, many members of the public, parliamentarians and his school principal argued that one mistake should not be allowed to spoil the rest of his life.

At the age of sixteen Majid Ahmed had pleaded guilty to a charge of burglary when he was found trespassing in an unoccupied house with two other young men. He claimed that he had been duped into entering the house. The offence resulted in a four-month community service order. Since serving his sentence, he has turned his life around, achieving top grades and doing voluntary and charity work. He said: 'At first I couldn't grasp that I am on the course this September – it's only a month away. I'm ecstatic. This shows people that determination and perseverance do pay off, and if you think you have been mistreated by a university, you should fight your cause. Now I see my future going somewhere, I just can't wait to be at medical school.'

C

Speaker: Model Naomi Campbell has been found guilty of assaulting a police officer during an altercation on board a plane at Heathrow Airport. The top-earning model, who previously served a five-day community sentence in New York for throwing a phone at her maid, was sentenced to 200 hours community service at a homeless shelter in east London.

In the incident, which took place earlier this year, the world-famous supermodel flew into a rage when one of her bags got lost at Heathrow. The trouble started when Ms Campbell was told that one of her bags hadn't been loaded onto the plane. She blew her top and started screaming abuse at the first-class cabin crew.

Airport police were called and Ms Campbell attacked one of the officers, who then had no option than to arrest her. A shocked first-class passenger reported, 'I simply couldn't believe what I was seeing. She was going berserk – spitting, punching and lashing out. The officer tried to use a softly-softly approach, but she was in a frenzy. She had to be arrested before she injured herself or someone else. I think she should get some psychological help.'

Unit 12 Different?

Track 1.18. Listening and Vocabulary

Speaker 1: I take a huge pride in my appearance – I like to be well turned out. I always have done. I don't mean I go for the latest thing – I prefer classic clothes. Y'know, well-tailored suits and smart shirts. I always go for the best quality even if it means saving for months. I can't see the point in buying something cheap and nasty that will fall apart in two weeks. My friends think I'm mad but I've got stuff I've had for years and it still looks good. I reckon quality never goes out of fashion. I suppose I'm a bit out of step with most people my age, but that doesn't bother me.

Speaker 2: Our degree course *Fashion and Textiles* has an international reputation for excellence. Graduates of the course are highly creative designers who have gone on to make an outstanding contribution to the worlds of contemporary fashion and haute couture, both in Britain and overseas. We are based in central London, one of the world's fashion capitals, and our goal is to develop creativity, originality and invention in our students. One of our core beliefs is that fashion both shapes and reflects the contemporary world. Graduates will leave the course with an in-depth knowledge of the subject.

Speaker 3: I've no idea what's happened to my son in the last six months. At the beginning of this year he was definitely a soap-dodger: I virtually had to beg him to take a shower or wash his hair. Now, he's never out of the bathroom! He spends hours in there preening before he goes out for the evening. I can't believe the amount he spends on hair gel and aftershave – he really has turned into a bit of a dandy. Although his personal hygiene has improved (thank goodness!), he still goes out in dreadful old jeans and T-shirts.

Speaker 4: In my circle of friends, it definitely isn't cool to wear the same clothes as everyone else. Don't get me wrong, we're all into fashion, but we customise our clothes. How it works is, we comb markets, designer outlets and vintage clothing shops to find interesting stuff and then we customise them – like these jeans I'm wearing, which I got in a designer outlet. I slashed the fabric and added these studs so they are unique. I got a 1970s denim dress a couple of weeks ago, and I've added a silk belt and some quirky buttons that I found on an old cardigan. It's a great way to have a distinctive style without spending too much.

Speaker 5: I really don't care what I wear – I think fashion is just daft. Some of the girls in my year are like the fashion police – they're forever criticising what other people wear, and one of them even offered to give me a makeover! The nerve! Not everyone wants to be a fashionista! And the other thing that annoys me is that they buy stuff, wear it once and that's it, they never wear it again. It's so wasteful. On the rare occasions when I do buy anything, I always check that it wasn't made by child labour and that the fabric is organic and fair-trade. I think if people knew more about why clothes are so cheap now, they would think twice about buying them. Treating clothes as disposable is just a waste of money and the world's resources.

Self-assessment Test 6

Track 1.19. Listening

Interviewer (I): I'm here in Peckham watching a gang of hoodies walking towards me. However, they aren't the hoodies of our nightmares, but rather normal teenagers who have chosen to wear this symbol of delinquency to show that teenagers should not be judged by the clothes that they wear but by who they are and how they behave. Melanie Jackson is one of the demonstrators. Hello, Melanie. What's going on?

Melanie (M): We are calling this the 'Don't Write Us Off' campaign. We're wearing hoodies because that is the item of clothing that adults are currently obsessed with, but it's nothing new. Throughout the last 50 years, adults have focused on teenagers' clothes and fashion as a sign that young people are dangerous troublemakers. It doesn't matter if it's the mini skirt or men with long hair, leather jackets, the wan complexion of goths, whatever it is, people judge us by our looks.

I: So what do you think people dislike about the hoodie?

M: People think that anyone wearing a hooded sweatshirt is a hooligan. Some shopping centres have banned people from wearing them. The shops in the centres sell them but, if you put it on, they can throw you out. They take our money, but they don't like us.

I: What do you want?

M: We want to be treated as individuals, not as teenagers. If we break the law, we should be punished, but if we don't, why should people think badly of us?

I: Isn't that natural? Don't you look at adults and think, oh look, he's wearing a suit, he's a boring businessman; she's wearing designer jeans, she's cool?

M: I don't. Well, I mean, it's natural that someone makes an immediate impression on us but, we then get to know them and react to them for who they are. With teenagers it's not like that. All teenagers, even completely normal-looking ones, are regarded with suspicion. Shops have signs in them saying: 'Only two teenagers allowed in at one time'. People mutter about us on the bus. I'm 17, I'm studying for my A-levels and I want to be a lawyer. I've never been in trouble with the police but I've got a nose ring. That makes me weird or repulsive to many people, even though I always wear very smart clothes, and they don't even try to hide that – or if they do try, they don't succeed.

I: What do you hope to achieve with this demonstration?

M: We're talking to people – people who may never speak to teenagers and who don't try to understand us. They're not scared today because there are so many police officers here looking after us so they listen and, despite arguing with us at first, they often start listening and agreeing with us.

I: Isn't that because you are nice, educated teenagers? How would you feel if a gang of real hoodies were walking towards you late at night? Surely you'd be scared and wouldn't be trying to find out what they were like as individuals?

M: Well, it depends. If they were acting aggressively, yes, I'd be scared, just like I'd be scared if a bunch of thirty-year-old drunks in suits and ties were coming towards me. What you have to remember is that I'm also a teenager. I know these people and I know that lots of them are OK. They're just wearing a uniform. It's a practical one, too. Hoods keep your ears warm in the evening. It's scary for you because you're from a different generation, but when you were younger I'm sure you were less scared by a gang of punks or metal fans than an older person would have been.

I: You could be right. Thank you, Melanie. So, there we are. That's the 'Don't Write Us Off' campaign and, with sensible, articulate spokespeople like Melanie, I'm sure we won't be writing them off just yet.